*American Sympathy*

CALEB CRAIN

# American Sympathy

MEN, FRIENDSHIP, AND
LITERATURE IN THE
NEW NATION

Yale University Press
New Haven &
London

Published with assistance from the foundation established in memory of Philip
Hamilton McMillan of the Class of 1894, Yale College.

Set in Sabon type by Keystone Typesetting, Inc., Orwigsburg, Penn.
Printed in the United States of America.

Library of Congress Cataloging-in-Publication Data
Crain, Caleb.
American sympathy : men, friendship, and literature in the new nation / Caleb Crain.
p.   cm.
Includes bibliographical references and index.
ISBN 0-300-08332-7 (alk. paper)
1. American literature — Male authors — History and criticism.   2. Men in
literature.   3. American literature — 19th century — History and criticism.
4. American literature — 1783–1850 — History and criticism. 5. Brown, Charles
Brockden, 1771–1810 — Characters — Men.   6. Emerson, Ralph Waldo, 1803 –
1882. Friendship.   7. Male friendship — United States — History.   8. Male friendship
in literature.   9. Sympathy in literature.   I. Title.
PS173.M36   C7   2001
810.9'352041 — dc21      00-011800

A catalogue record for this book is available from the British Library.

To Peter

# Contents

# Acknowledgments

Many people have helped me with this project. Michael Hardy of the University City Historical Society, Philadelphia, shared with me his discovery of the Leander and Lorenzo diaries. He was the first to see the human story hidden in these manuscripts, and I remain grateful that he allowed me to present it. John R. Holmes of the Franciscan University of Steubenville, Ohio, provided me with a draft of the *Letters of Charles Brockden Brown,* which he, Edwin J. Saeger, and Alfred Weber are in the process of editing. Their edition gave me access to dozens of Brown letters still unpublished and scattered in archives across the country; their notes made many obscurities clear. The Americanists' seminar held at Columbia University in 1996–98 gave me a forum to try out early drafts of many of these chapters; I always looked forward to the insightful responses of Andrew Epstein and Claudia Stokes. I depended on the encouragement of my friends Neville Hoad and Houman Sarshar, who were laboring with manuscripts of their own. Without Lucy B. Smith I would not have arrived at many of the insights here. At *Lingua Franca,* Hillary Frey, James Ryerson, Laura Secor, and Alexander Star were support-ive, if not indulgent, of their moonlighting colleague. My parents, Suzanne T. Carson and William R. Crain, have given me their steady support in this project, as in every other; so did my late grandmother, Mary Louise Crain. Finally, Andrew Delbanco and Robert A. Ferguson shared with me their insight and knowledge of American literature, and I am deeply thankful for their attention and trust.

I am lucky to have more formal kinds of assistance to acknowledge as well. The editors of *Early American Literature* published a version of Chapter 1 in 1998, which was awarded the Richard Beale Davis prize. I received helpful feedback when I presented talks based on this material to the Modern Language Association at a panel organized by Janice Knight in 1996, and at another organized by Sharon M. Harris in 1997. I also profited from the vital exchange of scholarship at Revising Charles Brockden Brown, a conference organized by Christopher Looby in 1998. A grant from the Andrew W. Mellon Foundation made possible my research in Philadelphia archives. A Jacob K. Javits Fellowship supported me when I began writing, and the Woodrow Wilson Foundation made finishing much easier with a Charlotte W. Newcombe Fellowship. Finally, my editors at Yale University Press, Lara Heimert and Mary Pasti, have my thanks for their improvements to my prose and their enthusiasm for the project.

The following libraries have graciously granted me permission to quote from manuscripts they hold: the American Philosophical Society, Bowdoin College Library, the Friends Historical Library of Swarthmore College, the Harry Ransom Humanities Research Center at the University of Texas at Austin, the Historical Society of Pennsylvania, the Library Company of Philadelphia, the Department of Rare Books and Special Collections at the Princeton University Library, the Quaker Collection of Haverford College, the University of Pennsylvania Rare Book and Manuscript Library, the Seeley G. Mudd Manuscript Library of Princeton University, and the University of Virginia Library. The owner of the first volume of the John F. Mifflin's diary has also kindly allowed me to quote from that manuscript.

This book is dedicated with love to my boyfriend, Peter Terzian.

# Introduction: The Ghost of André

*But all that can be said of friendship, is like botany to flowers.*
—Thoreau

In Washington Irving's tale "The Legend of Sleepy Hollow," the Headless Horseman is said to be the ghost of a Hessian soldier decapitated by an American cannon during the Revolutionary War. He may, however, be no more than a virile young prankster with a cape and a pumpkin. Terror or irony: Irving leaves it for the reader to decide. In either case, the Headless Horseman corresponds to the animal part of human nature. He is a body. Irving's antihero, the schoolteacher Ichabod Crane, has read too much Cotton Mather, and the Headless Horseman is what comes back to haunt the intellectual heirs, weak and strong, of American Puritanism.

But there is another specter haunting Sleepy Hollow. Unlike the Headless Horseman, this second ghost has a name. The name is familiar to Ichabod, who dreads crossing the terrain that belongs to it:

> [Ichabod] had never felt so lonely and dismal. He was, moreover, approaching the very place where many of the scenes of the ghost stories had been laid. In the centre of the road stood an enormous tulip tree, which towered like a giant above all the other trees of the neighbourhood, and formed a kind of land mark. Its limbs were gnarled, and fantastic, large enough to form trunks

for ordinary trees, twisting down almost to the earth, and rising again into the air. It was connected with the tragical story of the unfortunate André, who had been taken prisoner hard by; and was universally known by the name of Major André's tree.[1]

A page later, at a small rude bridge that is the "identical spot that the unfortunate André was captured," Ichabod first hears and sees the Headless Horseman. The Horseman is so closely attached to the landscape of John André's demise that a reader may wonder whether one ghost is haunting the other.

Why was the memory of John André — a handsome, young British officer caught and hanged as a spy just after he negotiated with Benedict Arnold for the betrayal and surrender of West Point — so persistent and disturbing? His is a difficult ghost for a modern reader to interpret. He belongs to a moment long since passed, but in his day he participated in a cultural experiment as powerful and novel as America itself. If the Headless Horseman represents the body, then John André represents sympathy, which in the first blush of Romanticism seemed to transcend the body's limits. That André was British hardly mattered; every American still felt British. André stood for a principle higher and more appealing than nationality, an ideal to which America as a nation aspired — the disinterested fraternity of men. Of course he haunted Irving. In antebellum America, the question he posed haunted all serious literature: Could this spirit survive in the United States?

In this book I argue that for a time the special task of American literature, like that of American politics, was the representation of bonds between men that kept men free — the provocation of sympathy, without any tethering of it. In John André's story are the seeds of many of the themes this book explores: the power of sympathy, its close relation to imposture, romantic friendship between men, writing as a vehicle for men's affections for one another, the conflict between sentiment and authority, and the peculiar fate of all these things in America.

There is something mysterious about sympathy. It allows us to bridge a gap that seems as though it ought to be unbridgeable. It allows us to feel emotions that are not ours. As Adam Smith noted in his 1759 summa of sympathy *The Theory of Moral Sentiments,* our senses "never did, and never can, carry us beyond our own person." Because the integrity of our bodies isolates us, no one can experience directly what another person feels, no matter how eloquently other people may describe the state of their hearts. But human beings do understand one another's feelings, well enough to respond to them with nuance and conviction every day. As Smith explained, although we have no direct access to our neighbor's sensations, we may "by the imagination . . .

The Unfortunate DEATH of MAJOR ANDRE

(Adjutant General to the English Army) at Head Quarters in New York. Oct.r 2. 1780, who was found within the American Lines in the character of a Spy.

*The Unfortunate Death of Major André*, by William Hamilton and John Goldar. 1783. Library of Congress, Rare Book and Special Collections Division, Continental Congress Broadside Collection and Constitutional Convention Broadside Collection.

place ourselves in his situation, . . . enter as it were into his body, and become in some measure the same person with him, and thence form some idea of his sensations, and even feel something which, though weaker in degree, is not altogether unlike them." Smith described sympathy as "changing places in fancy."[2] It is a work of fiction with real effects.

The object of a noble and intense sympathy is, we feel, our friend. As Thoreau explained, if sympathy is a fiction, then we tell our friend, "you are the fact in a fiction." In every friendship, there is a negotiation between life and art—a productive tension between a real person and a relationship that must be imagined. This is the paradox Emerson resigned himself to, half humorously, in his essay "Experience": "Let us treat the men and women well: treat them as if they were real: perhaps they are."[3]

In his 1711 essay collection *Characteristics,* the third earl of Shaftesbury proposed sympathy as the answer to Hobbes's pessimism about human nature. Shaftesbury believed that human beings had a sociable instinct as natural and perhaps as strong as their selfish instincts. (According to Shaftesbury, in publishing *Leviathan,* Hobbes had inadvertently proved Shaftesbury's point: Who but an altruist would take the trouble to warn others about the dangerous selfishness of human beings?) Somewhat punningly, Shaftesbury called this sociable drive "common sense"—a communal instinct that all humans shared. For Shaftesbury and for the Scottish Enlightenment thinkers who followed his lead, sympathy was therefore a political as well as a psychological principle, as it had been for Aristotle, who noted in the *Nicomachean Ethics* that "friendship . . . seems to hold states together."[4]

For a century and a half, sympathy had the force of a biological fact, as if it were as essential to human nature as sight, hearing, taste, touch, and smell. England's and America's most enlightened thinkers believed in what Francis Hutcheson called "this secret chain between each person and mankind."[5] Well into the nineteenth century, undergraduates at Harvard and Princeton studied it, under various names, in the treatises of Hutcheson and Dugald Stewart. Not until Darwin observed that competition, not cooperation, was the law of nature did its scientific prestige falter.

As a political force and a cultural ideal, sympathy was vital to the United States as it emerged. In *The American Crisis,* Thomas Paine wrote that sympathy alone had held the nation together in the moment of revolution. "We had no other law than a kind of moderated passion," Paine wrote, "no other civil power than an honest mob; and no other protection than the temporary attachment of one man to another."[6] The relationship that seemed to sustain sympathy best was friendship, and friendship in America became charged with a new meaning. The colonies' bond to England had been imagined as that of a child to a parent, or a wife to a husband. But as a metaphor and model for citizenly love, romantic friendship was more congenial to republican ideology than either filial or marital relationships. Romantic friendship was egalitarian. It could bind men without curtailing their liberty. (It could bind women, too, but because women were not full citizens, the political implications of their friendships were different.) Like confederation into civil society, friendship bestowed benefits that were other than financial or sexual.

"It is in war that the knot of fellowship is closest drawn," Shaftesbury once observed. And during the Revolutionary War, American soldiers expressed their love for one another in terms that may seem unusually frank to a modern reader. It was in this context that John André was so disruptive and appealing. André was highly lovable, but he was the enemy. To an idealistic young American soldier such as Alexander Hamilton, who prided himself on his noble-mindedness and emotional delicacy, André was exquisite torture. As Hamilton would confess, "My feelings were never put to so severe a trial."[7]

In any narrative of André, Hamilton figures prominently, because he was close to André during his imprisonment and because the two men shared an exceptional talent for expressing emotions. Hamilton's talent is well displayed in his letters to his friend John Laurens. Roughly the same age, Hamilton and Laurens served together as aides-de-camp to General Washington. Within the military-administrative unit of Washington's "family," camaraderie was high, but Hamilton and Laurens were particularly close. In December 1778, Hamilton seconded Laurens in a duel with the court-martialed General Charles Lee. In the spring of 1779, Laurens left Washington's family and traveled to South Carolina, where he hoped to convert slaves into American troops. Laurens's scheme was prematurely idealistic; the South Carolina legislature never approved his plan to raise a black battalion. But Laurens's absence gave Hamilton occasion to write about his feelings for his friend, and in his eloquent letters, he gave his sympathies free rein: "Cold in my professions, warm in my friendships, I wish, my Dear Laurens, it might be in my power, by action rather than words, to convince you that I love you. I shall only tell you that 'till you bade us Adieu, I hardly knew the value you had taught my heart to set upon you."[8]

This was unusually candid language, even for Hamilton, who usually adopted a bantering tone with Laurens. Later in the same letter, for example, he instructed Laurens to "advertise in the public papers" for a wife for Hamilton and provided a comic description both of himself ("mind you do justice to the length of my nose") and of the kind of woman he preferred ("She must believe in god and hate a saint"). On 11 September 1779, Hamilton twitted Laurens for having answered only one of the five or six letters he had written.

"Like a jealous lover," Hamilton wrote, "when I thought you slighted my caresses, my affection was alarmed and my vanity piqued. I had almost resolved to lavish no more of them upon you and to reject you as an inconstant and an ungrateful ———."⁹

The word to be supplied in the space Hamilton left blank was probably not a nice one. As Hamilton noted at the end of that particular letter, "On revising my work I find several strokes of the true School-boy sublime." Between two men so concerned for their honor that they periodically risked their lives in duels to maintain it, silliness was as much a sign of trust as emotionality. Hamilton goofed, whined, and postured, because he could rely on Laurens to be discreet. "My ravings are for your own bosom," Hamilton explained on 12 September 1780. To Laurens it was safe to confide a touch of grandiose despair: "In short, Laurens," Hamilton wrote on 8 January 1780, "I am disgusted with every thing in this world but yourself and *very* few more honest fellows and I have no other wish than as soon as possible to make a brilliant exit." Or he could indulge a whiff of sexual impropriety. On 16 September 1780, after boasting about the charms of his fiancée, Elizabeth Schuyler, Hamilton added, "My Mistress is a good girl, and already loves you because I have told her you are a clever fellow and my friend; but mind, she loves you *a l'americaine* not *a la françoise*." If he felt that he had to specify the style of love, there must have been a question in someone's mind. No wonder Martha Washington named her tomcat Hamilton.¹⁰

Hamilton's correspondence with Laurens was rich, capable of conveying with subtlety a wide range of sentiments. It was only natural, then, that when Hamilton found himself loving and esteeming a man whom his commanding officer insisted must hang, he wrote to Laurens with the story.

That story began with a secret correspondence — a correspondence "under feigned signatures and in a mercantile disguise," in Hamilton's turn of phrase.¹¹ Relying on two Loyalist poets as intermediaries, the American general Benedict Arnold and the British major John André wrote each other letters disguised in the vocabulary of commerce and encrypted in a numerical code keyed to various editions of Blackstone's *Commentaries*. By means of these ciphered letters, the two men arranged for Arnold to hand West Point over to the British in exchange for twenty thousand pounds. A face-to-face meeting, they hoped, would clinch the deal.

In fact, the meeting proved to be their undoing. On Saturday, 23 September 1780, three American volunteer militiamen stopped and strip-searched an unarmed man in civilian dress attempting to cross from American into British territory just above Tarrytown, New York. The militiamen may have been looking for loot; the neutral ground between American and British lines wasn't so much patrolled as marauded.

The man they stopped was five foot nine, twenty-nine years old, slender, and handsome, with a dark complexion. Under a large blue watch coat and cape, he was wearing "a purple or crimson coat with vellum-bound button-holes and garnished with threadbare gold-lace." He had the nankeen knee breeches and white-topped boots of a gentleman, and a beaver hat that had seen better days. When challenged, the man identified himself first as British, then as American. He presented a pass, signed by General Benedict Arnold, that authorized "Mr. John Anderson to pass the guards to the White Plains, or below, if he chuses." When the militiamen questioned whether the pass was genuine, "John Anderson" offered to pay them a ransom to release him.[12]

Put on guard by their prisoner's quick switch of story — and perhaps tempted by his boots — the militiamen led Anderson to a tulip tree, twenty-six feet in circumference, that stood just south of the bridge he had crossed. This was the tree that would one day frighten Ichabod Crane so badly.[13] Beneath it, Anderson — in fact, André — was searched. In his stockings, the militiamen found papers that detailed the strengths and weaknesses of the American fortifications at West Point. Most of the papers were in Arnold's handwriting. The militiamen decided to hand their prisoner over to the authorities.

The first officer who took custody of André believed that the Englishman must have stolen the papers from Arnold, and so he sent news to Arnold that the papers had been recovered. Later that day, a second, more savvy officer realized that because André was carrying a pass signed by Arnold, the general was complicit. Another letter was sent, this time to General Washington, due at Arnold's headquarters. Once he knew that Washington had been notified, André also wrote to the commander-in-chief, disclosing his identity, declaring himself to be an officer and requesting that he be treated accordingly. On Monday morning, 25 September, Washington was late to breakfast at Arnold's headquarters. The letter to Arnold arrived before Washington did, and Arnold fled.

As soon as Washington read the letter informing him of Arnold's treason, he sent Lieutenant Colonel Alexander Hamilton galloping after Arnold, but it was too late. Arnold was safely aboard the British ship *Vulture*. Upon his return, Hamilton wrote Elizabeth Schuyler with the news. Hamilton had witnessed an affecting scene highly suitable for sharing with his fiancée — the hysteria of Arnold's abandoned, apparently innocent wife. Sobbing, raving, and clutching her infant child, Peggy Arnold was a natural object of sympathy; she was a virtuous mother rendered miserable through no fault of her own. The tableau vivant gave Hamilton the opportunity to stress that he would never treat a woman as ungallantly as Arnold had. "Could I forgive Arnold for sacrificing his honor reputation and duty," Hamilton wrote, "I could not forgive him for acting a part that must have forfieted the esteem of so fine a woman."[14]

Hamilton wrote to Schuyler again on 2 October 1780, the day André was hanged. Again he turned André's story to sentimental advantage; this time Hamilton averred that he wished he possessed André's charms, in order to "endear me more to you."[15] But Hamilton did not address his more extensive narrative of the André affair to his fiancée. He sent her his account of Arnold's distraught wife, and with the same fine instinct for a sentimentally appropriate audience, Hamilton addressed a ten-page narrative of the affecting but manly distress of André to his romantic male friend, Laurens. His fiancée received a copy.

"Never perhaps did any man suffer death with more justice, or deserve it less," Hamilton wrote Laurens. As Hamilton explained, André had intended neither to cross into American territory nor to assume a disguise, but circumstances (and perhaps some negligence on Arnold's part) had forced him to do both. His life was therefore forfeit. André confessed this with "candor and firmness mixed with a becoming sensibility." Hamilton's letter described a man more concerned with the feelings of others than with any attempt to save his own neck. To the board of American officers who examined him, André "acknowledged the generosity of the behaviour towards him . . . in the strongest terms of manly gratitude." Concerned that his commanding officer, Sir Henry Clinton, might reproach himself for André's death, André requested special permission to write to assure Clinton that he was not to blame. When someone in the American camp suggested to André that he be exchanged for Arnold, whom everyone would have preferred to see hang, André refused to consider it. All he asked for himself was "to be indulged with a professional death." That is, he asked to be shot as a soldier rather than hanged as a spy.[16]

Washington refused this small mercy. To have granted it would have cast doubt on André's sentence, because if André had not been acting as a spy, then he must have been a British officer negotiating with his American counterpart under a flag of truce, who ought to be released. By denying André's request, Washington turned the execution into a moving and tragic scene and risked alienating the affections of many of the American officers around him. During the few days the Americans held him, André had won many hearts with his knowledgeable but genteelly diffident style of conversation and his pretty pen-and-ink sketches. "From the few days of intimate intercourse I had with him," Major Benjamin Tallmadge later recalled, "I became so deeply attached to Major André, that I could remember no instance where my affections were so

*Self-Portrait*, by Major John André. October 1, 1780. Yale University Art Gallery. Gift of Ebenezer Baldwin, B.A. 1808.

fully absorbed by any man." On the day of the hanging, Hamilton hastened to assure his fiancée that "I urged a compliance with André's request to be shot, and I do not think it would have had an ill effect; but some people are only sensible to motives of policy, and sometimes from a narrow disposition mistake it." A few months after the hanging, Hamilton quarreled with Washington over a minor rudeness and left the general's staff.[17]

Washington did not attend the execution. But Hamilton witnessed the condemned man's surprise at the sight of the gallows and heard his noble last words. Asked if he had anything to say, André answered, "Nothing, but to request you will witness to the world, that I die like a brave man." In the opinion of one Enos Reynolds, who served as a sentinel at the hanging, André "was the handsomest man I ever laid my eyes on."[18]

Lafayette, who like many others wept openly at the hanging, called Hamilton's account of André's imprisonment and death "a masterpiece of literary talents and amiable sensibility." Hamilton's letter may be the earliest instance in the young republic of the literary ambition this book explores: it is a piece of writing that aspires to represent a man's feelings for another man. The letter owes much of its poignancy to the reader's sense that Hamilton recorded his emotions on paper as an inadequate substitute for an action that could not be taken. He could write a letter, but he could not save André. "There was in truth no way of saving him," Hamilton wrote. "Arnold or he must have been the victim; the former was out of our power." This sense of the inadequacy of expression, however, draws the reader's sympathy all the more strongly, perhaps because sympathy itself is always an inadequate substitute, a fictional third term interposed between two people who are never fully present to each other. As Emerson would explain two generations later, "Souls never touch their objects"; in the realm of the emotions, sympathy is the best one can do.[19]

Hamilton's letter to Laurens resembles the works of literature this book investigates in another way as well: Hamilton could not have written it alone. His letter was the product of his intimacy with André and Laurens. The Federalist-era Philadelphia gentlemen whom I discuss in Chapter 1 kept their diaries for each other; Charles Brockden Brown's horror novels, discussed in Chapters 2 and 3, were nursed and disciplined by the young male friends in whose company he wrote them; Emerson wrote the poems and essays discussed in Chapters 4 and 5 about men he loved at crucial moments in his life; and two of the Melville novels discussed in Chapter 6 were dedicated to his old friend Jack Chase. Considered as an instance of sympathy, each of these literary works is a collaboration. The man who serves as muse appears to have a talent for inspiring sentiment, which the author usually feels obliged to credit explicitly. In the case of John André, that talent is surprisingly well documented.

An imprudent fondness for André appeared not only in the private recollections of American officers like Tallmadge and Hamilton but also in ballads and newspaper accounts. Washington's unsentimental decision caused so much disgruntlement and recrimination that nearly a year later, the *Pennsylvania Packet* was still complaining that "the high encomiums passed by American writers on a British spy, have been made use of to justify a charge of want of humanity in our excellent commander-in-chief, and the court of officers that condemned him."[20]

There is a quieter but no less remarkable testimony to André's sentimental appeal in the diary of the Philadelphia businessman Thomas Pym Cope. On 7 July 1801, Cope sailed up the Hudson River to Albany with a friend, the magazine editor and former novelist Charles Brockden Brown. At Tarrytown, Cope saw a melancholy sight. He recorded in his diary that what he observed "tended to revive the image of a man who was always dear to our family. His virtues made him so to others and perhaps no man ever met with a greater number of sympathizers. His hard & unfortunate sentence was lamented even by those whom the policy of war had created his enemies. Here, said my informant, Major André was taken. It was under that tree."[21]

In the hands of Washington Irving, André's tree inspired dread. No doubt Cope's friend Brown, more comfortable with the dark than with the light side of sympathy, would also have rendered it as a thing of horror. But Cope saw in the tulip tree an opportunity for pleasant, melancholy recollection. In early 1776, when Cope was seven years old, André had been billeted as a prisoner of war in the Lancaster, Pennsylvania, home of Thomas's father, Caleb Cope, "a Quaker gentleman of loyal proclivities." In Lancaster, André had whiled away his time by teaching a number of local children to draw. Among his pupils were Benjamin Smith Barton, the future naturalist, and Caleb Cope's oldest son, John. Until the end of his life, Thomas treasured a watercolor André had painted of a cozy English hamlet.[22]

In June 1803, Thomas P. Cope again had occasion to remember André. His brother John Cope, André's former pupil, had turned up in a Philadelphia public house "in a state of neglect & human degradation." Thomas moved John to the house of a widow who lived nearby, where a doctor and nurses were hired to care for him. John was too far gone, however. Evidently a longtime alcoholic, he died a few days later of "an infection of the liver."[23]

Thomas felt he could identify the crisis that had derailed his brother's life, and was spurred by his death to reflect on it. In 1776, when André had stayed with the Copes, John had been

> a youth of very promising talents. His mind was uncultivated by education & experience, but his heart was affectionate & pure, his person attractive & his genius versatile, active & powerful. His thirst for knowledge greatly exceeded his means of acquiring it. A similarity of taste & character ripened into a mutual & ardent attachment between him & André. They formed the resolution to spend the residue of their days together. London, as affording the best hope to rising genius, was designed as the place of their permanent abode. André made known their intentions to my father & craved his approbation. John also pressed the suit, but he pressed in vain; neither argument, solicitation nor tears availed. Father was inflexible. He would not part with his favourite child & André, when exchanged, was compelled to leave his friend behind him.

In 1776, André was twenty-five years old; John Cope, thirteen. According to André's biographer, André told John's father that he wanted to sell his commission and return to England and that taking charge of John's education would give him "a reasonable excuse for quitting the army." A Quaker who worked as a plasterer and had served as a town burgess, Caleb could hardly have been expected to give up his son to an artist's life.[24]

In March 1776, still a prisoner, André was transferred from Lancaster to Carlisle. He did not forget John Cope. Very properly, he kept up a correspondence with the boy's father rather than the boy himself. On 3 April 1776, he wrote to suggest that John come to stay with him in Carlisle. "He will be the greatest part of the day with us, employ'd in the few things I am able to instruct him in. . . . With regard to Expence this is to be attended with none to you. A little assiduity and friendship is all I ask in my young friend in return for my good will to be of service to him in a way of improving the Talents Nature hath given him." This offer, too, Caleb Cope appears to have refused on his son's behalf. But André continued to write, sending his compliments to "your son my disciple" and offering constructive criticisms of John's drawings when the father forwarded samples. On 2 December 1776, André still hoped that John "may once more be within my reach, when it will be a very great pleasure to me to give him what assistance I can." At the end of the year André was released in an exchange of prisoners; in January 1777 he was stationed in New York. No later letters between André and the Copes survive, but according to an oral tradition in the Cope family, André continued to write until his ill-fated trip to confer with Arnold.[25]

Was there more to André's letters to Caleb Cope than meets the eye? Were they accompanied by a secret correspondence with John? André liked skulduggery. For example, a few years later, when he and Arnold were trying to find a safe way to communicate, André offered to start up a correspondence with one of Arnold's wife's friends. André knew many women in Philadelphia high society because during the British occupation of the city in 1778, he had captured their attention by organizing an elaborate regatta and costume ball, the Mischianza, for which he designed the scenery and women's outfits. André suggested that his letters could "talk of the Meschianza & other nonsense," which would arouse no suspicion if intercepted. Meanwhile, interlined in the gossip in invisible ink, the two men would bargain for Arnold's treachery.[26]

Perhaps André had in 1776 indulged his penchant for conspiracy with John Cope; perhaps not. In any case, however formal and proper André's letters to the father may have seemed, they provoked a wild rebellion in the son. As Thomas Cope recalled in 1803, "Whether by a private understanding between them, or whether it was the offspring of his own motion alone, I cannot remember, but John soon attempted to follow his friend to New York. His escape was private, but would not long be concealed from his father, who went in search of him & having overtaken him before he reached the British lines, John suffered the mortification of being brought back & the bitter anguish of seeing his schemes of future greatness & happiness blighted by what he deemed a cruel interposition of parental authority." Thomas records that after this humiliation, John forsook art, grew sullen, and became dissipated. In Thomas's assessment, "the chagrin of disappointed hope" ruined his brother's life and perhaps André's, too. After all, André had offered to quit the British army to be with the boy. "Had John's inclination to follow the fortunes of

André been gratified," Thomas wondered, "what might not have been the present condition of both?"[27]

Ichabod Crane's heirs are careful not to make Ichabod Crane's mistake: scholars today think about the body. To a gay scholar in particular, a story like that of John André and John Cope is tantalizing. But the story belongs to a different era, when stories like it were not necessarily rare. What did it mean?

Did it mean they had sex? That is a valid and interesting historical question. It is not, however, a question I aim to answer. In antebellum America, men said little about sex between men. About their romantic feelings for one another, on the other hand, men were garrulous and subtle. For scholars, sympathy is a target of opportunity.[28] In this book I try to understand, in some detail, how a group of men in the United States wrote about what they felt for one another, and how in the process they created literature. Like its subject, this book is somewhere between life and art; that is, it shifts between biography and literary criticism. Although I intended to examine men's friendships only, the stories I choose to tell would be unintelligible without some discussion of such women as Deborah Norris Logan and Margaret Fuller. At crucial moments, sentimental male writers borrowed from the culture of women's friendships.

In Chapter 1, I tell a story similar to André and Cope's. The difference in age between John F. Mifflin and James Gibson was comparable to that between André and Cope. In both cases, the man's interest in the boy's career seems to have channeled an emotional investment, and although the boy's family regarded the friendship as innocent, to a modern eye there seems to be something equivocal and perhaps effeminate about the older man's gentility and solicitousness. But there is an important difference between the stories: unlike André and Cope, Mifflin and Gibson left behind writings that attest to their feelings. Under the names Leander and Lorenzo, they kept diaries for each other. That transition from life into literary art is the focus of my interest.

In one of his letters to Washington, André asked for "a decency of conduct towards me . . . as I was involuntarily an impostor."[29] Although Washington treated André graciously, he hanged him as a spy. Too much sympathy with André, the general recognized, was not in America's interest. There was something undemocratic about the desire to reciprocate André's "manly gratitude," a virtue that belonged, after all, to an aristocratic class that was not supposed to exist in the United States.[30] Sympathy may have assisted democracy when it bound Hamilton and Laurens, but it threatened the national cause when it linked a man like Hamilton to a man like André. André had corrupted Arnold. There were grounds for suspecting a sympathetic man of being a seductive impostor.

In his 1798 tragedy *André*, William Dunlap dramatized this danger by portraying an American soldier "so blinded by his love" for André that he wanted to desert.[31] Unfortunately, Dunlap did not engage the central ambiguity in the nature of sympathy. In the play, the character André is amiable and unequivocal. He even warns the hero not to justify immoral actions with high-minded sentimental motives.

Dunlap's friend Charles Brockden Brown, however, was fascinated by the mixed motives of impostors, and in a series of Gothic novels, Brown explored the terrors that Dunlap had sentimentalized. As an ambitious literary artist, Brown coveted the aesthetic power of sympathy, but as an American, he worried that it could compromise a citizen's autonomy. In Chapter 2, I examine Brown's letters, which chart his difficult evolution as a novelist. Brown seems to have learned how to turn sympathy into literature by using a circle of intimate male friends as guinea pigs for his experiments. Success brought him feelings of guilt and potency, and that ambivalence became the subject of his art. In Chapter 3, I read three of Brown's novels as parables of deformed sympathy.

Although Hamilton wrote Laurens that André could not be saved, Lafayette reports that Hamilton "was daily searching some way to save him." Hamilton may even have written a letter to Sir Henry Clinton that offered to exchange André for Arnold, although the letter was signed "A B" and the handwriting, if Hamilton's, was disguised.[32] Even though Hamilton took action, his letter does not ask the reader to. In fact, its pathos is enhanced by its air of stoic resignation. The reader is invited to appreciate melancholy feelings provoked by André's fate, but is excused from advocacy (which would come too late) or indignation (which would be treasonous) on behalf of André the man. The letter also derives sentimental power from an emotional misdirection; it describes feelings aroused by André, but shares them with Laurens. In Chapters 4 and 5, I argue that a similar separation and misdirection are the hallmarks of R. Waldo Emerson's prose, part of a sentimental strategy I call "hierotomy," the technique of separating one's feelings for a man from the man himself, in order to free them for literary use.

Like Major John André, the hero of Herman Melville's last novel did not dispute that he had committed the crime for which he would be hanged. And like André, Billy Budd was a beautiful young Englishman who treated his executioners with heartbreaking sensitivity and whose death seemed to cast a shadow across the paths of sympathy and democracy in America. I argue in Chapter 6 that *Billy Budd* is Melville's angry revision of the literary configuration this book describes — an exorcism, as it were, of André's ghost.

A young Thoreau once wrote in his journal that "a friend in history looks like some premature soul." Friendship is itself highly sympathetic, as Adam

Smith explained, because for a spectator of friendship, sympathy is "redou-bled."[33] Reading these diaries, letters, essays, and novels, I sometimes felt as though I were in the presence of a struggle I recognized despite my removal in time and sensibility. Some of that experience, I hope, has made it into the pages that follow.

## In the Pear Grove: The Romance of Leander, Lorenzo, and Castalio

On 1 August 1786, a Princeton undergraduate wrote of his twenty-seven-year-old friend, "After recitation [I] went to Leander — he gave me a hair ribbon and I promised to sleep with him to night."[1] More than two centuries later, it is hard to read this diary entry without either pooh-poohing or exaggerating its hint of sex. On the one hand, it might mean very little. After all, in the late eighteenth century, male friends often shared a bed, and many gentlemen were fastidious about their personal appearance. On the other hand, the entry must mean something. It does show a man flattering a boy's vanity, in a relationship where the two are easy and familiar with each other's bodies.

Gay love as we know it is modern, and as Thoreau wrote, "The *past* cannot be *presented*."[2] In the case of this particular undergraduate and his older friend, however, it is possible to examine at some length the language the men used to describe and convey their feelings. James Gibson (1769–1856) and John Fishbourne Mifflin (1759–1813) left behind diaries that offer a uniquely detailed and extensive chronicle of passion between men in early America. Under the cognomens of Leander and Lorenzo, Mifflin and Gibson wrote for each other and about each other. Two volumes (totaling 546 pages) of Mifflin's diary survive, and one volume (100 pages) of Gibson's. Read in conjunction with the family correspondence of a third young man, Isaac Norris III (known as Castalio), these diaries tell a story of affection between American men at a crucial moment: at the acme of the culture of sentiment and sensibility, when individuals first considered following the unruly impulse of sympathy as far as it would go. The men's writings also sensitively register the changing ideal of literary beauty: the diaries begin as gestures of refinement, like fancy ribbons that gentlemen might add to their coiffures, but they gradually become exposures of the self—attempts to let out something unexpected.

Where the Second Bank of the United States now stands—on Chestnut Street between Fourth and Fifth streets in Philadelphia, one block east of Independence Hall—the Norris family once grew a famously elegant garden. Charles Norris had built his house on the western edge of the city, but Philadelphia grew outward to meet the Norrises: by the 1780s their home enviably combined rural proportions with urban location. The Quaker matron Ann Warder recorded in her diary on 18 October 1786 that the Norrises "have a noble house and beautiful garden, which are rare in this city." Deborah Norris Logan, Charles's only daughter, remembered years later that "a walk in the garden was considered by the more respectable citizens as a treat to their friends from a distance, and as one of the means to impress them with a favourable opinion of the beauties of their city."[3]

The Norris garden was a mix of beauty and science typical of the eighteenth century. The Norrises — or rather the Swiss gardener they employed for twenty-five years—raised pineapples in their hothouse and medicinal herbs in their herbarium. Just outside the window of the back parlor, a palisade of roses and scarlet honeysuckle enclosed a terrace shaded by catalpas. Farther away grew willows, the first trees of this species brought to the region, a gift from Benjamin Franklin. To reach the garden proper, one descended a flight of stone steps into an area of "square parterres and beds, regularly intersected by graveled and grass walks and alleys." Espaliers of grapes led to a rustic-style cottage that lodged one of the women whom the Norrises were always too tactful to call a servant. The garden was a jewel. The balance and order of its design, the attention to previously unknown species, and the fastidiously kept grounds spoke of the Norrises' "taste and industry."[4]

On Saturday, 20 May 1786, John Fishbourne Mifflin rambled through the Norris garden alone, as he often did. He was slight, weighing 127 pounds, and carried a cane. He was very nearsighted. His powdered hair was gathered into a fashionable queue. Mifflin, at twenty-seven years of age, was the sort of man that children threw snowballs at—finicky about his appearance, mildly pompous in his manners, and too delicate to do much harm if he caught the

*A Party to Virginia*, probably by Elizabeth or Mary Rhoads. Circa 1777–1778. Historical Society of Pennsylvania, Rhoads Family Manuscripts, E-95.

offender. His father had been a successful merchant. The son, a lawyer with a trust fund, spent most of his days either sipping tea with Philadelphia ladies or trying to collect rent from his own or his half-brother's tenants.[5]

On this visit, as on most of his visits to the Norris garden, Mifflin headed to the pear grove. It was his favorite spot — "the scene of friendship," he called it in his diary. "Dear delightful spot," he wrote, "it ever sheds a charming influence over my spirits." As Richard Bushman has noted, an eighteenth-century genteel garden was meant to be "an extension of the parlor, a place where polite people walked and conversed." It was intended as a backdrop for highly staged, decorous socializing; if the garden was sufficiently scientific, it could provide a topic of conversation as well. Mifflin, however, did not visit the pear grove to show off his knowledge of botany or to court women (at least, not exclusively for these reasons: on another day he gathered hyacinths to catch the interest of young Mary Rhoads, who lived next door). He sat in the pear grove because "it always brings Lorenzo [James Gibson] very affectionately to my mind."[6] Mifflin came to meditate on a young male friend and on the pleasures of friendship.

This was a novel use of the garden. It was neither virtuous nor polite — the two behavior styles Mifflin's late father would have had to choose between. For much of the eighteenth century, American men had seen themselves reflected in *The Spectator.* They had defined themselves according to the challenge that the newfangled merchant Andrew Freeport presented to the old-style country squire Roger de Coverley. Sir Andrew represented progress and refinement, but no one was quite ready to dispense with Sir Roger, in part because it was with stodgy republican virtue that men like George Washington had won the Revolution. Never mind that America lacked a landed aristocracy on the English scale. The gentlemanly ethos that kept *The Spectator*'s Sir Roger insolvent was imposing enough to prevent even ambitious and unconventional Benjamin Franklin from assuming any pretensions to gentility until his moneymaking was decorously behind him. But under pressure of satire and bribed by dollars, virtue was gradually yielding to politeness. In Mifflin's day, the republican patriot seemed quaint, rustic, and out of touch. His deference to superiors and authority over subordinates no longer functioned well in a postrevolutionary society, where even parents could hope only to befriend their children, not command them. In Royall Tyler's 1787 play *The Contrast,* the old soldier Colonel Manly holds the moral high ground, although his overcoat is tattered, stinky, and years old. The audience would have snickered. As Tyler lamented in his prologue, with not quite heartfelt censure, "modern youths, with imitative sense, / Deem taste in dress the proof of excellence."[7]

The new politeness went hand in hand with the burgeoning of commerce, and the economic force behind this cultural shift was recognized even by those who did not welcome it. Politeness was polish, the natural result of the friction of marketplace collisions and exchanges. As Montesquieu observed, "Plus il y a de gens dans une nation qui ont besoin d'avoir des ménagements entre eux et de ne pas déplaire, plus il y a de politesse." Or, as Mifflin put it in his diary, "How civil & goodnatured people are when you are laying out your money with them." Politeness was venal, but it had the moral advantage over virtue that it was conceived in relation to others; it looked beyond oneself or one's own pride. However praiseworthy virtue might be, it was less social than politeness, and less useful. As Colonel Manly's sister disparagingly explained of her brother's goodness, "His heart is like an old maiden lady's handbox; it contains many costly things, arranged with the most scrupulous nicety, yet the misfortune is, that they are too delicate, costly, and antiquated, for common use." Politeness was a tool; virtue was a trinket.[8]

What then was Mifflin doing in the garden alone? As a man of commerce, he did not believe in solitary pleasures. He would have read in Edward Young's *Night Thoughts* that "Joy is an import; joy is an exchange; Joy flies monopolists: it calls for two" — a couplet that neatly entwined commercial values with the moral superiority of other-directed over selfish actions. To miss an absent friend when other companions could be found was both impolite and, in terms of social economics, imprudent. Mifflin's pear-grove meditation defied the application of market rules to the social sphere, but the blow it delivered to republican virtue was even more lethal. The last card that virtue had held in reserve over politeness was that virtue was inside. It was the constitutive weakness of the man of commerce that every property he had was alienable; no part of him was essential. He was smooth but perhaps soulless. People feared that under commerce's polish "the friction is so violent, that not only the rust, but the metal too, will be lost in the progress."[9] Virtue was supposed to be a kind of inner steel that would not corrode. But what Mifflin found in the garden trumped virtue. It too was inside — but like politeness, it was oriented toward others.

Sympathy — also called sentiment, sensibility, or compassion — posed as the most delicate possible refinement and the highest moral quality a person could exhibit, destroying the ethical systems it replaced by claiming to represent the acme of both. The seed of it may have been planted as early as the Restoration, in the optimism preached in England by latitudinarians trying to soften the Puritan concepts of an inscrutable, cruel God and an abject, fallen humanity. Shaftesbury, followed by the philosophers of the Scottish Enlightenment, discovered it operating deep within the human heart, a "moral sense" just as vital as the other five. This "innate principle of sociability" was a touchstone in a world loosened by Locke's environmentalism and Hobbes's cynicism. It grounded people; it said their hearts were naturally good. By providing a counterforce to self-interest, it allowed philosophers once again to explain altruism as not just possible but necessary to human happiness. But like any new force, it also appeared to be dangerous, which heightened its allure. In a testament to the power of sympathy, most of early American novels and many of the British imports in circulation documented its ability to seduce and ruin those, usually young women, who failed to understand its operations. Among a certain class, sympathy — irresistible, unruly, and mysterious — was all the rage.[10]

It fascinated Mifflin. His diary returns again and again to two concerns: his moods and his friendships. In colonial America, "friendship" had been a euphemism for patronage and dependence. Robert Munford had written in his 1744 play *The Candidates,* " 'Tis said self-interest is the secret aim, / Of those uniting under Friendship's name."[11] But by codifying and depersonalizing economic relations, commercial culture had paradoxically made a new kind of personal relationship possible. It had cut friendship loose from its financial duties. For the first time, friendship could be entirely disinterested.[12] Walt Whitman's much later desire to found an "institution of the dear love of comrades" should not be confounded with the eighteenth-century understanding of friendship as unfettered possibility: the new friendships seemed capable of anything because they had at last sprung *free* of institutions. Mifflin studied the vicissitudes of his libido as if it were a penned animal he had untethered for an experiment: it might serve its master; it might cause terrible damage. But in any case, from its tentative, unsteady motions he would learn something altogether new.

Mifflin's reveries in the Norris pear grove are among the earliest entries in his diary. They are a strange mix of emptiness and superfluity: an actorless stage cluttered with props. He was trying to take hold of someone who was not there; he was trying to produce an absence and then preserve it. In order not to lose his bittersweet longing for his friend, Mifflin wrote it down. Precious emotions had come over him in surplus, and he wanted to invest the excess back into the scene that had produced them.

Well read in British literature, Mifflin turned to a fragmented novelistic style to bank his feelings against the usury of time. In Richardson's novels, time had flowed fitfully, released in discrete, intermittent quantums. This stop-and-go pace had begun as a side effect of epistolary form, but writers were discovering in it new emotional possibilities. Sterne exploded the sequence of his scenes with ekphrastic commentary to see if the fragments could be made to cohere into a new emotional sense. The power of sympathy and the structure of plot had squared off evenly in Richardson, but sentimentalists increasingly sided with the power against the structure. They preferred to hover over what Wordsworth later called "spots of time." They wanted their emotions to accumulate. Because time and plot only squandered feelings, the sentimentalists described special scenes where a gap in time collapsed into a place, where "feeling comes in aid / Of feeling," never dissipated by result.[13] Mifflin's peargrove tableau thus marks him as a sophisticated belletrist, up-to-date on literary techniques evolving across the Atlantic and quick to adopt recent innovations as he constructs for himself an *aide-sentiment*.

Mifflin had first met his young friend Gibson at six P.M. on 14 March 1785; two years afterward he set down an account of the event in his diary, calling it one of his "happy anniversaries." On that early spring evening, Mifflin joined an audience of nearly eight hundred to hear a blind philosopher named Moyes who was visiting from Europe. "We happened to meet on the front row of the gallery at one of Dr. Moyes's lectures — It was on electricity — the gallery was crowded & I was indebted to my new friend for a seat — His gentle manners & modest politeness made me feel an immediate attatchment to him — when the lecture was over we returned home together — & at parting made an appointment to meet at the next lecture."[14] Fifteen years old, James Gibson was an earnest and quiet Princeton undergraduate. Although Mifflin probably attended Moyes's lecture because electricity was a voguish topic, Gibson would have gone because he took his education seriously. Mifflin wrote that Gibson was "a handsome lad" but not prepossessing. "My little friend is not a prominent or striking character, but of that amiable kind for which your esteem increases with your acquaintance." Gibson weighed about five pounds less than Mifflin, but people matured more slowly in those days, and Gibson would continue to grow for another decade (later that year, he wrote to his mother asking for "another pair of breeches as I have but too and they are both too short at the knees"). Like Mifflin, Gibson had a "taste for old fashioned queues," sometimes with a wig extension, but one gets the impression he was not quite as dapper as his older friend. For one thing, he did not have as much money to spend on his appearance. Although he employed a hairdresser named Barlowe, Gibson had to bargain to afford his services. Gibson's father, who was mayor of Philadelphia in 1771 and 1772, had died three years earlier, after losing most of his capital in a series of financial mishaps. Gibson's family was genteel but no longer wealthy. They lived in an "obscure and humble residence" that Gibson's sisters, who would soon be looking for husbands, viewed with "Mortification." This house stood at Chestnut Street above Fourth Street — on the same block as the Norris House.[15]

Gibson's family must have made considerable sacrifice in order to send him to Princeton; he appears to have tried hard to deserve it. In his diaries he is diligent to the point of overwork, itemizing his hours with strict economy. Mifflin reports hearing that Gibson was at the top of his class, although it is impossible to know whether this was fact or flattery. To relax, Gibson played battledores (badminton) and pitched quoits (horseshoes). His only rebellion against the numbing regime of rote memorization was an occasional dry comment, like this one the night before an exam: "Euclid is wished into non existence by many."[16]

When Mifflin wrote that Gibson had "a prudence beyond his years," he might have been putting a favorable spin on Gibson's adolescent awkwardness. Whenever the college boys roughhoused, it was always Gibson who got injured. His roommate, John Rhea Smith, who also kept a diary, was rowdier, more lackadaisical in his studies, and much more adept at provoking and then charming away the frowns of their tutor, Gilbert Snowden. "After dinner scuffle with Reed, Furman & Gibson in the entry," Smith recorded on 10 January 1786. "Enter the Room & lock the door on Gibson who bursts it open & falls — Gilbert sees him & enters the room immediately after — . . . He reproves it as imprudent & very wrong but at the same time scar[c]ely keeps from laughter." In a free-for-all pie-slicing competition on 12 June, Smith "came off not very successfully tho I had better fate than poor James my roommate who lost unfortunately part of his thumb in the fray." On 1 August, Gibson was "walking out in the campus when one of the Lads flung a stone and struck me on the Leg." Gibson was liked and accepted by his classmates — he was a member of the Cliosophic Society, a debating club — but the string of accidents suggests he was not entirely at ease with them.[17]

The klutzy and dutiful Gibson would have been an unlikely match for the sociable and dandyish Mifflin, but Mifflin was always on the lookout for a new friend. It was a habit, not a coincidence, for John Mifflin to strike up a new acquaintance in a public place. Consider, for instance, the adventure recorded in Mifflin's diary for 30 January 1787. Mifflin had gone to the theater alone. "I had no body near me that I knew to talk to which is very requisite to enjoy a play." Fortunately, Mifflin soon picked out from among the masses a "young gentleman . . . [who] was very genteelly dressed & seemed to be much in my own situation without any person he cared for near him — I touched him on the shoulder with my cane & made room for him between myself & a jolly looking dame of vulgar deportment." Since the young gentleman's previous benchmates had been crowding him and drinking grog, he was grateful for Mifflin's offer. "Upon the whole his getting next to me was an event 'to be wished'-for by us both — he was very clever & appeared to be in his teens — I found he was a Mr Coxe."[18] Together the two formed an island of cool gentility in the rabble. They ratified each other's delicacy, sharing severe criticisms of the performance that the other audience members were too lost in riotous enjoyment to appreciate. In the absence of Mr. Coxe, no one would have witnessed the insult to Mifflin's critical faculties inflicted by the pantomime sequence, which involved an elephant. Mifflin's meeting with Coxe is so similar to his first meeting with Gibson as to amount almost to a technique. Good manners gave sensitive young men a code by which to recognize one another.

Another important element in this code was the cognomen, or stage name, usually classical in origin. As David S. Shields, a scholar of early American high society, has explained, these "fixed personae" helped define a space of cultural play and "aestheticized conversation by distancing it from the mundane talk of familiars." When Gibson joined the Cliosophic Society, he was given the cognomen Decius. The renaming signaled that as a member, he would act, to some extent, as a new person. The new name also marked one aspect of Gibson's self as belonging in the club's domain; it was a part of his identity that the Cliosophists, but no one else, knew how to summon. In a similar way, when Gibson took the name Lorenzo, he surrendered a hold on his self to another group, one much more rarefied and flexible and powerful than any undergraduate fraternity: the society of well-educated, well-connected Philadelphia Quaker gentry. The Norrises, Logans, Wistars, Pembertons, Dickinsons, Fishers, and their friends and relatives prided themselves on their spirit as well as their station. Every young man and woman in their circle had a cognomen; the alias certified membership in a playful, intimate group with literary taste. Deborah Norris Logan was Ardelia; Sarah Wister was Laura; Sally Fisher was Amelia; George Logan was Altamont; Richard Wistar was Horatio. When Joshua Fisher courted Hannah Pemberton, he addressed his love letters to Cleora and signed them Philander. The names represented one's social persona, like a marker in a board game. The Cliosophic Society swore Decius to secrecy; if Gibson disclosed that identity, he betrayed his fellows. But Gibson did not need to hide Lorenzo; he needed to reveal him, selectively.[19]

Philadelphia's young smart set did not invent this literary style of masquerade. The public intellectual life around them was swimming with pseudonyms. In newspapers and pamphlets, a nom de plume accommodated both a gentleman's need for modesty and a politician's for canniness. Names such as Philodemos and Demophilus were commonplace. Casapipina (the Reverend Jacob Duché) had baptized Mifflin. The Farmer from Pennsylvania (the Delaware lawyer John Dickinson) was married to a Norris cousin. The Norris circle also knew older, British sources that depended on aliases for effect: Addison and Steele's *Tatler* and *Spectator,* and Trenchard and Gordon's *Cato.*

As teenagers, the Norrises and their friends at Robert Proud's Public Latin School had composed and handwritten pamphlets and newspapers inspired by these British models, plus Tom Paine and Ben Franklin. In "Letters to the Thompsonians" and "An Address to the Inhabitants of Latonia [1777–78]," Junius and Brutus appealed to their fellow citizens of Latonia to shrug off the yoke of tyranny imposed by the arbitrary decrees of the oppressive Toddites, in a goofy transposition of Revolutionary rhetoric to high school. The six numbers of the more ambitious "Universal Magazine and Literary Museum," published by S. L. Wharton, printed correspondence by John Curious and Inquisitive Queer, as well as Poe-like archaeological puzzles and essays about spiders. In 1780, "Amusement for the Circle"featured poetry by Ophelia and a regular column by the Pratler, who noted in his first contribution that "the Taste for disguising is very prevalent in both Sexes at present." When the Pratler wrote about "the Beau Monde," as the prospectus for the "Amusement" had promised, he was writing about his neighbors, siblings, cousins, and classmates. And since the beau monde he wrote about was the same beau monde he wrote for, the aliases concealed no one. Paradoxically, the masks reminded the readers how well they knew one another. Because the monikers both were and were not the people they represented, they fitted the new world of sentimental friendships neatly — free from the confines of being Deborah Norris, for example, Ardelia could try on any number of poetic poses and romantic alliances.[20]

Mifflin's nom de plume was Leander. In Greek myth, Leander swam the Hellespont every night to reach his beloved Hero, who lit a torch to guide him. One stormy night the torch blew out, and he drowned. Mifflin was not the only Philadelphian known as Leander at this time. In a private journal, Anna Hume Shippen gave her lover Louis Guillaume Otto, comte de Mosloy, the same name.[21] Shippen kept her Leander quiet, since she had a husband, but Mifflin was known as Leander to the Norris circle as early as November 1779, long before he met Gibson.[22] To Shippen, the name Leander connoted an ardent and persistent lover. (The story would famously inspire Byron to swim the strait in imitation.) The name fit Otto better than it did Mifflin, who in 1786 and 1787 flirted with women without devoting himself to any one in particular.

Lorenzo might have been named after the lover in the *Merchant of Venice,* but it is more likely that he was named after the reckless youth of Edward Young's *Night Thoughts.* Mifflin quotes Young's most famous line in his diary: "Procrastination is the thief of time." If Mifflin chose the name, it was probably not so much because Gibson resembled the character Lorenzo — who is giddy, indolent, and in need of reform — as because the poem addressed Lorenzo the way Mifflin wanted to address Gibson. "Thou say'st I preach, Lorenzo!"

Young wrote; " 'Tis confess'd."[23] The narrator's tone — sometimes hectoring, sometimes doting, always self-satisfied — is very much the tone Mifflin adopted.

Mifflin wanted to be Gibson's patron; he wanted to provide and help. Concerned about Gibson's public speaking, the older man wrote orations for him to deliver at his debating club. As graduation approached, Mifflin used his connections to find Gibson a job as an apprentice in Mordecai Lewis's countinghouse. Mifflin did not want Gibson to become a lawyer, Mifflin's own career choice, because he felt that lawyers were "a rapacious set of cormorants feasting & fattening upon the miseries & misfortunes of their fellow citizens," and he knew Gibson was too kindhearted to "brook such an ungracious ungenerous inurbane line of life, the prosperity of which depends on the wretchedness of thousands."[24]

There is something disingenuous about Mifflin's asking Gibson to be a purer sentimentalist than he ever was. Mifflin wanted to act as a father of sorts, but it is not clear that he understood what the role involved. Whereas Edward Young wanted to save his Lorenzo's soul, Mifflin's advice was at once more worldly and less practical: "My hopes & expectations of him [Gibson] are the highest that an affectionate friendship can form — Alas! should he not come up to them it will be sapping the foundation upon which I have built much *promised happiness* — But should he continue himself under the guidance of my *mentorship* I trust I shall pilot him safely thro' these shoals & rocks among which he will shortly be launched — & then, *ten years* hence I may look back with delight on *this days journal* & find all my hopes & expectations accomplished."[25] Gibson must have seen through some of the posturing, because he eventually became a lawyer despite Mifflin's "mentorship." Perhaps Gibson took Mifflin's friendship with a grain of salt. No doubt he knew that he was not the sort of Lorenzo that Edward Young railed against — one of

> Ye well-array'd! ye lilies of our land!
> Ye lilies male! who neither toil, nor spin,
> . . . Ye delicate! who nothing can support.[26]

Ironically, Young's rebuke matched Mifflin's case much better than it did that of his impoverished, industrious friend.

Although Mifflin and Gibson met on 14 March 1785, Gibson did not begin his diary until 6 February 1786. Mifflin began his even later, on 12 May 1786. Surprisingly, the idea of keeping a diary probably came from Gibson's Princeton roommate, Smith, who started his on 1 January 1786. Not introspective, Smith might have decided to keep a journal to figure out why his days accomplished so little. He intended his journal to be evidence of his good intentions to study longer and harder, but his resolve almost always failed, and the entries instead record the pranks and socializing that distracted him. In a typical entry, Smith sleeps late, tries to memorize a geometry lesson or write a composition until he admits that "my attention [is] diverted from study," arrives at recitation unprepared, gets caught in some collegiate misdemeanor, stays up late talking with his friends, and goes to bed realizing that he forgot to exercise.[27] It is a sociable diary. There are many friends and no cognomens, and Smith chronicles the politicking of the Cliosophic Society in detail.

When Gibson started his diary, he modeled it on Smith's. The layout of Gibson's pages is nearly identical: the day of the week and date, without the month, appear flush left, and the entry follows immediately in smaller script. In the beginning, Gibson also imitated Smith by using his journal more as a memorandum book than as an aid to self-reflection. Because Gibson was a straight arrow, compared to Smith the troublemaker, the plain-style reporting yields a fairly banal result: "5 o clock had a tooth-ach which prevented my studying much, but left me at 8 oclock, When I eat a hearty breakfast. Half after, had some cakes sent from Dr. Smiths, which being a rarity I liked very well at 10 went to recitation, recited 6 propositions of the fifth Book beginning at the second." Like Smith, Gibson used no cognomens, at least not in his early entries. On 8 March 1786, he prosaically referred to his friend as "Mr. Mifflin."[28]

The first entry in Mifflin's diary opens in a tone almost as perfunctory and mechanical: "Went with Lorenzo to wait on Dr Rush—not at home—talked with the ladies awhile and then withdrew—In the afternoon on business—very absent—Went twice out of my way—Drank tea with Mrs G.—took leave of my dear Lorenzo—God bless him."[29] Princeton separated Gibson from Mifflin. The merchant-lawyer had taken Gibson with him on several trips—in October 1785 to Lancaster, and in April 1786 to Nottingham—but Mifflin regretted that they could not spend more time together. He could compensate by visiting the boy's mother, Mrs. G., to gossip about James, but he still felt lonely. Mifflin later wrote that his journal "began by the desire of Lorenzo."[30] Gibson must have suggested it to Mifflin as a way to ease the pain of parting when he left for school on 12 May 1786.

Mifflin's first entry is colorless, but the words "very absent" hint at what will break out of the dry journalizing. The observation might mean that the debtors Mifflin was dunning were not to be found, but more likely it describes Mifflin's state of mind. Gibson would not have thought to notice such a thing, but Mifflin cannot help it. He lost his way twice because he was paying no more attention to his course than Laurence Sterne did when he wandered into Paris without a passport, forgetting, in his distraction, that England and France were at war. Mifflin's sympathies were drifting away from him, tugging him along, engaged by the person whose name begins and ends the entry — Lorenzo.

Mifflin never calls Gibson by his proper name. From page one Gibson is Lorenzo. In Mifflin's diary, Dr. Benjamin Rush appears undisguised, as do other respectable adult figures, such as Benjamin Franklin, Hugh Bracken-ridge, Thomas Paine, and James Madison. But grown-ups who are Mifflin's intimates get abbreviations, and young men and women who provoke Miff-lin's sentiments are given fanciful aliases. The widow Mary Parker Norris, proprietor of the Norris House and its garden, appears as Mrs. N.; her three sons are called Castalio (Isaac, the oldest), Josephus (Joseph Parker), and Carolus (Charles, the youngest). Deborah Norris had been Ardelia when she was single and writing to her girlfriends, but after her marriage to George Logan in 1781, she appears as Mrs. L. in the diary. James Gibson is Lorenzo, of course; his mother is Mrs. G.; and his younger brother John is Johannes or Jean. In the Rhoads family, who also lived on the Norrises' block, the wid-owed mother, Sarah, is Mrs. R.; her daughters, Elizabeth and Mary, are Eliza and Maria; and her twelve-year-old son, Samuel, is Ascanius. There are also a young woman known as Leonora, a deceased friend known as Eugenius, and a young man with the epithet "the young squire," none of whom I have been able to identify.[31]

In the early pages of his diary, Mifflin is restless with the knowledge that the diary is not an adequate substitute for the young man for whom he is writing it. "Not in very high spirits," Mifflin writes on day two. "In the morning rambled in the garden — missed my friend." Gradually Mifflin's heartsickness takes on a texture, and the absence of Lorenzo, dwelled upon, becomes an uneasy presence. "Read Biography & travels to pass away the time — not in a reading humour — After dinner in the figits — did not know what to do with myself — scribbled to Nort[h]ampton — walked about — tumbled over differ-ent books — dull dismal weather still continues — hope Lorenzo has a fire and takes bark — wish he or Castalio were here — such days lag heavily without a Friend." "How I want a confidant," Mifflin writes. Left alone, he seems agi-tated and overwhelmed by his sentiments. Freud might have explained Miff-lin's complaint as the depredations of unbound libido, erring without an ob-ject. Mifflin himself might have explained the remedy he wanted by quoting Cicero's words to Atticus: "There are many things to worry and vex me, but once I have you here to listen I feel I can pour them all away in a single walk and talk."[32]

Lacking an immediate auditor, Mifflin at first told his stories with abortive brevity. "Vexed at the insolence of *some people*," he writes in an early entry, declining to specify who offended or what the offense might have been. On another day, "Heard something in the evening which put me in spirits—a proposal of a friend which met my entire approbation"—again left unexplained. Mifflin's early diary is full of the unsaid, but Mifflin himself gives the key to the puzzles: "pland something . . . which I will tell Lorenzo when I see him." The ellipses are meant to provoke Gibson's curiosity. When they meet again, the two will read each other's diaries together; to spark conversation, the text is left deliberately incomplete. "This morning we examined the first volume of my journal," Mifflin writes after one such reunion, "& I explained to him certain blanks & other things which he did not understand."[33]

But one of the lessons a diary teaches is the stunning amount that one forgets. Mifflin might have discovered the hard way that he could no longer remember the anecdotes behind some of his earliest telegraphic entries, because after about a month, he struggles to get down the outline of the stories he wants to tell. Then he adds details. The diary gets richer. For example: "A visit from the 'Private Secretary'—has grown monstrous fat and lusty—alias *pinguid* (a newfashioned word) & think he bids fair to be big enough for an alderman." His vanity piqued, Mifflin also starts to fret about whether his diary is amusing. He spices up his vocabulary (*cozily* is another "new word") and rounds out his stories.[34]

By contrast, Gibson elaborates his narrative rarely in its first two months. Even when he passes on "a rumour that the Devile was seen in college wrapt up in a white sheet," his only follow-up is a laconic "I did not see him." April and May are missing, probably misplaced in one of Mifflin and Gibson's exchanges of diary installments by mail. But when the diary picks up again in June, something has happened: Gibson is calling Mifflin "Leander." He has started to use the abbreviation "N.B." at the end of his entries to introduce an entertaining detail that somehow got left out of the day's narrative—copying a writerly tic of Mifflin's. And he has a new refrain: "expected a letter from Leander though[t] of him"; "wished to hear from Leander and his journal"; "wished to hear from Leander and read his journal—intend to devote to morrow in writing to him—a fine Day—at five used exercise—thouthght of Leander."[35]

Gibson misses Mifflin with the same plodding, mechanical repetition that he does his chores, memorizes Euclid, and eats three square meals a day. Nonetheless it is a new element. Gibson is now studying and rehearsing sentiment with the same oxlike effort he applies to geometry. His textbook is Mifflin's journal; reading Mifflin's plaintive, lonely entries must have embarrassed Gibson into imitation. The boy's progress exemplifies an aphorism that Mifflin once quoted at a tea party: "a sentiment of Rochefoucault's 'that people would never be *in love* if they had never heard of such a thing.' "[36] Mifflin saw to it that Gibson heard of love, and taught him how to pine about it expressively.

But who taught Mifflin? Mifflin read widely, and friendship seems to have been one of his favorite topoi: he quotes Pope and Akenside on the subject.[37] He was practiced in journal writing (he had kept one as a boy) and in friendships (several young men had preceded Gibson). But Mifflin's most instructive apprenticeship may have been not to books or to other men but to a woman.

Mifflin was neither the first nor the only person to frequent the Norris pear grove in a sentimental mood. In 1780, Deborah Norris had set an ode to friendship in a "sylvan scene" resembling the grove. According to Shields, the garden as "an experimental haven for the heart" was at the time as conventional in genteel American women's poetry as neoclassical cognomens were. Shortly after her brother Isaac Norris III left for Europe in 1783, Deborah visited the spot before writing to tell him how much she missed him. "The House looks gloomy. I sat half an hour the other day under the pear tree in ye garden indulging a kind of pleasing Melancholy. I do not love to see things going to decay, and yet it raises ideas that soothe my mind." In the same letter, Deborah referred approvingly to Isaac's friend "Leander" (Mifflin), who had stayed behind in Pennsylvania.[38]

In their youth, John Mifflin and Deborah Norris had been close. She had called him "an agreeable friend of mine" despite the "poor opinion of platonic sentiments" other people held, carefully signaling that he was not a suitor. In 1779, Mifflin had pestered Deborah about the letters that she and her girlfriends were exchanging, until she was charmed into betraying their intimacies. "Thee will laugh at my folly," Deborah wrote to Sarah Wister; "indeed it is what thee can't avoid doing when I tell thee, that I have been prevailed upon to read part of this letter to J. Mifflin. I read (to divert too close an attention excuse me Sally) an extract of thine, he liked the style it was sprightly and interesting, he praised it had never been so happy before as to see any of thy productions see it, he did not, he sat at a respectful distance and I culld out the prettiest part of what thee wrote." He also asked Deborah to show him Sally Fisher's letters, but in that case Deborah claimed to her friend that "I did not satisfy his curiosity — Shall I do it, my dear!"[39]

Years later, when a cluster of young belles cornered Mifflin at a tea party and asked whether he kept a journal, he was vague about the details. "I acknowledged I kept a sort of a register of new ideas opinion & sentiments — & some incidents — but particularly travelling adventures — Miss R. seemed very desirous to know how it was conducted — (I thought with a view of

Sally Jones and Deborah Norris. Detail from *A Party to Virginia*. Historical Society of Pennsylvania, Rhoads Family Manuscripts.

regulating her own)."[40] In his sniffy reticence, Mifflin was conveniently forgetting how many of his sentimental habits he had learned by snooping on
women — on Deborah Norris Logan in particular.

In a groundbreaking essay, "The Female World of Love and Ritual," Carroll Smith-Rosenberg described an emotionally intense community of female
friendship in early America "in which men made but a shadowy appearance."
The story of Mifflin and Gibson suggests that that world had a male complement. But the interaction between Mifflin and Deborah Norris Logan further
suggests that the border between the two worlds may have been more porous
than Smith-Rosenberg estimated.[41]

Men and women shared their styles of same-sex intimacy, even when the
intimacy itself did not cross the line of gender. The pious Mary Dickinson, for
example, agreed with the sentimental notions of her young cousin Isaac Norris
about same-sex couples. "I join with thee in [believing?] that Real frdship is
the Balm of life." And she confided to him her own Emily Dickinson–like
passion: "The object of mine [i.e., of my friendship] was too Angelick to
remain long an Inhabitant here — I sometimes Indulge a thot, that if we were
not so wrapt in clods of Mortality we might see Angelick spirits hovering
round our dwellings, perhaps as Guardian Angels, but art has discovered no
Microscope — that can reach to this point . . . she will not return to me — but I
must follow her, — sure I am she is happy, and what I desire is to steer the
Course however rugged that will lead me to the same haven." It was probably
Isaac's close friendship with John Mifflin (discussed below) that prompted
Mary to recollect her girlfriend. The men's relationship may not have been as
celestial as hers, but she recognized that it was just as intense with emotion.
"He loves thee," Mary wrote to Isaac later.[42]

The names in Smith-Rosenberg's footnotes are in many cases the same as in
this chapter: she, too, cites Wistars and Logans; and a significant figure in her
essay, Elizabeth Bordley, was John Mifflin's half-sister. One should not make
too much of this overlap; by the end of their reign, the Philadelphia gentry
were as endogamous as any European royal house, and it would be difficult for
any two studies of their social behavior not to be linked by family. But these
kinship ties put the same-sex friendships of men and women in a wider context — the eighteenth-century upper-class preoccupation with sympathy.

Smith-Rosenberg felt that her readers in 1975 would find early American
female friendships "an intriguing and almost alien form of human relationship."[43] In the two decades since the publication of her essay, lesbians and gays
have become highly visible, yet the relationships Smith-Rosenberg describes
remain alien. What distances them is not the homosexuality of their eros but
its peculiar strength. They provoke a kind of jealousy in us. From the vantage

of our era, it is difficult to appreciate the cultural experimentation of the eighteenth century—which encouraged individuals to follow a sympathetic attachment as far as it would go. They dwelt in possibilities that we cannot help but reduce to prose. Whether or not a couple had sex is a natural question to ask, but the answer will not allow us into the private meaning of their bond.

Smith-Rosenberg established that female friendships, far from being stigmatized, amounted to a cultural norm in antebellum America. Because research on male friendships is scantier, it is unclear whether John Mifflin's chronic friendliness was a rule or an exception, but the obstacle to interpretation here is not a scarcity of material but an overabundance. "As rational equalitarian friendship was neither habitual . . . nor dangerously passionate," Jay Fliegelman has observed, "it was hailed in numerous eighteenth-century volumes as the ideal relationship." Friendship was everywhere during the period; every surface that men exposed to one another is coated with cottony, saccharine rhetoric.[44]

It was not unusual in the eighteenth century for a man to keep a journal expressly for another man. Boswell hoped that his London journal would "be of use to my worthy friend Johnston, . . . while he laments my personal absence," and mailed it to him in installments. Nor was it unheard of for gentlemen to exchange the word *love*. In 1779, Alexander Hamilton wrote to John Laurens that he wished it were in his power "to convince you that I love you." Daniel Webster proposed bachelor marriage to James Hervey Bingham in 1804, vowing, "Yes, James, I must come; we will yoke together again; your little bed is just wide enough; we will practise at the same bar, and be as friendly a pair of single fellows as ever cracked a nut."[45] In both cases, although the affection seems genuine, the tone is somewhat arch. Hamilton and Webster are addressing the language of courtship to a male friend; they relish the misapplication, but the extravagance of their conceits signals that they know, and their readers know, that it is a misapplication. In both Webster's and Hamilton's correspondence, vows of friendship were accompanied by political news, delivered with a touch of melodrama, and by in-depth analysis of their personal careers—the same distinctive mix to be found in Cicero's letters to Atticus. To some extent the young men were posing as passionate young heroes of the republic.

Mifflin records his social milieu in such detail that if he were shunned as deviant, his diary would betray it. I have not been able to find any evidence that polite society considered Mifflin's behavior outside its norms. The few incidents that might indicate a raised eyebrow turn out, on closer examination, not to amount to much.

On 19 January 1786, for example, John Rhea Smith recorded how awkward he felt when Mifflin visited Gibson, his roommate, in their quarters at Princeton: "Read Higginson Abiel & Duff in the Room when Mr Mifflin comes in — I feel a little embarassed & sorry for James's sake, we soon get settled & into conversation & then I felt very easy — Mifflin conversant & easy . . . James goes to the Tavern to sleep with Mr Mifflin." Why did Mifflin's presence cause Smith to feel embarrassed on Gibson's behalf? Did he and the other students suspect something funny was going on between Gibson and Mifflin? Probably not. Smith and Mifflin liked each other; Smith himself went to see Mifflin at Mrs. Knox's tavern at least once. In the context of Smith's diary, it seems more likely that Read, Higginson, Abiel, and Duff were in the room because the boys were goofing off together, and that when the older gentleman entered, they felt sheepish. They were supposed to be studying. Smith felt bad because Mifflin was seeing studious James in the company of slackers — not because the slackers were seeing James with Mifflin.[46]

More incriminating is this piece of unsolicited advice from Benjamin Rush recorded by Mifflin: "Dr Rush came in — he was rather queer — & not in the usual soft complimentary strain — he told me very bluntly that 'he thought it was time for me to be married' — I told him I thought so too — for I did not want to be an old batchelor." In statistical terms, Mifflin was not overdue to marry. The average age of a Quaker man at first marriage was 26.8; when Rush made his comment, Mifflin was not quite 28. (Gibson did not marry until age 47.) But there are several perfectly heterosexual reasons for Rush's bluntness. By his own admission, Mifflin was courting more than one woman. In December he rather inconsiderately bragged that hints from the sisters Leonora and Eliza "give me to understand that *nothing is in the way* but my *indecision* & a spice of diffidence." Diffidence won out, and by March fickle Mifflin's "attentions to Maria were beginning to be talked of." Rush may have intended to warn Mifflin that Philadelphia had only so much patience with young men who toyed with daughters' expectations.[47]

It remains possible that Rush saw other reasons for marrying Mifflin off, reasons neither he nor Mifflin could have discussed. However, to judge by the attitudes of the mothers and guardians of the young men whom Mifflin befriended, Rush would have been alone in any suspicions he might have had. Mifflin's friendship with Gibson was no secret. Gibson had to ask his Princeton professors for permission to spend the night with Mifflin when he visited. In Philadelphia, Mifflin was a frequent guest of Gibson's mother; he was welcome to sleep in James's bed whether or not James was at home. Mrs. Gibson enclosed Mifflin's letters to her son inside her own. When Mifflin failed to write, Gibson asked his mother for news of him. Mary Parker Norris, the mother of Mifflin's friend Isaac, also welcomed Mifflin into her house and her son's bed. She mentions Mifflin's new friendship with Gibson in letters to family and friends and goes so far as to call Mifflin "my adopted son." In fact, Mrs. Norris was so far from disapproving of Mifflin's influence that she encouraged him to take her youngest son, Charles, under his wing. "I am greatly obliged to J Mifflin for the notice he takes of him," she wrote to Isaac, "as I think it is of advantage to Charles, and introduces him to proper acquaintance." The middle brother, Joseph, was also "happy to hear of Leanders kind Attention to Charles." The experiment failed, however. "Charles is too volatile," Mrs. Norris wrote to Isaac several months later, "to engage his attention and friendship." Unable to accept Mifflin's guidance, poor Charles eventually made a misstep that got him written out of his mother's will and shipped off to Asia as a sailor.[48]

Yet despite the lack of overt censure, the modern reader senses that there was something odd about Mifflin. This may be an effect of perspective — of looking at one man's story closely instead of reviewing a set of case studies. Smith-Rosenberg deliberately moved away from scrutiny of the psychic pathologies of the women she studied. "The scholar must ask if it is historically possible and, if possible, important to study the intensely individual aspects of psychosexual dynamics. Is it not the historian's first task to explore the social structure and the world view that made intense and sometimes sensual female love both a possible and an acceptable emotional option?" Her shift in focus avoided the anachronism of judging early personalities by late psychosexual standards, and it recovered some of her subjects' dignity. But it also had a cost. In tossing out the foul bathwater of psychopathology, Smith-Rosenberg also lost the baby of individualism. As Kierkegaard observed, it is error — departure from the norm — that flushes the self out of abstraction: "The category of sin is the category of individuality." As a historian, Smith-Rosenberg was right to study the norm, but literary scholars might want to approach Mifflin and Gibson as diarists characterized by what Kierkegaard calls earnestness: "The accent of earnestness rests on the sinner, who is the single individual."[49]

As a piece of the historical record, the Mifflin and Gibson diaries give evidence that at the height of sympathy's reign, American men could express emotions to each other with a fervor and openness that could not have been detached from religious enthusiasm a generation earlier and would have to be consigned to sexual perversion a few generations later. But Mifflin's diary, in particular, is also the record of an individual with a distinctive personality who seems to be pushing the limits, admittedly broader then than later, of male-male emotions.

What makes Mifflin a vivid character is that he wants a friend desperately and holds on tenaciously to the men he finds. What makes his diary a good read is that Gibson is not the only man he is courting. The story is a love triangle even before the diaries begin. Mifflin met Gibson "at a time when Castalio [Isaac Norris III] was in Europe, & I being left rather friendless & forlorn without a *confidant,* was more open & disposed to be impressed with his merit." As early as day three of his journal, either oblivious to or solicitous of the jealousy he might be provoking in Gibson, Mifflin notes that he "recieved letters from my dear Castalio; & sat up very late talking about him — hope soon to welcome him to his native shore."[50]

Repeatedly, Mifflin invites Gibson to worry about whether Mifflin will remain faithful. In the same entry in which Mifflin fondly remembers Gibson in the pear grove, he draws "a comparison between him [Gibson] and the young squire," the burden of which seems to be that the young squire would make just as good a friend. A few days later, Mifflin returns to the pear grove with Ascanius (Samuel Rhoads III), and they discuss "many plans & schemes . . . respecting his [Samuel's] destination," evincing the same sort of amicable paternalism that Mifflin indulged with Gibson. A week later, he praises Gibson's younger brother, John, this time making explicit the game he is playing: "Think he will stand a chance to rival the negligent inattentive Lorenzo in my affections."[51]

Added to the number of young men Mifflin pursues is the intensity with which he seems to need their affection. Mifflin may not have been much more labile than the people around him, but he was undoubtedly more aware of his volatility. "I wonder if every body thinks as much & as *constantly* as I do," he once complained. Mifflin's thinking was not profound, but he did monitor his fluctuating feelings with a vigilance that amounted to an innovation. On some days he treated the matter with a light touch borrowed from Sterne: "It is *inconsistent* to pretend to be always *the same.*" But on other days it perplexed and annoyed him: "Rather in dull spirits & did not talk much there is no accounting for these taciturne moods." Usually, though, Mifflin did know how to account for his moods, or at least how to solace them: he turned to his young male companions. They protected him from depression. If Mifflin grew sad, he could remind himself, in terms of almost biblical rapture, "Have I not my Castalio left . . . & have I not acquired my Lorenzo! . . . In them have I cause to rejoice." When they failed him, he was left miserable. "I was in wretched spirits & wanted him [Isaac Norris III] to come home with me — but he would not — & I do not remember when I wanted more the exhilarating society of a friend."[52]

Mifflin's raw neediness cut against the grain of contemporaneous political rhetoric. When Mifflin falls, he wants someone else to catch him. He longs to be vulnerable under the protection of another man. In the Philadelphia of 1787, these were counterrevolutionary desires. Reciprocal but unequal relations had guided colonial society, but the American Revolution upset that deferential system. Christians no longer advocated submission and dependence; ministers like Jonathan Mayhew equated freedom from British authority with freedom from sin. Mifflin's emotions, however, betray a nostalgia for hierarchy. Mifflin liked to play the role of Gibson's patron. The role moved him deeply. Once, while discussing James's career options with Mrs. Gibson, Mifflin's "heart was so full I was obliged to go into the other room to give it vent." Something of a valetudinarian himself, Mifflin was happy when Gibson came down with a toothache because it gave Mifflin a chance to nurse his friend. "Never do I feel the calls of friendship stronger than in sickness."[53] The tenderness possible between a stronger and a weaker party aroused Mifflin. Exchanges of mutual benefit to two equal parties could be left to the unsentimental marketplace.

Mifflin had never known his father, who died several months before he was born; perhaps Mifflin role-played with Gibson to rehearse a wished-for identity with his missing parent. Or he may have been revisiting a more recent trauma — the friendship with Eugenius interrupted by death. If Eugenius was Jabcz Maud Fisher (1750–79), then Mifflin and Fisher would have been friends while Mifflin was a teenage student at the College of Philadelphia (University of Pennsylvania) and while Fisher was a merchant in his middle to late twenties — this is almost exactly the same age difference that obtained later between Mifflin and Gibson. Fisher left for London in 1775, the year Mifflin graduated from college, so their later friendship would have depended on correspondence, as did Mifflin and Gibson's.[54]

Whatever Mifflin's motives, he wanted a friendship that hearkened back to a less egalitarian past. Younger and poorer Gibson obliged. Mifflin acted as pedagogue; Gibson eagerly, if somewhat coarsely, mimicked his teacher's moonings over the absence of his friend, and his pique when he felt that he had been treated coolly. The physical maintenance of the diaries reflects their unequal status. Gibson is caretaker of the diaries. During one of Mifflin's visits to Princeton, Gibson "marked Leander's Journal by placing the names of the months on the top of each page." He also sewed the journal leaves together into fascicles. When Mifflin complained that it was "very troublesome" to cut paper to fit in his book, Gibson helpfully "added four blank leaves to my dear Leander's journal and trimmed it." He further promised that "I will always agree to make Leanders journal papers provided he pays me well and my price is that he will not grow tired but always continue to write *long* journals."[55] Ever so gently, and even as he affirms that he likes the game they are playing,

Gibson is ribbing his older friend. He is reminding Mifflin that according to the economic terms that prevail in the world at large, the disparity of their roles is something of a joke, a relic of hierarchy that cash (which labor could purchase) would quickly dissolve.

At the start of his diary, Mifflin was living not in his own quarters on Second Street but at the Norrises'.[56] All of Mrs. Norris's children were away from home; Isaac and Joseph were touring Europe, Charles was banished to Asia, and Deborah, by then married, had retired to Stenton. At Mrs. Norris's invitation, Mifflin had taken up residence as "gaurd of the house." The Gibsons lived next door. The Norris property — Deborah Norris Logan once jokingly called it Norris Castle — cast a long shadow, and Mifflin at first saw Gibson only in this shadow.[57] Gibson was a fallback friend. Mifflin first loved Isaac, also known as Castalio, scion of the Norris family. Although Mifflin began his diary for Gibson, what gives it an almost novelistic drive is the question of whether it will remain Gibson's. The rise of Gibson's star is nearly eclipsed by Isaac's rather spectacular fall.

Less than a year younger than Mifflin, Isaac Norris III was Mifflin's emotional and intellectual peer and ever so slightly his social superior. In 1779, Isaac and Mifflin were already so close that when Mifflin came down with a fever, Isaac spent the night to "condole" him — "I wonder what they will dream!" Isaac's sister Deborah commented. Castalio, Isaac's nom de plume, appeared in the children's handwritten newspaper "Amusement for the Circle" as early as 1780. He may have been named after the lover who ended unhappily in Thomas Otway's play *The Orphan* — "the gentle lover who was all tenderness," as Boswell called him — but his name might also have been a masculinized version of Castalia, the spring on Mount Parnassus sacred to the Muses, named for the woman who plunged into it to avoid rape by Apollo.[58] The alias suited Isaac: he never married, and he was a poet. In a cartoonish watercolor of him, probably painted by one of the Rhoads girls, his face is childlike and abstracted, his delicate figure perched on his seat.[59] His cousin Mary Dickinson, admittedly partial, wrote that he was "without exception the handsomest young man I know."[60]

The same cousin encouraged Isaac to send her his poetry. "Thy little pieces of poetry soothe my soul," she wrote him; "I have a small collection hall be happy if thee will enlarge it." To one of her letters he appended a note listing which poems he had already mailed her, to avoid repeating himself: "Ode. when February / Sonnets. To thee O pity & Down a sloped hill / Inscription for Queeny [?]." One of his poems survives, probably saved by his sister Deborah, in a manuscript blotched with what may be tears. "Say what is Life if Frenzy

Betsy Wister and Isaac Norris. Detail from *A Party to Virginia*. Historical Society of Pennsylvania, Rhoads Family Manuscripts.

clouds the Mind," the poem asks, and its confused answer seems to come from a heart that couldn't quite bear the ups and downs of either human luck or emotion. "Passions wreck him with continual War," the poet despairs. Since neither pleasure, power, nor wealth can bring peace to the "compound creature Man," the poet longs for the moment of release when his "Nobler Part" will "leave the shatterd Tennement behind."[61] Werther's embrace of death was defiant and rebellious, but Isaac's case resembles that of Harley, the emotionally fragile, aristocratic hero of *The Man of Feeling*. He gives the impression of not having been altogether of this world.

Mary Dickinson asked Castalio for poetry, but on other occasions she used her privilege as an intimate to remind Isaac of his duties as a Norris. Isaac had been named after an illustrious uncle (1701–66) and grandfather (1671–1735). As the eldest son of the eldest son in a great house, Isaac III was expected to rise to meet formidable expectations. "I do believe thy bearing the name that I have *always* so loved, & reverenced, is a cause of my loving thee yet more," Mary wrote in a saccharine tone that would make almost any young man queasy and evasive. She could threaten more directly and ominously when she wanted to: "Consider the station in which thy Creator has placed thee among the creatures here — the Eldest son of a worthy Father and family, who fixed their hearts on thee — God has showered great Blessings on thee — where my Child are the returns — He expects fruits." Isaac was trapped by his inheritance; it raised the stakes while skewing the psychological odds against him. America no longer followed Norrises just because Norrises had been accustomed to lead. Isaac could not live on the estate that came with his name except by selling it off. If he entered the world, he had a great deal to lose — his pride as well as his money — and thanks to his patrician ethereality, he most likely stood to gain nothing in return. Erik Erikson described the similar plight of rich young easterners of privilege in the twentieth century: "The grandsons know that in order to find an identity of their own they have to break out of the mansion, so to speak, and join the mad striving which has engulfed the neighborhood. . . . These men, of the once highest strata, join those from the very lowest ones in being the truly disinherited in American life; from where they are there is no admission to free competition, unless they have the strength to start all over."[62] Like Harley, Isaac would never find a way out of his socioeconomic predicament, but his aporia would attract the sympathy of everyone around him.

On 5 June 1783, Isaac set off to take the Grand Tour of Europe. Travel was "the last Step to be taken in the Institution of Youth," as *The Spectator* put it. The trip was supposed to teach Isaac gracious and cosmopolitan manners, give him knowledge of the wider world, and welcome him into manhood. Mifflin expected to follow his friend soon; they planned to rendezvous in England. Mifflin "is extreamly anxious to go," Deborah wrote her brother two months after his departure. "I think nothing is wanting but his Fathers consent, it would cement your Friendship and you would lay in a kind of joint stock of ideas to serve you in future life."[63]

It was a time for both congratulations and admonition. Charles Thomson, secretary of the Continental Congress and a cousin by marriage, did Isaac the favor of supplying letters of introduction to Thomas Jefferson and John Jay. In exchange, Thomson had license to inflict on Isaac some grandiose advice: "You are now in the situation of Hercules, just stepping into life and left to yourself to follow unrestrained where passion leads or prudence points the way. Before you, lie the rough ascent of virtue on the one hand, and the flowery path of pleasure on the other. I hope and trust you will with him make the glorious choice." The Choice of Hercules was a parable often presented to young men in the early American republic. In 1776, John Adams had proposed an image of it for the Great Seal of the United States. "The Hero resting on his Clubb. Virtue pointing to her rugged Mountain, on one Hand, and perswading him to ascend. Sloth, glancing at her flowery Paths of Pleasure, wantonly reclining on the Ground, displaying the Charms both of her Eloquence and Person, to seduce him into Vice."[64] As Isaac discovered, it was harder to discern the path of virtue than Adams's neat image suggested.

To Isaac, Thomson wrote of prospects. To Jefferson, however, Thomson wrote of fears. "As he is a young man of an amiable disposition and considerable fortune, I am anxious he should return as uncorrupted as he went." Jefferson thought he knew exactly what sort of danger Thomson was hinting at. "It is difficult for young men to refuse it where beauty is a begging in every street," Jefferson commiserated.[65] Overall, at least for others if not for himself, Jefferson assessed the education that Paris had to offer as not worth its risk to sexual morals.

Even Isaac's mother fretted over the chance that away from home, Isaac might marry or start a liaison with someone inappropriate. "I have a Confidence in my dear Child that he will not form any plan for his future life without the knowledge of his affect: mother, I think thee will comprehend my meaning." None of these people knew Isaac very well. If the family had heard the rumors circulating in Philadelphia even before Isaac embarked, they would not have worried about Isaac's id but about his superego. According to a report filed years later by a committee of the Arch Street Monthly Meeting, Isaac "had joined with the People called Roman Catholics." Although Isaac did not advertise the fact and may have deceived his family to hide it, "previous to his leaving this Country he had been initiated into that society by the Ceremonies they make use of for that Purpose."[66]

It was no small matter for a Quaker to defect to Catholicism. The Norrises were lax churchgoers, but they were prominent in the Friends community. Once abroad, Isaac ceased to conceal his conversion, and the scandal spread quickly back across the Atlantic. When Robert Morton reported the news to a friend in Philadelphia, he commented, "I believe its the first instance of a person who had known anything of the principles of friends, changing them for Romish — I am sorry he is so deluded, and in hopes he will shortly see his errors." Isaac's conversion sent the Norrises into a panic, chronicled in the family letters. In the end, sympathy (and blood) triumphed over doctrine. Mary Norris's letter of 30 October 1784 to Isaac presented the family's final consensus on the issue: capitulation. When she had rebuked her son mildly, he had responded with silence. Now she wrote to retract her criticism: "I have been greatly disappointed that I had no letter, if in any of my late letters to thee I may have wrote any thing concerning thyself, my dear Son must attribute what I have wrote to my anxious concern for what I think is for his happiness, but altho' wee may differ in our religious sentiments, I hope that will not lessen our affection, & love, and my dear Child may depend on it that his mother will leave him to his Christian liberty at his return which She hope[s] will be by the next Spring."[67] The Norrises were too afraid of losing Isaac to want a quarrel.

The Norrises lost Isaac anyway, to something rather darker than Catholicism. His conversion seems to have been only one component of a nervous breakdown. A censorious voice emerged in Isaac. All of England came under its interdict — "it is an expensive, dissipated place," he wrote — and he fled to a monastery in Liège. This aspect of Isaac judged all pleasures harshly. Explaining his changed travel plans to his sister, he wrote that "from various circumstances on a nearer view I conceived a disgust to the pleasures which formerly my imagination had drawn a false picture of, — & this disgust is since improved into an entire conviction of their falsehood and vanity, and an entire adieu to them." In another letter, he was at pains to correct any notion she might have that "we travellers live in perpetual rounds of amusement." To set the record straight, he meticulously catalogued his increasingly rare sallies into public. When he gave his sister the reasons for his conversion, he omitted any points on which Catholicism and Quaker doctrine differed. What brought him to Roman Catholicism, in his telling, was a new awareness of his sinfulness — "we are not placed in this world for nothing, or merely to amuse ourselves" — couched in the terms a young heir might use to reproach himself for failing to live up to the family name. Perhaps, as Isaac's boyhood ended and he realized he would never satisfy manhood's demands, his ego-ideal became crueler. What Erikson would have called his psychosocial moratorium was drawing to a close, and he may have felt more and more acutely how far he was going to fall from his forefathers' standard. He himself admitted that if he had felt more confidence, he would not have needed to convert: "More satisfied with myself I might have placed happiness in myself."[68]

For all his new austerity, however, Isaac stayed in Paris because he liked it. "I find by Isaac's letter that he is in good spirits and says that he prefers one week in Paris to a year in London," Isaac's cousin Hannah Thomson gossiped to Mifflin. (Hannah sympathized; she liked living in New York because of its Parisian manners. "In this city as in France Nobody grows Old," she wrote. "Every body is young while they can Visit & keep their Infirmities to themselves.") Even though Isaac had chosen his new religion with ascetic logic, in his daily routine while abroad he consulted nothing but his pleasure. His brother Joseph wrote home that Isaac "still preserves the same Whims, Notions, likes & Dislikes as formerly — this Day he eats heartily — to morrow he will only take Tea or some such Slop — this Night he sleeps remarkably well, the next some great Noise has prevented him from closing his Eyes — & he still preserves the old Custom of taking things going to Bed to make him sleep — With regard to his time of rising it is not regular sometimes at 10, he shows himself & often am told it is near twelve." Isaac detached himself from everything worldly, but the enthusiastic young convert did not realize that this detachment was itself a pleasure and temptation. "The less one goes out, and sees of the world, the more I think what we do see interests us," he wrote to his sister. Joseph could not wait to get back to Philadelphia, but Isaac postponed his return again and again. As Joseph reported, Isaac's "attachment to this vile *dirty hole* is astonishing — Without friends, without Acquaintances, cubbed up in a little pittiful dark Chamber he prefers it to his native place."[69]

The amused tone with which Joseph relayed his brother's eccentricity sounds somewhat forced. Isaac's sleep pattern suggests depression, as does the social isolation he increasingly preferred. Isaac's "old Custom of taking things going to Bed to make him sleep" likely refers to the use of opiates. Mifflin describes in his diary how, with only a fever and mild dysentery, he practically had to fight off prescriptions of laudanum from Doctors Hall and Rush. Once, when Mifflin explicitly "desired there might be no opium in" his medicine, Dr. Hall duped him. Dr. Rush laughed when he heard about his colleague's behavior; "he said it was one of those things which the physicians termed 'pious frauds.'"[70] It would have been easy for Isaac to start taking opium; and, confused about his goals and lacking self-discipline, it would have been difficult for him to stop.

Mifflin had intended to follow his friend Isaac to Europe, but soon after Isaac's departure, Mifflin delayed the transatlantic voyage in order to woo a young woman in Maryland. The courtship came to nothing, but just as it ended Mifflin came down with the ague. Because of his poor health, Mifflin decided not to travel to Europe. By 1786, the two had been "separated longer than thrice the annual coarse of the sun," and Mifflin was anticipating Isaac's return in verse.

> Fly swift ye hours, you measure time in vain
> Till ye bring back Castalio again:
> Be swifter now & to redeem that wrong
> When he & I are met, be twice as long.[71]

Mifflin knew his friend had converted; he may have had some inkling of his other troubles, too. Just before they were reunited, Mifflin dreamed of the reunion. In the dream, Isaac "was so altered both in person & manners that he appeared quite a new being to me — his face was flat & sallow, his figure long & gangling — & he had a careless swaggering air."[72] The dream suggests that Mifflin was afraid that the sensitive poet had turned into someone with jaundiced skin and selfish manners — an opium eater perhaps.

Mifflin's anxiety about Isaac prompted him to take the strange precaution of testing his friendship with Gibson. No other episode in the Mifflin and Gibson diaries shows so markedly the peculiar, vivid attention Mifflin devoted to his friendships.

In July, Mifflin dropped a mysterious hint: "Mem—Something to break to Lorenzo, which perhaps he little dreams of—however it must be borne." Gibson suspected nothing. When Mifflin traveled to Princeton several days later for an extended visit, innocent Gibson was ecstatic. "Very happy on seeing him," Gibson wrote on 29 July. "Spent the morning till Dinner in rumaging his trunk—talking to him, and in reading his journal—how time flies away when a person is engaged in such a manner!" Faced with Gibson's unambiguous goodwill, Mifflin took to bed on 31 July with a suspiciously vague complaint.[73]

Mifflin diagnosed his sickness as caused by "low spirits," but Gibson sensed there was more to it. After noting that he was "very sorry" to hear about Mifflin's headache, Gibson confided to his diary that "I conceit he has not quite as much regard for me now as he had some time ago—returned to college but could not study on account of thinking of him."[74]

The next day, Mifflin "wrote a long letter to Lorenzo, with a plan which my heart did not dictate—a trial of his affection—& almost wept at the conclusion of it." The letter spoke contrary to Mifflin's heart, as he unconsciously protested during a visit he paid to the Rush and Stockton families that afternoon. When he apologized to his hosts for not having been a more diligent correspondent, unintended words slipped out of his mouth, which "entirely perverted" his apology. Just as Mifflin declined to report the content of the letter, he omitted to specify his slip of the tongue.[75]

He described at length, however, the delivery of his letter to Gibson, and that description is worth quoting. Mifflin "sent word by [Mr. Brown] to Lorenzo that a letter was at Mrs Knox for him—I placed it on the table up stairs with a candle by it & then shut myself in the back room to wait his arrival." When Gibson failed to respond to this summons, Mifflin left his hiding place to send another messenger to Gibson.

> I resumed my Station & he soon made his appearance—there was something mild & uncertain when he looked at the letter, he seemed to open it hesitatingly & his eyes flew precipitately over every page & then to the cover before he began to read—he had perused but a few lines when his countenance fell & he deliberately drew a chair & sat down—as he read I believe he heard me breathe & lookd for a few seconds earnestly at the door—all was hush'd. & he again returned to his letter—when he had finished, he folded all up slowly—& as he went down I thought I heard a sigh—My heart felt a melancholy sadness & I almost repented of my scheme—I followed & overtook him just as he had enterd the college gate—the sound of my voice so unexpected made him still more at a loss to account for what he had read—I asked him to return & told him I would explain the whole affair—when we

had retired, I told him my fears about Castalio & that in case they should be realized that all my hope would rest on him & that the letter was only a trial [of] what dependance I might have on his friendship & affection—the dear fellow seemed hurt at the experiment, but gave me the fullest assurances of his attachment—& I felt mine doubly renewed to him by the consciousness he testified of his own sincerity.[76]

Gibson's account corroborates Mifflin's; the only information it adds is that the incident baffled him. When Gibson read the letter, he was "very much surprised at it and could not understand it."[77]

If one takes Mifflin at his word, he felt some compunction over toying with his friend's feelings, but not enough to stop. His guilt was outweighed by his desire to know how strongly Gibson was attached to him. The modern reader sees at once Mifflin's voyeurism and the narcissistic reward he engineered at the cost of Gibson's pain. (Mark Twain understood that Tom Sawyer had to stumble into hearing his own funeral elegy; to have calculatedly managed it would have been inexcusable even in a rascal.) Mifflin's fictional letter must have been cruel, perhaps announcing a rupture in the friendship. There is something unschooled about Mifflin's sadism here, like a child's torture of an animal. The strength of his own emotions preempted consideration of the emotions he was provoking. But whether or not Mifflin's explanations speak well of his character, the episode does show that the pleasures and dangers of friendship between men were compelling enough in the eighteenth century to motivate some rather elaborate behavior.

As with his pining in the pear grove, Mifflin staged the scene at Mrs. Knox's inn not only for his immediate gratification but also for the revisitable pleasure he would find in recording it. Fixed in Mifflin's diary, the scene testifies forever to Gibson's sweet, gullible loyalty. But without Mifflin's intending or entirely recognizing the fact, it also testifies to the inadvertent damage caused by artists who work with human emotions. Charles Brockden Brown discovered similarly ambiguous results when his ventriloquist hero Carwin experiments with the feelings of the Wieland family by counterfeiting their voices. Mifflin's manipulations do not lead to anything as dire as psychosis or murder; his case more closely resembles the delicate negotiation of asking a lover who does not like to pose to stand still for a snapshot. A photographer who bullies his lover and ignores his discomfort procures a sentimental token that is unreal, but time and a sort of economics are on the photographer's side. The snapshot will outlast the lover's annoyance. A photographer with a strong faculty of forgetting will be able to enjoy the still image of his lover for years, cherishing it for the happy concord that the lover at that moment could hardly bear to represent.

Gibson, however, never gave Mifflin's tableau the lie. Later that month,

Mifflin recorded that Gibson had written "informing me (& oh! how consolatory) that I 'need not labour under any apprehension from him on the score of rivalship.'" Mifflin had not made any attempt to put Gibson at ease on this issue. It didn't occur to either party that Gibson might resent Mifflin for showing him his status as Mifflin's second choice. The lopsided arrangement seems to have suited Gibson; he preferred not to challenge those who adopted a fatherly attitude toward him. Years later, a lawyer colleague noticed this deference in Gibson and regretted it as a handicap: "Mr. Gibson is afraid of Tilghman [with whom Gibson had read law]. He believes him infallible, and dare not risque opposition to him, but if he means to be a *great lawyer* he should glory in opposing the whole *Bar,* and of all men his *old Master.*"[78]

Secure in Gibson, Mifflin was prepared to face the return of Isaac, rising to the occasion as a valetudinarian. "My sickness comes very untimely for his arrival — but he has arrived very opportunely for my sickness," Mifflin noted, with almost too much insight to qualify him as a hysteric. When Isaac reached Philadelphia, the Norrises sent their carriage to fetch Mifflin from his sickbed. He dashed into the Norris parlor feverish and sweating, "with all my invalid drapery flowing after me." In the happy flush of reunion, Mifflin felt that Isaac "was the same Castalio he was three years & three months ago" — an assessment time showed to be untrue. As soon as the two men were left alone, Isaac "told me he was determined we should never part again — 'I will give myself up to you' said he 'I will go wherever you go — & one shall not go without the other.'" Mifflin could not leave this avowal alone, of course; for Gibson's benefit he added this query to his diary entry: "Have I another friend that would make such a declaration?"[79]

Fortunately for Mifflin, he did. Whatever was troubling Isaac in France persisted, and probably worsened, when he returned to America. Isaac continued to sleep late. "I am very uneasy at his leading such an inactive life," Mifflin wrote when he discovered Isaac still in bed at one in the afternoon. "I went up and talked to him — I found he had taken an anodyne the night before — a practice I have repeatedly reprobated." New rumors circulated about Isaac in town; Mifflin attributed some of them to the scandal caused by Isaac's conversion, but others seemed blacker, although Mifflin spells nothing out. Several weeks after his return, Isaac was already hinting that he wanted to go back to Paris. It became difficult to persuade him to leave the house. "I think if he would exert himself more, & mix a little more in the world he would be better," his mother wrote a friend, "but he excludes himself too much, he converses with nobody hardly, but his friend John Mifflin." Isaac's silent spells exasperated even Mifflin. "He seems never easy but when I am with him," Mifflin observes, "& frequently when we are together he will not talk." Gibson was often quiet, a trait Mifflin saw as charmingly modest, but Isaac "was uncommonly mute . . . almost as if he had been *stricken*."[80]

Isaac's decline was gradual. When Gibson returned home from school at the end of the month, it briefly looked as though the three young men — Leander, Lorenzo, and Castalio — might join in musketeers-style unity. Mifflin flitted between the Norris and the Gibson houses in a game of musical beds that sometimes found all three men spending the night together. But when Mifflin left his two friends alone, they had little to say to each other. One day he came upon them sitting wordlessly in the Norris dining room. "I opened the door & found the brace of male Epicenes sitting at the west-window in as profound silence as if the God of *it* were holding his fingers to their lips — I soon broke up their 'mum-chance' — rattled them a while during which Lorenzo had a sort of an inkling to let Castalio see the journal — I did not second his motion." The word *Epicene* was probably a malapropism; it is unclear what Mifflin meant by it. More intelligible is the question of the privacy of Mifflin's journal. When Isaac had asked to see it on 27 September, Mifflin had put him off by saying he needed to ask for Gibson's permission because he kept the journal for Gibson's sake. In this scene, Gibson gave his assent, and Mifflin was forced to own that he did not want Isaac to read it. A week later, as if to cement his decision, Mifflin admitted Gibson to his "sanctum sanctorum": he showed Gibson "some of the letters of my dear departed Eugenius — to whom he has succeeded."[81] Isaac remained a close friend; no matter what the whisperers said, Mifflin stayed loyal. But Mifflin never opened his sanctum sanctorum for Isaac. Mifflin and Gibson, by contrast, grew more and more intimate.

The expression of their intimacy took several forms. Gibson gave Mifflin *"a to[ken] of friendship,"* and when they were apart, Mifflin remembered his friend by "putting it to my lips." When they were together, intimacy between the two could take the form of a shared, inviolate space. During a visit to Gibson's Princeton quarters, they walled themselves off from Gibson's classmates to achieve this. "We locked ourselves in my study," Gibson wrote, "and I fixing my gown across the window (to prevent the students seeing us) we looked over papers and talked till the dinner bell rang." Whenever the two spent the night together, the hours of talk that came between retiring to the bedroom and falling asleep were precious. A second bout of intimate conversation always took place the next morning, before leaving the bedroom for breakfast. Sometimes the two did more than talk during these private moments. On a trip together to Nottingham, Mifflin recorded that "in the evening as I was wrestling with Lorenzo I fell on the side of my head & hurt myself a little." A few days later this injury blossomed into a black eye.[82]

"I love & esteem him," Mifflin wrote of Gibson. Whether or not the two expressed their affection in sex, they held each other in a regard that we would call sexual. Mifflin dreamed of Gibson often. In one of his dreams, he appears to have been struggling with images of shame and loss of control that a direct relation between their bodies could have brought on.

> Dreamt a very odd dream last night—I thought Lorenzo & I (& I know not whether there was another person or not) were in a very small boat inside of a long kind of pier-wharf which was a great way into the river—I thought we had neither oar paddle or anything else to guide our course & we were driving fast into the current which was very strong but just as we got almost to the outside of the pier I caught hold on something to stop us & then pushed our boat from one thing to another till we reached the wharf—the people on shore all the time hallowing to us & very anxuous for our safety—I climed up the pier (which was very high) & then drew Lorenzo up after me—he seemed to be Stark naked & as we were [?] running along hand in hand to the place where his cloaths were—I awaked—greatly agitated by the danger from which we seemed to have escaped.[83]

If the river in Mifflin's dream represents the sentiments carrying the men along, then the lack of an "oar paddle or anything else" might represent an attempt to navigate their passions without recourse to what makes their bodies sexual and male. Rudderless, they find the current dangerously unmanageable. Once Mifflin finds something to hold on to, they are saved, but then the pier rises to a massive height, and Gibson and Mifflin are exposed—"hand in hand"—on the very thing that saved them.

A dream is not evidence of sexual conduct, but there is enough detail to the story of Lorenzo, Leander, and Castalio to make the question of did they or didn't they somewhat irrelevant. It is not inconceivable that they did, but they never said so. Nor is it inconceivable that they didn't. An eighteenth-century friendship felt like a bold experiment because it was not subject to the compromises of either marriage or commerce. "Is friendship in love more to be depended on than friendship in trade?" Mifflin asked. "Not so much perhaps." Mifflin thought his friendship with Gibson was purer than love as well as purer than trade—it was friendship for its own sake, freed from the duties and compensations a man looked for in either a wife or a business partner.[84]

More interesting is the evidence that Mifflin's pier-wharf dream gives of his evolution as a writer and self-analyst. He has moved far beyond his early elliptic comments; he tells the dream with a thoroughness and honesty that leaves him vulnerable. It is not easy to become intimate with the page, but Mifflin has learned how. He recognized that the journal gradually ceased to be only a means for communicating with Gibson. After several months of diary keeping, Mifflin noted that "it has now become an amusement to me." The writing process itself offered unexpected rewards. It gave shelter, for example, from unsentimental company. "Indeed this journal of mine is a resource in lonely hours & against stupid people." With a journal to compose, Mifflin could retreat from society without fear of ennui. It bothered and fascinated Mifflin that his spirits were "subject to such extremes," and so it pleased him to discover that the regular examination and statement of his emotions had the effect of both amplifying and taming them. In the end, the intermediary of writing served as a more reliable solace than the friend it stood in for. It acted "to counterbalance many things I have to displease & trouble me," including Gibson's occasional inattention. It steadied Mifflin by letting out the unsteadiness that his sympathies made him subject to. "It hath served as a barometrical diary of my hopes & fears my distresses & happiness — Many have been their vicissitudes, & at this moment I feel a gratitude for being preserved thro' such a variety of moods & dispositions."[85]

Gibson was not married to Mifflin, nor was he apprenticed to him. No writing bound them. But their writing, like the sympathy that played between them, was not altogether free, either. It was decorous, nostalgically deferential, and unself-conscious about artifice. It was not common, but it was decidedly not radical. Yet Mifflin does unburden himself as the diary moves forward. In the pear grove and at Mrs. Knox's inn, Mifflin struggled to represent the sentiments between Gibson and himself in scenes he could not quite stage-manage smoothly. But by the time he records the pier-wharf dream, he has left this struggle behind. Maybe he felt sure, at last, of Gibson's love, sure enough to realize that sympathy could not be proved by any display that he engineered, ornamented, and transcribed, but was best enacted by writing itself. The diary showed sympathy, barometrically; Mifflin only had to learn how to take a reading. Sharing a dream about sex was risky and intimate, riskier and more intimate than sex itself, because the dream, unlike sex and unlike Mifflin's scenes, could never have been scripted beforehand. Like a literary fiction and like love for another person, a dream is both under and beyond its author's control. As Mifflin dreams about losing his oar or paddle, he is almost ready to ride the current. In his diary he is moving from a notion of sympathy as sentimental control toward a style of writing that invites sympathy by the sincerity and open-endedness of its attention.

The last page of Mifflin's diary breaks off in midsentence on 17 April 1787; a stray single page from 11 May 1787 survives, bound into the volume at the Historical Society of Pennsylvania out of chronological order. Gibson's diary also ends midsentence, on 1 October 1786. Perhaps further pages or even volumes of either diary will someday come to light. In the meantime, however, other documents can give a sketchy finish to their story.

Isaac Norris continued to deteriorate. "Piety is not confined to cloisters," his cousin Mary Dickinson warned, but no amount of moralistic hectoring would persuade Isaac to return to the world. In January 1790 he abdicated the role of eldest son by transferring ownership and management of the family property to his brother Joseph. In May 1790 he left a second time for Europe; this trip lasted less than a year. In 1793, Isaac was mentioned in family letters as an object of pity and frustration. "My poor dear Isaac," his mother lamented from her home in Chester, "why will he not come to see me?" A few months later, when yellow fever hit Philadelphia and the Norrises were evacuating all friends and family from the city, Mrs. Norris instructed her daughter, Deborah, to "invite [Isaac] to your house, he will not come near mine."[86]

By the mid-1790s the family were writing about Isaac as though he were a child. In the family letters, paragraphs referring to Isaac after 1786 have been systematically crossed out by a later hand, but some can be reconstructed. "I am pleased thee called on thy poor Brother," reads one such passage, written by Mrs. Norris to Deborah on 9 March 1796. "I think he might have got up to have seen thee, but so it is with him, Josey wrote me that he had been with him & was quite as he always ought to be, the day before." By 1798, Isaac was making irregular visits to his mother, and her letters fall into a pattern of saying how improved he looks after a stay under her supervision and that she hopes he won't relapse when he leaves her. "He has lived regularly & soberly, which has been a Comfort to me, but I fear he will not continue so to do."[87] The same year, cousin Mary wrote to Isaac that "thee appears to be buried from all thy friends." In the end Isaac saw no friends, not even Mifflin. In the last letter Mrs. Norris wrote before she died, Isaac appears to have returned to a state of infancy. "My Son Isaac is with me & has been since the latter end of Augt: & his conduct in all that time has been highly satisfactory to me, he has never once deviated & looks much better then when he first came down." Isaac died, unmarried and childless, on 7 October 1802, at the age of forty-two.[88]

On 18 June 1788, roughly a year after his extant diary breaks off, Mifflin married Clementina Ross, the eighteen-year-old daughter of the merchant John Ross. Mifflin and his wife had six children, none of whom had issue. As an attorney, Mifflin's major commission was as the Philadelphia representative of John Penn and later his widow, Anne, who became unhappy with Mifflin's performance.[89]

Gibson was admitted to the bar on 28 September 1791. He worked closely with the financier Robert Morris and became heavily involved in real estate speculation. In 1796 he moved his mother and sisters to a more fashionable house, a few doors away from their old home.[90]

After Mifflin's marriage, Mifflin and Gibson successfully translated their

*Portrait of Elizabeth Beale Bordley (Mrs. James Gibson),* by Gilbert Stuart. Circa 1797. Courtesy of the Pennsylvania Academy of the Fine Arts, Philadelphia. Bequest of Elizabeth Mifflin.

private friendship into the semipublic sphere of volunteer service on committees and associations. Both men were elected to the American Philosophical Society: Mifflin on 15 January 1796, Gibson on 17 April 1807. Both served, too, as trustees of the University of Pennsylvania, sitting, for example, on the Committee to Obtain a Master of the Grammar School. In both cases, Mifflin appears to have introduced Gibson, who then worked diligently free of charge as a fund-raiser, behind-the-scenes organizer, and legal adviser. Socialite Mifflin was also a member of the Sons of Washington and recruited members for the Philadelphia Agricultural Society of his stepfather, John Beale Bordley.[91]

Mifflin died on 13 May 1813. Four years later, at age forty-seven, James Gibson finally married. He chose as his bride Mifflin's half-sister, thirty-nine-year-old Elizabeth Bordley. The couple lived together happily for almost four decades, until Gibson's death in 1856. They had no children.[92]

On 23 April 1788, not yet a recluse, Isaac Norris wrote to his cousin Mary Dickinson. He mentioned that John Mifflin was away on a trip — perhaps related to Mifflin's impending marriage, only two months away — and that he missed Mifflin badly. To ease his mood, Isaac's thoughts turned to the family garden. The famous Norris garden, however, could no longer reassure him. It was being divided into parcels, probably in order to rent the land to raise cash. The spring had been warm and quick, Isaac noted. "I enjoyed the fine weather but somehow in a melancholy way, at the idea of the garden being cut up, and the Catawba & Willow trees in the lot taken away, — as the parting of friends calls up all their tenderness, and makes them sensible of an attatchment which perhaps lay latent in them when they were daily together so the change in this scene of my youth and farewell to every well-known tree & shrub makes me regret their loss and think them more beautiful than ever." The street's charm would be diminished, he felt, when the Norris trees were cut down. His mind wandered back to his childhood, and he recalled his sister picking flowers in the garden for her bonnet, and children playing in the lot at sunset.[93] Even the duck pen brought back memories, and to break his sorrowful train of thought, Isaac decided to tell Mary a joke: "A Gentleman of our acquaintance lost his wife lately, in the heigth of his grief, before the funeral, a friend visited him and found him in the greatest affliction, — in the midst of his tears a servant came into the room & said 'Master the jack wants winding up' — he left all, — went & wound up the jack, & returnd to his company. for it was a *patent jack* & none could wind it up but himself."[94] Isaac presented the vignette to Mary as a non sequitur, but it wasn't. Isaac was hinting at what he knew: to survive in a world of accelerating losses, sympathy had to be managed, coolly. In America, a sentimental man was in danger of collapsing in on his emotions unless he could bring himself to believe, wrongly but comically, that the impersonal machine outside required his special intervention. In combination, Mifflin's friend and his journal had acted like a wick to tap the fuel of his sentiments in an even, steady flow. But Isaac never found what would take him out of himself; his lamp went out.

# 2

## The Decomposition of Charles Brockden Brown: Sympathy in Brown's Letters

In Philadelphia in 1787, while John Mifflin was keeping his diary, a sixteen-year-old boy named Charles Brockden Brown finished his studies at Robert Proud's Friends Latin School and was apprenticed to Alexander Wilcocks to study law. Like the Norrises and the Gibsons, the Browns were Quakers, but their status in society was lower, and their finances were often precarious. Charles's father, Elijah Brown, had been arrested as a profiteer during the Revolutionary War and jailed for debt in 1784. The family indulged young Charles with a first-class education because they expected great things of him.[1]

Brown began his legal career seriously — he was earnest enough to join a law society, where he served at least one five-week term as president — but the study of law was soon at war with a different ambition. Like Mifflin, Brown was captivated by literature — and by the new sentimental style. But whereas Mifflin regarded writing as a recreation and sympathy as a pleasure, Brown aspired to make writing a profession and experienced sympathy as a seduction into horror. Charles Brockden Brown became, as Leslie Fiedler famously observed, "the inventor of the American writer."[2]

Brown's development as a writer is harder to track than Mifflin's because it is more chaotic. Both men discovered themselves as writers by addressing young male friends. In the judgment of Paul Allen, Brown's first biographer, Brown's susceptibility to friendship was "by no means an ordinary case."[3] And

*Portrait of Charles Brockden Brown,* by James or Ellen Wallace Sharples. Circa 1795–1800. Independence National Historical Park, Philadelphia.

at times both Mifflin and Brown used the emotions of others in ways that may seem manipulative. But Brown's ambition to write for a living complicated the process of putting his feelings into words by raising the stakes. Mifflin may have enjoyed provoking sighs and tears, but Brown hoped to live off them. Brown had to work more artfully than Mifflin because he was crafting an aesthetic technique for public rather than private consumption and because his announced ambition put his friends on notice to expect deceit. He had to hide the tools that Mifflin left exposed. Brown's early correspondence is therefore a game of camouflage and cloaks; it is the chronicle of an artist's self-creation and, in itself, constitutes a transitional literary form, somewhere between autobiography and fiction. Its themes are imposture and infection, and the personality that we meet there is adolescent — charming, exasperating, and disorganized. We wonder about Brown as we wonder about any teenager: Will he find a way to live out his ambition? In his case, the challenge is particularly steep. Will he find a way to become a novelist in a culture without novelists?

While apprenticed to Wilcocks, Brown devoted his nights and other stolen moments to a diary entitled "The Journal of a Visionary," where he recorded his impressions and meditations, taking d'Alembert and Diderot as his intellectual models.[4] When Wilcocks left town on business, Brown confessed to a friend that he took advantage of his master's absence to write hundreds of lines of verse inspired by Alexander Pope. One of Brown's couplets derided law as antisympathetic, in the same terms that Mifflin had derided it to Gibson: "How mean and sordid is the lawyer's mind / That joys from others woes can only find."[5]

Brown's best friend during this period was a young man named John Davidson. Davidson may have been a medical student and was probably a schoolmate from Proud's academy. In a poem Brown wrote at age fifteen or sixteen about "some of his School fellows," which Brown's father transcribed into one of his commonplace books, a marginal note identifies as Davidson a friend who the poet prophesies "shalt eclypse a Cullen's fam'd name." In a letter to Davidson, Brown once wrote that he could not understand "the dialect of medicine" in an essay Davidson had written — another hint that Davidson was studying to be a doctor.[6]

Between them, Brown and Davidson created the Belles Lettres Society, a group that met to encourage its members "to improve in composition and eloquence." The birth of the society involved a certain amount of gamesmanship. According to Allen, the impetus for the group came from a letter Brown wrote to Davidson, asking him to clarify "the relations, dependencies, and connections of the several parts of knowledge."[7] Perhaps wary of undertaking to answer such an encyclopedic question by himself, Davidson countered by suggesting a club instead. Brown agreed and recruited several friends, only to have Davidson back out of all organizational responsibilities.

In recounting the genesis of the Belles Lettres Society, Allen several times refers to Davidson's "indolence." No doubt Allen is echoing an annoyance that Brown expressed in letters and journals, since lost, about what he felt to be Davidson's bait-and-switch. "The mere negligence of a friend," Allen writes, led to the society. Brown's club redeemed "a mere occasional apology for indolence in his friend."[8] But Allen's (that is, Brown's) annoyance is hardly fair. Davidson failed to follow through on an intention that had originated with Brown. Brown, not Davidson, wanted to sort out all human knowledge. Somehow Brown palmed his ambition off on Davidson, whose failure to consummate it obliged Brown to step in to the rescue.

Unfortunately, we know little about Davidson, who died in December 1790. From the few facts that Brown relates, he emerges as a contradiction: notably hardworking and notably lazy. Brown piously recollected him as so assiduous that it was unthinkable to picture him wasting time on "insignificant amusements" like chess or cards. He describes Davidson's early death as "the period of my intellectual progress."[9] He used Davidson's memory much the way Mifflin used Eugenius's—as a standard to hold new friends against. But Brown also recalled Davidson as such an indolent, faulty thinker that he felt compelled to start a debating society to address the questions that Davidson would not. Like later friends, Davidson served as the vessel of a duality that Brown felt within himself.

Brown inflicted on Davidson not only his ambivalent sense of himself (indolent versus hardworking) but also his ambivalent understanding of literature (true-to-life versus invented). In the summer of 1788, Brown composed a series of love letters between "C.B.B." and Henrietta G.—one of Brown's earliest surviving works of fiction. But the final letter in the series, addressed to "J. D——n," suggests that Brown intended Davidson to read the letters as *non*fiction. (Whether or not Davidson was fooled, Brown succeeded in deceiving at least one of his twentieth-century biographers.)[10] Davidson seems to have been the first victim of Brown's experimental attempts at transmuting life into fiction. In a pattern Brown would repeat, Brown chose a doctor to hear his intimate confessions; then instead of confessions, he delivered lies.

The Henrietta letters are tepid and conventional. No reader would guess that spree murders, ventriloquism, and Indians lurk in their author's imaginative future. Indeed, no reader would learn anything about Brown, except that he was somewhat vain and, like most adolescent boys, fascinated by breasts. ("That bosom which it is criminal to name, thinkest thou that I shall not be tempted to touch, to gaze with too much greediness at its enchanting undulations?") The character C.B.B. is such a cookie-cutter imprint of the sentimental lover that Brown felt obliged to apologize for his hero's flatness—for his curious reluctance to "reveal domestic incidents" to the woman with whom he claims to wish to share all.[11]

The only intriguing conflict in the letters is whether they ought to exist at all. C.B.B. pretends that he wrote the letters in order to enjoy his feelings for Henrietta while she was absent. But when he scrutinizes this motive according to the logic of romance novels, he concludes that if his sympathy for Henrietta is real, then the effort of writing is unnecessary. Language merely obstructs. "Are not my ideas fettered and degraded by the poverty of language? Is she not actually present? . . . Her soul mingles with mine." Insofar as the emotion is real, the writing that derives from the emotion is clutter. Furthermore, these extraneous words might not interest Henrietta. "O my beloved, whither are now thy thoughts straying?" From the inadequacy of his writing, C.B.B. infers an inattention in Henrietta. That is, the expression of his sympathy leads him to wonder about his competence as a writer, which in turn leads him to doubt that his beloved is as attentive as he is. He is forced to conclude that he writes for conflicting reasons: because he hopes he is in sympathy with Henrietta and because he cannot trust that he is. "I discern with astonishment and horror that thou art absent."[12] Out of this paradox, however, Brown has not yet created art. Brown frets about the relation of sympathy to expression as if it is a puzzle. The sympathy in question is ideal rather than real — altogether safe. Neither Brown nor C.B.B. is ready to explore how make-believe might induce corrupting feelings that *do* exist.

Another friend and classmate from the Friends Latin School, Joseph Bringhurst Jr. (1767–1834), comes into sharper focus than Davidson, because more than two score of Brown's letters to him have survived — as many as Brown is known to have written to his wife.[13] Four years older than Brown, Bringhurst was studying medicine while Brown studied law. Brown addressed him half-jocularly as "O great Physician" at the close of one of his letters, and in another called him "conversant with the medical Science, and its mournful trappings and appendages of Skeletons and livid Carcases." Bringhurst later practiced in Wilmington, Delaware, where he had been raised, and ran into professional difficulties, including imprisonment, probably for debt.[14]

Bringhurst's family were pious Quakers. When a yellow fever epidemic hit Philadelphia in 1793, Bringhurst's father took a hard line. In the senior Bringhurst's opinion, the plague had not administered as much divine wrath to the capital's sinners as they deserved. "Something yett more dreadfull may be in Righteous Indignation ordered for the Sorrowfull Humiliating of this Wicked proud people, many of whom look as if they scarcely thought the ground good enough for them to walk upon." Joseph Junior inherited a touch of his father's moralism — in arguments with Brown, he defended Christianity against atheism, refused to condone suicide, and warned Brown to desist when his intimacy with a married woman began to look adulterous. But Joseph lacked his father's austerity. In fact, he was vain and worldly enough to play the fortepiano and to woo his fiancée, Deborah Ferris, with the literary conceit that he was "a quaker Petrarch" courting a Laura. In the spring of 1791, under the pseudonym Birtha, he contributed sonnets to a poetical correspondence published in the *Gazette of the United States*. Bringhurst belonged to the Belles Lettres Society and to the Society for the Attainment of Useful Knowledge, which succeeded it. Literate, Quaker, and romantic, Bringhurst shared Brown's background and many of his ambitions.[15]

Brown felt his affinity with Bringhurst so intensely that he sometimes described it as a kind of rapture. "O take me to thyself, thou best of friends!" Brown gushed in one letter. "My Bringhurst! Suffer me to call thee by the tenderest appellations. My heart is open to divine and softening impressions. I am soul all over." Brown imagined that he was on Bringhurst's mind even while Bringhurst slept. "He dreams of me. His lips inarticulably and involuntarily utter my name. My idea flows across his fancy and he smiles. . . . Heavenly Sympathy! I feel thy influence!"[16]

Brown's declarations of sympathy must be taken with a grain of salt. In the same letter that he quiveringly professed to be "soul all over," Brown was struggling to answer an accusation from Bringhurst that Brown had been ridiculing him. Unable to confront his friend's anger directly, Brown deflected the accusation with a silly caricature of regret. If Bringhurst could believe that Brown was mocking him, then Bringhurst had failed to appreciate the fervor of Brown's devotion. "Alas!" Brown exclaimed with campy offendedness, "where has the delicacy of exalted friendship vanished!" Then, as if afraid that Bringhurst might take this complaint seriously, Brown clowned further, drawing elaborate attention to his impish, hyperemotional style. "Surely I am haunted by some malignant daemon, who wrests from me the dominion of my pen. . . . What makes me write thus strangely? Is it this gloomy and unpropitious hour? Midnight is the season of Insanity. It borders upon three. Tick! Tick. Tock." The image of their souls' magic dream-union follows this passage. It is the last flourish in a complex erasure of their disagreement. The passage was overwritten because its motive was overcompensation.

The strategy worked. Bringhurst wrote back to say that Brown's letter had moved him deeply. Brown replied that to move Bringhurst was "the felicity after which I languish." And then, inspired perhaps by his previous success, Brown repeated his melodramatic performance. His bliss took a hairpin turn into melancholy. "I am no longer master of myself—I weep involuntarily. . . . Stretch out thy hand, again, my guardian angel." The impression is of a teenager intoxicated by his expanding vocabulary and what he has read of Rous-

*Portrait of Joseph Bringhurst (1767–1834)*, by Robert Fulton. 1786. Rock-wood Museum, New Castle County Government. Photo courtesy of Frick Art Reference Library.

seau. He is not experimenting with his emotions so much as with the expression of them: the novelist-to-be has not yet learned that sobbing and noting your sobs as stage directions do not induce the same reaction. Variety makes up for insincerity, a predicament that Brown almost acknowledges in the self-epitaph concluding the letter: "Here lies, who was born to prove the extremes of joy and woe."[17]

Only a fellow adolescent could have kept up with the zigzags in Brown's moods. Brown's self-esteem could rise and fall precipitously according to the tributes his friends paid to his talent. He lacked a consistent sense of himself and looked to Bringhurst in particular, the friend who had known him longest, to tell him who he was and what he was worth. Throughout their friendship, Brown threw at Bringhurst wildly varying self-images, as if to dare his friend to confirm or deny them. Brown could claim that "in my own opinion, no one of this same age that ever lived has seen, has read, has written, has reflected more than myself." But he could also speak of himself in the third person as "a *grave* formal *wretch*, difficult to please and easily offended, whom a sneer will sink into despondency, and a wand of deceitful approbation or a smile of artful complaisance, will raise into confidence."[18]

Sometimes Brown's volatility must have charmed Bringhurst. It would have been hard not to smile at Brown, aged twenty-one, lamenting his plight as a has-been. "Thou seest before thee the ruins of a man: and yet think not that thy friendship will be either unacceptable or useless."[19] He seemed to find a wild fun in his own despair, and to be as unself-conscious about it as Mr. Micawber, who was crushed and abject at every arrest for debt but also gleeful at the chance to turn it to epistolary advantage. What David Copperfield's aunt said of Mr. Micawber applies to Brown: "I believe he dreams in letters."

At other times, these mood swings must have been hard to take. Reading over Brown's journal entries, now lost, Allen felt that he was in the presence of something like a split personality: "Any one who perused them would with difficulty be persuaded that so much excentricity, and so much irregularity were the productions of one man; much less would he believe them to have proceeded from the same source with the interval of a few moments only." As Brown himself put it, "Am I not uniform in contradictions, and invariable in vicissitude?" The trick accomplished by all this vagary was that Brown was able to hide in plain sight. Garrulous and entertaining, his letters revealed nothing about their author—not his real emotions, not even accurate news. There were no concrete details. Allen described the odd lopsidedness of the correspondence as follows:

In his own letters he sedulously avoided the mention of himself. . . . His correspondence therefore with his most intimate friends, wears a curious cast. On their side is the utmost frankness in the disclosure of all the little circumstances affording them delight; on his part he joins in their joy, and revels in their intellectual hilarity; presents these circumstances again in a more fascinating shape, and makes his page the depository of all the benevolent sympathies in which he so munificently indulges. . . . Now in requital for all this frankness and confidence, what is communicated on his part? Literally nothing.[20]

Sympathy, in excess, erased Brown's self from his letters. He fused with the friend he was responding to, to the point of vanishing himself. As Brown proudly lamented, "No one whose character is . . . less known to those that know him best . . . ever existed." In his sympathetic ecstasy, he also lost touch with the comforting solidity of things that is usual in eighteenth-century prose. We never get any sense of where the writer is. If he mentions his pen, it is to launch a bagatelle about quills. A mention of his desk gives way to an invocation of a winged Muse. He pretends to write from London or Switzerland. There are no facts, only voices.[21]

It haunted Brown to think that despite his flurry of emotionality he might not make any real connection. In a letter in which he expressed envy of Bringhurst's relative ease of expression, Brown described his own soul as "a toad enclosed, alive and active in the Centre of a rock." There is nothing very rocklike about Brown's letters — they are not still, they are always cracking open — but their surface did imprison an angry inner self that loudly and ceaselessly claimed to be a prince, no matter how ugly it looked. Years later, Brown probably drew on this sense of an occluded, underappreciated self when he created his hero Arthur Mervyn, who loftily pretended not to blame his country neighbors for despising him. Mervyn knew that his neighbors were able to see only the toad. "It was not me whom they hated and despised. It was the phantom that passed under my name, which existed only in their imagination, and which was worthy of all their scorn and all their enmity."[22]

In another letter to Bringhurst, Brown cast himself as a rural boy playing on a riverbank, misjudged by hunters passing by. The passage is remarkable not only for what it reveals about Brown's self but also for the precocious experiment he makes with stream of consciousness and disjointed subjectivities.

Do you see (says one sportsman to the other) that boy upon the bank. He is not above fourteen years of age. He would be

---

Cursed! Cursed! Cursed, who can help it! Let him send — perdition seize him — tears of joy would I shed upon his grave — no sweeter music than his funeral dirge. — fye — fye upon thee. How easily ruffled? — How quickly will it pass away — tomorrow it will only be remembered — lend me a staff to drive him from my toes — This — This black ox, according to the vulgar metaphor —

It would be amusing to discover what are his reflexions at this moment. Nothing (says the other) but a country bumpkin, illiterate and unreflecting. A short interval from work he snatches to amuse himself with thoughtlessly wandering in the Sunshine. I wonder where his fishing Rod is. He can be suited to no other employment, mean rustic and ungainly.[23]

The frenzied, poetically turned thoughts of the boy prove him to be both better read and more vengeful than the smug adult hunters suspect. But the hunters can appreciate neither his superiority nor his malice, because the toad is encased in rock. When they try to sympathize, they completely mistake him. Successful sympathy would bring them in contact with near psychotic rage. Instead, they condescend to think that his reverie looks quaint, which aggravates.

Why would you let your friends see that on the inside you are still an unkissed toad? If they gently ask about your feelings, how could you reward them with frustrated ambition fermenting into bitterness — with the complaint that they have never realized your true worth? But this is what sentimental piety required of Brown: to offer the ugly self with the pretty one, to say "the good and the bad with the same candor," as Rousseau would swear before God on Judgment Day that he had done in his *Confessions*. As Brown explained to Bringhurst, "A mask became . . . habitual to me" over the years, but in his romantic correspondence with his friends, he felt "a childish and precipitate eagerness to be more explicit," to drop the mask and reveal the hidden truth about his life, with "all its degrading contracts and all its calamitous vicissitudes."[24]

Brown said he dropped the mask. But when he claimed to be most sincere, he could be least relied on. He strained so hard to render his confessions satisfyingly degrading and calamitous that he lied. To meet the expectations of the genre that Rousseau had set forth, Brown distorted facts. In one letter to Bringhurst, Brown "confessed" a heart-wrenching untruth: "O Bringhurst! Thou *shalt* be master of my heart. . . . Thou shalt know all in spite of thee. That I *loved* that I *wedded*. That, ere a lunar revolution was accomplished death snatched from me the object of my vows." No evidence outside the letters has come to light to confirm the story of this child-wife. It hardly seems likely that the marriage could have been kept secret in a community as tightly knit as that of the Philadelphia Quakers, especially from a friend as intimate and long-standing as Bringhurst. Brown continued to prompt his friend to weep over his blighted marriage for nearly a year. He even related a Spenserian dream that his supposed wife had shared with him, a premonition of her own death, in which a black knight snatched her out of Brown's arms.[25]

It is not clear how Brown understood his lies. There are hints that he thought of them as a game. He wrote once that he hoped Bringhurst "derives amusement from my imperfect narratives, of fictitious adventures." But this probably referred only to the narratives that Brown clearly acknowledged to be made up, such as the letters he wrote as if he were in London collecting law books or in the Alps wooing a Swiss maiden named Jacquelette. On another occasion, after announcing that he had almost finished transcribing a letter series, Brown added, "I think I have already assured you that those letters are genuine," as if he could not remember what truth-value he had claimed for them earlier and as if it did not much matter one way or the other so long as the game was played as though they were genuine. But Brown did want the emotions he expressed to be taken as real, even if the stories were not. In the fictional series of love letters to Henrietta G., Brown described his psychological state upon first meeting her face-to-face: "In a short time I discovered with rapture and astonishment that those emotions which I had hitherto delighted to feign had suddenly become real."[26] Within a letter that counterfeits authentic emotions, Brown is describing a moment when counterfeited emotions became authentic. Perhaps Brown blurred the difference between real and imagined emotions in order to hide toadlike feelings about his own inadequacy. Perhaps he wanted to obscure the strength of his attachment to male friends. Perhaps he was perversely thwarting what Leslie Fiedler calls the Sentimental Love Religion, with its demand to produce emotion as if it were a commodity, and its unlikely expectation that the emotion produced will always reflect well on the soul it comes from. Or perhaps he was merely unscrupulous in his ambition to win the trophy of a sentimental writer's success: his readers' tears.

To make Bringhurst cry, Brown did not hesitate even to threaten suicide. He seems to have discovered almost by accident that hinting at it was an efficacious tearjerker. The Society for the Attainment of Useful Knowledge was debating a common Enlightenment controversy: whether suicide should be understood as the destruction of an immortal soul, always to be damned, or whether in some circumstances it was a rational, even noble sacrifice, after the manner of Addison's Cato.[27] Bringhurst wrote Brown a description of a suicide, presumably to diminish the Roman glamor by highlighting the sorrow it brought to others. Brown admitted to Bringhurst that the scene made him weep, but he maintained that "such is the darkness and perverseness of my understanding that I think them [suicides], if the truth must be honestly avowed, wholly justifiable!!! that their conduct is such as a slight accident once prevented me from imitating." Bringhurst reacted strongly, fearing that Brown still had thoughts of killing himself, and he thereby launched a new bad habit in Brown. Once Brown knew the idea of his killing himself would set off Bringhurst's waterworks, he could not resist dark hints. In the same letter that he pooh-poohed his friend's anxiety ("Do you fear that I shall ever kill myself *merely* because I *think* it justifiable?"), he dilated on an earlier flirtation with death ("I was once on the very point of perpetrating this crime"). Brown was shameless enough to close one letter with the morbid suggestion that he might have departed this world between his writing of the letter and Bringhurst's reading of it: "Farewell and possibly FOREVER! who knows but before the return of morning I shall be no more. Death may seize me ere I sleep!"[28] Brown always promised not to do himself in, but his reassurances left open the possibility that if he were slightly more depressed, he might. One hopes that Bringhurst had strong nerves and did not take his friend too seriously.

If a character such as Carwin in Brown's *Wieland* may be read as a figure of the author, it seems that Brown experienced his romantic impulse and his urge to tell stories as imposture: as a deceitful manipulation of others, which their credulity and his powerful imagination seduced him into, almost against his will. In his letters Brown acted this imposture out, literally deceiving Bringhurst. But in his fiction, oddly, he could not yet act the imposture out; he tripped over the immorality of it. In his first published prose, a series of Addison and Steele–style newspaper essays entitled *The Rhapsodist,* Brown opened by turning the useful fiction of a persona into a moral quandary. In Addison's first number, Mr. Spectator introduced himself and promised to disclose so much personal information over time as "to Print my self out, if possible, before I Die." Brown's Rhapsodist, in contrast, explains that despite the conventions of the genre, he could never discuss his own person without "somewhat disguising the truth." Because that would be wrong, the Rhapsodist chooses to withhold nearly all information about himself but promises nonetheless that "the sincerity of my character shall be the principal characteristic of these papers." He then works himself into a dudgeon on the virtue of honesty: "Wherever I perceive the least inclination to deceive, I suspect a growing depravity of soul."[29]

In order not to compromise his sincerity, then, the Rhapsodist vows to reveal little or nothing of his own heart, yet it is this absent personal character and these suppressed private sentiments that are supposed to interest the reader. Discretion wins; the reader of *The Rhapsodist* loses. Moral indignation about lying is somewhat at odds with the practice of fiction. Brown blew a lot of hot air while trying to vent his ambivalence. Neither indignation nor anxiety, however, prevented Brown from including a letter from a flattering, invented correspondent who wrote in to praise the Rhapsodist's intelligence and talent.

In a letter to Bringhurst written several years after *The Rhapsodist,* Brown's fictional impulse and moralism stand in a slightly different configuration but are still unresolved. Pretending that the fictional Henrietta G. had asked him to rewrite Rousseau's *Julie,* Brown offered Bringhurst "a sketch of the plan" of the novel he supposedly produced for her, "The Story of Julius." Henrietta had found Rousseau "pernicious and seductive" and wanted his influence corrected. Brown promised to repair the romance plot so that virtue would "triumph . . . over the most lawless and impetuous passions." But nothing about "The Story of Julius" is quite what Brown promised. According to Brown's plot outline, Julius half-obeys his mother's deathbed wish by not marrying the woman he wanted, but he half-defies her by not marrying the woman she wanted, either. The denouement — Julius's death of a broken heart — can be read as the triumph "of duty over inclination" only if one is willing to read Werther's death not as a protest but as a triumph of morality over desire. Brown had claimed that the relationship between Julius and his twin sister, Julietta, would be the book's great innovation, for "Rousseau and Richardson had only described that friendship which may subsist between two men or two women, and have given us no striking pictures of sisterly and fraternal love."[30] The plot he sketched, however, had almost nothing to say about the love between the twins. With its conventional, sentimental plot, the book, if written, would have been a failure on all counts: it would have lacked artistic originality, and it would have failed to satisfy Henrietta's moral strictures.

Brown nonetheless found narcissistic pleasure in thinking about the novel: he admitted that he had "often sat upon the rocks of Schuylkill, and shutting my eyes, imagined myself to be the identical Julius." He made Julius everything he wanted to be — "at this time my ambition extended no farther than to act and speak like *Julius*" — and this sympathetic identification was the chief reward of his fantasy.[31] But if Julius, the learned but impetuous lover, was one half of the self that Brown projected into the fiction, Henrietta represents its complement. The "pernicious and seductive" nature of Rousseau, which Henrietta loathed, was what first attracted Brown, but in the parable that Brown tells of composing "Julius," it was Henrietta who pushed him to write. Unfortunately, the only way the Henrietta and the Julius in Brown could successfully collaborate on a romance, at this stage, was by not writing it.[32] As a fantasy uncompromised by execution, "Julius" could bring Brown a daydream of literary glory without the penalty of any aspersions on his morals. The letter to Bringhurst about the novel is itself a fiction — the only fiction about Julius that Brown ever wrote. There is no reason to believe either Brown's claim to have finished writing half of "Julius" or his claim that "Julius, when complete, would run to "twenty duodecimo volumes." Julius never existed, neither as a person nor as a novel, any more than Henrietta did. In 1792, Brown had managed to become only an impostor of a novelist; not until he wrote *Wieland* did he become a novelist of impostors.

For all its hysteria and duplicity, the love that Brown felt for Bringhurst was "not so violent: so tender: so impassioned" as the love he felt for another young man, William Wood Wilkins. Wilkins came to Philadelphia in April 1788 to study law with John Todd. He had been to school in Woodberry, New Jersey. Only fifteen years old when he arrived, Wilkins was two years younger than Brown and six years younger than Bringhurst. As a child, Wilkins had been the unjolly, eerily tranquil sort who strikes adults as likely to grow up to become a preacher or scientist — not unlike Brown, whose teacher had advised him to relent from studying his books and maps and get some exercise. New to the capital, Wilkins was lonely. "For many months," Bringhurst wrote, Wilkins "remained . . . entirely a stranger, without acquaintance to allure him to healthful relaxation." He overworked himself and fell into a depression. Then Bringhurst discovered him. In July 1789, Bringhurst invited Wilkins to recuperate in the companionship and the "elegant indulgence" of the Belles Lettres Society.[33]

Wilkins was handsome — "a young man of singular beauty and animation," according to William Dunlap. Witty and high-strung, he shared the aesthetic and intellectual enthusiasms of the society. When his turn came to deliver an address to the group, he described how one evening, walking through a park, it overwhelmed him to hear by chance a man playing music. He found himself "sunk in a Delirium of indescribable pleasure. . . . I had forgotten everything but myself. I now forgot myself." As a fellow law student who could appreciate "the softest — weakest — most irresolute Sensations — Extravagant, inexplicable," Wilkins stole Brown's heart. Wilkins was Bringhurst's friend before he was Brown's, and Brown swore, "Never will I bereave Bringhurst of his friend. Never will I take his Wilkins from him." But Brown fell in love. Allen wrote that out of "an acquaintance formed in the first instance by the casual meetings of the society," the two soon became "inseparable companions." Brown himself described their meeting more passionately: "No sooner did I see and converse with him, than I felt myself attached to him by an inconceivable and irresistable charm that, like the lightning of love, left me not at liberty to pause or deliberate."[34]

The two adolescents believed fervently in the ideal of romantic friendship. In a letter to a New Jersey schoolmate, Wilkins had written that in friendship "we find those delights that kindred souls can enjoy, soul locked to soul, and mind touching in heavenly sympathy with mind." Brown wrote to Wilkins about his own conviction in similar terms: "Friendship is, perhaps, more pure but certainly not less violent than love. Between friends there must exist a perfect and entire similarity of disposition. . . . Soul must be knit unto Soul. The fictions of Romance must be realized — They must adhere to each other, by a kind of magnetical influence." By this credo, true friends ought to think and live so close as to admit no room for dissension. Merely human, Brown and Wilkins never quite achieved this unity of spirit, but in their attempt they did strike a pitch of emotion even higher than Brown's soul-melting love for Bringhurst. They always presented their desire, however, as unsatisfied. Their union never seemed to be as perfect as they wanted it to be. Wilkins protested that Brown refused to grant him the title of friend. Brown complained that Wilkins did not love him as much as he loved Wilkins. "What a woman, what a child am I!" Brown lamented. "What affection can Wilkins have for me? *I* am never sought by *him*. It is I that hunt his footsteps." At times Brown seemed to envy Bringhurst's friendship with Wilkins. He asked Bringhurst, "Do you think that friendship can subsist between three persons?" in much the same spirit that Mifflin had hoped that Norris, Gibson, and he could share their affections without jealousy. But at other times, Brown confided to Bringhurst his criticisms of Wilkins, as if to skew the triangle away from the romantic lawyer toward the pious doctor. In the end, Wilkins died in the arms of Bringhurst, not Brown, and it was Bringhurst who delivered Wilkins's elegy to the Society for the Attainment of Useful Knowledge. But that may have been because Wilkins's romance with Brown was too fiery not to burn itself out.[35]

In their correspondence, Wilkins and Brown could be giddy and playful. "I will overwhelm you," Brown warned Wilkins, "with a torrent of exhaustless though perhaps inspir'd gayety." The would-be novelist invented scenes of a distraught lover weeping over his mistress's letters and of a spy trespassing in a scholar's study. As in his letters to Bringhurst, Brown sometimes pretended to write from abroad. Rather than report that the dinner bell had rung, Brown would lark that "I audiate a vocation to Concoction." Wilkins in this spirit could sign his letters "William O'Wisp." In doggerel verse, Brown honored their lighthearted hours with this description:

> But sitting securely together
>     We order the door to be shut
> We pass from the news and the weather
>     To shuffle, to deal, and to cut.
>
> In tale of fictitious distress
>     In study or converse the day —
> In ombre or chequers or chess
>     The even shall vanish away.

But the two could also wallow in each other's melancholy. They wrote many lines protesting that they did not want to burden each other with the full weight of their unhappiness, but burden each other they did. "There is something unaccountably consoling in complaint; in pouring one's sorrows into the bosom of a friend," Brown wrote Wilkins, clarifying the pleasure they took in sharing their sadness. To soothe Brown's misery, Wilkins once offered to show Brown the poetry he had written while depressed. The bond between them was so gratifying, it did not matter whether the mood of it was pleasant or painful. In either case, they could turn it into sympathy and verse.[36]

At the height of the young men's romance, they expressed their love with physical, as well as spiritual, gestures. "I wanted to take your hand last evening," Wilkins confessed in a short note one morning, adding with a touch of lover's modesty, "Excuse this hasty nonsense." Brown told Bringhurst that at the sight of Wilkins "I can scarcely refrain from embracing him. Tears of affection start into my eyes." For a while, the two were roommates. "Charles, I shall now live with you," Wilkins wrote, breaking the good news that his father had granted him permission to board with Brown while studying in Philadelphia.[37]

In the ditty above, Brown admitted to Wilkins that his tales of distress could be fictitious. Except for the occasional reference to Henrietta G., Brown seems never to have tried to convince Wilkins that a fictional letter was genuine. Brown had lied to Bringhurst about his past, as if to hide himself. Brown's intimacy with Wilkins was no less threatening, but his defense took a different form. He treated Wilkins as he had treated Davidson, whom Wilkins succeeded in Brown's heart. Brown made false assessments of Wilkins's character, which turned out to be true insights about himself. In an early letter to Wilkins, Brown made his trouble explicit through a half-joke: "If I am not permitted to write about my own self," Brown asked, "will you suffer me to talk about my other self!" No one had forbidden Brown to discuss himself. Wilkins, among others, begged him to, to no avail. "Why, my dear Charles, will you not talk to me about yourself?" he pleaded on 27 November 1792. But Brown could not bear to comment on himself directly. Through his bond with Wilkins, however, he found an indirect means: projection. As his other self, Wilkins was pelted with the accusations that Brown heard pounding in his own ears. In a retrospective letter to Wilkins, trying to decide what had driven them apart, Brown fixed the blame for their separation on the "misfortune . . . that our foibles were too nearly alike." Wilkins protested that Brown felt this likeness of faults more strongly than he did, but Brown's letters made a sort of novel out of his life, and he insisted on seeing Wilkins as his sympathetic hero. He fiercely identified with Wilkins's successes and failures, as he had with

Julius's — as if they were his own. He could not see Wilkins from any other vantage.[38]

Brown accused Wilkins of imposture, that is, of behaving in contradiction to what Brown thought was Wilkins's real nature. The charge took three forms. First, Wilkins failed to develop his literary talent; he used laziness to hide his true ambition. Second, he yielded too readily to prudence, conforming to social mores to gain worldly success as a lawyer — a venal compromise with his romantic nature. Third, he disguised his real emotions, distracting himself and others with levity when he should have confessed his sorrow. In each case, the imposture took a form that Brown himself was struggling to resist as he looked for the courage to leave behind a secure career as a lawyer for the risky life of a novelist.

If it weren't for Wilkins and Bringhurst, Brown liked to pretend, he would never have condescended to enjoy vulgar pleasures such as checkers and cards. But with "Will and Joe," a game of loo could become an opportunity "for the indulgence of celestial Sympathy," and so Brown made an exception. Early in his friendship with Wilkins, this conceit of Brown's turned into an accusation that Wilkins was addicted to the trivial amusements into which he inveigled Brown. Writing to Bringhurst, Brown harped on Wilkins's "*levity* and *thought-lessness.*" Wilkins's curiosity was content to answer the legal questions assigned to him. Once he had mastered them, he looked only for diversions. For Brown, who wanted to emulate the French encyclopedists, this was intolerable. Brown fretted about the "indifference with which he [Wilkins] regards those sublime objects of Juvenile and rational ambition. . . . Why will he thus pertinaciously slumber?" He felt that although Wilkins's talent was superior, he himself worked harder. "I have no reason to condemn myself for negligence or inactivity," Brown preened. If Wilkins were to cultivate his native capacity as diligently as Brown cultivated his, he would soon achieve renown.[39]

Wilkins was sensitive to the charge. Like Isaac Norris and many other young men in late eighteenth-century America, Wilkins saw himself as facing the Choice of Hercules: his fate depended on his choice between the easy pursuit of gratification and the stern path of virtue. On occasion, Wilkins lapsed into visiting the theater and other "resorts of Pleasure," but he always returned from his bouts of hedonism with renewed dutifulness. One night, for example, he gave in to the bad example of some gluttonous colleagues. (When Bringhurst reported this lapse in his eulogy, he palliated it with this explanation: "Perhaps there are no professional persons by whom the debaucheries of excessive eating & drinking, are so continually followed, as by N[ew] J[ersey] Lawyers.") Wilkins repented properly. The next morning he swore "never again to be present at their indecent revelries," and there is no reason to believe he broke his vow. He gave the issue enough thought to publish an essay on the topic: "On the Regulation of the Passions" appeared in Carey's *Museum* in April 1791.[40]

To dismiss Brown's charge of indolence, it probably suffices to note that before Wilkins's death at not quite twenty-two, he had passed the bar in Pennsylvania and New Jersey and was running a successful law practice in Philadelphia. In addition to the essay mentioned above, he had published a series of "Trifles," as he called them, in the *New Jersey State Gazette*. But Wilkins himself gave Brown a straightforward reply. He was not a writer, he explained, not in any serious way. He was a lawyer. Brown's expectations of him were "friendly and flattering, but very erroneous. . . . I have an understanding as capable perhaps of cultivation as those of the majority of mankind, but . . . an inexhaustible invention, keen perception, exquisite taste, and lively sensibility . . . belong to my friends, Bringhurst and Brown." Please, he seems to have been asking, do not saddle me with your aspirations for yourself. In the same letter, Wilkins politely but firmly turned the accusation of laziness back on Brown: "When will the moment arrive when Charles will lay aside that indolence and despondency which is unworthy of him and do justice to the talents which nature has bountifully bestowed upon him?"[41]

It was a good question. Brown never passed the bar, and his fiction did not see print for another five and a half years. And Wilkins needed to defend himself. As he put it, it was "flattering," if aggravating, for Brown to charge him with neglecting his literary talent. But Brown's second charge, leveled at Wilkins's compliance with the conventional limits of a career in law, was somewhat darker, somewhat suggestive of wanting to tear down a friend's achievement. It is one thing for a friend to encourage you to think of yourself as a writer when you suspect you are not, but it is another to have this friend disparage your career as a lawyer while you are working hard at it. Taken together, the two rebukes amounted to a request that Wilkins erase himself for Brown and substitute Brown's desires for his own. This would have made sense to Brown, who wrote Wilkins that "my hopes are transferred from myself to my friends."[42] That this transfer involved a kind of obliteration — like a father bullying his son into becoming the high school football star he never was — Brown did not see. As Brown was accusing Wilkins of imposture, he was, unwittingly, asking Wilkins to become an impostor of himself. Brown probably intended his identification with Wilkins to be sweet and self-effacing, but the Gothic novelist in him must have sensed the attempt to violate and control his friend.

Even while they were both still students, Brown needled Wilkins for his dedication to the law. "Is your reading altogether legal?" he asked. "Surely such constant and invariable legality is not indispensably necessary." Brown joked that it would be no crime to read a novel, because novels were beginning to feel criminal to Brown, and it was a sore spot he needed to itch. The hero of his *Stephen Calvert* would maintain that a novel by Madeleine de Scudéry was responsible for making him "fickle and fantastic . . . a thing of mere sex." Brown knew he was under fiction's influence and wanted some indication that he was not alone in his ambivalence toward the law. In a letter to Bringhurst, Brown pretended to be a stuffy legal conservative, gone to England, the Holy Land of precedent, to collect volumes for his private law library, which at his death would be burnt so the ashes could be inserted Egyptian-style into his hollowed-out skull. Brown's friends appreciated his humor, but they disapproved of his reluctance to take up adult responsibility. Allen records that Brown first protested that to practice law would be even duller than studying it. The objection sounds honest, but it failed to impress Brown's friends, so he then claimed to be appalled by the immorality of law. He did not see how he could vigorously defend someone whom he knew to be a criminal. "What must be the feelings of a lawyer if he had become auxiliary to a decision of injustice?" Mifflin had taught Gibson to turn up his nose at the commercial amorality of law, but both men had understood the lesson as a genteel attitude, not meant to interfere with practice, and Gibson went on to specialize in land speculation. Deploying the rhetoric of emotions and sympathy, Brown turned a gentlemanly aversion to dirtying one's hands into a matter of principle.[43]

Brown stepped up his attack on Wilkins's profession after autumn 1792, when Wilkins passed the bar in Pennsylvania, moved out of Brown's home, and left for New Jersey to study for the bar in that state. Brown insinuated that Wilkins was in it for the money. To Bringhurst he sniffed at Wilkins's "grasping at gain," and to Wilkins himself he diffidently observed that "our intellectual ore is apparently of no value but as it is capable of being transmuted into gold." He claimed not to see why Wilkins was in such a hurry to qualify as a lawyer, especially since, in Brown's opinion, Wilkins could stand to improve his skills as a thinker, writer, and orator. He suggested that Wilkins delay for two or three years in order to mature — seven years would be even more advisable, and there was an argument to be made in favor of twenty or thirty.[44]

Wilkins liked Brown enough to rise above such envious nonsense. Wilkins explained himself with a candor that even today would put in place any slacker who whined that a former roommate had sold out. "I wish to be *rich*, Charles," Wilkins wrote. Wilkins's parents were not wealthy, and because they had six children, he could not expect any inheritance sizable enough to live on.

"I wish to be independent. I wish to be respected. I wish to be able to be hospitable, charitable, and generous. I wish to please those that wish me well and save those that love me. I wish to offer to some dear affectionate female . . . an eligible settlement." The explanation sounds honest and plausible. Wilkins drilled his point home by asking repeatedly when (and whether) Brown would complete his legal apprenticeship. "Indeed, Charles, you are so indifferent at present about what ought materially to interest you that I am afraid to ask you whether you intend to apply to December term next for admission" to the bar.[45] It was not a question that Brown was prepared to answer.

Brown seems to have been unable to relate to Wilkins once Wilkins asserted a goal of his own. As their careers diverged, the sympathetic identification between them peeled apart. The correspondence broke off soon after this difference of opinion; at least, no letters between them later than spring 1793 survive. Brown continued to send Wilkins his love, but only at the end of letters to Bringhurst. Wilkins returned to Philadelphia in January 1794 to take over the practice of his former master, John Todd, who had died of yellow fever, but Brown and he were no longer close. Brown's comment on his old friend's return to the capital was dry: "If in grasping at gain he does not lose his health or his friends, he may be esteemed happy."[46]

A third strain in the young men's dispute is worth examining. Brown's distaste for Wilkins's single-minded devotion to law involved, as a corollary, the notion that Wilkins was hiding his true feelings. Brown could not believe that Wilkins was as cheerful as he appeared to be. Surely his suppressed yearnings for literary glory and dissatisfaction with law should have rendered him sullen. Seeing Wilkins happy, Brown resented Wilkins's decision not to confide these secret sorrows.

A dispute was triggered when Wilkins poked fun at Brown's stagy moping. Brown indignantly reported the incident to Bringhurst in a letter that Wilkins was not allowed to read. Wilkins had subjected Brown to "mirth and ridicule" on a serious topic, Brown complained. Brown was furious that his precious and delicate melancholy had been jeered. "The anguish which certain reflexions produce to me, is only embittered and exasperated by a Jest," he wrote, threatening to retaliate by moping harder and deeper than ever.[47]

To defend Wilkins and repair the breach between the friends, Bringhurst appears to have suggested, though not disparagingly, that Wilkins was a hypocrite. Bringhurst was claiming that Wilkins made light of serious matters in order to conceal sorrow felt at a deeper level. As Ian Donaldson has noted in his essay "Cato in Tears," this was a common and approved formula for handling emotions in eighteenth-century literature. When struck with misfortune, a man of feeling was expected to contain the expression of his grief, either to prevent distress in his friends and family or to attain virtuous transcendence of his bad fortune. The hero never succeeded in his stoicism; his sadness always broke out. As Donaldson explains, "That the attempt fails is the final guarantee of his goodness. It was decent of him to try to behave like a Stoic; it was heroic of him to fail in the attempt."[48]

Brown had presented his own emotional state in this light only a month earlier. To Bringhurst, he had written, "I have been . . . accustomed . . . to the affectation of gayety and unconcern, at times when my bosom was agitated by the most violent Emotions." With Wilkins, too, Brown had given an outward impression "of equanimity and fortitude" and then had taken care to reveal an inner self, hidden from others, where his mind roiled with "phantoms of imaginary midnight and apparitions of unreal horror." But now, suddenly and perversely, Brown refused to excuse the same behavior in Wilkins. He even pretended not to understand it: "You ask me if I think that he [Wilkins] is always internally gay when he is apparently so. Why should I adopt a different opinion? Is there any uncommon merit in counterfeiting gayety? . . . You tell me that he is often sad in the midst of mirth and gayety. That is very strange and wholly unaccountable." Brown's lack of self-awareness would be comic if it had not led so directly to the end of a friendship. When Brown proceeded in his next letter to ask the rhetorical question "What is he that seeks to amuse only by the wildness of his contradictions and the novelty of his absurdities?" he seems to have been castigating himself by means of his friend and repudiating his own juvenile sensationalism through a scapegoat.[49]

Wilkins responded coolly. He asked Brown "whether by maintaining on all occasions [my] real sentiments, [I] have forfeited [your] regard."[50] Wilkins seems to have felt not so much misunderstood as dictated to. Brown's demand for sympathy was tyrannous. There was some desperation in Wilkins's insistence that the sentiments he was struggling to express were, despite Brown, "real."

When Wilkins died several years later, Brown in his eulogy focused on imposture as Wilkins's most signal trait. "To hear him talk," Brown wrote of his friend, "one would think that he never had a serious moment in his life. . . . To see the effusions of his pen, one would imagine that he was a stranger to smiles, that he was forever steeped in tears and wrapped in melancholy." Brown returned in this eulogy to a conventional understanding of eighteenth-century pseudo-stoicism. He was no longer attacking Wilkins; his tone was fond. But it was a strangely hollow conclusion to such a passionate friendship. As the couple broke apart, Brown vowed to Wilkins that "I most sincerely love you," but in commemorating him, Brown felt he could sum up his friend's character best by pointing to his genteel insincerity. Brown's only other surviving comment on Wilkins's death, in a letter to one of his own brothers, was to cite it as an excuse for postponing the bar exam yet again.[51]

"Whether talking or writing," Brown once complained, "I cannot get rid of myself."[52] With Bringhurst, the attempt to get rid of himself had led Brown into imposture: fantasy preserved a fictional self (Brown as an American Werther-Rousseau) while hiding the factual self (a talented shirker) from his friend's scrutiny. With Wilkins, the same attempt led Brown to compel a sort of imposture on another, in the puppetlike way an immature author might think he could enter and control one of his characters. When Wilkins rebelled, the friendship ended. Brown did not understand why. He was left behind as if caught in an endless game of tag, where he was all the players at once and not sure who was It. In his novels, this nescience of himself manifests itself as a profound uncertainty about who the villain is and who the hero. His villains often have to be told what they have done wrong, and his heroes never know themselves well enough to exempt them from suspicions of fraud, slaughter, or rape. Arthur Mervyn, for example, must prove he is not a minion of Welbeck's, whose bad faith he is improbably slow to understand. Because Edgar Huntly does not know he sleepwalks, perhaps he does not know he scalps, either. Even in *Wieland,* a reader may wonder whether the emotionally disjointed Clara, who sometimes cannot distinguish waking from dreaming, might turn out to be handy with an axe.

In December 1792, as he was losing Wilkins, Brown repeatedly asked Bringhurst to be his mirror. "Let me put your sincerity to the test, your friendship," Brown requested. "Set my picture before me. Let me know in what estimation I am held by others and by yourself." It was perhaps disingenuous of Brown to ask someone he had worked so hard to delude to discern his true self. But Brown was in crisis. Wilkins's success at the bar and departure for New Jersey set off by contrast Brown's failure as a lawyer—a more and more deliberate failure, although Brown did not yet feel he could admit this. As his friend Thomas P. Cope wrote years later, Brown's family and friends "pressed him continually to the practice of the law. . . . He had too much good nature to deny them flatly; he gave expectations of compliance but, without sufficiently explaining his objections, he secretly fostered a determination adverse to their wishes & was fully resolved never to appear at the bar." No one could tell Brown's secret back to him; impostors, like vampires, do not reflect. Bringhurst asked to be excused from the responsibility; Brown relented but did not give up. He justified his desire for Bringhurst to play his mirror, writing that "a wish to know the opinions of others, is certainly a natural and reasonable wish." And before the month was out he asked again: "Wilt thou, my Bring-hurst, be my enlightened and impartial monitor?"[53]

I have been using the word *imposture* to describe both the lies that Brown told to Bringhurst and the duplicity he believed that he detected in Wilkins. If understood as a psychoanalytic term of art, however, the label may not be accurate in either case. Phyllis Greenacre provides one of the clearest defini-tions of imposture in the clinical sense: "An impostor is not only a liar, but a very special type of liar who *imposes* on others fabrications of his attainments, position, or worldly possessions." According to Helene Deutsch, the psycho-dynamic motive for imposture is "the friction between [the impostor's] patho-logically exaggerated ego ideal and the other, devaluated, inferior, guilt-laden part of his ego." The impostor tries to relieve this friction by swindling the world into believing that his ego and his ego-ideal are the same. As Deutsch points out, an impatient wish to have reached one's internal standard of suc-cess is normal and common. It is probably our sympathy with this wish that makes stories of successful imposture so enjoyable. More difficult to under-stand is the impostor's insistence on fakery. This need to win by deceit and only by deceit, Lucy LaFarge notes, is what distinguishes imposture from other kinds of psychopathology. "The impostor cannot be happy with the real thing; his pleasure requires artifice and deception to be complete."[54]

Brown's behavior differs from these classic definitions in a number of ways. His lies to Bringhurst did not enhance his stature. To say that you were wid-owed young or that you have flirted with suicide does not exaggerate your "attainments, position, or worldly possessions" — unless we consider that in Brown's eyes, these lies gave him an aura of special suffering that in the terms of Romanticism did constitute an attainment. Brown's claim to have written half of a twenty-volume novel about Julius is grandiose in a way that is more typical of imposture, but Brown is far from pretending that he himself is Rousseau. In fact, what launches the fantasy is Henrietta's imaginary request that Brown distinguish himself from Rousseau. That signals an artist's pride, not an impostor's eagerness to abandon an uncomfortable ego. The elision that tempts Brown is not between himself and an existing, successful author, but between himself and Julius, a fictional character of his own creation. In the Julius letter, Brown as a young artist is trying on an identity that is still too much for him. What restrains him from claiming to have completed the novel, or from attempting to write it, seems to be garden-variety neurotic guilt. Also, Brown did not remain content merely to pose as a novelist. Unlike an impos-tor, Brown wanted to and later did become an author under his own name.

Furthermore, although my exposition of the erratic and hyperemotional character of Brown's relationships with Bringhurst and Wilkins puts Brown in an unflattering light, his friends do not seem to have judged Brown harshly. Perhaps they understood his volatility as playacting or as a wildness linked to his artistic nature. In any case, almost no one expected Brown to conform to normal social codes. Brown's friend Cope, for example, recognized that Brown could not be relied on even to keep a date, but he did not hold a grudge. In his notes of an 1800 visit to New York, Cope describes an evening when Brown stood him up:

> Half past five & no Charles — I expected as much — Polly suggest[s] the idea of his being ill — This is not improbable — however I will go & see —
> Have been to visit C & found him lolling at ease in his chair — He had not been to look for a carriage, & forgot to tell his frd W. Johnson of our invitation to join us in the excursion.[55]

Cope shrugs off his disappointment and does not attempt to rebuke Brown. Instead, he writes that Brown's unpredictability is "just in character."

Upon discovering that they had been misled, Brown's friends reacted with tolerance and amusement. These are not the "disturbed and humiliated" feelings that a classic impostor leaves with victims aware that they have been deceived.[56] Nor does Brown's own reaction to his deception resemble that of an impostor. Brown's friends were puzzled by his outbursts of self-hatred, which probably stemmed from his concealed decision not to practice law. In classic imposture, however, a successful lie reinforces and strengthens the impostor's sense of coherent identity; the audience's response encourages the impostor into greater and more elaborate lies. Brown's anguish therefore belies a diagnosis of him as an impostor.

Brown's relationship with Wilkins fits the psychoanalytic definition of imposture no better. Brown accused Wilkins of not being his real self. But even if this accusation is understood as a projection and is transposed back onto Brown, it fails to satisfy Greenacre's criteria for imposture. Pretending to be a lawyer when you are at heart a writer is not like pretending to be a prince when you are really a goatherd. In some ways it is the opposite case, in that Brown was hiding his lamp under a bushel. Writing, Brown felt, was much more glorious than law — so much more glorious that rather than admit his ambition directly, he guiltily transferred it to Wilkins.

If Brown was not an impostor, why bother to retain the term? Because even though the diagnosis of impostor does not accurately describe Brown, the term is useful for understanding Brown's villains and heroes, such as Carwin, Arthur Mervyn, and Ormond. Through the figure of the impostor, Brown expressed anxiety and ambivalence about the power that writing gave him.

Brown's letters have an eel-like wildness that must have frightened him even as it mesmerized his friends, but this wildness belonged to a writing self distinct from Brown's personal self. "I cannot when personally present with my friend, give utterance to my feelings," Brown wrote in an early letter to Wilkins. "My pen is the best Interpreter of my Sentiments." Brown with a pen, however, was so much better an interpreter of sentiments than Brown without a pen that the two states felt like two different people, or like the revelation of a real person beneath a fake one. Brown in person was "accustomed to reserve: . . . to counterfeit Sentiments to which my heart was utterly a stranger."[57] The self revealed by writing pierced this mask, but it raised the question of which self was real — the apparent self or the self that writing created. Brown may have feared his artistic gift, and that gift may have felt most unholy when he used it to play with the people closest to him.

In the essay "The Relation of the Impostor to the Artist," Phyllis Greenacre tries to understand what attracted Thomas Mann to such impostors as Felix Krull. Adapting an idea of Proust's, Greenacre posits that "every artist is at least two people, the personally oriented self and the artistic one." While an artist is still struggling to come to terms with a gift for art, she wrote, the disjunction between the personal and the artistic selves may produce "seemingly unreliable or even chaotic behavior which is likely to be regarded only as perverse or psychopathic until the strength of the artistic demands have brought about some definite fruition."[58] Unfortunately, in Brown's early letters we see only the unreliability and the chaos — the criminal side — of his talent, not yet the work that would make that disorder seem worth enduring.

Brown himself once suggested that he was aware of two foci in his psyche. The itinerant actor John Bernard made an observation to Brown reminiscent of Brown's attack on Wilkins: in person, Brown was such "a very cheerful if not an entertaining companion" that the "sombreness of his writings" came as something of a surprise. Brown conceded the point and went on to explain himself in terms similar to Greenacre's.

> I am conscious of a double mental existence. When I am sufficiently excited to write, all my ideas flow naturally and irresistibly through the medium of sympathies which steep them in shade, though the feelings they bring are so pleasing as to prevent my perceiving it. The tone of my works being thus the necessary result of the advancement of those truths or discoveries which lead me to composition, I am made so happy by it for the time as to be ignorant of its real effect upon my reader. This I term, therefore, my imaginative being. My social one has more of light than darkness upon it, because, unless I could carry into society the excitement which makes me write, I could not fall into its feelings.[59]

This passage must be treated cautiously, because it is only reported of Brown, not written by him. But if accurate, the quotation goes far toward explaining how sympathy, writing, and selfhood came together in a way that felt like imposture. Brown says here that he experiences his imaginative being and his social being as distinct. The imaginative being takes pleasure in sympathizing with even the darkest emotions. Sympathy is a skill, a component of writing, which so engrosses the practitioner that he loses himself in his work; the author does not feel the emotions he is deploying, even though he must at some level be calculating their effect on his reader. The social being, on the other hand, is more brittle. His tone must be light, not dark — a condition that implies that his ability to sympathize is limited. If Brown "could carry into society the excitement which makes me write," his social self would be able to handle a wider range of feelings. But he can't. The act of writing charges Brown's imaginative self with a kind of pleasure that insulates him while he writes; unfortunately, no such pleasure protects Brown while he does not write. The social Brown is easily wounded by the "darkness" that is the imaginative Brown's material. And so the social (or, in Greenacre's term, personal) Brown never knows the feelings about which the imaginative (artistic) Brown writes with authority and sophistication. The richest emotions he touches only indirectly, through art, by faking them.

As described by Greenacre, the relation of Mann to Krull resembles that of Brown to Carwin: the writer is seeing his talent as a crime. In the figure of the impostor, the author works through the conflicts within him between compliance and authenticity, between keeping in touch with others (sympathy) and expressing himself honestly (sincerity), between copying (artistic death) and originality (personal danger). There is something poignant about an artist who treats his gift with suspicion when it also serves as the only way for him to reach his feelings. But as a literary device, the impostor is a sign of an author's mental health — an astute way of exploring the side effects and drawbacks of sympathy as a literary ideal and as a literary tool.

In late 1792, Brown had achieved no literary work to set in the balance against his sinking law career and his degenerating friendships. His power of sympathy had led him into hollow poses. He was impatient with masquerade and needed a new discipline. He wanted to know who he was, but he would settle for knowing what was wrong with him. The same month he demanded that Bringhurst mirror him — December 1792 — Brown wrote three times in letters to Wilkins and Bringhurst the phrase "my principles are uninfected."[60] For him to repeat them in such quick succession the words must have resonated for him. In all three instances, their manifest meaning was a defense: although his conduct was censurable, he knew he was doing wrong. He seems to have been referring to his poor progress as a law student, but his self-criticism was broad enough to amount to a general self-hatred: "I despise myself. I am the object of my most unbounded pity." A core of himself had been protected, he maintained. At least he knew the truth about himself: "I do not miscall my depravity virtue." No influence had contaminated his inner judgment.[61]

One could, however, perversely read the sentence as a complaint. Brown's letters had succeeded too well as masks for it to matter what his untouched principles were. Neither Bringhurst nor Wilkins had been astute enough to resist or challenge Brown's fictions. Sympathy flowed between them too easily to teach Brown anything about himself.

The sentence might also be read as a warning. My principles are uninfected because the toxin has not yet reached my heart, but it will. And it did. Within a year, Brown became a deist and an anarchist. A foretaste of life as a literary man rendered it impossible for him ever to return to law. He came under the influence of two strong personalities, Elihu Hubbard Smith and William Godwin. And the yellow fever epidemic that struck Philadelphia gave him details and story lines for a new major rhetorical figure for representing sympathy between men: infection.

Personable, intimidating Elihu Hubbard Smith proved to be Brown's truest and most honest friend. In his diary, Smith recorded this caricature of himself as a twelve-year-old Yale sophomore hazing a freshman:

> Imagine to yourself a figure four feet high, whose fat limbs & jolly person might become a cloathed Bacchus, & whose round, smooth & ruddy visage was surmounted by a large, three-cornered, cocked-up hat, & terminated by a long, flaxen *queue*. A long, white wand, the emblem of command, was florished with his right hand, & a dutch pipe, whose stem nearly equalled the length of the holder, & which seemed to have been just removed from his lip, struggling to suppress a smile, graced his left. A voice shrill & clear, laboring after the tone of dignity, sharply demanded, if a freshman who had lately come to College was not there.[62]

When Brown met him, Smith was twenty, just eight months younger than Brown. Smith's baby fat had no doubt vanished by then, because as an adult, he was a vegetarian and fiercely hardworking. But the boy's wand (an "emblem of command") and voice ("laboring after the tone of dignity") signaled a character that remained legible in the man. In his struggle to make himself into a medical and literary authority, Smith could be something of a martinet. In 1791, Timothy Dwight's academy at Greenfield Hill and Yale College were behind him; Smith was in Philadelphia studying medicine with Benjamin Rush. His diary testifies to his daunting regimen: for the three years he kept it, Smith used his diary to monitor his intellectual productivity, assigning himself tasks by week or by month and then at intervals summarizing his progress with lists of the reading and writing he had accomplished. This steady self-exaction brought results. Robert A. Ferguson has catalogued Smith's achievements thus: "Smith founded the *Medical Repository,* the best American medical journal of the day; he wrote a biography of the Connecticut Wits, scientific essays, and an opera; published an anthology of American poetry; was the moving force within a number of academic and literary societies; and maintained both an extensive correspondence and a private journal that reached to more than two hundred thousand words." No board games or cardplaying for Smith. Here was the man whose steel was hard and burnished enough to mirror back to Brown the harsh truth about himself. The playwright William Dunlap, a friend to both men, put the contrast between them sharply: "Brown was without system in every thing; Smith did nothing but by rule." The opposites attracted.[63]

It was probably Bringhurst, a fellow medical student, who introduced Smith to Brown. The earliest evidence of the trio's friendship is the poetical correspondence in the *Gazette of the United States,* where Smith's cognomen was Ella. Brown was the last of the three to enter the correspondence, and in a letter to Bringhurst dated 22 April 1793, Brown refers to Smith as "your [Bringhurst's] admirable friend." But as had been the case with Wilkins, the friendship between Smith and Brown soon burned brighter than that between Smith and Bringhurst. To describe the symbiosis that linked Brown and Smith, Brown's biographer Harry Warfel resorted to a simile: "Their lives became intertwined much as a Virginia creeper drapes itself upon a strong oak."[64]

Smith was as romantic as he was diligent. Like every sensitive intellectual young man of his era, he fervently believed in friendship. When Smith's proselytizing for deism threatened his relationship with the more orthodox Theodore Dwight, for example, Smith assured Dwight of his affection with passionate language: "You must not . . . be surprized if . . . I use rather the expressions of a lover than a man; for I feel for you all that Jonathan felt for David." To remind his cousin Elnathan Smith of their mutual love, Smith asked by letter, "Have we not often held each other's hand, & looked one at the other, hours, in silence? And, how expressive is such silence!"[65]

In the spring of 1793, Brown needed a love as strong and practical as Smith's. Smith had invited Brown for a visit to his native Connecticut, and although it is always difficult to distinguish the actual state of Brown's emotions from his histrionic expression of them, a letter Brown wrote to Bringhurst a week before departure suggested that he was near despair. He claimed to be almost unable to put pen to paper, because the process of writing had become "intolerably irksome" to him. "Writing or reading is certainly not the business of human life," he told Bringhurst. "I, for my part, can not any longer read nor write." But to cure his writer's block was not the avowed motive of his trip. Instead, Brown claimed that he wanted "to find a grave" — the grave of his (almost certainly fictional) dead wife — and he hinted that he might expire happily next to her remains. "O! my friend! I am wrong, very very wrong indeed, in desiring to visit Connecticut. . . . This journey will either confirm me a wretch forever, or restore me to some degree of tranquility." In closing, Brown asked that Bringhurst "not let my family know that I intend going farther than New York, or staying longer than a fortnight or three weeks." Brown was running away.[66]

The hint of suicide in Brown's letter provoked Bringhurst to his usual earnest concern, and so to calm his friend, Brown in his next letter invented an allegorical dream (mentioned earlier in this chapter) that he said his dead wife had related to him. In the dream, a giant knight in black armor seized his beloved and carried her across a stream, but before a despairing Brown could drown himself in the stream, Brown's mother snatched him back from the brink. Brown drew the moral: "Never till I forget that I have a mother, of whose afflictions my death would compleat the sum, shall I voluntarily cease to live."[67]

It is unclear whether Brown's despair was any more real than his widower-hood, but perhaps the dead wife buried in Connecticut represented Brown's literary ambition — the Henrietta G. who had asked him to rewrite *Julie*? — closely associated with Smith. If so, then Brown's mother functioned as an icon of traditional responsibility who by guilt (if not physical force) prevented him from joining his chosen one. In any case, the dream, as an invention, augured well: under the prospect of a visit to Smith, Brown's great lost love, fiction, was already reviving.

Connecticut exceeded Brown's expectations. Not only Smith but all Smith's circle welcomed Brown as an author and a peer. "I was surprised," Brown reported back to Bringhurst, "to find that among this Ella's [Elihu's] friends you and myself were almost as well known as in our native city." Smith had provided first-rate advance publicity for his poetry- and essay-writing friend from Philadelphia, and so Smith's introductions granted Brown entrée into the most refined and literary homes that Connecticut could offer. Brown gushed his appreciation: "Sicily or Switzerland can afford nothing that surpasses it." He felt as though he was living in a Rousseau novel. "You have read Eloisa," he boasted to Bringhurst. "You recollect the situation of St. Preux in Wolmar's family. Such, believe me, my friend, is mine in this."[68]

"In the midst of lettered elegance and domestic refinement," as Brown phrased it, his wish to write fiction grew stronger than ever. Connecticut in the summer of 1793 intoxicated Brown by recognizing him as the artist he had not yet become. Under Smith's wing, Brown could learn and his talent could grow. Under the implicit promise of the environment, Brown felt both restored and vulnerable. As he confessed to Bringhurst, he felt old regrets and new longings merge within him and rise to the surface:

> At a very early age I began to reason on a plan of study and to make some preparation for gratifying my literary propensities, with advantages, but I had scarcely formed a plan before passions, violent, absorbing passions, interfered, equally detrimental to study in their gratification and disappointment. How I doat upon the scene which now presents itself to my imagination! With what transport would I hail the return of tranquility! my heart melts within me at the prospect of residing in Connecticut, at the soothing consolations, the inchanting enjoyments of social and studious retirement. . . . Once more would I resume the study of Shorthand, ascend the Heaven of invention, and riot at the banquet of the muses, and in the sweets of fancy. . . . What a picture this is! but yet I am sure that I could realize it.

If Brown could stay in Connecticut, he felt, he might make good on his literary ambitions.[69]

But Brown could not stay in Connecticut; he was too poor. "Money! Money! is the Spring of my Machine, the want of which is the first of miseries."[70] Brown didn't dare live on the generosity of Smith, who in any case couldn't afford it, and the support of Brown's parents depended on the pretense that he would some day pass the bar, a pretense that would be unsustainable if Brown idled for too long in another state. As his holiday ended, Brown's despair returned, as did the ghost of his fictional dead wife. But Connecticut had changed the meaning of her death. Before, she had seemed to represent a hope he thought he had lost. Now, her death was the door Brown shut on a traditional life of marriage and law.

"Genuine felicity," Brown dutifully recited to Bringhurst, "is only to be found in the arms of love in the bosom of a wife and children." This was the happiness that Wilkins had set forth when he declined to be an author. But this happiness could never be Brown's, allegedly because death had taken his young make-believe wife. Brown claimed that the "hand of an inexorable destiny" had deprived him of any possibility of conventional wedded bliss. "No! Since I am cut off forever from the hope of nuptial enjoyments, which alone my heart is formed to receive, life indeed has lost its principal charm, but is there no consolation to be derived from the Society of the good, and the Sympathies of friendship? . . . Shall I not regain my relish for the delights of composition and invention? . . . But that it seems is not to be allowed me.

Occupation agreeable to my inclinations, would shut out disagreeable remembrances, or soften their asperities, or make them subservient to my peaceful and unamibitious views but alas!!"[71]

My desires are normal, Brown lies. Of course I want nothing more than to be married. But fate has forbidden me wedded bliss, he disingenuously laments, and it seems gratuitously cruel for fate to forbid me a career in fiction, too. If only I could be permitted the leftover, second-rate happiness of life as a bachelor novelist.

Before Connecticut, imaginative writing had stood with Brown's imaginary wife on the far side of the river that separated life and death. But sometime during Brown's visit with Smith, writing crossed to the side of life. He still could not aver that the life of an unmarried artist was as worthy as the life of a married careerist. It was only good enough to serve as a consolation, which is why Brown needed the fiction of widowerhood to rule marriage out. With his fib, Brown was insisting that he could not marry, because in his case he would be marrying death. What he could not quite say openly was that in the place of "nuptial enjoyments," he wanted a life filled with the "Sympathies of friendship" and the "delights of composition." Perhaps for financial as well as psychological reasons, as a writer he preferred the sympathy of friends to the love of a spouse. Upon his return to Philadelphia, Brown undertook to write fiction in earnest, encouraged by Smith's example to "believe that application will perform any thing." When a letter from Bringhurst challenged him, Brown promised "to put my skill to the test." Prefacing his attempt with a formulaic lie — "the following story is strictly true" — Brown wrote Bringhurst an epistolary short story. What he produced was not a lie about his prowess as a writer, like the Julius letter; nor a fearful avoidance of the power of make-believe, like *The Rhapsodist;* but a very genuine, very bad piece of fiction. By the time he reached the end of the story-letter, he recognized it as invented. He forgot his earlier claim that it was "strictly true" and asked Bringhurst, "Tell me shall I read this imaginary letter before the Society next Saturday."[72]

Like Walt Whitman's early tales "The Child's Champion" and *Franklin Evans,* this first honest fiction of Brown's was a temperance melodrama. Late one night, while reading, inquisitive Mr. Waring hears cries of distress coming from the house next door, where an Irish family named Cooke has recently moved in. Mr. Waring, like any good Brown character, is willing to let curiosity lead him into a compromising situation, and so he sneaks up to their kitchen door to eavesdrop. There he hears a woman's voice moaning, "For God sake Jackey don't expose yourself" — the cue that behind the door is something vile, exciting, and worth a peek. Mr. Waring rushes in to behold Mr. Cooke, drunk, lashing his wife with a horsewhip while their four adult daughters look on. The demon-drink plot that follows is fairly predictable: Mrs. Cooke perishes, and Mr. Waring gets a chance to use the horsewhip on Mr. Cooke. The story is a pastiche of ethnic stereotype, voyeurism, and sadism, but however awful, it has the advantage of being *echt* Brown, which *The Rhapsodist* and the Julius letter were not. The vexed moral position of the observer who wants to meddle became the meat of Brown's best work, and graphic violence and illicit snooping were his favorite spices.

In his next letter to Bringhurst, Brown wrote that he had "already imagined the leading incidents and general outlines of a tale," although he was unsure he had the stamina or tranquility of mind to complete it. He was launched, however. Over the next five years, Brown's correspondence with Smith, Bringhurst, and Dunlap shows him strenuously trying to write novels — between lapses of despair. To someone unfamiliar with the process of becoming an artist, these years could look rather vacant. Brown's no-nonsense friend Cope described this period:

> For several years after he attained the age of 25, his time was spent not absolutely in listless idleness but without that regular application to business which is necessary to the acquirement of steady habits & to the formation of a settled character. His hours were spent in seclusion from the world & were principally devoted to reading & the society of a few select friends. He was poor, nor had his parents the means of conferring on him anything beyond a bare subsistence in their family. . . . While in this state of mental perplexity he became acquainted with the poisonous writings of the celebrated Godwin.

Cope wrote this passage at Brown's death in 1810. On the basis of Brown's correspondence, I would argue that Cope slightly misdates the period he is describing — that Brown's apparent idleness reached a crisis three years earlier, in 1793, when Brown was twenty-two rather than twenty-five. Brown tried to convince his brothers that he would someday practice law until at least 1795, but to his intimate friends he dropped the pretense of a law career in the summer of 1793. For example, in a letter dated 25 July 1793, he told Bringhurst that he might pass the bar by age forty but that "to speak seriously I am convinced, my friend, that my present situation cannot long continue unchanged. I must of necessity form some determination."[73]

By and large, Cope saw only the professional career that Brown was shirking, not the artistic career whose false starts and experimental failures Brown was working through. But Cope did accurately seize on two elements crucial to this period of growth without visible achievements: "the society of a few select friends" and William Godwin.

Godwin's *Political Justice* was published in 1793; extracts were published in

*New York Magazine* in July of that year. A comprehensive rethinking of political philosophy, the book argued that government was an evil less necessary than ruling classes had led people to believe. Godwin believed fervently in altruism — an instinct for benevolence was the motive at the center of Godwin's conception of human nature — but he thought that where government was concerned, people set aside their self-interest too readily. "Individuals are everything," Godwin wrote, "and society, abstracted from the individuals of which it is composed, nothing." Permanent political institutions and their nationalist or partisan ideologies discouraged people from using their minds to think about their own interests. If women and men would exert themselves to speak honestly and understand their relationships critically, they would soon achieve the "true euthanasia of government."[74]

The subject matter of two dated documents by Brown suggests that he read the book the year it came out, while in Connecticut, probably prompted by Smith. In what appears to be a letter to Susan Godolphin, dated 2 July 1793, Brown included a dialogue with a fictional Conswould wherein he explained Godwin's theory of promises, although he does not mention Godwin by name. Consider these parallel passages:

> GODWIN: What I have promised is what I ought to have performed, if no promise had intervened, or it is not. It is conducive, or not conducive, to the generating of human happiness. If it be the former, then promise comes in merely as an additional inducement.

> BROWN: What I have promised to do is either just or unjust, independantly of the promise: If it be just it is my duty to do it whether I have promised or not. If it be unjust it is my duty not to do it.[75]

In another apparent letter, dated 29–31 August 1793, Brown demanded of a friend named William C. — Holmes and Weber, the editors of Brown's letters, supply the last name Coleman — that he confess himself according to Godwin's theory of sincerity, though again without invoking Godwin explicitly.

> GODWIN: Reserve, deceitfulness, and an artful exhibition of ourselves take from the human form its soul." "How much better would it be if . . . every man were to make the world his confessional?

> BROWN: Ruses, distance, Secrecy, are the enemies, of all my Schemes." "Thou must disclose to me all the Circumstances of thy present condition.[76]

(A caveat: Both the Susan Godolphin and William C. documents might be fictions rather than letters to actual people. No other letters to or from Godolphin or William C. survive, and the length and intimate tone of the texts suggest correspondents whom Brown knew well and wrote regularly. The biographer Steven Watts considers the William C. letter to be a fragment of a novel titled "Ellendale." In that case, even the dates written on these texts might be invented, perhaps chosen to match the date of publication of *Political Justice*. But their strong echo of Godwin suggests that whenever the texts were written, Brown was excited by ideas that he had probably just read for the first time.)[77]

It was no accident that Brown's extracts from Godwin dealt with promises and sincerity. On both topics, Godwin said things that Brown needed to hear. Godwin believed a promise was like an amputation. It was always evil to lose a leg, although it might be a lesser evil than death from gangrene. "The case of promises," Godwin wrote, "is considerably similar to this." A man who rigidly kept a promise cut himself off from the use of his mind from the moment he swore the promise until he executed it. In between, he lost permission either to acquire new information about what he had promised or to come to a new understanding of it. Promises "depose us . . . from the use of our own understanding," Godwin charged. "There may be cases in which they are necessary and ought to be employed: but we should never suffer ourselves by their temporary utility to be induced to forget their intrinsic nature."[78]

To a young man who had prematurely promised his family that he would become a lawyer, these were welcome words. According to Cope, Brown espoused Godwin's skepticism of promise keeping, and then some. "Having at an early period become contaminated by Godwin's Political Justice," Cope complained in 1806, Brown lacked "that delicate respect for his plighted word which would give dignity to his other accomplishments."[79]

Brown had to feel free to break promises in order to obey another commandment of Godwin's that he found congenial: to live sincerely. To Brown, stuck in a dead end of imposture, Godwin's description of the insincere man must have hit home: "In youth . . . he accommodates himself with a pliant spirit to the manners of the world. . . . Observant of the game that goes forward around him, he becomes skilful in his turn to elude the curiosity of others, and smiles inwardly at the false scent he prompts them to follow." Godwin demanded that people break out of this sterile system of pretense. Sincerity was a prerequisite for the success of anarchy. In the best of futures, governmental surveillance, control, and punishment would be discarded as unnecessary once citizens learned to confess their faults openly and exchange criticisms of one another's behavior in a spirit of generous moral support. In Godwin's ideal universe, all citizens would volunteer to tell their own stories in the manner of Rousseau. Those who contemplated a crime would have to stop and ask themselves "whether they chose to be their own historians, the future narrators of the scene in which they were acting a part."[80] Most commentators in the late eighteenth century condemned novels as degrading to public morals, but Godwin claimed the opposite: narration was a moral tonic.

Godwinian sincerity gave license to Brown's narrative impulse. As a corollary to the political use to which he put sincerity, Godwin denied a right to privacy, and so he also licensed Brown's Peeping Tom brand of curiosity. "The imputation of inquisitiveness, impertinance of a restless propensity to pry into the affairs of others affect me not," Brown could now tell Coleman. Best of all, Godwin's philosophy seemed to endorse Brown's agonized wish to reveal himself as he really was.

Brown may have responded so strongly to Godwin's philosophy in part because it paralleled the Quaker teachings of his youth. Both Godwin and the Quakers felt the truth that came from deep inside the heart to be powerful and transformative — almost holy. Godwin called the true opinion of the people a "temple"; "if it be polluted," he wrote, then "there is no longer anything sacred or venerable in sublunary existence." Godwin may not have been as mystical as the Quakers, but he shared their belief that heartfelt speech would spread love. If everyone practiced sincerity, Godwin wrote, "hatred would perish from a failure in its principal ingredient, the duplicity and impenetrableness of human actions. . . . If our emotions were not checked, we should be truly friends with each other. . . . Every man would be inured to the sentiment of love." Almost religiously, Godwin believed that the release of the truth would lead inevitably to what the Quakers would have called a Society of Friends.[81]

Quakers premised their meetings on a faith in the soul's spontaneous gesture. Congregants waited in silence for the spirit to move them to speak, with the understanding that it was difficult to listen to this inner voice and that its emergence was unpredictable. Some Sundays the time passed as a silent meeting. In his diary, for example, Mifflin recorded that the preaching of the visiting English Quaker John Storer so impressed him that he attended meeting steadily for the next three weeks in the hope that Storer would preach again. He did not.[82] In our era, when religious services appear on scheduled television shows, it is hard to understand the radical patience of waiting for words that often did not come.

When the itinerant Quaker preacher John Woolman began his journal, he explained that he started to write because he had "felt a motion of love" to do so. This was the only motive that ever counted for Woolman, and he acknowledged in it an authority he would never have arrogated merely for himself. A motion of love, for example, drew him to Virginia, where he clandestinely paid the slaves who waited on him and openly told the Quakers who hosted him that they were wrong to own other human beings. It was difficult for Woolman to rebuke Friends who were older than he and of higher standing in the community and to whom he owed favors. But Woolman remained faithful to the "drawings in my mind," however revolutionary and socially awkward they might have been. It was a virtue that Godwin also championed when he asserted that sincerity must overrule the "artificial delicacy" of polite conventions. To find the courage to write what he was not supposed to, Brown reached—through Godwin—back to the Quaker faith, which held that the voice that emerged from an opened heart was God's. In Woolman's *Journal,* an Indian named Papunehang epitomizes this Quaker attitude toward language: after listening without the aid of an interpreter to Woolman at prayer, Papunehang says with appreciation, "I love to feel where words come from."[83]

Elihu Hubbard Smith also recognized this syncretism of anarchy and Quakerism. When Smith wrote the passionate letter to Theodore Dwight with "the expressions of a lover", the more conventional Dwight bridled at the "baldface stile" in which Smith had addressed him. Smith defended himself by saying that he had picked up the habit almost unintentionally from his Quaker friends. "It had become habitual for me, in respect to Brown, Bringhurst, and Wilkins (who were educated in Quaker habits) and I believe some others— before I thought of it's being more proper than any other," Smith wrote. But Smith would have known that "this simple stile of address," however untheoretically acquired, conformed to Godwin's principle of sincerity; after all, an apologia for *Political Justice* filled the rest of his letter to Dwight.[84]

*Political Justice* was Smith's favorite book; he pressed it on nearly all his correspondents. Strangely, he did not read it from cover to cover until 1797, when he acquired the second edition. Perhaps he was concerned that its influence over him was already too great; perhaps he was afraid that it would disappoint him if he examined it too closely. In any case, for years *Political Justice* was a gospel to thump rather than thumb. "Tho' I have not read his Book," Smith wrote in his diary, "my friends, who have read it, pronounce my opinions to resemble, in many respects, those therein contained." Smith, Brown, and Dunlap were probably the philosopher's greatest American fans. Dunlap corresponded with Godwin on the group's behalf. In a surviving letter in reply, Godwin attempted with some amusement to answer Dunlap's "singular question, whether I am an honest man."[85]

In America, this would not have been thought a singular question. Cope, for example, called Godwin's writing "poisonous . . . visionary & pernicious."[86] But it was Godwin's poison, administered by Smith, that made an honest man of Charles Brockden Brown. Unlike Wilkins or Bringhurst, Smith refused to indulge Brown's evasions and tale-spinning. He held Brown to strict Godwinian standards of sincerity. By forbidding Brown to confuse his life with make-believe, Smith forced him to mature as an artist. It may seem unlikely that a stern rebuke could work beneficently on a man as childlike as Brown. And how could a stricture against lies help a novelist develop? But I would argue that for as long as Brown's fantasies stood between Brown and his friends, they stagnated. They clotted the flow of emotions among the men and stuck to Brown too closely for him to work on them: as long as he needed them as decoys and disguises, he could not afford them the free play of fiction. When Smith barred these fantasies from his relationship with Brown, he shunted them onto more fertile ground, where they could develop into art.

During this fallow period of Brown's, Smith's letters show the difficult process of correction in some detail. When Brown wrote a foggy, mysterious letter claiming that he had "been the child of passion, & inconsistency; the slave of desires that can not be honorably gratified; The Slave of hopes no less criminal, than fantastic," Smith lost his temper.

> What, my friend, is the meaning of all this? . . . If you meant that we [Dunlap and Smith] should understand you, why were you not explicit? If you had no such intention, where was the necessity of introducing such a passage? Charles! you know we love you. Your heart has told you so, a thousand times. . . . You are well aware of the value of sincerity; you see that we stand, as it were, isolated from the rest of mankind; & you must be convinced, that if we are not true to ourselves, & true to each other, we can not hope for aid, correction, & instruction, — candidly & affectionately administered — from any one beside.[87]

Either tell us or don't tell us, Smith ordered with exasperation, but if you're not prepared to tell us, don't lie and don't tease. To Smith the doctor, Brown's problem with "mystery" looked like an illness. "Is it the disease of Will?" Smith speculated, "or of Habit?" A diagnosis came in Smith's next letter: Brown was infected with imposture. The source of the contamination was Rousseau, whose writing "had too many charms in your eyes, not to captivate you, & incite you to imitate him." Like a teenage smoker, Brown had started young on an unhealthy habit that addicted him before he could understand its consequences. "You were pleased to have others believe those misfortunes to be real, which you knew how so eloquently to describe. The transition is natural — & to a mind of sensibility almost unavoidable: you began to fancy that these fictions were real; that you had indeed supposed, enjoyed, known, & seen, all that you had so long pretended to have experienced; every subsequent event became tinctured with this conviction & accompanied with this diseased apprehension; the habit was formed; & you wandered in a world of your own creation." It was Brown's mental illness to live in a novel but not write one. According to the metaphoric logic of this diagnosis, the effective but painful medical treatment for Brown's "diseased apprehension" was sincerity.[88]

Smith referred to Godwin's precepts gently but firmly. Part of Brown's illness, however, was to think that merely to read and recite Godwin sufficed. As Smith caricatured Brown's premature sense of relief: "*Godwin came, & all was light.*" To cure his friend, Smith had to apply sentences that stung even as they cleansed. As if to justify his harsh tone, Smith wrote, "He deserves not the name of Physician, who, thro' fear of giving pain, temporizes with his Patient. . . . To wound, is to save; to delay, is to destroy." So Smith listed his friend's errors. He chastised Brown for muddling his news with such fancy language that Smith could not tell from Brown's letters whether Bringhurst was in jail literally or metaphorically. Within a world of personal fantasy, the question would not matter, but to Smith, who lived insistently in the real world, it mattered a great deal. The ambiguity infuriated him. (At the time Bringhurst's imprisonment was only metaphorical.) It also got on Smith's nerves that Brown could never simply give the titles of what he had been reading but always rendered his experience of books as images of himself — "with visionary step printing the sands of Arabia, hovering over the hills of Swisserland on wings of imagination, & exploring the wilds of America with the eye of fiction." Most damningly, Smith wrote that he was giving up on any attempt to filter the truth out of Brown's autobiographical lies. Brown had admitted that he sometimes made things up, and his stories about himself were full of internal contradictions. Impatiently, Smith declared, "I know not what to believe."

Much biography and criticism of Brown points to his friendships — and particularly to his friendship with Smith — as crucial to his identity as an author. Most commentators, however, have seen Smith as more of a squelcher than a liberator of Brown's creativity, in part because of the schoolmarmish tone of these letters of correction. Some blame for the poor figure that Smith cuts is due to Dunlap, who muddied the history of Brown's friendships and writerly ambition very early on. In the first published biography of Brown, Dunlap dated Brown's decision "to become exclusively an author" to December 1798, several months after Smith's death. "He at this time carried into effect," Dunlap wrote, "the plan which had long been forming in his mind of becoming an author by profession; of devoting his life to book-making, and trusting his future fortunes, as well as fame to the labours of his pen." The sequence presented in Dunlap's biography implies that *Alcuin* and *Wieland,* the first of Brown's books to see print, were the fruits of a new, post-Smith resolution. It suggests that Brown did not dare to think of himself as a fiction writer until Smith was safely six feet under.[90]

In fact, *Alcuin* and *Wieland* were written and published while Smith was alive, with his encouragement and supervision. The dates that Dunlap gives in his diary and elsewhere in the biography — as well as the dates provided by Smith's diary — belie the story line that Dunlap constructs. Also, as I suggested above, Brown had acknowledged to his friends, if not his family, that he was abandoning law for writing much earlier, probably in 1793. December 1798 is, more accurately, the date when Brown modified his writerly ambition to include editorship of a magazine.

Although incorrect, Dunlap's chronology has persisted because it appears to solve a psychobiographical puzzle. It offers Brown's critics an explanation — morbid but compelling — for what Leslie Fiedler calls Brown's "feverish bout of creative activity." Brown's four major novels — *Wieland; Ormond; Arthur Mervyn, First Part;* and *Edgar Huntly* — were published in 1798 and 1799. "The rapidity of Mr. Brown's compositions," wrote Dunlap, "can scarcely be paralleled." To explain how Brown could write so many novels so rapidly, most critics have imagined a pent-up energy that was suddenly released. Following Dunlap, Fiedler suggested in *Love and Death in the American Novel* that what "cued" this outburst was, in part, Smith's death. In a more inflected and careful reading, Robert A. Ferguson has seen Smith as a "perfect model," whose life inspired but intimidated Brown and whose death in a fashion liberated him.[91]

Smith's letters to Brown make it clear that he treated the novelist with a daunting mix of encouragement and condescension. But if one constructs a timetable of Brown's writing, the evidence shows that Smith must have been far more of an enabler than an obstacle, because Brown's burst of creativity was well under way when Smith took ill with yellow fever.[92] I would divide Brown's writing into three phases. In the first phase, before Smith's death, Brown wrote the dialogue *Alcuin,* the lost novel "Sky-Walk," *Wieland,* the essay-fiction series *The Man at Home,* the "Series of Original Letters," twelve chapters of *Arthur Mervyn, First Part,* the novel fragment "Memoirs of Carwin, the Biloquist," and at least part of *Memoirs of Stephen Calvert.*[93] In a second phase, after Smith's death and before Brown met his future wife, Elizabeth Linn, Brown wrote *Ormond,* the rest of *Arthur Mervyn, First Part* and *Edgar Huntly,* and probably the short story "The Death of Cicero."[94] Since *Edgar Huntly* was a rewrite of "Sky-Walk," and *Ormond* borrowed liberally from *The Man at Home,* no major novel of Brown's was conceived after Smith's death. The keynote of Brown's second phase was the completion of projects begun while Smith was alive — no small achievement, but a different kind of creation than that of imagining new novels. In a third and final phase, during his relationship with Elizabeth Linn, Brown wrote *Arthur Mervyn,*

*Second Part; Clara Howard;* and *Jane Talbot*—Richardsonian fictions that most critics have felt to be a falling off.[95] Smith's death, rather than freeing Brown, may have cut him off from the source of his creative innovation. Without Smith, he reverted to sterilized romances in the spirit of his unwritten "Julius."

By Brown's fruitful production, then, we know Smith to have been a propagator of fiction. Furthermore, we know Brown welcomed Smith's criticism. A few days after Smith berated Brown with questions such as "Wherefore are you so vigourous, so firm, in thought; & so weak, so vacillating in action?" Brown wrote to Bringhurst about the gratitude he felt for Smith's reprimand. "I have just received a most charming letter from Elihu," Brown wrote. "It is full of censures, indeed, but these censures manifest a soul, glowing with benevolence and dignity. I cannot tell thee how much those proofs of moral improvement delighted me." Brown understood that Smith was performing the role that Godwin called the "ingenuous censor." The role was exchangeable, not static; Brown in turn asked permission to perform it for Coleman. The criticism was not intended as hostile, nor was it received that way. As both corrector and corrected understood from their reading of *Political Justice,* "true sincerity will be attended with that equality which is the only sure foundation of love."[96]

This is not to say that Brown did not resist. At least once, Brown tried to dismiss the gravity of Smith's rebuke by accusing his friend of moodiness. In a letter dated 16 July 1796, Smith refused to allow Brown to get away with this. "You are mistaken," Smith wrote. "I experience, for the most part, a temperate flow of spirits." He went on to take Brown to task for continuing to withhold personal details from his letters. "My several questions still remain unanswered; tho' my desire to know how you are? what are you doing? what you wish to do? What is proposed for you to do? & What you expect to do? — continues as vivid & anxious as ever."[97]

Brown's old whine cum boast — "no one whose character is . . . less known to those that know him best . . . ever existed" — was at last being challenged. If Brown's friends did not know who he really was, Smith sternly observed, it was no one's fault but Brown's. Furthermore, it was a little rude of Brown to insist on reminding them of it. After the scolding, Smith proceeded to offer "an example of what is becoming in a friend." To show Brown how sincerity ought to be practiced, Smith devoted the remaining paragraphs of his letter to information about himself. Of course, the revealed truth about Smith's life was more flattering than the truth about Brown's would have been: Smith detailed his recent decision to become a vegetarian and the self-imposed regimen according to which he was studying medicine and French — a confession that was hardly compromising.[98]

But in the rhetoric that structured Brown's friendships, Smith's unbosoming was provoking a crucial shift. One metaphor was replacing another. Self-consciously, Smith was posturing as a model, but he was not quite inviting Brown to mimic him. Brown was supposed to act as Smith did — but remain Brown. In the past, Brown had avoided confronting his friends' demands by vanishing into imposture, but Smith had cut off this escape route. It would not do for Brown to pretend to be Smith, because Smith could tell whether Brown was faking, and he was willing to call Brown's bluff. Rather, something of Smith had to enter Brown. Brown had to become vulnerable to Smith's influence, as Smith had been vulnerable to Godwin's. The cure for imposture, I suspect, felt like another disease; it worked because the stronger poison drove out the weaker. Where Brown had once been infected with imposture, he would now be infected with Smith.

The new infection seeped through Brown's correspondence. It changed the way Brown wrote to Bringhurst about Christianity. Back in May 1792, Brown's doubts about his faith were an ambiguity he could exploit for melodramatic effect. Rather than avow and defend his deism, Brown invited Bringhurst to wash it away by flooding their friendship with emotion. "Dost thou wish me to become a convert to your doctrine?" Brown appealed. "Make me convinced that thou art certainly my friend, and thy temper and opinions and pursuits will instantly become my own." Even earlier, in the Henrietta letters, love had rendered the religious skepticism of C.B.B. similarly flimsy: "Formal argument was indeed wholly unnecessary. . . . For my conversion to your doctrines was effected by a single word." This was the way an impostor handled a difference in opinions: love me, and I'll pretend to agree with you. Up until his departure for Connecticut in 1793, Brown preferred to promise Bringhurst that he would eschew arguing with him and "be henceforth, if possible, a votary of mild and heavenly Religion."[99]

By 1795, Brown no longer pretended even to *want* to agree with Bringhurst's piety. "I once thought . . . that religious belief were desirable, even if it were erronious," Brown wrote his friend. "I am now of a different opinion." Godwin had taught him that religion (like monarchy and aristocracy) was a system of imposture. At best, politicians who knew the truth encouraged religion's lies because they hoped these lies would restrain the foolish masses from vice. But Brown was through with imposture. Like Godwin, Dunlap, and Smith, he now believed that only understanding and sincerity led to virtue. You could not trick someone into being good. On the contrary, Brown now maintained, "the belief of the divinity of Christ and future retribution, have been pernicious to mankind." It was manipulative to try to convince someone that a statement was true because a god had said it or because disbelief would be punished in the afterlife. Faced with Bringhurst's orthodoxy, Brown was now combative rather than appeasing — sincere rather than sympathetic. Brown's principles were infected, and he would not pretend differently. In fact, he tried to corrode Bringhurst's faith as well, to infect his friend just as he had been infected. To indoctrinate Bringhurst, Brown quoted a disquisition by Dunlap that condemned religious imposture in Godwinian terms, and he conferred with Smith on the best arguments to win Bringhurst over to "our Philosophy."[100]

As discussed above, Brown's letter of 29–31 August 1793 to William C. may be a piece of fiction. But although he may never have mailed it to anyone, the text shows Brown's understanding of sympathy at an important crossroads between imposture and infection. In the letter, Brown demands that masks be dropped to expose corruption — moral corruption as well as physical corruption. He mixes a demand for intimate knowledge of a friend with both evangelical anti-Christianity and hints of an actual infectious illness.

Much as he had once upbraided Wilkins, Brown opens the letter by reprimanding "my dear William" for hiding his real anguish beneath phony raillery. On Godwinian principles, Brown urges William to reveal his true self. Secret melancholy is like an infected wound; it will heal only if exposed and ventilated. "My friend, thou must explain to me thy disease," Brown writes. "Allow me to judge the improbability of a Cure."[101]

Brown anticipates that his correspondent will return the critique. "Why, thou sayest, does this vaunting soul of mine, linger still in obscurity?" And so Brown promises that soon he will reveal himself — not only to William C. but to the world. The promise has a millennial air. Brown hints that he will step forward as a kind of deist and anarchist prophet — as a "new Champion of duty: and Ambassador of Heaven." The man who as a teenager once compared himself to a toad trapped in a rock is now imagining himself as a messiah unacknowledged by his people. Brown predicts that America will give the world a "new Mecca or Nazareth." In 1793, Brown was twenty-two, and in this letter he compares his own hesitation to embrace his fated career to Jesus': "He, whom thou knowest I account an excellent example, did not enter upon the office of instructing mankind till he had seen ten years more than I have." (This comparison strengthens the case that the 1793 date on the text is reliable.) Brown admits the delay makes him anxious, because he will never be able to fulfill his destiny if "our globe may chance to be confounded in the thundering career of a Comet while I am hiding under a bushel the lamp that is destined to illuminate mankind." With stunning immodesty, Brown frets that it would be a shame if his ambition were preempted by apocalypse.[102]

But perhaps the most remarkable aspect of this letter is its conflation of the mental illness of emotional masquerade with a real and particular physical disease. "Art thou in health, my brother?" Brown writes. "Art thou forever exempt from the groans and tossings of disease?" From the sentences that follow, it seems that Brown is asking about his friend's psyche, encouraging William to put aside a mask of hilarity and confront his depression. But from the place and date at the head — Ellendale, along the Schuylkill River, 29 and 31 August 1793 — the question must also allude to yellow fever, which had then become epidemic in the nation's capital. At the end of August, the plague was twelve days old, and nearly everyone who could was fleeing Philadelphia for the countryside. Brown was evoking the metaphoric "groans and tossings of disease" while friends and neighbors were literally dying in their throes.[103]

Over the next five years, Smith complained often that Brown failed to apply himself to any one writing project for very long. "He starts an idea; pursues it a little way; new ones spring up; he runs a short distance after each; meantime the original one is likely to escape intirely." Smith listened patiently to Brown's utopian political romances, littered with ominous-sounding names and European conspiracies — "his Aloas & Astoias, his Buttiscoes and Carlovingas," Smith called them. But there was one plot that Brown returned to again and again, that he managed to sustain a focus on, and that raised Smith's hopes whenever he heard that Brown was working on it. In September 1795, Brown mentioned this project to Dunlap, informing him that upon returning to Philadelphia he had planned out "a work equal in extent to [Godwin's novel] Caleb Williams."[104]

There is no way to know for certain what this novel was about, but two clues point toward yellow fever. On 24 September 1795, Smith recorded in his diary that he had told his colleague Amasa Dingley the story of a boy orphaned by yellow fever who then succumbed himself. Afterward, Smith "mentioned my friend's (C.B.B.) plan, for a Tale — & was surprised to see the tears trickle down Dingley's cheeks; & to find him, for several minutes, unable to make a reply." The second clue also comes from Smith's diary, the entry of 13 February 1797. Brown had been living in New York with Dunlap since 30 August 1796; he was due to return to Philadelphia in mid-March, and as if fearing it was his last chance, he spent his final month in Manhattan working feverishly in Smith's apartment. "Charles has . . . recommen[c]ed his Phila. novel; so fiercely undertaken in the Autumn of 1795," Smith recorded. Brown had returned to the material that had made Dr. Dingley cry. Although the majority of Brown's fiction is set in the Philadelphia area, the pieces of fiction that feature the city prominently enough to be called a "Philadelphia novel" — *Arthur Mervyn, Ormond,* the "Man at Home" — all concern themselves with the yellow fever epidemic. The story line that best focused Brown's developing creative energy dealt with the plague, perhaps embroidered with an anti-Christian message.[105]

Smith took pleasure in his friend's difficult ambition. He enjoyed thinking about the impact that Brown's autumn 1795 novel would have when Brown presented it to the world. Smith looked forward to sharing the opprobrium as well as the glory of his friend's achievement. "What different sentiments will it excite! And how much rancour, & misrepresentation must he encounter! And not he alone, but all those who are united to him, by the ties of friendship, & bonds of resembling opinions." As the friend of a writer who agonized about his writing, Smith behaved almost perfectly. Unlike Wilkins, he never reminded Brown of his unfinished commitment to law. He gently dissuaded Brown from other occupations as well. When Brown considered nursing, for example, Smith argued against "devoting yourself to the care of the sick." He repeatedly asked Brown to continue writing and to show him what he had written. He expressed some frustration when Brown diffused his energy into many projects, but he never disapproved of any given story. In fact, he greeted every new work that Brown gave him with more enthusiasm than the last. He and Dunlap both offered Brown physical as well as psychological shelter, housing (and perhaps feeding) the impoverished writer for months at a time. It cannot have been easy for a man as proud as Brown to accept all this assistance.[106]

On 7 August 1796, while staying at Dunlap's house in Perth Amboy, New York, Smith, Dunlap, and Brown took a walk in the countryside. Their stay in Perth Amboy was a summer vacation of sorts; while there, even diligent Smith put aside his studies in favor of unstructured conversation and companionship. "From conferences such as these," Smith wrote, to excuse his lapse from routine, "new intellectual, as well as moral, energy is derived." The year before, the three friends had discovered a "three-partile Tree, emblem of our friendship," and on their walk they revisited it. "We had some doubt which stock belonged to each. For each of us had fixed upon his own. We readily agreed that the slenderest one, & which grew in the middle, must be Charles's."[107]

This three-part tree is perhaps also a fit emblem of how Brown's art grew from his friendships. Like the slender trunk that represented him, Brown's art was frail and required support. The more vigorous beings on either side might look as though in their strength they threatened to pinch him right out of existence, but they also held him up. Like the sapling positioned in the middle, Brown's art grew in a space that was in between. In the narrow ground between friends, emerging from the stuff that connected them to one another, pushing the same stuff away in order to find air and light, it struggled to grow.

Brown became an author in a nurturing and competitive community of men who sheltered and contained him. The lines of their growth hedged and trained his. During an early phase, marked by a rhetoric of imposture, Brown lied to these men and manipulated their emotions; during a later phase, marked by metaphors of infection, he let their influence cross into him, although this felt like a dangerous corruption of himself. Brown's letters are marked by the struggle to take nourishment from his friends' affection without mistaking their lives for his, to sympathize without becoming someone else or losing himself. In his letters, Brown is trying to cultivate a new style of language in a cramped place. To speak this new language, Brown needs friends as badly as he resents and fears his need of them. Out of the fight between this need and fear grew the terror and insight of Brown's fiction.

## The Transformation, the Self Devoted, and the
## Dead Recalled: Sympathy in Brown's Fiction

Charles Brockden Brown spent the autumn of 1797 incommunicado
in Philadelphia. He was writing "something in the form of a Romance." In
September, Elihu Hubbard Smith begged for details, but Brown would offer
none; he would not even say whether he was reviving an old project or launching a brand-new one. Months passed, and Brown's New York friends heard
no news. On 30 November 1797, Smith mailed Brown a one-line reproach:
"Charles! are you dead?"[1]

Brown finished his manuscript on the last day of 1797. For the first time, he
had written a novel all the way to its conclusion. "I hardly know how to regard
this exploit," Brown wrote in his journal. "Is it a respectable proof of per-
severance or not?" Brown was as surprised as anyone that he had completed a
book. The achievement left him ambivalent. It did not compare favorably to
*Caleb Williams*, he confided to his journal; but for a first novel, perhaps it was
acceptable.[2]

The very next day, New Year's Day, 1798, Brown wrote an extraordinary
letter to his friend William Dunlap. Brown had lived with Dunlap in New
York from August 1796 to March 1797, but the two men had not corresponded since Brown's return to Philadelphia. Histrionic and melancholy,
Brown now interpreted Dunlap's silence to mean that Dunlap had given up on
him. "I lived with you six months," Brown wrote. "During that time you no

*Portrait of Dr. Elihu Hubbard Smith, B.A. 1786 (1771–1798)*, by James Sharples. 1797. Yale University Art Gallery. Gift to Yale Medical Library through Dr. Herbert Thoms by Mrs. Frances G. Colt.

doubt scrutinized my conduct & character with accuracy." Brown felt sure that Dunlap had disapproved of what he had seen. After his intimate observation of Brown, Dunlap must have concluded that "my infirmities & follies were too rooted for you to hope their cure." Brown maintained, however, that no one — not even he himself — was beyond the reach of Godwinian sincerity. Dunlap ought to have told Brown honestly how degraded he had become. "Whatever was my depravity, it did not sink me below deserving a mere verbal effort for my restoration."[3]

Brown chastised himself severely, writing, "I think upon the life of last winter with self-loathing almost unsupportable." But it seems unlikely that Dunlap had as low an opinion of Brown as Brown did of himself. Even Smith at his harshest had accused Brown of nothing worse than laziness and a desire to be willfully obscure. When Dunlap had read a similar letter of self-reproach by Brown in August 1797, he had noted in his diary that he found Brown's "charges against himself as to his conduct towards me . . . mysterious & unintelligible." When Dunlap saved the New Year's Day letter from Brown in his files, he appended this palinodic comment at the foot: "So at certain moments could think & write one of the purest & best beloved of men." Dunlap deliberately signaled to posterity that he neither hated Brown nor looked askance at his behavior.[4]

What sort of depravity Brown had in mind is hard to determine. "I shall die, as I have lived, a victim of perverse & incurable habits," Brown wrote. But which incurable habits — indolence and mendaciousness? What about sodomy or masturbation? The sensational rhetoric of this letter echoes the self-reproaches with which Brown had exasperated Smith a year and a half earlier, when he had claimed to be the "slave of desires that can not be honorably gratified." When a modern reader reads a confession of perverse habits and dishonorable desires, he wonders: perhaps Dunlap, during his six months as Brown's roommate, witnessed some sexual deviance of Brown's. Dunlap may have used the word *purest* in his postscript to fend off a sexual reading of Brown's letter, and where there is smoke, there may be fire.[5]

However, sex is not the only field in which one may be depraved or pure. In his biography of Brown, Dunlap listed the faults he thought Brown had: improvidence with money, slovenliness in dress, and social awkwardness. Only the first would seem a weighty enough charge for self-castigation this dire. During the winter he spent with Dunlap, Brown seems not to have held a job. Smith records that Brown worked on a number of writing projects that season — during February 1797 his diligence impressed even Smith — but he brought none of them to completion. Brown must have lived off Smith's and Dunlap's largess and the piecework he did as a scrivener. Brown was "poor:

absolutely destitute," Smith told Joseph Dennie in July 1797 in order to coax some pity and cash out of the editor of the *Port Folio*. "His pen is his only support; & he chiefly employs it mechanically."[6]

Perhaps indolence was all Brown meant by depravity. If so, nothing would have shown up the writerly shiftlessness of the previous winter so well as this winter's bout of industry. The morning after he finished the novel, rather than congratulating himself, he rebuked himself. Not even Dunlap knew what for, but it might have been for not finishing his novel sooner. Brown may have regarded his old self with such intense hatred and disgust because, for the first time, it seemed within his power to leave that self behind. Brown's New Year's Day letter to Dunlap is an avowal of hope worded as despair. "As I am you despise me," Brown wrote. "How can I remove the burthen of your scorn but by transforming myself into a new being?" But even as Brown claimed this transformation was beyond him, in the same paragraph he told Dunlap, elliptically, that the transformation had already taken place. He cued Dunlap to ask Smith about "the transactions of the last four months," that is, his completed novel. Dunlap seems to have understood that the self-deprecation and the achievement were the two sides of a coin. In his diary, Dunlap summarized the communication thus: "I yesterday received a letter from Brown full of self condemnation, particularly for his conduct last winter: in one to Smith he says he has finished a novel or romance."[7]

Brown excoriated himself as if to peel off a molting self. With his novel, Brown had completed the metamorphosis of his identity. In 1793 he had given up on law. In 1794 he had held the position of "Master of the Friends' Grammar school," which came to nothing. Unlike his friend and future brother-in-law John Blair Linn, Brown was too much of a deist to find a haven in the church as a poetry-writing minister. To Smith's relief, Brown had only toyed with a "wild project of devoting yourself to the care of the sick" before discarding it. He was now neither lawyer, teacher, minister, nor nurse, but author. He "describe[d] himself as assiduously writing Novels & in love." When he returned to New York on 3 July 1798 to live with Dunlap, Brown had finished "Sky-Walk," all four parts of *Alcuin,* most of *Wieland,* and enough of *Arthur Mervyn* to have begun serial publication in the *Weekly Magazine.* He was writing at a furious pace, and manuscripts in hand, he was returning to Manhattan in triumph.[8]

To realize his ambition, a young man must struggle with the ghost of his father. He has to figure out a way to be and not to be the man his father was — to be like him without being merely a lifeless semblance of him. A son cannot simply take his father's place. Freud described the double bind thus: The superego's "relation to the ego is not exhausted by the precept: 'You *ought to be* like this (like your father).' It also comprises the prohibition: 'You *may not be* like this (like your father) — that is, you may not do all that he does; some things are his prerogative.'"[9] In Shakespeare's best-known play, Claudius went about this problem the way a younger brother would, which was all wrong. Of course Claudius turns out to be no more like Hamlet's father than Hamlet was like Hercules. When the thirty-year-old prince contrasts this pair of contrasts, he is signaling with his self-deprecating humor that he appreciates the difficulty: direct analogies between fathers and sons, though inevitable, never put sons in an advantageous light.

The novel *Wieland* is America's first *Hamlet*.[10] Like Shakespeare, Brown writes about sons who feel themselves troublesomely fathered not so much by men as by language. Along the Schuylkill River, as in Denmark, words seem either too swampy or too sheer to build on them a house of one's own. When Hamlet puns, Claudius objects: "These words are not mine." "No, nor mine now," Hamlet answers, tauntingly. Words can belong to anyone, and therefore they belong to no one. Hamlet protests too much when he claims to his mother that "I know not 'seems,'" because *seems* is everywhere, and Hamlet with his north-by-northwest sanity knows this better than anyone else in his play. Carwin and Wieland are also enmeshed in webs of seeming, and although Carwin spins his webs himself, the literary problem he does not solve is the same as Hamlet's and Wieland's: how to speak in a voice that answers the father who haunts it. In these works, an artist is trying to respond to the authority of the father without killing himself, that is, to honor the struggle passed on from the father, which killed the father and which it is the artist's responsibility to be killed by also — a responsibility he would like respectfully to avoid.

The artist would like, in other words, to speak in sympathy with his father. He would honor his father by sharing his feelings while avoiding his fate. When Hamlet attempts to sympathize with his father's ghost, what comes out is delay, which combines, in complicated succession, both refusal and obedience. Delay makes Hamlet first an antic impostor and only later a destroyer. Brown splits Hamlet's two responses into separate characters, the impostor Carwin and the destroyer Wieland. Carwin refuses his father's spirit, and his unhaunted voice becomes dangerously plastic, susceptible to all the other voices in the world. Wieland obeys his father's ghost too literally and loses this world, which he can no longer speak to but must kill.

In his early notes for *Wieland*, Brown named most of the characters in the novel after himself: Theodore, Clara, and Catharine Wieland were originally Charles, Caroline, and Charlotte. The only major figure not named a variant of Charles in these drafts was Marcrieve, who eventually became Carwin, a name that (like Clara) echoes "Charles" and its Latin form "Carolus" (427).[11] It is a commonplace that authors write aspects of themselves into their characters, but there is something appealing and brutally simple about Brown's compositional technique here. Names mattered to Brown. His notes include pages of nothing but lists of names, and when he liked a name — Colden or Clara, for example — he recycled it. To name every character in a novel after oneself, even in draft, is to build a crude but sturdy bridge of narcissism between text and writer.

Narcissism, however, does not usually lead to art. Brown had never finished his "Julius" novel, because the pleasure of imagining himself as Julius had been too direct. It had distracted him from the task of mere writing. Julius was a perfect Romantic hero; it would have been pointless to write him down, because language would necessarily have failed to capture him. But the central concern of *Wieland* is the failure of language. By 1798 the flaws in writing intrigued Brown enough to lead his sympathetic identification with his characters along a more circuitous (and productive) route; he cast himself into language and then took himself out in new forms, as if to see what damage happened in the translation.

In *Wieland,* reading and writing do not correspond to each other in the seamless way of fantasies uncommitted to words. When Clara complains that she should not have to spell out what she feels for Pleyel — "when minds are imbued with a genuine sympathy, are not words and looks superfluous?" (79) — she echoes the sentimental pieties that Brown had once exchanged with his young friends Wilkins and Bringhurst. But Clara's plaint also cues her reader to expect her comeuppance, because in this novel, a Godwinian dystopia, there is no magic to sympathy. Any communication that is not sincere and explicit goes wrong, but so do several communications that *are* sincere and explicit. When the characters in *Wieland* speak to each other, their words often mislead them, sometimes because language is treacherous, sometimes because they want to mislead. Maybe Brown's own impostures had to fail before these failures could provoke his art. As in his early letters, Brown saw himself in his fiction as the arch impostor, the Charles who could speak as Charles, Caroline, Charlotte, and Carwin. But the artistry of *Wieland* as a novel is self-conscious. It reflects not only Brown but itself, telling a story about imposturous creation as Brown creates a story by imposture.

The novel opens with a series of begats that is an account of writing and reading as well as a genealogy of three generations of the Wieland family. Grandfather Wieland, a nobleman, married as he pleased, not as he should have, and so lost his inheritance and was forced to write "sonatas and dramatic pieces" to eke out a living. Like Melville's Pierre, Grandfather Wieland made a choice of wife that forced him to professionalize an amateur love of literature. And like Pierre Glendinning, Grandfather Wieland died young, in abject poverty. In artistic terms, however, his life was a success. Brown's narrator writes that the eldest Wieland "may be considered as the founder of the German Theatre," honored for the "fruitfulness of his invention" and the "soundness of his taste" (7). In human suffering, the cost of Grandfather Wieland's integrity was high, but most of that cost would be borne not by him but by his surviving orphan son.

That boy — Father Wieland — grew up in "mercantile servitude." As an apprentice and clerk, his "duties were laborious and mechanical" (7). He was unhappy, but his unhappiness had nothing to do with a frustrated wish for cultural refreshment or for the freedom to express himself in art. His was the generation that the Wieland creative intellect skipped. According to his daughter, "he entertained no relish for books, and was wholly unconscious of any power they possessed to delight or instruct" (8). License had lost Grandfather Wieland his patrimony, and so Father Wieland avoided it instinctively. Writing had no place in his life; reading, however, became a sort of religion for him. One day Father Wieland's unfixed melancholy was solved by an accidental glance at a French Protestant tract. "Seek and ye shall find," the book read, quoting Matthew. Father Wieland mysteriously and irrevocably decided not to seek any further. He decided he had found what he did not even realize he had been looking for. Narrow, rigid, ardent reading of this Protestant tract and the Bible became the focus of his life. "A thousand scruples to which he had hitherto been a stranger" now hemmed him in, leaving him "alternately agitated by fear and by ecstasy" (9). Persecuted for his idiosyncratic convictions, Father Wieland left the Old World for America, where he exhausted himself with attempts to convert Indians. Whereas Grandfather Wieland had suffered the fate of the Writer, making himself up and committing himself to words with an indifference to consequences that destroyed him, Father Wieland suffered the fate of the Reader; his life was filled and ruled by a stranger's voice, his great anxiety was whether he had understood and obeyed what he had read, and, as if to suppress his doubts of the writer's authority, he made his readings ever more strictly faithful.

For his God, Father Wieland built a plain, domed temple on a high rock not far from his house along the Schuylkill River. Every noon and midnight, he prayed there. But his devotion could never alleviate his sense of guilt. A Reader can never know for certain that he has read truly; he can never be sure that he has not sinned by writing something in, himself. So eventually Father Wieland came to feel that his God had condemned him. He hinted to his family that "a command had been laid upon him, which he had delayed to perform." In the interim of this delay, Hamlet played out the whole tragedy of his life, but Father Wieland's melancholy was not antic. Refusing to tell anyone in his family what this mysterious command had been, he said only that it was too late now. "He was no longer permitted to obey. . . . All that remained was to endure the penalty" (13).

Late one August night, the penalty came. Distraught, feeling as though "his brain was scorched to cinders," Father Wieland went alone to his hilltop temple (14). Watching anxiously from the window of their house below, his wife saw bright, strange lights and heard an explosion and shrieks. The family went running. Father Wieland was discovered in the temple bruised and naked, his clothes burned to ashes. He said that a man with a lamp had struck him, and a spark had set his clothes afire, but his story did not sound convincing. Within hours, fever, delirium, and noisome infection had killed him, and his family was left to wonder whether his death was a case of spontaneous combustion or the "stroke of a vindictive and invisible hand" (19).

After the prologue of Grandfather and Father Wieland's demises, the curtain opens on the third generation of Wielands: the siblings Theodore and Clara. In their lives, instead of either the extravagance of writing or the slavishness of reading, an Enlightenment balance now prevails. Father Wieland's austere temple has been softened by a harpsichord and a bust of Cicero—the icon of a writer who knew his duty and a reader who could think critically. Where once Father Wieland had retreated in pious solitude, now "the social affections were accustomed to expand, and the tear of delicious sympathy to be shed" (24). Theodore's personality is as somber as his father's, but "the mind of the son was enriched by science, and embellished with literature" (23).

In Brown's novel, Theodore's sister, Clara, plays the role of Horatio, Hamlet's friend. Modest and with an independent spirit, she takes reason as her touchstone, and through the horrors and marvels that follow, she will survive to narrate the tale. In the first paragraph of her story, Clara hints at the threat to the young Wielands' precarious balance. "The tale I am going to tell," Clara asserts, "is not intended as a claim upon your sympathy" (5). Throughout the novel, Clara pauses from time to time to master or dissipate the feelings that her story evokes in her. When she first mentions Carwin, for example, the memory troubles her, and she stops to "take a few turns in my chamber" lest "dire remembrance . . . subdue my courage or baffle my design" (49). To stay coherent and rational, Clara suppresses her sympathies deliberately and often. Her self is hermetic. She writes her diary in shorthand to make it more difficult for others to read. For no very compelling reason, she has chosen to live separately from her brother and his wife, Catharine. Her apologetic explanation is that she is "an economist of pleasure. Self-denial, seasonably exercised, is one means of enhancing our gratifications" (22). Clara likes boundaries. She likes, in particular, to know where her brother ends and she begins. Unfortunately, by the end of the novel, her diary will be read without her permission, her house will burn down, and her brother will try to kill her.

Clara's self-possession obstructs her love for her brother-in-law, Pleyel. She pretends not to care for him in order to maintain her dignity. "I must not speak," she vows. "Neither eyes, nor lips, must impart the information" (79). In this sense, Clara is the first impostor the novel introduces, the first shaper of words whose speech is designed not to reveal her true self. As a woman, however, Clara represents a part of Brown that is spared from always having to choose whether to follow or defy his father; her imposture is therefore relatively mild. To see the truly toxic effects of this forced choice, one must turn to the male characters.

An early clue that Theodore Wieland's equilibrium is not as stable as might be desired comes in his attitude toward Cicero. Wieland not only reads Cicero's orations, he performs them with finicky attention to proper pronunciation and gestures. We know he is near the edge when he turns into an obsessive textual scholar. "He was diligent," Clara tells us, "in settling and restoring the purity of the text" (24). Wieland's attention to Cicero's words is pious rather than thoughtful, let alone playful. Although for a time his wife's skeptical, humanist brother, Pleyel, restores some perspective by teasing Wieland on the subject of the "divinity of Cicero" (25), Theodore comes to repeat his father's way of reading. Very soon Cicero will not seem a figure absolute enough for this kind of veneration.

To copy the father is not to honor him. In cases of imposture, this is easy to see. When the thief, jailbreaker, and counterfeiter Stephen Burroughs borrows his father's sermons in order to impersonate a preacher, he is not out to flatter his father. In fact, Burroughs in his *Memoirs* makes it clear that he turned to the ministry because he considered it the one profession a man without any skills or recommendations might resort to. By no accident, almost the last fact in Burroughs's *Memoirs* is that after years of being gulled, "the disappointed and dejected father . . . lost all confidence in his son." Hamlet intended no compliment when he forged Claudius's handwriting to put Rosencrantz's and Guildenstern's names on the death sentence originally written for him. Expressing a consensus in psychoanalysis, Phyllis Greenacre identifies Oedipal conflict as a major component of imposture: "Insofar as *the imposture* is accomplished, *it is the killing of the father through the complete displacement of him.*"[12]

The case of Theodore Wieland is not, however, one of imposture. His is another kind of mimicry. Like imposture, it takes a repetition of the father's identity to an extreme that distorts, but unlike an impostor, Theodore does not keep in reserve a self that sneers at anyone who is fooled by it. He commits himself utterly to fulfilling the command that he feels he has inherited from his father, namely, the command that he destroy everything he loves. Wieland's illness is a psychosis, but because Brown sees in it a special danger to his art, I would like to distinguish it further by giving it the name *copyism*.

A copyist is a self whose creative impulse has been destroyed as a sacrifice to authority. The sacrifice is in a sense a gift of love. The copyist would rather not be himself or herself than lose the approval of the one he or she copies. But in the thoroughness of the destruction, there is an implied reproach. The salt sewed at Carthage does not speak well of Rome. Copyism may begin as Dora imitating her father's cough, as a neurosis where "identification has appeared instead of object-choice, and . . . object-choice has regressed to identification."[13] But in copyism it is as if Dora proceeds to become nothing but cough. If her need for her father is strongly mixed with rage, then the obliteration of her self relieves the guilt her rage provokes, while also giving her the secret satisfaction of a rebuke: I am what you are, and you are a cough, not a man.

While Brown was struggling to succeed as a writer, he earned his living as a copyist in another sense of the word. To repeat what Smith told Joseph Dennie, "His pen is his only support; & he chiefly employs it mechanically." It seems likely that Brown despised this kind of work. In a dialogue on music, Brown once wrote that "low, indeed, must be that ambition, which is satisfied with pleasing by mere mimicry, by putting off every distinctive property, every thing that constitutes *themselves;* and, warbling the words of others, and running through unmeaning, unappropriate, unintelligent notes." Brown could not appreciate musicians whose art lay in the interpretation of others' compositions. To him they were no better than plagiarists. His anxiety over the originality of art was too intense for him to see them any other way.[14]

Brown was named after a copyist, his great-uncle Charles Brockden, whom Benjamin Franklin described in his *Autobiography* as "an eminent Scrivener or Conveyancer in the Town." Anyone who reads the Brown family papers in the library of the Historical Society of Pennsylvania sees at once that copying pervaded the mental environment of the home Brown grew up in. Charles's father, Elijah Brown, also worked as a conveyancer. In an elegant, controlled hand, he wrote out legal documents. The collection of Brown papers at the historical society consists mostly of Elijah's copybooks. The material in them written by Charles was preserved almost by accident. When Elijah came across a notebook that Charles had scribbled in haphazardly, he would fill with copies every available space left in the margins of his son's writing. Elijah copied anything he came across: newspaper stories, real estate notices, Mary Wollstonecraft on the French Revolution, excerpts from Godwin's *Political Justice,* Quaker doctrine, Louis XVI's last will and testament, and dialogues, poems, and letters written by his son. It is fairly easy to distinguish Elijah's hand from Charles's. The son's penmanship looks lax and rushed; the father's is dainty and precise, and it fills every crevice, like the delicate web of an indefatigable spider. At the front of one of his copybooks, Elijah inscribed this disparaging note: "The paper Coarse, & Writing bad." In fact, the handwriting is flawless. In another volume, Elijah wrote, "Extracts made by E. Brown then under bodily pain — in order to divert it — but with tremulous hand." Copying might have terrified Charles, but to Elijah it was soothing. He took pride in it, because he earned his living by doing it well.[15]

Elijah's penmanship exercises may seem harmless and quaint today, but to his son, they must have appeared poisonous. They resembled Father Wieland's obsessive-compulsive rituals — only a gentle eccentricity to most people around him but the cause of a psychosis in young Theodore. There is another reason why Elijah's copying would have disturbed his son. Charles must have sensed that his father, as a copyist, was a broken man. As the historian Peter Kafer has discovered, the young Elijah Brown was a more promising and more ambiguous character, not unlike Arthur Mervyn: he aspired to wealth, tried to marry into it, and became involved in business transactions that to an impartial eye looked rather shady. In 1768 the Philadelphia Monthly Meeting censured and disowned Elijah for "want of adhering to the Principle of Truth" in his financial dealings. In 1770, Elijah smuggled tea for his brother-in-law. In 1784, when Charles was a young teenager, Elijah was imprisoned for debt, ending his career as an unreliable businessman. Elijah failed as a man of his word. Charles saw him become, instead, a man composed only of words — others' words at that.[16]

Charles eventually found that the mechanics of copyism gave him the means to overthrow it. Like Hamlet, he at first held it "A baseness to write fair and labor'd much / How to forget that learning." But once detached from authority, the skill of perfect compliance can be turned to profoundly selfish and rebellious uses. Again like Hamlet, Brown changed his opinion of the ability to make a flawless copy, because "It did me yeoman's service."

Along the Schuylkill River, the agent of irresponsible invention — and the author's proxy — is Francis Carwin.[17] Brown lets Carwin enjoy his author's bad habit of imposture for most of the book, teaching him his lesson only in the closing chapters. At the climax of the novel, in moral outrage Clara exclaims of Carwin, "He is able to speak where he is not." This insulting skill — a combination of imposture and projection — is the force that Brown opposes to copyism. It is a semblance of the suspect, emerging voice of literary art.

Like Clark Kent, Carwin was raised by a peasant who did not satisfy him as a father. As a boy, he began to deceive in order to escape the jealous limits his father set on his intellectual development. Like Stephen Burroughs, Carwin first appears as an impostor of his father. Burroughs preached; Carwin begs a cup of buttermilk from Clara's maid while dressed as a "clown" (50). Both men unnerve their audience by not quite suiting their clothes. Burroughs regretted that his dandyish suit looked wrong on a minister, because it betrayed his recent past as a rake. In Carwin's case, however, seeming to be a little better than his rustic outfit is part of the act. To advertise his Romantic sensibility, Carwin lets his eyes roam appreciatively over the landscape outside Clara's house, and she takes the bait. Soon she is indulging in "airy speculations" about enlightened farmers who dream as loftily as poets (51).[18]

Clara never recognizes Carwin. "I know you well," Clara claims just before she opens her closet door to discover Carwin, but she opens the door because she is sure the man hidden inside is her brother (88). Even when she witnesses Carwin in the act of ventriloquism — when she sees his face contorted in the muscular effort of projection at the same moment she hears the words *"hold! hold!"* — she does not put the voice and the face together (147–48). When in the end Carwin flees Philadelphia, Clara rather optimistically imagines that "he is now probably engaged in the harmless pursuits of agriculture" (239). Left to her own devices, Clara likes to think Carwin is better than he is. As if to correct her, Carwin prefers to trick her into thinking he is worse. Caught in a relatively innocent prank, Carwin chooses not to explain that he can throw his voice but instead pretends he was going to rape her, but her guardian angel — heard in his thrown voice — intervened. "For the sake of creating a mysterious dread," Carwin later explains, "I have made myself a villain" (209). When he discovers Catharine's strangled corpse, he leaves a note for Clara that suggests he was responsible and would have murdered Clara if she had been available. The truth obscured by Carwin's grandiose badness and Clara's wishful thinking is that Carwin's force is amoral. Carwin is a confused and frightened young man who does not know how to handle his gift. A Hamlet who knows he is not going to become king of Denmark after all, Carwin is a little lost because he no longer understands what his princehood consists of.

In the character of Theodore Wieland, Brown dramatizes the hazards of a self responsible to authority for its voice. Carwin's trick, by contrast, is *not* to establish an identity anchored in sympathy with the father. That kind of fixity and confidence would suffocate art, which must remain open to sympathy with anyone. By means of imposture, Carwin plays copyism against any authoritative sympathy. If he were to become the man his father would have been proud of, he would have to give up his devilish skill. Responsible people do not even recognize the sort of thing Carwin does as a skill; Hamlet would have.

When Hamlet challenges his stepfather's flunkeys to play the recorder, he is twitting them for their failure to understand this kind of talent. "It is as easy as lying," Hamlet taunts. In fact, lying is not easy at all. But it is hard for the righteous to appreciate the work that goes into evil. To Clara, the pleasure Carwin takes in misleading earnest Pleyel sounds not aesthetic but infernal: "To deceive him would be the sweetest triumph I had ever enjoyed," Carwin exults (210). Clara does not hear this as a statement about craft.

One night, upset by the inexplicable voices that have been threatening her and by her inexpressible love for Pleyel, Clara turns for comfort to a piece of writing that is securely fathered—to her father's manuscript memoir. "The narrative was by no means recommended by its eloquence," Clara admits, yet "its stile had an unaffected and picturesque simplicity" (83). But when Clara goes to her closet to retrieve the memoir, she finds Carwin. The ventriloquist has come to read the same text in hopes that it can provide information useful to his machinations. One of the lessons of the novel is that a desire for plain and representative language always collides with the potential of the plainest language to betray. Clara's own homely diary arouses jealous fantasies in Pleyel when he reads a few stray words over her shoulder (125). The same diary betrays her "inmost soul" to Carwin's eyes (206). Yet every character longs for words still somehow pure. In a project reminiscent of "Julius," Pleyel has been "not[ing] down, in writing, every particular of [Clara's] conduct" in order to create a prose pattern of female perfection that as nonfiction will be more instructive and inspiring than any novel. "Here there was no other task incumbent on me," Pleyel says, "but to copy" (122). Even Carwin hopes to write a "faithful narrative of my actions" that will vindicate him (212).

A plain style appeals because it offers to channel sympathy between reader and writer in a straightforward way. Father Wieland's memoir, Clara's diary, Pleyel's paragon, and Carwin's vindication are (or would be) written in hopes of winning their readers over. To believe in plainness is to believe that language need not get in the way; copyism will put an equals sign between writer and reader; emotions will transfer directly between persons. But there is nothing direct about sympathy. It is not *feeling* but *feeling with,* because as Adam Smith explains in his *Theory of Moral Sentiments,* we can never experience directly the sensorium of another person: "It is the impressions of our own senses only, not those of [another person's], which our imaginations copy."[19] Copying alone is sterile. An act of sympathy requires something more—the self-deceit of imaginative projection. This substitution and indirection appear to be impurities. Although Hamlet uses the impurity of fiction to set a dramatic mousetrap for Claudius, it bothers him that artificial stories provoke real feelings. As Hamlet asks of the actor who brings tears to his own eyes,

"What's Hecuba to him or he to Hecuba, / That he should weep for her?" When Clara first hears Carwin's voice, she, too, cries. "When he uttered the words 'for charity's sweet sake,' I dropped the cloth that I held in my hand, my heart overflowed with sympathy, and my eyes with unbidden tears" (52). Clara cannot tell Pleyel, a man she has known for years, that she loves him, but she sobs for Carwin, a stranger and a hoax.

The subtitle of *Wieland* is "The Transformation." Brown never spells out what this means, but the word *transform* occurs in the novel three times, once each for Theodore, Carwin, and Clara. Each time, the word signals a change in a character's identity that is not simply an exchange of place or role. And in each case, the kind of change is different. A look at the use of this word may serve as a summary of the story that *Wieland* tells about copyism, imposture, and sympathy — about the different styles of self that may result from sharing another person's feelings.

The most sudden and violent changes in the book are Theodore's. Either Carwin's ventriloquism or Theodore's own schizophrenia "changed him who was the glory of his species into worse than brute," to borrow Clara's words (197). To Theodore, though, this madness feels like transfiguration. On the fateful night, as he walks to his sister's house, his mood surges from contentment with his earthly state into a rapture of pious gratitude. He would give anything, he prays to God, for "the blissful privilege of direct communication with thee" (167). In answer, Wieland is bathed in light, reminiscent of the fire that scorched his father just before his death. "Some powerful effulgence covered me like a mantle" (167). Wieland is granted a contact with the Deity so immediate that it clothes him. A sacrifice would turn this garment into a self. God speaks, demanding the death of Theodore's wife. The father's divine mantle, glowing with power and beauty, turns out to be the command that killed his father when he tried to shrug it off. Uninsulated sympathy with ultimate authority has an effect about as subtle as sticking a finger in an electric socket. To obey perfectly, Wieland must kill everything he loves.

Brown does not use the word *transform* to describe Theodore's exaltation into madness; he reserves the word for his fall out of it. Carwin's final act of ventriloquism completes the cycle of Wieland's changes. To save Clara's life, Carwin counterfeits the voice of Theodore's angel, which he denies having counterfeited before. "Man of errors!" he says to Theodore. "Shake off thy phrenzy, and ascend into rational and human. Be lunatic no longer" (230). Clara, as narrator, points out the logical inconsistency in this command: this latest voice from above "might as justly be ascribed to erring or diseased senses" as the earlier voices it claims to discredit (230). But by raising the question of authority, Carwin's final order erodes authority. Once the mysterious voices begin to say things like "Pay no attention to the man behind the curtain," the game is over, and the voices that Theodore hears must be copies, not divine. Clara observes that, deprived of his delusion, "Wieland was transformed at once into the *man of sorrows*" (230).

Theodore's transformation happens in the passive voice. It happens not to Theodore but to Wieland, the name he shares with his father. The passive verb and the patronymic reflect in linguistic form the psychological trouble with copyism, which distorts the operation of sympathy by omitting its middle terms — the selves of the spectator and the sufferer. In Adam Smith's formulation, we sympathize "by changing places in fancy with the sufferer," but Theodore does not change places with his father.[20] Rather, he tries to cancel both his father's place and his own in order to equate them at zero. Theodore does not sympathize with his father's predicament, that is, with the whether to obey or not, but with the principle of fatherhood in his father — the principle that Father Wieland died resisting, as near as the reader can tell. Theodore's word for his resistance to murdering his wife and children is "selfishness" (172–73). To Theodore, to obey the divine command means to reduce his self to nothing by killing off its desires — a meaning spelled out clearly in Brown's notes for the novel, where the Theodore Wieland character destroys a series of increasingly loved objects: "1 some favourte inanimate object. an organ / 2. greyhound. / 3. children 2. / 4. Ward. / 5. Wife. / 6. Sister" (433). He hopes that if he destroys his self, he will become one with the force of patriarchy that his father never quite merged with. Like Laertes, he thinks a murderous fury will answer Claudius's baiting question about paternity: "What would you undertake / To show yourself in deed your father's son / More than in words?" Like Dora's cough, Theodore's murders accomplish a number of tasks at once: they bring Theodore an omnipotent sense of union with the father; they vent his rage against his father; they punish Theodore for his rage by hurting and removing loved ones; and they cast a nasty, backhand aspersion on God the Father, whose brutal nature they reveal.

In Christian iconography, "man of sorrows" is the name given to representations of Christ crucified but not triumphant. It derives from a passage in Isaiah often read as an antetype of the Messiah: "He was despised and rejected by men; / a man of sorrows, and acquainted with grief."[21] Theodore's breakdown takes the form of an identification with a person in the Trinity. That identification has shifted, however, from the sacrificing Father to the sacrificed Son — from Abraham to Isaac. In Theodore's final transformation, the middle term of sympathy, the self, is resurrected. The rational, Ciceronian Theodore returns, though too late. The father did not want the sacrifice that he seemed to be asking for. As Theodore's self returns, so does his sympathy with the world and an emotional understanding of what he has done. Unable to bear this understanding, Theodore again destroys his self, this time by suicide — the honorable, pagan, and highly sympathetic exit of Cato.

In Theodore's case, Brown's use of the word *transformation* is wrenchingly serious. Set next to it, the case of Carwin appears trivial. Early in the novel, Pleyel tells Clara that he met Carwin before. He knew Carwin in Spain, where he appeared as a Roman Catholic under a Spanish name. At that time he was "highly intelligent and communicative" (67) on every subject but one: "On topics of religion and of his own history, previous to his *transformation* into a Spaniard, he was invariably silent" (68).

Brown (or perhaps his printer) italicized the word *transformation* to draw attention to it, but the emphasis is incongruous. It is a rather grandiose word for an arbitrary and ephemeral disguise. Neither Carwin's Catholicism nor his Spanish identity matter in *Wieland*'s plot again. But this triviality may be the point. Theodore ruins his self by attempting a direct sympathy with the most significant being in the universe. By contrast, Carwin refuses to link his self to anyone significant to him. Who Carwin pretends to be — whether Spanish grandee, Pennsylvania rustic, or angel — has no importance to his identity. He has denied that it is a problem to be fathered — that there is a command that defines him by either his obedience or his defiance. The only escape from this double bind is into insignificance — the mask of gaiety that Brown accused his friend Wilkins of wearing. As an impostor, Carwin chooses hollow identities. He may mimic a Roman Catholic believer or even the voice of God because he is already a deist. Whereas Theodore was transformed involuntarily, Carwin elects his change and controls it, in the compact form of a noun rather than a moving verb. He does not change selves in fancy with the object of his imposture; he hides his self behind or inside another artificial self. If one thinks of Theodore's copyism as sympathy without a middle term, then perhaps Carwin's imposture may be seen as sympathy with one middle term too many.

That extra term, a false self, resembles literature in being constructed deliberately out of language. Many critics have wondered why Brown slapped a classic seduction onto the end of *Wieland*.[22] A modern reader finds Mrs. Stuart's seduction by Maxwell extraneous to the central plot. What do the too trusting affections of a lonely young wife have to do with ventriloquism and religiously tinged psychosis? Brown himself gives the answer. To him, the two plots were of a piece. Maxwell and Carwin were both writers who created stories by creating false selves out of words, which then misled two naive readers: Mrs. Stuart and Theodore. As Brown notes in Clara's voice, "The evils of which Carwin and Maxwell were the authors, owed their existence to the errors of the sufferers" (244). In the end, ventriloquism is only the disembodied male-male version of the sweet nothings a rake whispers in a young wife's ear. As Jay Fliegelman has written, relating Carwin's vocal skill to the force of rhetoric in the young republic, "Eloquence was a male equivalent to the power of female beauty to create desire, to solicit something akin to an involuntary sexual response."[23] The novel as a genre derives its interest from the dramatic irony of exposing a seducer's sweet nothings to readers outside the novel who are more sophisticated than the Mrs. Stuarts and Theodores within it. We always know better than Pamela what Squire B. is up to, but she ends up surprising us as well as Squire B., when her own sentimental education wreaks a transformation, by sympathy, on her seducer. In generic terms, then, the puzzling thing about *Wieland* is not that Theodore is seduced by Carwin but that he never marries him. Theodore learns to read ironically only moments before dying, and no one reintegrates Carwin into the social order. All the sentimental education devolves onto a third character, Clara.

A false self is not a work of art, as the posturing of Brown's private correspondence demonstrates. Like *Hamlet, Wieland* stages instead the destruction by and of false selves. The true reader in both works is the survivor whose heart has followed the turns of the story but has not been consumed by it. Carwin ends up too guilty; Hamlet may prove that neither his mother, the king, nor he himself are who they seemed to be, but he dies in the proof. Rather, Horatio, who has seen the ghost but is not its son, lives to report the cause aright, and *Wieland*'s lessons about reading and writing accrue to Clara, the daughter who lives in a separate house. When Clara insists that Theodore and Mrs. Stuart committed "errors," she draws the hermeneutic moral of the book. God speaks and lovers tell the truth only in genres less realistic than the novel.

For Clara, Brown puts the word *transform* not in a declarative sentence but in a question. After her uncle explains that Theodore is insane and that insanity runs in the Wieland family, Clara begins to worry about her own mental health. After all, she, too, has seen a vision and heard unexplained voices. "Was I not likewise transformed from rational and human into a creature of nameless and fearful attributes?" Clara asks. "Was I not transported to the brink of the same abyss?" (179–80).

Clara fears her sympathy for her brother, Theodore. Her pity for him and his love for her are threatening. She intuitively senses this early on, when she dreams that he is beckoning her into an abyss (62) — a dream not unlike the fictional Henrietta's, in which Brown was tempted to follow Henrietta across the river of death.[24] When Theodore escapes from jail, it is the sympathy between brother and sister that imperils Clara. Thanks to their closeness, he has a special wish to murder her. "Had I been a stranger to his blood; had I been the most worthless of human kind," Clara muses darkly, "my safety had

When Brown began to write *Arthur Mervyn*, in late spring or summer 1798, yellow fever was, however, more than a memory or a literary device. Almost every autumn during the 1790s, the cities of New York and Philadelphia saw recurrences of the epidemic, with varying severity. It was a presence in the lives of Brown and his friends. Smith, for example, maintained a correspondence with his former teacher Benjamin Rush on the origin, vectors, and treatment of yellow fever. It is not quite a coincidence, therefore, that Brown's novel about the Demon — as he once referred to yellow fever in a letter to Dunlap — seemed to summon it.[29] There is no sure evidence that Brown experienced the Philadelphia plague of 1793 firsthand, but when the disease came to New York in 1798, it killed Brown's best friend and changed the course of his life.

On 25 August 1798, Brown wrote to his brother James that yellow fever had broken out in New York City. He assured James there was no reason to worry, because it had not reached his neighborhood and because he had adopted Smith's protective regimen: vegetarianism and teetotaling. Two days later, however, Smith confided to his diary that he had been "subjected to more than ordinary fatigue," and on 4 September, Brown had to admit that the redoubtable Smith was sick. Nonetheless, Brown reiterated to James his faith in Smith's ability as a doctor to keep his friends and himself safe. "E.H.S. has extensive and successful practice in this disease. Through fatigue and exposure to midnight airs, he is at present somewhat indisposed, but will shortly do well." At this point, Brown decided not to leave his friends, no matter how bad it got. A sense of mutual responsibility, he felt, now bound him to the group of young men he lived with in New York. "If when this fever attacks our neighbourhood I run away, I am not sure that I shall do right. E.H.S. at least, probably Johnson, will remain, at all events; and if I run the risk of requiring to be nursed, I must not forget that others may require to be nursed by me, in a disease where personal attentions are *all* in *all*."[30]

This network of duty and support had been carrying the weight of Brown's new identity as an author, but the network was too fragile to hold up under the strain of an epidemic. In retrospect, the last straw would seem to have been the burden of caring for a man who was a relative outsider. Joseph B. Scandella, a doctor from Italy, had first paid Smith a visit on 22 January 1798. He shared Smith's professional curiosity about yellow fever, and Smith compiled for him a list of U.S. publications on the subject. On 11 September 1798, Scandella returned from a visit to Philadelphia in poor health. Because he was already sick, no boardinghouse would lodge him, and no nurse could be hired to care for him. Smith therefore brought Scandella into his own home to attend him personally. Although Smith had not altogether recovered from his own bout of infection, he assured Benjamin Rush by letter that "Dr. Scandella of Venice . . .

is now in my house, & all that the faculty of N. York can do for his relief will be attempted."[31]

No one begrudged Scandella this care. "Of an opulent and distinguished family," Scandella had made himself vulnerable to infection by caring for "an amiable family of helpless females" in Philadelphia. The Italian's intelligence and gentility made his case particularly affecting. "Poor Scandella has excited all my apprehension & sympathies," Smith wrote in his last diary entry. "The history of this most accomplished, & most unfortunate man is calculated to awaken the deepest interest & foster the profoundest regrets." Brown called Scandella "an Italian gentleman of great merit," whose illness led Brown to regret that "the victims to this disease have been in innumerable cases, selected from the highest and most respectable class of inhabitants." Unfortunately, on Saturday, 15 September, Smith suffered a relapse, perhaps triggered by the stress of treating Scandella. On Sunday, 16 September, Brown reported to his brother that "our Italian friend is dead." Brown added that Smith, in his remaining lucid hours, had had second thoughts about his altruistic decision to take Scandella in. "Before his last attack E.H.S. became sensible of the disproportionate hazard which he incurred."[32]

Smith himself died on Wednesday, 19 September 1798, just after noon. "He saw the last symptom of the disease, black vomit, pronounced the word 'decomposition' and died." Brown, also ill, had been staying in Dr. Edward Miller's house since Sunday; Smith's death left him distraught. "The die is cast," Brown wrote to his brother. "E.H.S. is dead. O the folly of prediction and the vanity of systems."[33]

*Decomposition* — it was the last word of a scientist, who was struggling toward understanding even as his self dissolved. But Smith lost the struggle. Order had been routed, and the process of making reality into sense reversed. William Johnson echoed Brown's lament of system when he broke the news to Dunlap. "How fallacious is hope!" Johnson wrote. "How vain is theory!"[34] Smith's intellectual force had mustered and held together a community of thinkers with the courage to explore anarchy and deism, as well as science. But Godwin and vegetarianism had not saved Smith. His radical vision of society had held a place for Brown as an author. Now, however, this authorial identity seemed likely to disintegrate, decaying as if in sympathy with the corpse of the man who had helped Brown to realize it. Sympathy for Scandella had killed Smith. Would sympathy for Smith kill Brown?

"The survivors of the sacred fellowship," as Brown called them, gathered at Dunlap's country home in Perth Amboy in the immediate aftermath. Yo-yoing between Philadelphia and New York, Brown remained in their society — and in communion with Smith's spirit — for several years. But with the loss of

Smith, the group retreated from theory and systems. Just a week before the tragedy, Dunlap had dropped hints of Christian belief, and now Smith's parents were inquiring through a third party whether their son had died a deist. Brown presented a copy of *Wieland* to President Jefferson in December, but a few years later, he had left his radicalism so far behind as to write pamphlets for the Federalists.[35]

Charles Brockden Brown wrote slipshod plots, and *Arthur Mervyn* contains one of his worst. Dunlap listed a few of its narratological offenses: "making Mervyn perfectly resemble both Lodi and Clavering, without any necessity for his resembling either; exciting an interest in Mrs. Wentworth, and leaving her and her story, like Butler's bear and fiddle; keeping Welbeck's servants quietly asleep in the house, while pistols are discharged, murder committed, the dead body buried, etc." Nor was this list comprehensive. Dunlap elsewhere pointed out that although what Arthur saw in Welbeck's attic "furnished matter which my curiosity devoured with unspeakable eagerness," the reader never finds out what it was (213).[36] Dunlap also drew attention to poor Eliza Hadwin, who for seven-eighths of the novel looks to be the heroine, but whom, in the last fifty pages, both hero and author ruthlessly ditch—"abandoned," Dunlap says, "in a manner as unexpected as disgusting." Dunlap might have added that according to chapter 2, all the Mervyn men die of a congenital illness at age twenty, but the book ends before Arthur reaches twenty-one. When the Quaker diarist Elizabeth Drinker read the book, she recorded her disappointment tersely: "Arthur Mervyn, or memoirs of the year 1793. Said to be written by Charles Brown, son of Elijah Brown—It ends without finishing."[37]

There is, however, order in Brown's chaos—a structure somewhat obscured by its own decomposition. Whereas *Wieland* stages the dangers that sympathy with a father poses for a child's voice, *Arthur Mervyn* stages the dangers to which sympathy with another man exposes a citizen's body.

Brown presents the series of implausible plot fragments as a novel, but it may be more profitable to read them as a dream—that is, as the disguised fulfillment in fantasy of a disavowed wish. For method, a reader might turn to Freud's hint about narrative disfigurement in the Dora case: "The patients' inability to give an ordered history of their life in so far as it coincides with the history of their illness is not merely characteristic of the neurosis. It also possesses great theoretical significance."[38] Freud felt that a narrative with gaps and doubts was still susceptible of cure. Left untreated, the patient's conscious and unconscious disingenuousness eventually smoothed the story over with lies. But a narrative voice still struggling against repression would waver and omit. The questions to answer, then, are the following: With his gaps and non sequiturs, what is Arthur Mervyn (or through him, Brown) trying not to say? And why doesn't he say it?

The novel opens in the autumn of 1793. A plague of yellow fever has overrun Philadelphia. One evening the kindly Dr. Stevens happens upon a young and attractive male fever victim sitting in the street. An upstanding citizen of the eighteenth century, Stevens is filled with sympathy. "I scarcely ever beheld an object which laid so powerful and sudden a claim to my affection and succour," he says (6). The sight of Arthur appeals to Stevens as suddenly and overwhelmingly as the voice of Carwin moved Clara Wieland. But Stevens does not immediately act on his sentimental impulse — the first sign that this is a thoughtful rather than a pious novel. He consults his wife, and they weigh the pros and cons. If Stevens brings home this strange young man, he risks infecting himself and his family. Is the young man worth it?

It may help to put Stevens's sympathetic reaction in context. Social philosophers such as Francis Hutcheson and Adam Smith had brought forward sympathy as the antidote to Hobbes's cynical and Locke's amoral views of human nature. Spontaneous, irrational, and nearly automatic, sympathy prompted men to do good almost in spite of themselves. Also called benevolence, it was defined by Hutcheson as "a real internal undissembled desire of the welfare of others." For these philosophers, the altruistic impulse was an article of faith, although usually it was presented as a self-evident fact of human nature, as a matter of common (that is, shared) sense. In Adam Ferguson's example, "it is unthinkable that a mother in presenting the breast to her child has in view some future returns." Although Adam Smith saw sympathy as an imaginative transposition of selves, he did not believe that sympathy therefore derived from self-love, and to prove his point, he, too, chose an example from domestic life. "A man may sympathize with a woman in child-bed; though it is impossible that he should conceive himself as suffering her pains in his own proper person and character." According to these commonsense philosophers, our most intimate emotions are naturally selfless, and human nature is therefore essentially good.[39]

But if the eighteenth century's faith in sympathy was fresher than our own, so was its sense of the dangers. Once duty yielded to sympathy, a young woman in a sentimental novel was invariably ruined. Sympathy was contraindicated for doctors, too. During the 1793 yellow fever epidemic, Benjamin Rush wrote to his wife that he struggled against sympathy in order to stay healthy: "I do not neglect to use every precaution that experience has discovered to prevent taking the infection. I even strive to subdue my sympathy for my patients; otherwise I should sink under the accumulated loads of misery I am obliged to contemplate." When the bereaved mother of a fever victim embraced him, Rush, "finding myself sinking into sympathy, tore myself from her arms." When Rush finally did catch yellow fever, he attributed his infection in part to "a *last look* from a beloved friend who had been killed by a [Frenc]h physician. I never can forget his [fran]tic cries to me in his last moments [of] 'help — help.'" It may or may not be a coincidence that this beloved friend's name was Mervin.[40]

It was a commonplace in the eighteenth century to compare the spread of sympathy to the spread of disease. "All our affections and passions," Francis Hutcheson wrote, "seem naturally contagious."[41] When Arthur Mervyn's tears cause tears in a benevolent old Quaker, Arthur observes that his own "sympathy . . . had proved contagious" (151). But what if sympathy were not only as insinuating as disease, but as lethal? Described in Brown's novel as "a poisonous and subtle fluid" (144), the contagion of yellow fever acts in the novel as an objective correlative for the dangers associated with highly charged emotions.

Yellow fever acted this way in real life, too. For a few months, the actual epidemic of 1793 turned everyone in Philadelphia into a Charles Brockden Brown character, allergic to conventional sympathy and pitching wildly between suspicious isolation and abject dependence. During the plague, most of the usual, social forms of physical intimacy seemed too perilous to indulge. Philadelphians stopped shaking hands. They avoided barbers and hairdressers, whose occupations brought them into regular contact with many people, and even bought their own lancets to avoid contact with doctors. The streets were nearly empty. Susanna Dillwyn wrote to her father that "servants are unwilling even to go to a pump for water, and those who walk the street hold handkerchiefs wet with vinegar to their faces, and fear to speak to each other." According to the merchant John Welsh, "At present there is not much satisfaction to be derived from Society — distrust seems to pervade those that were near & familiar companions. . . . The people shun each other as if death was the inevitable follower of a touch, or, as if they perceiv'd a baneful fume breathed from the others nostrils." Dr. Rush claimed that "if it was the season of vegetation the Grass would grow in the streets."[42]

The sick were the most feared. Although the coffinmaker Joseph Price did a brisk business, he would not enter the houses of his customers. He described one coffin delivery in his diary thus: "Set off took the Coffin there did not go withing 25 yd. of the house & used a spung & venegar rue & Garlick to smell at." To avoid ostracism, people tried to hide any symptoms that might indicate infection. When a cigar made Elizabeth Drinker's son Henry nauseous, "he made shift to get into G Hessers Orchard, where he discharg'd his Stomach, he was fearfull of doing so on the road, least he should be suspected of having the prevailing disorder." Those who nursed fever victims often found themselves rewarded with the status of pariah. There were stories of husbands leaving sick wives, children abandoning unhealthy parents, and servants and masters precipitately packing each other off to the hospital. Even within families who continued to care for one another, the infected and the uninfected were kept as separate as possible. Caspar Wistar Haines was not allowed to enter the room where his mother was dying. "I have not yet seen her," he wrote to his wife, who was safely out of town, "& she has requested I woud not attempt coming in to her Room but pro poses her getting to the Window to look at me which however hard shall for the present put up with." To indicate that the letter carrying this news was safe to read, Caspar marked on the outside that it had been "well smoked." Since horses were harder to fumigate, the letter also bore instructions to "tell Felty to turn this Horse into the Pasture & then nobody go near him."[43]

In Brown's novel, it is, in other words, an act of exceptional courage and generosity for Dr. Stevens to offer to house and care for a fever victim he has found on the street.[44] It is so extraordinary, in fact, that Arthur resists. Either suspicious or desperate, Arthur asks, "Why should you risk your safety for the sake of one, whom your kindness cannot benefit, and who has nothing to give in return?" (7) No one can answer this question. Stevens's response, "Let us try," obliges Arthur to produce the narrative that follows, to attempt to justify the trust that Stevens has extended without warrant.

Stevens acts out of faith and love. Reason is never up to the task of explaining emotions, but this is not the only difficulty that Arthur's narrative has to struggle with. Faith and love themselves seem to frighten Arthur, who riddles his story with faults and self-doubts as if to fend them off. His specialty is the unsolvable moral puzzle describing a choice that no one would have held against him if he hadn't brought it up. When he accidentally crosses the toll bridge into Philadelphia without paying his fee, for example, he considers turning back to wake up the toll collector even though he is penniless. It is as though he wants to call attention to the moral compromise that his financial and social vulnerability has produced. Arthur incriminates himself again and again with a candor that makes it impossible to believe he is merely a criminal. He admits that he watched a will be burned and did not try to stop the crime — but he admits this to the beneficiary of the burnt will, now disinherited. "I can scarcely tell whether this simplicity be real or affected," the matronly Mrs. Wentworth observes in exasperation (359). Arthur's lover, Achsa Fielding, has a more gentle explanation, which Arthur paraphrases: "Ordinary rules were so totally overlooked in my behaviour, that it seemed impossible for any one who knew me to adhere to them. No option was left but to admit my claims to friendship and confidence, instantly, or to reject them altogether" (397).

In other words, Arthur does not negotiate faith or love. Either they spring forth fully formed or not at all. He is incapable of gauging whether someone is trustworthy and likewise incapable of following the social conventions that would signal to others that *he* is trustworthy. For a young man who arrives in a metropolis without friends or money, these defects are disastrous. But at this point I ought to return to the question of gaps and incoherences, lest like Arthur's, my narrative be accused of making promises it does not keep.

In the preface, Brown promises to "depict . . . in lively colors the evils of disease and poverty," but once Arthur starts to tell his story, there is no mention of the plague for more than a hundred pages (3). Instead, Arthur describes men unworthy of his dependence, on whom Arthur nonetheless becomes dependent — nightmare rehearsals for his redemptive relationship with Dr. Stevens. The most important of these figures is Welbeck, the villain — an impostor, seducer, murderer, and forger to whom Arthur will be more or less apprenticed. But before Welbeck, there is the odd case of Wallace.

Flat broke, Arthur is moping in a tavern when Wallace approaches him. With genteel clothes and polite manners, Wallace makes a good first impression. He buys Arthur dinner. Then he invites Arthur to come home and share his bed. Arthur is suspicious. "I saw no reason why I should be treated with benevolence" (32). But Arthur second-guesses himself. Because he knows himself to be suspicious, he decides to err on the side of inappropriate trust. He is too poor to rob, and maybe Wallace sees in Arthur a man with a future, whom it would pay to befriend. As Arthur puts it, "I was not devoid of all mental and personal endowments" (33). So Arthur follows Wallace home.

What happens next is fascinatingly odd. Wallace sneaks Arthur into the bedroom of an opulent mansion, blows out the candle, orders Arthur to undress, and vanishes. Arthur discovers a baby sleeping in the bed, hears footsteps, and hides in the closet. While Arthur eavesdrops, the baby's natural father comes in to kiss it, and then fetches his wife, to whom he pretends the baby is a foundling. Duped, she adopts it. Once they fall asleep, Arthur tiptoes out of the house in his stocking feet.

The most remarkable thing about this episode is that man, wife, and child resurface only once more, a hundred pages later, dead of yellow fever. In other words, they have nothing to do with the rest of the book. Reflecting on the adoption, Arthur is amazed at "the slightness of that thread by which human passions are led from their true direction" (39). But a reader might also be impressed by the slightness of the plot device that leads Arthur and Wallace away from the direction of their initial passions. The conclusion of this scene is no more legitimate than the baby in it. The reader as well as the wife is fooled into accepting something whose origins should perhaps be more closely examined.

What would have happened in this bedroom if no baby had been there and if no heterosexual couple had intruded? What if Wallace had carried out his first intention and shared his bed with Arthur? Wallace himself was later unable to account for his mischievous decision to put Arthur in his master's bed rather than his own. Perhaps Wallace's initial motive was sexual, but then he lost his nerve, and the episode degenerated into a prank. Arthur later excuses Wallace for introducing him into "a situation so romantic and perilous" by attributing to him the motive of "juvenile wantonness" (136). But juvenile wantonness does not quite explain away what looks to a modern eye like a narrowly averted homosexual seduction.

Sex may be merely what a modern reader projects onto a blank when confronted with an unexplained intimacy between strangers. Onto the same blank, Brown wrote a deformed parable of heterosexuality. The blank was located in the "perilous precincts of private property" — to borrow Arthur's gratuitously alliterative phrasing — between two men, in age and social rank more or less equals, linked by a desire that Arthur could not identify, which Wallace later qualified by saying, "I meant only to sport with your simplicity and ignorance" (175).

Willy-nilly, Arthur was vulnerable to other men. He welcomed intimate dependence on Dr. Stevens, who was older and who was clearly established as Arthur's social superior. He despised intimate dependence on Welbeck, which he could write off as a regrettable mistake, a relationship he was forced into by poverty and friendlessness. But an increasingly democratic society demanded of Arthur something more frighteningly ambiguous: intimacy and reliance on someone who was neither hero nor villain, someone as ambitious, impulsive, unstable, dependent, opportunistic, and fluxional as Arthur himself. Arthur cannot take his place in the deferential order of betters and worses that had structured colonial society; after the Revolution, there are only peers, like Wallace, for Arthur to count on and commit to.

Interdependence is too scary, and so, by a trick of the plot, Wallace vanishes, along with Arthur's shoes. He reappears much later, when Arthur discovers that he and Wallace are suitors to a pair of sisters, Eliza and Susan Hadwin. (The women link the men, but they also neatly heterosexualize the link.) In what is probably not an accident, Wallace's return to the narrative coincides with the reappearance of the plague. Wallace is at the epicenter of the yellow fever, in downtown Philadelphia. Safe in the countryside, Arthur decides to find and rescue Wallace, not because he loves or esteems him, but because they are scheduled to become in-laws: "His welfare was essential to the happiness of those, whose happiness had become essential to mine" (133). The question that needles Arthur, though, is the same question he asked Dr. Stevens about himself: Is he worth the risk? "The preservation of this man, was my sole motive for entering the infected city, and subjecting my own life to the hazards, from which my escape may almost be esteemed miraculous. Was there arrogance in believing my life a price too great to be given for his?" (270).

Like many of Brown's idées fixes, the notion of comparing the worth of human beings derives from Godwin. It was a peculiarly elitist component of Godwin's system of anarchy that Godwin did not believe all men were created equal. "In a loose and general view I and my neighbour are both of us men; and of consequence entitled to equal attention. But, in reality, it is probable that one of us is a being of more worth and importance than the other." To demonstrate his point, Godwin proposed a thought experiment. Suppose Fénelon and his valet are trapped in a burning palace, and I can save only one. Whom should I rescue? "In saving the life of Fénelon, suppose at the moment he conceived the project of his immortal Telemachus, I should have been promoting the benefit of thousands who have been cured by the perusal of that work of some error, vice and consequent unhappiness." Even if I myself were the valet, Godwin continued, justice would require me to prefer Fénelon's survival to my own. If the valet were my father or my brother, Fénelon should still be my choice. As a young author struggling to convince himself that his work counted, Brown must have been captivated by this example: the writer with a book in his head trumps all other cards.[45]

Unfortunately, marketplaces rarely rate unpublished authors as highly as Godwin did. An occluded sense of oneself as promising cannot be meaningfully priced. Society will pay for scriveners but not for unproven authors, and so when Arthur volunteers to Welbeck that he is qualified to work as a "writer," Welbeck hires him as a forger. In *Wieland,* Theodore became a copyist of his father, sacrificing his self for the sake of union with patriarchal power. In *Arthur Mervyn,* the problem is slightly different. Arthur's brothers, he explains, were the "copyists of the father, whom they resembled in temper and person" (343). But Arthur himself is in danger of becoming the salaried impostor of anyone who comes along with enough cash. If Wallace offers him dinner and a bed, Arthur has no choice but to go home with him. One night may not be too much to pay, but a lifetime is costly.

This anxiety explains another of the great non sequiturs in the novel. Looking for Wallace, Arthur returns to the same room in the same mansion where their earlier assignation did not take place. As he approaches the bedchamber, "a vapour, infectious and deadly," assails him. Arthur feels the shock of infection overtake him, and he knows "the work of corrosion and decomposition to be busily begun." He does not quail, however. "This incident, instead of appalling me, tended rather to invigorate my courage" (144). With nothing to lose, Arthur draws back the curtains of the sickbed to discover whether Wallace is dying or already dead.

But instead of Wallace, Arthur finds a man unexpectedly noble and beautiful. "Was he not one in whose place I would willingly have died?" Arthur wails, grateful for a plot twist that, like a neurotic fantasy, reassures him that he has not become infected with the yellow fever merely for the sake of a fellow democrat but rather for a scion of European royal blood (147). This beautiful, ethereal man, named Maravegli, dies fast, and he vanishes from the plot just as rapidly. But his meteoric appearance serves a function; he represents an untenable nostalgia for hierarchy, for a world where power relations between men were unequal but reciprocal and where a sacrifice like Arthur's held meaning. Arthur greets the apparition with an ecstasy that is almost erotic. "The life of Wallace was of more value to a feeble individual [Susan Hadwin], but surely the being that was stretched before me and who was hastening to his last breath was precious to thousands" (147). The excess emotion that Arthur spills for what is more or less a pretty corpse marks him as something of a decadent.

Although this sudden Italian beauty violates the principles of dramatic unity and narrative economy, he is not irrelevant. Within the novel, he falls into a class of not quite this-worldly men on whom Arthur has a crush. Remember Dunlap's complaint, quoted above, that Arthur resembles Clavering and Vincentio Lodi for no good reason. All of these men are upper class; none of them are hardy; all of them provoke a hollow, sexualized sympathy as they expire. They seem to resemble Arthur not so much out of physical coincidence as because they have no firm identity of their own that would prevent them from drifting into his mirror. Maravegli and his fellows present a comforting illusion: it is a more beautiful version of yourself that you are dying for, they seem to say. But in fact you are dying for Wallace — the other fellow, different from but no better than you.

In *Wieland,* sympathy had to navigate between the Scylla of copyism and the Charybdis of imposture. In *Arthur Mervyn,* imposture is still one of the hazards; Welbeck is Carwin gone professional. When Welbeck asks for a writing sample to test his skill as a forger, Arthur "by some inexplicable connection" quotes the apothecary in *Romeo and Juliet:* "My poverty, but not my will consents" (50). The line makes Welbeck sob, because he recognizes in it his own identity: imposture motivated by greed.

But the opposite hazard in *Arthur Mervyn* is not copyism. Copyism does kill in this novel, but it is a quiet, mediocre sort of death. Copyism, too, has become professional, and it is what happens to men like Carlton, a debt-ridden, tubercular scrivener, whose pen is eventually "usurped by his sister" (261). In *Arthur Mervyn,* the live hazard is not copyism but infection. Like

Theodore Wieland's madness, infection collapses the middle term of sympathy. Instead of a fiction that imagines two men in unity, the link is direct. The contagion moves from one body to another. Just as contact with God raised Theodore's spirits, contact with the effluvia of yellow fever exalts Arthur. Once infected, he may "execute without faultering, the duties that circumstances might create," because he has nothing left to lose (144). But this is as far as the parallel between infection and copyism will go. Although infection may be represented in language, it happens without language, and so it falls into a different category of hazard. The danger it poses to identity cannot be resolved by a parable about reading and writing.

If infection in *Arthur Mervyn* seems at times to resemble the invasion of the self during love, this is perhaps because Brown structured his book to prove the lesson that the only cure for an illness caught by intimacy is more intimacy. As initially planned, the novel describes a sick man who gets well because another man nurses him and listens to his story. Smith himself promised Brown that intimate care would reduce mortality. As Brown relayed to his worried brother, "E.H.S. . . . answers for me that not more than one out of nine, when properly nursed, die." It was also the moral of Mathew Carey's history of the 1793 plague: "Almost all the remarkable cases of recovery are to be ascribed, under providence, to the fidelity of husbands, wives, children, and servants, who braved the danger, and determined to obey the dictates of humanity." A little more than a week before he died, Smith wrote to Rush that "I have seen no one hesitate to nurse a sick friend"; he was proud that people around him were behaving bravely and hopefully during the epidemic.[46]

The reader of the early chapters expects to watch Arthur's psychological health improve, too. At first, Arthur can't trust, and he provokes mistrust, as if he fears that his need will destroy anyone whom class status has not set apart as his irrevocable superior. Under the tolerant guidance of Dr. Stevens, however, Arthur is supposed to learn that his needs will not necessarily destroy those he takes from. He should learn not to make equals like Wallace vanish from his plot, and he should give up the sexualized idealizations that he attaches to fictional superiors like Clavering or the Italian fever victim. But for this recuperation to occur, Stevens must survive the attacks of the illness that Arthur carries.

I suspect that Smith's death, while Brown was composing the novel, threw these lines of development into doubt. Stevens survives, but he never comes into focus as a character. His offer to train Arthur to be a doctor does not settle Arthur's anxiety. As if he senses that Stevens is no longer strong enough to ground him, the Arthur of the second half of the book rushes from woman to woman, attempting rescues and seeking money without a sense of purpose.

It would be misleading to force the two parts of this novel into an organic whole. The second part of *Arthur Mervyn* was written a year later than the first — a crucial interval for Brown. Part 2 was not written while Brown mourned Smith but during Brown's post-Smith life as a magazine editor and Elizabeth Linn's fiancé. To some degree, the uxorious Arthur of part 2 belongs with the heroes of *Clara Howard* and *Jane Talbot* more than he belongs with the earlier version of himself. By spanning two phases of Brown's literary and personal development, the book registers in its disjunctures Brown's generic shift from Gothic to sentimental fiction and his protagonist's psychological shift from dependence on men to dependence on women.

Arthur manages to tell his story, but it is not clear that Arthur's final psychic state is healthy. He might, instead, be more coherently fraudulent; that is, it may be that he smoothly and volubly avoids saying the things he stammered over in his first chapters. After all, Freud's thesis about the flaws in his patients' plots, quoted above, has an unfortunate corollary predicting that the narrative of an incurable neurotic, whose lies have grown to fill every awkward silence, would be indistinguishable in its seamlessness from that told by someone in perfect psychic health. There is no evidence, for example, that Arthur learns to accept his resemblance to Wallace. In fact, he damns Wallace for failing to follow through on his engagement to Susan, when Arthur himself drops his engagement to her sister Eliza with just as little thought. Nor does Arthur give up his sexualization of dependence. His marriage to Achsa Fielding merely combines all the elements of his crushes on male aristocrats — Achsa is European, older, wiser, and richer — with a heterosexual object. Arthur is not altogether comfortable with heterosexuality, however. The prospect of union with Achsa provokes the only reported dream in the novel, about Achsa's husband, Mr. Fielding, "a champion of the people" who was destroyed by the French Revolution that he had helped to foment (426). In the dream, the radical politician returns from the dead and in a jealous rage stabs Arthur with his "shining steel" (437).

On the last page, Arthur puts down his own weapon. Love for Clavering inspired Arthur to write "a few elegiac stanzas" (30), but love for Achsa leads him to condemn writing as "pen-prattle" (446). "I *will* abjure thee," Arthur tells his pen, "so let *this* be thy last office." The novel thus ends with another gap, placed to be invisible.

A form of eros underlay the sense of trust that was being established between citizens in America's new democracy, and in the novel *Arthur Mervyn,* the stress of the 1793 and 1798 plagues has flushed anxieties about that attachment into expression. During the plagues, mourning and shock may have rendered Brown's personal attachments to men more poignant and more frightening, thereby troubling his new identity as an author, which their society had nurtured. As a result, in this book Brown's expression of male-male eros takes the form of evanescent idealization and suggestive indirection — a far cry from Whitman's brash and utopian adhesiveness half a century later. Because Brown feared that sympathy with a male equal might cause the self to disintegrate, corrupted by either market forces or infectious agents, in the end he chose marriage to a woman, and silence. In Brown's fiction, plague makes love for fellow citizens a risk that is experienced with charged and ambivalent emotions.

Brown was not the only writer suspicious of sympathy in 1790s America. Writing under the name Peter Porcupine, William Cobbett liked to point out that the Jeffersonians' communal solidarity had a nasty side. He mocked the anti-Federalists for their knee-jerk resentment of traditional social distinctions and their infatuation with all things democratic, including the new French Republic. Conspiracy theories about unscrupulous political radicals fascinated both writers. Cobbett thought he detected Jacobin sedition lurking in Irish immigrant groups in the United States; Brown's villains flaunted connections to such organizations as the Society of the Illuminati. Brown feared what sympathy would do to the American self; Cobbett feared that American political culture would be corroded by sympathy with the French Revolution. Both men abruptly switched their politics as the century turned — Brown from left to right, Cobbett from right to left.

Like Brown, Cobbett suggested that sympathy might not be as benevolent as it seemed. For instance, Cobbett loathed Dr. Benjamin Rush for his unctuous, showy compassion. "To see and hear him, you would think he was all friendship and humanity." He also despised Rush's "silly sans-culottish" politics. To puncture this smiling mask and debunk the people's-servant pose, Cobbett harped on Rush's intransigent belief in the efficacy of bleeding and purging. He listed the colleagues that Rush's stubbornness had alienated and the patients that Rush-style treatment had probably killed — including George Washington. To a New York newspaper that called Rush "a man born to be useful to society," Cobbett answered, "And so is a *musquito*, a *horse-leech*, a *ferret*, a *pole cat*, a *weazel*: for these are all *bleeders*, and understand their business full as well as Doctor Rush does his." Cobbett refuted the admiration of those who saw Rush as a hero of the 1793 plague by correlating mortality tables against Rush's claims of cure. Where Brown's mode was Gothic, Cobbett's was satiric. But both writers used the deaths of the yellow fever epidemic to give the rhetoric of sympathy the lie.[47]

Cobbett's attacks on sympathy and left-wing politics mirror Brown's novelistic explorations; and like a mirror, Cobbett's picture of the world reverses Brown's — Cobbett loathed the utopian politics that appealed to the young

Brown — but in that reversed image, some connections are easier to see. Cobbett's jokes, for example, explicitly link same-sex intimacy and anarchic rebellion. For Cobbett, too close a sympathy with one's fellow man was not only politically dangerous but also sexually ridiculous. Although sexual orthodoxy was not Cobbett's prime concern, his attacks on the Democratic-Republic clubs are to a modern reader mildly homophobic. He taunted club members with the prospect that women would resent the enthusiastic new democratic intimacy between men: "Must not their gander-frolicks, and their squeezing, and hugging, and kissing one another, be expected to cause a good deal of pouting and jealousy [among women]?" Elsewhere Cobbett mocked the new democratic vocabulary for the clumsy way it tried to preserve gender differences while erasing all other social distinctions: "Our good ancestors had not foreseen these days of equality, and had therefore never thought of a termination to express the *feminine* of a *free-man*. To say that *citizen* A. was married to *citizen* B. would have had a brutal sound, even in the ears of a Jacobin, and therefore the ingenious news-man invented a termination, and his paragraph ran thus: 'On —— *Citizen* —— was married to *Citess* —— by *Citizen* ——.'" The snicker here is to suggest that thanks to all this French-style leveling, the wedding of Citizen Jacques to Citizen Pierre is not far off.[48]

Cobbett's gibes reveal, I think, why Arthur Mervyn dreams of a man the night before he proposes to Achsa Fielding. Cobbett's ridicule and Brown's horror both derive from a fear (coexistent in Brown's case with a denied wish) that political anarchy might lead to sexual anarchy — that during a revolution, gender and sexual desire might cease to be governed by traditional restraints. As a deputy to the French National Assembly — "the adherent of violent measures, till the subversion of monarchy" — Mr. Fielding represents political disorder.[49] And that political disorder carries a sexual charge. Just as a woman like Achsa represents authority, by means of her wealth, age, and British citizenship, a man like her husband represents rebellion. In the end Arthur chooses Achsa because in his imagination, marriage to (female) authority averts the stab you might receive from friendship with (male) rebellion.

Similarly, in Brown's *Memoirs of Stephen Calvert* the divide between the twins Felix and Stephen has both an erotic and a political valence. When the novel opens, Stephen is having trouble obeying the sexual norms of his culture. "I am fickle and fantastic," he says, blaming a libertine French novel, "not a moral or rational, or political being, but a thing of mere sex" (192).[50] But Stephen's dirty mind may not be the novelist Scudéry's fault. It may be due instead to the fantasies inspired by his separation from his twin. As an infant, Stephen emigrated to America with the boys' properly Protestant parents, but Felix remained behind in England with their grandfather, a Catholic Jacobite who plotted an overthrow of the British king synchronized with a French invasion. Stephen thinks of Felix as a lost part of himself. When he imagines a reunion with his brother, he sounds a little like the Aristophanes of Plato's *Symposium,* mourning the curse that split contented four-legged beings into discontented two-legged ones. "For want of experience I imagined that there was something peculiarly sacred and tender in the bond of brotherhood, and that this tie was unspeakably enhanced by the circumstance of being ushered into being together; of being coeval in age, and alike in constitution and figure" (97). That Felix was reared by a would-be regicide enhances his mystique. Felix actually committed the adultery that Stephen is only accused of, and when Felix is sighted in America, he appears to be as comfortable with his sexual amorality as Stephen is tortured by his attempt to conform.

Written just before Smith's death, the fragmentary *Stephen Calvert* is the one piece of his fiction where Brown broaches the topic of sodomy. When, in the passage quoted above, Stephen uses the word "unspeakably" to describe his enhanced tie to his twin, he may be exaggerating for vague Gothic effect. But he may also be prompting the reader to think of the sin known for its lack of a name. "Unspeakable" is how Clelia Neville describes what she caught her husband doing with other men. "Under a veil of darkness, propensities were indulged by my husband, that have not a name which I can utter. They cannot be thought of without horror. They cannot be related" (204).

There is nothing peculiar about how Clelia words her shock; preterition was the conventional way to represent sodomy. But it is peculiar that two pages after she walks in on her husband in flagrante delicto — "I cannot utter it" (205) — Clelia uses the same words to describe her affection for her aunt, Mrs. Keith. "I looked after my beloved friend with unspeakable longings," Clelia says. She wants terribly to follow her aunt to America, but "this desire I never dared to utter, and made haste to stifle so flattering a gratification" (207). Brown uses the same phrasing to indicate both the horror of sodomy and the intensity of affection in a same-sex friendship. In his hurried style, Brown often repeats stock sets of words, but the coincidence is telling, even if caused by inattention rather than deliberate choice.

*Stephen Calvert* brings same-sex sympathy to the brink of something else. The book ends just as Stephen is about to meet his twin for the first time since infancy. "My heart throbbed as if I were on the eve of some fatal revolution. The suddenness of this occurrence, the meeting with a brother so long severed from my side, and whose mode of birth made him, in some sort, an essential part of myself, seemed like passage into a new state of being" (272). Brown never finished *Stephen Calvert,* perhaps because Smith's death derailed this line of exploration. But perhaps Brown could never have said what this new state of being would have consisted of. Radical politics promised that extreme sympathy would change the world, and so Brown described crossing this threshold as a revolution. But he may have described this revolution as fatal because he could imagine no life — and no narrative — after it.

Death, as a literary figure, may have represented a decision not to imagine where sympathy between men might lead. But the actual death of a friend presented a different kind of problem to a writer whose works explored and exploited the ambiguities of sympathy. If literature is a play of language between two friends, what game is possible once your playmate is dead? Brown survived Smith. Surprisingly, in the immediate aftermath of Smith's death Brown's writing survived, too. Brown's professional life was steady and fruitful. In the autumn and winter of 1798, he wrote the novel *Ormond; or, The Secret Witness*. And, to his novel writing, Brown added the project of editing a new magazine, which he launched in April 1799. Robert A. Ferguson has suggested that to gain a further reprieve from his family's expectations, Brown may have exploited the pity they felt for his loss of Smith, much as in 1795 he had pleaded Wilkins's death as an excuse for not taking the bar exam. Brown was working hard to consolidate his literary career. As Dunlap wrote in his biography of Brown, "He at this time carried into effect, the plan which had long been forming in his mind of becoming an author by profession; of devoting his life to book-making, and trusting his future fortunes, as well as fame, to the labours of his pen." The plan of professional authorship was in Brown's mind in large part because Smith had helped to put it there. Brown had been writing prolifically well before Smith fell ill. But Smith's death made the matter urgent. Brown now *had* to succeed, because he had lost the person who in the past had picked him up and dusted him off when he had failed.[51]

Brown eventually discovered that "*authorship* is not a *profession*" in America. But in a letter to his brother Armit on New Year's Day, 1799, Brown still hoped that it was. The contrast between this letter and Brown's New Year's Day letter of 1798 is striking. Brown in 1799 greets the new year calmly, grateful for a life that is uneventful and productive. He opens by sidestepping the suggestion that he ought to be shouldering "conjugal and paternal cares." He goes on to describe his daily schedule, as if to prove that writing is a job like any other, with its own rhythms and rewards, however modest. "As to me, the surface of my life would be thought, by most observers, tolerably smooth. I rise at eight, am seated by a comfortable fire, breakfast plenteously and in quiet, and with a companion who is a model of all the social and domestic virtues. All personal and household services are performed for me without the trouble of superintendence and direction. The writing occupation is pursued, with every advantageous circumstance of silence, solitude, pure air, cleanliness and warmth." No longer is writing a crime, furtively committed in stolen hours. It is now an "occupation" — "my voluntary and variable task," Brown calls it. It has a certain heft. But although Brown is rejoicing, quietly, that his avocation has at last become his vocation, the letter ends on a note of valediction, if not resignation: "It is time to end this letter. To write it was the first employment of the new year, and will be the sole employment of the kind, that will take place on this day. . . . On this day, all the world is busied in visiting and congratulation and feasting. I believe I shall, in this instance, act, in some degree, like all the world."

On the first day of 1798, Brown had asked, "How can I remove the burthen of your scorn but by transforming myself into a new being?" One year and three novels later, Brown's anxiety and self-hatred have so far dissipated as to allow him to take comfort in acting "like all the world." But to act like all the world means, in this letter, not to spend the day writing.[52]

By the summer of 1799, Brown had finished *Edgar Huntly*, a rewrite of his lost first novel, "Sky-Walk." It was the last novel of Brown's second phase — the last book that modern critics consider artistically serious and the last to contain "gloominess and out-of-nature incidents," as Brown himself put it a year later, when explaining to his brother James why he had abandoned the Gothic style. On 26 July 1799, Brown wrote to his brother that yellow fever was creeping back into New York. This time, Brown and his friends had no intention of staying in the city to face the danger. Everyone planned to flee. "Those friends who then [in 1798] were as hard as myself are already alarmed, and all those whose safety is particularly dear to me, will vanish from this scene as well as myself." Heroic solidarity had given way to realistic fear. The self who had written novels as though they were stronger than the plague now seemed like a stranger to Brown. He looked back on this self "with astonishment." "That I could muse and write cheerfully in spite of the groans of the dying and the rumbling of hearses, and in spite of a thousand tokens of indisposition in my own frame, is now almost incredible." Brown no longer understood how he could have made art in the midst of death.[53]

In *Edgar Huntly*, Brown mourns both his friend Elihu Hubbard Smith and the fiction he had written for Smith — in particular, "Sky-Walk." To revise an old novel and to write about a dead friend present similar challenges to an artist: in both cases, the artist must extend sympathy to something that was once dear but is no longer living. Both exercises feel painfully artificial. It also feels cruel that the unacceptable text and the friend's corpse, however cherished they were when alive, must now be discarded, if not destroyed. As acts of mourning, both processes stir up ambivalence toward the lost object. Putting a friend down on paper certifies that the friend is gone; it may feel like participating in that death. And no one kills a piece of writing so authoritatively as a writer who undertakes a new draft.

The death of a friend brings our true feelings about the friend to the surface, because on the one hand, there is no longer any reason to pretend more affection than one actually felt, and on the other hand, deep grief demands to be let out. But any demonstration of affection after a friend's death is futile as far as the friend is concerned. The interlocutors in Cicero's "Laelius: On Friendship" examine Laelius about his feelings for Scipio Africanus just after Scipio's death. Cicero chose this moment because Laelius would be free to say how he really felt, but the freedom of the text is linked to its uselessness. "Of course I am upset," Laelius admits. But he praises Cato's refusal to cry for his son, because death hurts only the living, not the dead. "I do not believe Scipio himself has suffered any misfortune. If anyone has suffered a misfortune, it is myself." If there is any point to sympathizing with the dead, it is a selfish one. The high-minded thing to do is not to mourn; but as Freud and Klein have noted, it is the disavowal of mourning's selfish ends that renders it morbid.[54]

When Adam Smith described the process of sympathizing with the dead, his prose turned as grotesque as anything Brown ever wrote. When we feel sorry for a friend who has died violently, Smith said, "we enter, as it were, into his body, and in our imaginations, in some measure, animate anew the deformed and mangled carcass of the slain." Mourning turns out to be an act of Gothic fiction. We imagine something that we know is untrue; we imagine that a corpse feels. "It is miserable, we think, to be deprived of the light of the sun; to be shut out from life and conversation; to be laid in the cold grave, a prey to corruption and the reptiles of the earth; to be no more thought of in this world, but to be obliterated, in a little time, from the affections, and almost from the memory, of their dearest friends and relations." These fantasies are painful. The decaying body disgusts us. It forces us to separate from what we loved. We have to acknowledge that we cannot share the feelings of a corpse. In fact, it reminds us, we never really shared the feelings of the friend, either. Mourning appalls in part because it forces us to admit that all sympathy is fiction.[55]

Freud described mourning as a struggle between reality's demand that love be withdrawn from an object that no longer exists and love's reluctance to give up its object. Mourning hurts because it feels like a betrayal to admit that sympathy is only a story we tell, and we can find other stories to tell that will continue to relate us to the world even though our friend is dead. Also, it pains us to unwrite the story we wrote about our friend. As Freud explains, the process of separating love from the lost object requires us to parse the narrative of our love, examining it "bit by bit": "Each single one of the memories and hopes which bound the libido to the object is brought up and hyper-cathected, and the detachment of the libido from it accomplished."[56] Mourning is a line-by-line revision, by an editor who forces you to cross out your favorite passages in a sentimental fiction that you wrote only for your own pleasure.

Nonetheless, this abandonment and refashioning is what Laelius concludes we must do when a friend dies: "Since everything that is mortal is precarious and transient, we ought always to go on and on searching for people who can receive our love and be loved by us in return."[57] I suggested above that one of the questions that *Arthur Mervyn* tried to answer was whether sympathy for Elihu Hubbard Smith would kill Brown. In *Edgar Huntly*, the answer is yes. Sympathy for the dead will kill you because it prevents you from telling new stories to connect you to the world. Sympathy with the dead is perhaps the only nonfiction sympathy, in the sense that the death of emotions is faithful to a dead friend with a fidelity that living emotions for living friends can never match. This fact tempts you not to mourn. But as the narrative of *Edgar Huntly* demonstrates, refusal to mourn sentences you to live out continuously the horror that Adam Smith described, of experiencing yourself as a corpse — of being buried alive.

The characters in *Edgar Huntly* cannot shake off their troubling relationships to the dead and dying. Edgar compulsively revisits the elm where Waldegrave was shot, although he cannot bear to sleep in the bed where Waldegrave breathed his last breath. Clarice postpones her wedding to nurse a girlfriend expiring of tuberculosis. Weymouth believes his "existence and property were . . . inseparably united" to Waldegrave's life, now lost (141).[58] Mrs. Lorimer has similar fears: she is convinced that whenever her evil twin, Wiatte, dies, she will die, too. And Clithero's psychosis consists in believing Mrs. Lorimer's phobia to be literally true. When Clithero accidentally kills Wiatte, he decides to kill Mrs. Lorimer as well for her own good — "to accelerate thy journey to rest," as he puts it (83).

The death of the virtuous Waldegrave triggers much of this anxiety. Edgar can't get it out of his head. Its resemblance to Clithero's murder of Wiatte provokes Clithero to sleepwalk. But who is Waldegrave? Brown does not provide many clues. Scrupulous, benevolent, and indigent, Waldegrave "was teacher of the Negro free-school" (143). A passionate freethinker, Waldegrave argued for deism in a series of letters to Edgar. Edgar now sees this packet of letters as both toxic and precious: they could corrupt the religious principles of Waldegrave's sister, but they also represent Waldegrave at his most vital and intelligent. Although Waldegrave converted before he died, Edgar remains a deist. "I did not entirely abjure the creed which had, with great copiousness and eloquence, been defended in these letters" (133).

In a letter to Samuel Miller, responding to that writer's *Retrospect of the Eighteenth Century,* Brown saw deism as crucial to the intellectual history of the previous hundred years. In more personal terms, "French Atheistic Philosophy" had linked Brown and Elihu Hubbard Smith in vigorous discussion. Smith wrote at length to Brown and others about his loss of faith, describing his evolution from "an early & rigid Calvinistic education" to a renunciation of prayer of any sort as "inconsistent with the notions I entertain of the structure & constitution of the Universe." While Smith lived, Brown had followed him in believing that " 'Political Justice' contains a purer system of morals than the Bible." But after Smith's death, Brown defected from deism. In his fiction, infidel villains such as Ormond and Ludloe gave way to reformed heroes such as Waldegrave and *Jane Talbot*'s Henry Colden. Like Smith and Waldegrave, Colden has left a trail of correspondence that betrays his radical past as a Godwinian unbeliever: "These letters showed Colden as the advocate of suicide; a scoffer at promises; the despiser of revelation, of providence and a future state; an opponent of marriage, and as one who denied (shocking!) that any thing but mere habit and positive law, stood in the way of marriage; nay, of intercourse without marriage, between brother and sister, parent and child!" But Colden today, the novel assures us, is a responsible Christian. Characters like Waldegrave and Colden may be emblems of Smith, but they may also represent an earlier self of Brown's. After all, Smith did not live long enough to recant. Brown did. In 1803, in an editorial announcing himself as a "willing champion of the Christian religion," Brown wrote that "I should enjoy a larger share of my own respect, at the present moment, if nothing had ever flowed from my pen, the production of which could be traced to me." In the fictional *Edgar Huntly,* it is the surviving friend, strangely enough, who does not change his mind about the past. In the dead penitent Waldegrave and the living apostate Huntly, the dead apostate Smith and the living penitent Brown have to some extent switched places.[59]

When *Edgar Huntly* opens, the dead Waldegrave survives only in his letters and in his friends' memory of him. He was an author; he is now a ghost. And a ghost is a sympathetic fiction that must be unwritten. The process of mourning must revise it into a corpse, which is neither fictional nor sympathetic. Like *Wieland* and *Arthur Mervyn, Edgar Huntly* explores a deformation of sympathy — of the fictional transposition that relates spectator to sufferer — but here the case is not imposture, copyism, or infection, but haunting. The sufferer is dead, and the fiction consists in supposing him not to be. The danger to

Brown's creative process is that in ridding himself of the ghost, he may also rid himself of fiction. As he investigates what it means to love a ghost, Brown buries his characters alive. He risks smothering what he feels for them.

Whoever or whatever he may represent, Waldegrave is in a grave. His is not the only body that Brown buries in *Edgar Huntly*. Bill Christophersen has noted another pun on interment: Solebury, the name of Huntly's native town, seems to denote "the wilderness in which the soul lies buried" (142). And Norwalk, the name of the surrounding region, sounds as though it could be the second half of some pronouncement about the dead ("they shall neither sleep nor walk," perhaps). Sometimes what gets buried is not a person but a person's textual remains. While sleepwalking, Clithero buries an apologia written by Mrs. Lorimer, whom he feels obliged to kill, and Edgar similarly secretes Waldegrave's letters in the rafters of his attic. Other burials are of people not yet dead. Edgar discovers Clithero lying passed out in a pit in a hilltop—in a sort of mausoleum with a sunroof. When Edgar awakes from his episode of sleepwalking, he finds himself in a lightless underground cave where "I imagined myself buried alive" (162). Later Edgar lies in "a rift, some-what resembling a coffin in shape, and not much larger in dimensions" (217).

Like Clithero, the novel buries and unburies compulsively. "Was it a grave that he was digging?" Edgar asks when he first spies Clithero at work with a spade in the middle of the night. "Was his purpose to explore or to hide?" (10) One could ask the same question of Brown's novel. It seems obscurely to express some kind of grief, but is Brown's purpose to explore or to hide this grief? Is he trying to find something that is under the surface, such as a feeling or an insight into what a lost friend means to a writer? Or is he trying only to dig a hole, to carve out an emptiness where he may deposit a way of writing and feeling that is now dead to him?

*Edgar Huntly* is told in the interrogative mode. It is a narrative that doubts itself at every step. "For what purpose have I come hither?" Clithero asks when Edgar confronts him (35). "Is it to relate my story? Shall I calmly sit here, and rehearse the incidents of my life? Will my strength be adequate to this rehearsal?" Every dozen pages or so, the text breaks down into one of these sorites of questions (e.g., 41, 74, 80, 92, 156, 160, 171, 175, 198, 201, 220). Neither Brown's grief nor his novel know what they are about, and that is because grief is in part a reluctance to face the fact of loss. When Edgar asks a farmhand whether the Huntlys are dead, he receives this answer: "Huntly? Yes. No. He did not know. He had forgotten" (234). This, in a nutshell, is the state of knowledge in *Edgar Huntly* and during mourning: for as long as the ego will allow it, the id affects either not to know or to have forgotten that the beloved is dead.

It is a mark of the morbid nature of Brown's grief that *Edgar Huntly* is such an imperfect revision of "Sky-Walk." Bits persist of the earlier versions that Brown could not quite relinquish, and they constitute the most glaring flaw of the book. (They also cause the textual decenteredness that appeals to post-modern readers.) *Edgar Huntly* is a murder mystery when it starts. The reader is cued to expect a solution to the question Who killed Waldegrave? Suspicion falls on Clithero, spotted digging where Waldegrave was shot, and on Edgar, whose sleepwalking and persecution of Clithero suggest a guilty conscience. But the book turns out to be a great big shaggy dog story. These two trails of evidence are not so much red herrings deliberately strewn by Brown as unre-vised traces of earlier plots. In Brown's short story "Somnambulism," the sleepwalking narrator (the Edgar Huntly–like character) was the murderer. Brown retained several elements of "Somnambulism" in *Edgar Huntly,* in-cluding a narrator who anxiously discouraged the victim from riding out so late on the night in question and a conspicuous tree that marked the spot in the road where the deed was done. On the other hand, in "Sky-Walk" the mur-derer was probably the Clithero-like character, if the attention given to him in the extract published in the *Weekly Magazine* and in the comments about "Sky-Walk" in Dunlap's diary is any indication. If he was not the culprit, why would he have figured so prominently? If a sleepwalker was not to blame, why would the subtitle have been "The Man Unknown to Himself"?[60]

In *Edgar Huntly* proper, the murderer turns out to be an Indian whom we never meet, whom Edgar may have killed anonymously.[61] We do not learn his name; we are not sure that justice was done. In a way this is a darker ending than a murder by either Clithero or Edgar would have been, and it is Brown's artistry to have hit this unexpected note, whereby all the sensitive psychology of European Romanticism is rendered futile and irrelevant amid the arbitrary cruelty of race warfare. At the cost of narrative unity, Brown turns the haunt-ing of *Edgar Huntly* by its earlier drafts to advantage. This end also achieves an attitude toward Waldegrave that is almost as satisfactory as successful mourning: it leaves Waldegrave behind. By the end of the book, Waldegrave does not matter to the plot. The long distraction of Clithero's story has driven him from the reader's mind. Except for providing a corpse, his death holds no meaning. The disjointed structure of the novel does not resolve the feelings stirred up by the loss of Waldegrave but instead fractures, disperses, and buries them.

It buries these feelings in the ground. The landscape of *Edgar Huntly* comes alive because its hero hides and rediscovers there his feelings toward a male body lost to death. Like the landscape of W. H. Auden's famous poem "In Praise of Limestone," Norwalk's geologic basis is limestone — "a substance that eminently abounds in rifts and cavities," Brown explains (22). Auden loved the "stone that responds" and gave this description of the landscape that it and water created:

> . . . Mark these rounded slopes
>    With their surface fragrance of thyme and beneath
> A secret system of caves and conduits; hear these springs
>    That spurt out everwhere with a chuckle
> Each filling a private pool for its fish and carving
>    Its own little ravine whose cliffs entertain
> The butterfly and the lizard. . . .

Brown's Huntly also found "a mountain-cave and the rumbling of an unseen torrent . . . dear to my youthful imagination" (22). Auden's setting is more or less explicitly an allegory of sexual love between men, featuring a "nude young male who lounges / Against a rock displaying his dildo" and brotherly rivals who "climb up and down / Their steep stone gennels in twos and threes, sometimes / Arm in arm, but never, thank God, in step." I would argue that Brown's limestone landscape is also homosexual, with the caveat that whereas Auden was consciously proposing a model of gay community as well as eros, Brown's Huntly experienced Norwalk as a trap he did not understand or recognize.[62]

Edgar Huntly is precise about geographic detail. The northern half of Sole-bury, he explains, is uncultivated wilderness. He asks Mary Waldegrave to "imagine a space, somewhat circular, about six miles in diameter, and exhibiting a perpetual and intricate variety of craggy eminences and deep dells" (96). A valley that threads erratically through the uneven terrain serves as a sort of road. This is Norwalk.

Huntly roamed Norwalk as a boy to collect berries and nuts (97). Then, as a young man, he returned with his tutor Sarsefield. During their peripatetic lessons, Sarsefield dispensed "moralizing narratives or synthetical reasonings" to his pupil (97). In other words, Huntly has been here before. In fact, he repeatedly boasts that no one knows the region better than he, although Clithero and the Indians repeatedly prove him wrong. It is a familiar landscape, but not one he has mastered. Mastery is something of a problem, as it turns out. Huntly may have come here for childish pleasures, but as Sarsefield's student, his boyish sense of his own prowess in the woods had to yield to the older man's expert knowledge. Norwalk's topology is not democratic. Sarsefield himself considered Norwalk perilous because it was "a scene of inequalities, of prominences and pits" (249). And as in an aristocratic society, there is often no way to move from pit to prominence, at least not in the open air. The climber might make progress, however, by knowing the subterranean routes — information Sarsefield did not offer, although Clithero will.

Norwalk is also sterile. "To subsist in this desert was impossible," Huntly notes (95). "Rugged, picturesque and wild," Norwalk contributes nothing to the nourishment of Solebury (19). If Clithero stays long in Norwalk, Huntly figures, he will have to starve, beg, or steal. Geographically disordered and agriculturally barren, the vista of Norwalk is thus a kind of masculine sublime — violent and nonreproductive, untamed by civil society.[63] Only men come here, and nothing they do here will benefit the republic.

Norwalk is a place where men meet to no good purpose, and its dark caves and steep-cliffed hills may represent, in aggravated form, the parts where the male body is vulnerable and threatening, that is, the anus and the phallus. Sarsefield had been "fond of penetrating into these recesses," but Huntly in his pursuit of Clithero penetrates deeper than Sarsefield ever had (97). He enters the caves, which Sarsefield never did. He there discovers "dark and untried paths" (128), which make accessible regions he previously thought could not be reached. The power of this secret knowledge appeals to Huntly. When he emerges from a cave to discover an impressive, oddly shaped hill, Huntly thinks he is the only person ever to have set foot in this particular place. "Since the birth of this continent, I was probably the first who had deviated thus remotely from the customary paths of men" (103). Of course, in the next paragraph, Huntly finds that someone else has thus deviated — Clithero, the man he has been pursuing.

Brown describes the form of Clithero's hill carefully: a hollow cylinder surrounds a taller cylinder that rises from inside it. Between the inner and outer cylinders runs a ring-shaped hollow. From the top of the inner cylinder rushes a stream, and the whole sight impresses Huntly with its "desolate and solitary grandeur": "A sort of sanctity and awe environed it, owing to the consciousness of absolute and utter loneliness" (103). The note of loneliness is wrong. Huntly came here to find Clithero, and Clithero is present. The cylindrical rocky hills cannot represent solitude. I suspect they represent a different kind of oneness, that of union: the form and position of the two hills suggest one phallus inside another — one hiding the other, or one buried in the other — and yet at the same time kept separate by the same hollowness that makes the union possible. Huntly stands on the hollow outer cylinder; an abyss separates him from Clithero; but if Huntly can pass through the right cave, or if he can chop down the right tree, he can join Clithero. This image resonates with other images of Brown's imprisoned self: the toad trapped inside the rock, the intellectual hidden in the rural fisher boy, the hardworking scholarly Mervyn invisible to his neighbors. It is a sculpture in limestone of one man imagining himself inside another, or imagining another inside himself.

But what happens if, while you are united with him, the man inside you dies? According to the psychoanalyst Melanie Klein, mourning in an adult causes the same kinds of anxieties that an infant experiences when it first tries to take into itself a representation of what it loves. The baby is struggling to assemble an inner psychic world for the first time, whereas the mourning adult is shoring up a world that death has threatened to undermine, but their tasks are similar. Just as a baby worries that when it takes inside itself an image of the mother's breast, its aggressive desire might destroy the breast's goodness, so a mourning adult worries that the death of a beloved proves that hostile, persecuting forces inside the mourner have killed the good objects he or she has taken in. Both babies and adults, Klein explains, experience the psychic process of internalization as a deep, unconscious fantasy, elaborated with concrete details. For example, a baby may feel his parents "to be live people inside his body," in danger of being digested.⁶⁴ Mourning reactivates these primitive, psychotic anxieties. When Huntly wakes up bruised and cold in a pitch-black cave, it is as though he has woken up inside his own fantasy of how Waldegrave's death might destroy him. He is buried alive, as he imagines Waldegrave to be. But he is also in a cave that represents his own inside, where Waldegrave is buried. Klein might phrase the fantasy anxiety this way: Since the beloved has died inside me, will everything inside me die, including my self?

To overcome this anxiety, Klein wrote, the mourner must strengthen his "belief in goodness — his own and others' " — until he feels sure enough of the existence of goodness "to surrender to his own feelings, and to cry out his sorrow about the actual loss." If the mourner cannot achieve this level of faith, however, he or she may resort to a manic defense, that is, an attempt to save goodness by isolating it from badness. Klein gives as an example a mother who "took to sorting out [her dead son's] letters, keeping his and throwing others away. She was thus unconsciously attempting to restore him and keep him safe inside herself, and throwing out what she felt to be indifferent, or rather hostile."⁶⁵

Huntly was sorting through Waldegrave's letters just before his sleepwalking episode. Like the grieving mother in Klein's example, he was trying to separate the good Waldegrave from the bad one by copying over for Mary Waldegrave not all her brother's letters but only "such as were narrative or descriptive" and free of pernicious atheist reasoning (133). This censorship triggers Huntly's first act of sleepwalking: at night he hides the letters from himself, as if he senses that as representatives of Waldegrave, they need to be protected from his own somewhat vengeful wish to revise them.

The waking Huntly feels the loss of all Waldegrave's letters, bad and good, as persecution by a force he cannot identify: "A whispering intimation that a relique which I valued more than life was torn forever away by some malignant and inscrutable destiny" (135). Having banished from his conscious mind his own hostility to Waldegrave's memory, Huntly has become a little paranoid. And then Weymouth arrives to deprive Huntly of Waldegrave's other legacy, seventy-five hundred dollars. "What remained?" Huntly lamented when the letters vanished (134). On the surface, Huntly consents to the loss of Waldegrave's money with good grace, but it must seem like a final blow. Now nothing remains. It is after this loss that Huntly ends up underground.

"What I loved him for was his goodness," Laelius says of Scipio, "and this is something that has not died."⁶⁶ But with the loss of his correspondence and cash, it is as though Waldegrave's goodness *has* died. Huntly is left alone in the cave of himself where only greed and hatred have survived. Just as he takes up his tomahawk to kill himself, however, Huntly spies two eyes glowing in the dark. "The weapon which was so lately lifted against my own bosom, was now raised to defend my life against the assault of another" (166). At the last minute, Huntly spares himself by attacking a panther.

This is the second panther in the novel. After Huntly watched the first plunge to his death, he recalled that a local farmer had reported "two marauders in his field, whom he imagined to be a male and female panther" (126, 128). But although Brown has primed the reader to expect the first panther's mate, the second panther is also male. In the curiously narrated scene that ensues, Huntly kills this panther and eats him raw. "I will not shock you by relating the extremes to which dire necessity had driven me," Huntly says, as if the eating of raw cat broke some fearful taboo. In case the reader has missed the hint of cannibalism, he spells it out: "If this appetite has sometimes subdued the sentiments of nature, and compelled the mother to feed upon the flesh of her offspring, it will not excite amazement that I did not turn from the yet warm blood and reeking fibres of a brute" (167). As one of a male-male pair and the subject of a cannibal feast, the panther appears to stand for Waldegrave — a vengeful ghost, which Huntly's tomahawk hastily revises into a corpse.

Huntly's "abhorred meal" gives him a nearly lethal case of indigestion. "My stomach was seized by pangs whose acuteness exceeded all that I ever before experienced" (167). After the prolonged gastrointestinal agony, however, Huntly wins, the panther fragments inside him lose, and "that which I had eaten . . . had been of use" (168). Huntly finds his way out of the cave, and he begins to kill Indians methodically.

This is the turning point of the novel. By means of "a banquet so detestable" (167), Huntly has mastered his grief for Waldegrave. Rather than an extended mourning — a slow teasing apart of his feelings and a forgiving realization that

Waldegrave was both bad and good and that both aspects will be missed —
Huntly has torn a panther to pieces and chewed him up. An angry digestion
has separated the useful from the painful. What entered the cave alive as
if through the bowels of sympathy has been aggressively reingested, through
the mouth. What follows is the new Edgar Huntly and the new *Edgar Huntly*.
The novel's genre switches from meandering Gothic to fast-paced action-
adventure. Edgar the Indian killer still has the pathologically sympathetic
impulses of the earlier Edgar, but they no longer trip him up. The old Edgar
Huntly thought that if he offered Clithero a good weep, he would cure his
psychosis. "To set by him in silence, to moisten his hand with tears, to sigh in
unison, to offer him the spectacle of sympathy, the solace of believing . . . that
one at least among his fellow men regarded him with love and pity, could not
fail to be of benign influence" (106). In contrast, the new Edgar Huntly sympa-
thizes by means of gory, execution-style murder. "Pity" compels him to extend
a coup de grâce to an Indian he has mutilated but not quite killed. "To kill him
outright, was the dictate of compassion and of duty" (201). In a remarkable
piece of "cruel lenity," Huntly's second bullet also misses and he has to finish
off his victim with a bayonet (202).

The moral of this bloody benevolence — Huntly's fifth Indian corpse in one
day — is that what attracts sympathy must be killed. Will I die if my friend
dies? Huntly's psychotic yes urges him to kill his friends. Mrs. Lorimer worried that her brother's death would cause her own by sympathy. Not to know
what will become of this worry is to mourn, but mourners can relieve the
tension of not knowing by deciding that if it doesn't kill them, it should.
Thus mad Clithero promises to make sure Mrs. Lorimer does die (289). When
the death of Elihu Hubbard Smith fails to equal the death of Brown's fiction, Brown forces the equation. Like Clithero murdering Mrs. Lorimer, like
Huntly murdering his panther, Brown kills his fiction deliberately. Guilt and
anger lead him to wish they did equate: Does Brown's fiction deserve to outlive
the friend who encouraged and supported it? Also, the death of fiction protects Brown from sympathy, which fiction communicates. Clithero's triumphant and psychotic rage, the last consequence of loss, must then be locked
away. And the temptation to set him free, like the temptation to take Waldegrave's letters out of the drawer, must be resisted.

In March 1800, Brown met Elizabeth Linn, the woman he married. In April,
Brown wrote to his brother James that in his future novels he would be "drop-
ping the doleful tone and assuming a cheerful one." But Brown would not be
leaving copyism, imposture, corpses, or sodomy altogether behind him. In his
love letters, he promised to be Linn's "copyist" and had to struggle to convince

her not to "relapse into the old belief of my imposture, my duplicity." Linn might be forgiven for doubting the sincerity of a lover who could recycle a poem he had presented to another sweetheart six years earlier. In his pamphleteering, Brown continued to ventriloquize, counterfeiting the voices of an adviser to Napoleon and of Thomas Jefferson. Images of the living dead haunted his literary criticism — ghosts of the creative work he had left behind. A superficial elegy for Washington, for example, reminded Brown of a skeleton dressed up in fancy clothes: "We wished to find, under a mantle of such glossy texture and luxuriant folds, a body, graceful, vigorous, and well proportioned. A meagre, distorted, tottering and limping frame covered with tissue and embroidery, is always a mournful, and sometimes a disgustful spectacle. . . . Yet may it not be said, that a shewy garb is of more value to the skeleton than to the perfect man?"[67]

In the afterlife of his fiction, sodomy, too, recurred, not as a compelling horror but as a matter of sophisticated disparagement. In an essay about Anacreon's odes, Brown warns his readers that "the passion which inspires the greatest part of all this *love,* and all this poetry appears not to have even *woman* for its object." "Fough!" cries Brown — although it is not clear how seriously to take the disgust, because the review ends with a friend named "Tom" interrupting the author's tirade with "a severe invective against my prudery."[68]

Brown's writing after *Edgar Huntly* is to some extent a continuation of the Gothic by other means, but rather than end on this note, I would like to close with a story that I believe is Brown's farewell to serious fiction.

To represent his dying art, Brown returned to Cicero, the virtuous pagan whose writing, both artful and republican, had seemed the ideal balance of feeling and reason in *Wieland.* In late 1799, Brown's publisher Hugh Maxwell appended the short story "The Death of Cicero" to the last volume of *Edgar Huntly,* then in print.[69] It was probably the last "doleful" work Brown composed. Like another of Brown's stories, "Thessalonica," which he had published in the *Monthly Magazine* in May 1799, "Cicero" is a parable of the downfall of Rome.

Brown claimed in the essay "Walstein's School of History" that the purpose of historical fiction was "to exhibit, in an eloquent narration, a model of right conduct" and that the advantage of fiction over mere exhortation was its ability to show how different situations conditioned the sort of conduct that was right. Like his make-believe scholar Walstein, Brown researched "The Death of Cicero" carefully, and what Brown boasted of for Walstein is true of his own work: "The facts are either collected from the best antiquarians, or artfully deducted from what is known, or invented with a boldness more easy to admire than to imitate."[70] Where Brown differs from Walstein is in the moral effect at which his story aims. It does not offer a model for right conduct. Much darker, it describes a situation where no right conduct is achievable — where society has come to a moral dead end. In corrupt Rome, there are no longer any meaningful choices for an individual to make.

"The Death of Cicero" consists of a letter written by Cicero's freedman Tiro to Cicero's friend Atticus describing how Mark Antony's tribunes hunted down and executed Cicero. There is a curious motionlessness to the story, not unlike the stillness of Melville's *Billy Budd*. The reader knows from the start how it will end — the title and the first line remind any readers deficient in Roman history — and the characters' only struggle is the struggle to surrender.

Cicero himself has already surrendered. "Let their executioners come," he intones. "I am willing to die" (120).[71] This haughty renunciation exasperates Tiro, who is still trying to save Cicero. Brown took this conflict between a master's death wish and a servant's desire to deny it from his sources. Plutarch writes that Cicero's servants tried to carry him to a getaway ship "partly by entreaty, and partly by force." And the Elder Seneca quotes Livy's report that Cicero "grew weary of flight and of life" and that when "his slaves bravely and loyally showed readiness to make a fight of it, . . . Cicero himself . . . ordered them to put down the litter and suffer calmly the compulsions of a harsh fate." It was not self-evident even to the ancients that Cicero was right to have resigned himself to death. The Elder Seneca presents his material about Cicero in the form of a suasoria, a rhetorical exercise in giving advice. In Suasoria 6, "Cicero Deliberates Whether to Beg Antony's Pardon," some rhetors advise Cicero to imitate his friend Cato and choose suicide, but others, such as Varius Geminus, urge him to flee to Brutus and Cassius in Macedonia, arguing that Cicero "had lived long enough for himself — but not long enough for Rome."[72]

It was probably this debate that attracted Brown to the incident. Brown's narrator Tiro argues, like Varius Geminus, that "to despair of himself or the republic while the seas were open, and while Cassius was in arms, . . . was unworthy of [Cicero's] understanding and his virtue" (123). Brown's Tiro is willing to call Cicero a "recreant and coward" to his face rather than give up (127). Like Mrs. Lorimer to Wiatte, Cicero is linked sympathetically to Rome. "With the life of Cicero," Tiro believes, "was entwined the existence of Rome. The stroke by which one was severed, would be no less fatal to the other" (130). Waldegrave's death threatened only Huntly, but now sympathy for a friend's death could bring about the fall of the whole republic. That Rome did fall punctuates Brown's conclusion.

According to Plutarch, Cicero died "clasping his chin with his left hand, as was his wont," and from Plutarch, Brown takes the detail that Cicero "stretched his neck forth from the litter" as if to meet the executioner's blade.[73] But Brown then describes the corpse in a manner all his own. "One blow severed the devoted head!" Tiro writes. "No sooner had it fallen, than the troop set up a horrid shout of exultation. Laenas grasped the hair and threw the head into a large bag, held open by one of his companions for that purpose. . . . Nothing but the headless trunk, stretched upon the floor of the litter, which floated in blood, remained. I approached the vehicle without being fully conscious of my movements, and gazed upon the mutilated figure" (131). Cicero has become a headless trunk, a body without reason, the remains of an orator whose voice has been taken from him. Like the dismembered panther, the decapitated Cicero horrifies. "My thoughts were at a stand," Tiro writes, "as well as my power of utterance suspended." The great speaker has fallen, and in the face of his mutilation there is nothing for anyone to say.

Silently, Tiro asks a series of questions about Cicero:

> Was there cowardice or error in refusing to mingle in the tumults of war? In resigning to younger hands, innured to military offices, the spear and the shield? Is it more becoming the brave to struggle for life; to preserve the remnant which infirmity and old age had left, than serenely to wait for death, and encounter it with majestic composure? Is it dishonourable to mourn over the triumph of ambition, and the woes of our country? To be impatient of life, when divorced from liberty, and fated to contemplate the ruin of those schemes, on which his powers had incessantly been exercised, and whose purpose was the benefit of mankind? (132–33).

Like *Edgar Huntly,* this story is a reaction to the loss of a loved man, and as in that novel, the emotion that death arouses is not so much sorrow as fury. But Huntly had panthers and Indians to vent his fury on, and there is no one to take the blow in "Cicero" but Cicero. Tiro's fury is therefore impotent. Tiro, devoted to the "devoted head" of a "headless trunk," cannot bring himself to anger. He is as much without a tongue as Cicero is, and thus his answer to his own questions does not make sense: "Yes. The close of thy day was worthy its beginning and its progress. Thou diest with no stain upon thy virtue" (133).

This is a "Yes, we have no bananas" answer. Was there cowardice in refusing to fight? Yes, thou diest with no stain upon thy virtue. Is it more becoming the brave to struggle for life? Yes, the close of thy day was worthy its beginning. The language of Brown's Tiro has become infected with something that has destroyed its structure. Like Smith on his deathbed, Brown here seems to be trying to say something about his own decomposition, about his ceasing to use language. His confusion expresses a deep ambivalence about the feelings between men that bind together a nation, about the devotions to one another that trap them together in a nation's rise or fall. "The termination of thy course was coeval with the ruin of thy country. Thy hand had upheld the fabric of its freedom and its happiness, as long as human force was adequate to that end. It fell, because the seeds of dissolution had arrived at maturity, and the basis and structure were alike dissolved. It fell, and thou wast crushed in its ruins" (133).

Not Cicero but Rome died. Cicero could live only in sympathy with Rome. Or maybe it is the other way around, and Rome is a feeling inspired by Cicero, which must die with him. I think that Brown is writing about a voicelessness he was left in by Smith's death. Like Tiro after Cicero, Brown had been living since September 1798 as a sort of caretaker, not writing but revising and finishing the novels he had begun while Smith was alive. The autumn of 1799 was the first anniversary of Brown's loss, and what catches in Brown's throat here is anger. He never speaks it; he loses touch from now on with the dark side of sympathy; he becomes a sentimentalist in love and a cynic in politics. It is as though Brown excused Smith instead of forgiving him. Not Smith but America died, the parable about Cicero suggests — or, rather, Smith's radical idea of America died, an idea Brown had fallen in love with. The tenuous republic of sincerity and affection has dissolved. "An unexampled concurrence of sentiment," Thomas Paine called the nascent American republic. "Concurrence" (*consensio*) was also the word that the historical Cicero picked to define friendship: "an accord in all things" or "a complete identity of feeling," depending on the translation. But a *consensio* is not permanent; it is a happy accident. Paine worried about depending too much on "the temporary attachment of one man to another." With Smith's death, the attachment in Brown's heart dissolved. His Gothic style, in which he had expressed that attachment with rich ambivalence, dissolved as well. Brown imagined the end of America rather than imagine what he had lost in Smith. To put it another way, in order to protect himself from what he felt for Smith, Brown lost his art, and America, too.[74]

# 4

## The Unacknowledged Tie:
## Young Emerson and the Love of Men

In 1840, Alexis de Tocqueville noticed that Americans were Cartesian in all but name. "Everyone shuts himself up tightly within himself," Tocqueville observed, "and insists upon judging the world from there." This near solipsism was first articulated as a philosophy by Descartes, Tocqueville explained, offering the unscholarly Americans a footnote to themselves. Now, in the young United States, it appeared that social conditions had conspired to make the French philosopher's radical skepticism practical and relevant. Thanks to the rough parity of economic and political power that obtained here, no citizen was obliged to trust any other citizen. Everyone was free to adopt a wait-and-see approach. "A noble doubt," Emerson called it in *Nature*, and in his essay on Montaigne, Emerson's statement of nonfaith sounded almost regal: "I neither affirm nor deny. I stand here to try the case. I am here to consider, *skeptein,* to consider how it is." What in the seventeenth century had been a French thought experiment became, in the nineteenth, the usual state of the American mind.[1]

This distrust had helped to spark the Reformation and dethrone kings, but it worried Tocqueville, because the intellectual fire wall that it raised between Americans and their world isolated not just minds but hearts. The European aristocrat had friends ready to hand—his lord, vassals, and clan. Aristocrats "often sacrifice[d] themselves for other men," Tocqueville noted. The code of chivalry required a man to lay down his life for another, in an act of political love. But a democrat possesses no natural friends. "In ages of equality every man naturally stands alone; he has no hereditary friends whose co-operation he may demand, no class upon whose sympathy he may rely." Tocqueville feared that without sure allies, the democrat—however intellectually impregnable—would be politically vulnerable. Democratic sympathy was different: more diffuse and less demanding. "In democratic ages," Tocqueville wrote, "men rarely sacrifice themselves for one another, but they display general compassion for the members of the human race."[2]

This more abstract sympathy had its advantages. Because aristocrats sympathized locally, they felt no outrage at the torture of people not allied to them by blood or oath. Democrats, distributing their sympathy by general rule, could be as upset by distant torture as if a neighbor were on the rack. But because democrats felt sympathy so promiscuously, their emotions were spread thin. Aristocrats could be counted on to shed blood on their friends' behalf. Would democrats ever care enough about any single person or principle to be willing to leave their armchairs? "In democratic times . . . the bond of human affection is extended, but it is relaxed."[3] In Tocqueville's opinion, uniform sympathy came so close to indifference that a new kind of despotism could easily insinuate itself.

Democracy had changed sympathy irrevocably. Rather than cry down a jeremiad in favor of antique virtue, Tocqueville pointed out that the New World had a new recourse. Through the press, democrats could appeal to humanity as aristocrats had appealed to their intimates. Printed and then dispersed, words could stir up outrages and loves that would bring citizens together in associations, which could then act in concert to reform society. Tocqueville seems to have had the abolition movement and its newspapers in mind, but he phrased his observation as a general insight about the role of the press in America. "The only authors whom I acknowledge as American are the journalists," Tocqueville decreed, and in the newspapers they wrote for, he discerned a holy mission: "They maintain civilization." In Tocqueville's sociology, one of the high functions of democratic literature is to focus and transmit enthusiasms that would otherwise dissipate.[4]

Couple this role with the entertainment needs of a people with busy lives and uneven educations, and Tocqueville predicted that the style of democratic literature would be "fantastic, incorrect, overburdened, and loose, almost always vehement and bold." Whereas aristocratic literature had tried to please and charm, democratic literature would astonish and arouse. Aristocrats had used language as a frame, to order and contain experience, or as a microscope, to hold the world under a glass while it was investigated, while its symmetries and lusters were revealed. With democrats, however, literature smelled a little of utility. Tocqueville predicted that democrats would use language as a device for piping sympathies from one soul to another: "Nothing but a newspaper can drop the same thought into a thousand minds at the same moment," he remarked. Democratic literature amplified rather than moderated; it distorted more often than it smoothed. At best, it could be a weapon; at worst, a diverting toy.[5]

Tocqueville's notion of democratic literature was hypothetical. He was describing an end-state toward which literature was evolving but which even in the United States had not yet arrived. The poles of his logic predict both the turgidity of the newsletters that members of Congress mail to their constituents (a medium that is relational but does not feel like it) and the glittery, emotionlike intensity of Hollywood movies (a medium that feels relational but is not). But for Tocqueville in 1840, these disasters were in the distant future. He still looked forward to a moment of poise, when the two worlds of literary style would balance each other as they came and went. "Such epochs are transient, but very brilliant," Tocqueville noted. They would combine the formal elegance of the aristocratic style with the urgency of the democratic. As if he had foreseen the American Renaissance for which R. Waldo Emerson would stand as the advent, Tocqueville wrote that these epochs "are fertile without exuberance, and animated without confusion." No doubt he was thinking of Wordsworth and Chateaubriand when he wrote that during these periods of transition — as poets lowered their eyes from gods and kings, but before they had fallen so far as to see only themselves — they would take nature for their muse. But perhaps *Nature*, the book Emerson published anonymously in 1836, had managed to reach him.[6]

"Our strength is transitional," Emerson celebrated. The artist, he felt, must yield to the ecstatic flux that was the only government of the world, what he called the "Method of Nature": "If anything could stand still, it would be crushed and dissipated by the torrent it resisted, and if it were a mind, would be crazed; as insane persons are those who hold fast to one thought, and do not flow with the course of nature." Emerson was temperamentally suited to the moment of literary transition that Tocqueville anticipated. He was by disposition an experimenter, and he knew when to abandon a literary form. With canny timing, he deserted the sermon for the essay and the lecture, genres whose financial rewards were as yet obscure. His taste ran toward styles of writing where spontaneity had burst form, as he once explained to a too lady-like poet whose work he rejected. "The verses you sent me are uncommonly smooth & elegant, and happily express a pleasing sentiment," Emerson wrote, "but I suppose I should prize more highly much ruder specimens from your portfolio, which you, perhaps would as much underrate, which recorded in a way you could not repeat, some profound experience of happiness or pain."[7]

In 1840, Charles Brockden Brown had been dead for three decades. America had changed, and Tocqueville's simply worded theories about democracy help explain two of its transitions in particular: in literary style and in the style of relationships between men. By 1840 authorship had at last become a profession, but as if in a strange kind of compensation, passionate love between men had become more problematic. As Tocqueville noted, democracy tended to attenuate the emotions between any two particular men. A democrat rarely wants to die for another democrat. When Charles Brockden Brown had flirted with that wish in *Arthur Mervyn,* he had already felt obliged to cast it as a horror, then to avert it with a sudden plot twist that substituted an aristocrat for a plebeian. A generation later, Emerson knew that this kind of selfless love for another man had vanished from his culture. In a letter to his aunt regretting the death of the elder William Ellery Channing, Emerson wrote, "Our broad country has few men; none that one would die for; worse, none that one could live for." The shape of sympathy had changed, as had the nature of men. As artisans gave way to factories, the personal commitment of man to man gave way to diffuse, impersonal associations. Like Tocqueville, Emerson recognized that modern men resembled each other more and more but affected each other less and less. "There must be somewhat analogous in the factories of heaven to those of earth," Emerson once wrote Margaret Fuller, "and as we make all of cast iron now & not of wrought, so are the men now made run in molds, but do not yield or expand." Tocqueville suggests why democracy made the expression of love between men both difficult in society and imperative in literature. It is this tension that gave much of early American literature its distinctive color.[8]

Every story can be told from several angles. Tocqueville's sociology may elucidate why the evolving literature of the world's first successful modern republic might — given that only men were citizens — concern itself with the emotions that passed between men. But another way to tell the story is to focus on homosexual desire. Recently it has been unfashionable to imagine that in earlier ages, there were some people whom nature and nurture disposed to feel romantic love for their own sex; such thinking is dismissed as "essentialism." Yet, although the terms and words and social categories have changed, I suspect that because such people exist now, they existed then. As Emerson put it, "One nature wrote and the same reads." As James Creech has written, any gay critic who uses projective identification as a tool for reading risks the label "vulgar." But like Creech, I am afraid that poststructuralist gay critics have outwitted themselves; wishing to be more impartial and abstract than their homophobic opponents, they have deprived themselves of a homely, human tool. Emerson was himself a great advocate of the notion that if we have any right or reason to read at all, it is in our vulgar selves. "There is no event but sprung somewhere from the soul of man," he wrote in "Literary Ethics," "and therefore there is none but the soul of man can interpret."[9]

From this perspective, then, one could imagine a convergence of the story told by Tocquevillean sociology and a story that focuses on homosexual desire. The joined story might run something like this: In America as it democratized and industrialized, literature came forward as a way to exchange emotions between increasingly separate men. Meanwhile, men who were aware that they loved other men found it harder and harder to express their feelings to each other. They gravitated to literature as an outlet because of its license to express links between men. This license gradually became one of the markers that distinguished poetic language from standard language, in line with Jan Mukařovský's theory that poetry distinguishes itself from ordinary speech by "the intentional violation of the norm of the standard."[10] Mukařovský hypothesizes that "the function of poetic language consists in the maximum of foregrounding of the utterance." If, as Tocqueville and modern cultural historians agree, the direct expression of love between men became stigmatized in the culture at large as the nineteenth century advanced, then the persistence of a male-male romantic style in poetic speech might have served as a marker of "literariness." It would foreground the utterance not only formally, by violating normal speech codes, but also structurally, by bringing forward the psychodynamics of speech between men that normal discourse automatized. The cultural logic that granted literature this dispensation to express homosexual sentiments, not permissible elsewhere in public, would coincide with the attraction that this literary exception must have had for men who felt tabooed homosexual sentiments in private. These two processes, working in tandem, might explain why it is the rule, rather than the exception, that the canonical works of the American Renaissance have as their theme love between men — a rule that literary history would accentuate, rather than soften, as time passed and the canon was refined.[11]

This, however, is a generalization, and as Emerson might have objected, "there is properly no history; only biography."[12] Individual writers lived out these contradictory historical forces as best they could. For Mifflin, Gibson, and Norris, nostalgia camouflaged with a courtly, upper-class manner a romance that claimed not to fit the new hermetic individualism because it was too good for it. They claimed that their friendships were exceptional not because they were immoral or criminal but because they were traces of a vanishing class's grandeur. A decade later, Brown's love and dependence on his friends provoked anxieties about his manhood and self-integrity, which in turn fueled experiments with language as a means of imposture or vehicle for infection. When love between men surfaced in his fiction, it appeared — conservatively transformed — as horror. Neither the early Philadelphians' nostalgia nor Brown's horror would have been plausible as disguises or compensations for a writer like Emerson: he was too modern and too enlightened. And, to rework Henry James's old complaint, American culture seems to have been too scant and thin to permit the masquerades of eccentricity and hypocrisy possible in Britain. In America, literature was transparent. So in the Emersonian moment, writing expressed desire between men through transparence, invisibly, by itself becoming that desire. For the Philadelphian diarists, language had described and moderated their love; for Brown, language had deformed that love into correspondent nightmares. In the moment of transition, in Emerson's hands, literature aspired not to describe or disguise but to *be* the relationship between two men — to enact it through words alone.

Homosexual eros is the motive and structuring metaphor of his work, and at times it is his explicit topic. To most ears, this assertion may sound likely for Whitman but novel as a claim for Emerson. The expression of love for men was not Emerson's exclusive literary motive, and he probably never realized a love affair with a man. But this brand of eros was a crucial force in Emerson's life and writing, as an examination of two moments in his career will show: in this chapter, his early crush on another college student; and in the chapter that follows, his writing of the essay "Friendship" in 1839–40.

"Mr. Somebody, will it please your impertinence to be conscience-struck!" Emerson pleaded, in parentheses, at the end of a journal entry about his crush on a fellow Harvard student named Martin Gay.[13] A couple of times, after confessing to the page his continuing fascination with Gay, Emerson threatened to burn his diary. Happily he did not. But, distrustful of Mr. Somebody's conscience, either Emerson or his son Edward later blotted and scribbled over most of the entries about Gay. Emerson's first mention of the crush by name was hidden by a later hand, which went so far as to cut an entry from elsewhere in Emerson's journal and tip it over the page as a veil.

Serendipitously, the journal passage that was used as a veil concerned the alteration of morals by circumstances. And circumstances, as it turns out, have altered our view of the morality of what Emerson was trying to hide. The impertinent somebodies who edited the sixteen volumes of Emerson's *Journals and Miscellaneous Notebooks* were so intent on ferreting out an accurate text of everything Emerson wrote — even what he wished he had not written — that they photographed one canceled sentence and studied it "under magnification of about 19 power."[14] Ever since Jonathan Ned Katz collected some of Emerson's more provocative entries in his *Gay American History,* information about Emerson's college crush has been widely available. But with a few important exceptions, including Erik Ingvar Thurin, Julie Ellison, and Christopher Newfield, scholars have kept this news bracketed off from their gestalt of Emerson as a man and from their understanding of his philosophy and writing.

In fact, the feelings that came to Emerson during his crush on Gay provoked metaphors, ideas, and psychological compromises that became crucial to his mature philosophy and writing. To appreciate their intensity and complexity, one must trace the story of Emerson's crush in the journals he kept as he struggled through this "queer acquaintance."[15]

Sketches of men's heads, almost always in left profile, riddle Emerson's early journals. Like the books of physiognomy popular at the time, his notebooks were encyclopedias of male faces, of all ages and types: soldierly, Falstaffian, jolly, elegant, chubby, and wise. Perhaps the doodles were a way of imagining what sort of man he himself would become. On or around 9 August 1820, the seventeen-year-old Emerson turned to words rather than images to explore his feelings for a new face to which his thoughts insisted on returning. "There is a strange face in the Freshman class whom I should like to know very much. He has a great deal of character in his features & should be a fast friend or a bitter enemy. His name is Gay."[16]

According to the modern editors of Emerson's journals, Martin Gay was a young man roughly Emerson's age from Hingham, Massachusetts. Although as a sophomore, he helped to lead an undergraduate rebellion against Harvard authorities, he eventually grew up to become a respected Boston doctor and chemist. He had entered Harvard as a freshman in the autumn of 1819, when Emerson was beginning his junior year.[17]

Because the college was a small community, the two boys had no doubt noticed each other much sooner than the end of the academic year. An attraction to Gay was likely behind an earlier entry of Emerson's, dated 7 June 1820. Something had been bothering Emerson on that occasion, and he turned to a *sortes Virgilianae,* or "Virgilian lot," for advice. A Virgilian lot was a kind of Magic Eight Ball for Augustan tastes. To administer it, one let a book of Virgil's poetry fall open to a random page, and the first passage to catch one's eye was then to be interpreted as an oracle. Emerson wrote:

> A very singular chance led me to derive very sensible answers to the two questions I proposed to Virgil. For the first I opened to the line
>
> O crudelis Alexi, nihil mea carmina curas
> [O cruel Alexis, care you naught for my songs?]

for the other I opened to a line, Dryden's translation of which is

Go let the gods & temples claim thy care.[18]

Although Emerson did not specify his two questions, they may well have been about homoerotic feelings, given that Emerson considered the shepherd Corydon's lament — about his neglect by the "beauteous boy" Alexis — apropos.

Emerson may have interpreted the second of the two Virgilian lots as a recommendation to reinvest his affections in loftier concerns. He was not, however, able to manage such a sublimation yet, and in late October 1820, another set of diary entries about Gay emerged. This time Emerson wrote that Gay's face so transfixed him that "I begin to believe in the Indian doctrine of eye-fascination": "A dozen times a day & as often by night I find myself wholly wrapped up in conjectures of his character & inclinations. We have had already two or three long profound stares at each other. Be it wise or weak or superstitious I must know him."[19]

That month, Gay was rusticated for his part in a dining-hall riot, and news of this rowdiness left Emerson with mixed feelings. "My opinion of ☞ was strangely lowered by hearing that he was 'proverbially idle.' This was redeemed by learning that he was a 'superior man.'" The pointing hand that Emerson drew indicates a scrap-paper portrait, probably of Gay, that Emerson sketched and attached to the lower half of the page. In the sketch, Gay is a Caesar, with high forehead, Roman nose, and full lips. On the bound page underneath the portrait, Emerson inscribed two quatrains that distilled his feelings:

> Perhaps thy lot in life is higher
>    Than the fates assign to me
> While they fulfil thy large desire
>    And bid my hopes as visions flee
>
> But grant me still in joy or sorrow
>    In grief or hope to claim thy heart
> And I will then defy the morrow
>    Whilst I fulfil a loyal part.[20]

The poem bears the date "October," and the entry about Gay as "proverbially idle" and "superior" is dated "Nov. 1." Probably Emerson composed the lines and painted the sketch while in the thrall of his eye-fascination with Gay, and when the news of Gay's rustication reached him, the fancy's power over him broke somewhat. The November diary entry undermines to some extent the idealization and romanticization of the October poem. The facts may have brought the idea of the boy to ground.

*Sketch of Martin Gay,* by Ralph Waldo Emerson. 1820. By permission of the Ralph Waldo Emerson Memorial Association and of Houghton Library, Harvard University. MS AM 1280H (5) Wide World 2.

Still, the split in Emerson's idea of Gay is intriguingly drastic. Gay was always at an extreme in Emerson's mind, but which extreme is a toss-up. In Emerson's first mention of Gay, Gay could turn out to be either "fast friend or a bitter enemy." At the moment when Emerson committed portrait and poem to his journal, Gay was either unreachably above Emerson or a profligate much below him.

A man both "idle" and "superior" sounds as far from Emerson's own ever-striving and self-critical character as one could imagine. The two adjectives suggest an aristocrat — someone whose high status is a matter of essence, not effort. One thinks of the Virginian gentlemen whom Henry Adams encountered at Harvard a generation or so later, who aroused in him a mix of envy, affection, and scorn. Trying to explain these gentlemen's popularity and lack of achievement, Adams suggested that the Virginians had been raised with a "habit of command." But "the habit of command was not enough, and the Virginian had little else. He was simple beyond analysis; so simple that even the simple New England student could not realize him. . . . As an animal, the southerner seemed to have every advantage, but even as an animal he steadily lost ground." That these cosseted breeds soon weakened did not make them any less perplexing to a New England temperament. Even in middle age, Emerson, too, would find this type of southerner hard to handle. "Bladders of conceit," he called them; but he also admitted that, armed with a southern style of unexamined confidence, "a snippersnapper eats me whole."[21]

The collegiate Gay was not from the South, but as a leader of young rebels rather than a studious goody-goody, he belonged to the same type — a type that attracted but baffled Emerson all his life — the born leader. "There are men, who, by their sympathetic attractions, carry nations with them, and lead the activity of the human race," he wrote in his chapter on power in the *Conduct of Life*. Of this type, Emerson's Napoleon was an intellectual species, as Melville's Handsome Sailor was a species of the same genus with the intellect degraded. In Emerson's personal mythology, the heroic man administers his power to his admirers through his eyes, as described in Emerson's essay "Character": "A river of command seemed to run down from his eyes into all those who beheld him, a torrent of strong sad light." The cocksureness of the "Napoleon temperament," as he sometimes called it — "impassive, unimpressible by others" — was one that Emerson envied and always wished he had. Conceit, like sexual appetite, seemed to Emerson to be a trait that Nature flouted Christianity by favoring. Emerson compensated for his lack of it by writing. "Even in college," he remembered, "I was already content to be *'screwed'* in the recitation room, if, on my return, I could accurately paint the fact in my youthful Journal."[22] According to the *Oxford English Dictionary*, the word *screw* in early nineteenth-century U.S. college slang meant "to examine rigorously" — as if a tutor put his pupil in thumbscrews — but the word also had then the sexual meaning it has today. In the journal passage, the act of writing was Emerson's revenge for having fallen into a submissive role in an encounter with another man. But the two quatrains Emerson wrote beneath Gay's image show that while in college, Emerson could also use writing to find pleasure in deferring to another man if he could link himself to that man with love.

Emerson's first quatrain explains that Emerson has every right to envy Gay's superior prospects while his own "hopes as visions flee." But this he refused to do. In a 28 May 1826 journal entry, Emerson denied on philosophical grounds that envy of a friend's success was inevitable. "You love your friend for your sake, not for his own, might say Hobbists & wolves, for you would not have that good fortune befal him that should raise him above your reach of your society." Emerson had read Dugald Stewart, and he believed in Francis Hutcheson's "moral sense" — an innate altruism not reducible to self-interest. "I please myself that I can dimly see how it would gratify me to promote that very good fortune of my friend."[23]

In fact, as Emerson's second quatrain asserts, Emerson finds a renewed hope for his own future by making an affectionate identification with his successful friend: "I will then defy the morrow / Whilst I fulfil a loyal part." After Emerson transforms envy to hope, the residue is not a lingering resentment but an almost mystical joy. "In God's name what is in this topic?" Emerson asked when his May 1826 philosophical exercise yielded him an unexpected rush of pleasure. "It encourages, exhilarates, inspires me. . . . I *feel* immortal."[24]

Common to all of Emerson's entries about Gay is a concern with merit and rank, on the one hand, and with affection, on the other. A good word for the fork of this dilemma is *emulation,* the eighteenth-century ideal that continued to bring young men into associations in Emerson's day and beyond. To emulate meant both to imitate and to rival. Adam Smith defined it as "the anxious desire that we ourselves should excel . . . originally founded in our admiration of the excellence of others."[25] Young men joined Societies for the Attainment of Useful Knowledge because they hoped they were alike in sharing the same lofty ambitions and because they hoped that by coming together they would prove their difference — that competition between them would spur some to higher achievements. The ambiguity in the meaning stands nicely for the ambivalence at the heart of these motivations. If you admire a fellow, you ought to want to be like him, and then surpass him; but to accomplish these goals, you have to get to know him, which requires intimacy rather than oneupmanship. Anxiety about one's place in the world could thus be both motive and impediment to friendships with other young men.

Like Charles Brockden Brown with his friend William Wood Wilkins, Emerson seems to have responded to this double bind by projecting a character that he wished for himself onto Gay, and then reacting with anger and disgust when reality disappointed imagination. What makes Emerson's case even more peculiar than Brown's, however, is that in April 1821, after a year of mutual glances, the two "friends" had not yet "exchanged above a dozen words."[26]

That month, a rumor reached Emerson that Gay was "dissolute." "I shall have to throw him up, after all, as a cheat of fancy," Emerson wrote on 1 April 1821. Emerson did not record the anecdote that showed Gay to be "more like his neighbours than I should wish him to be," but he did write out the details of the fancy that Gay's dissipation had shattered: "Before I ever saw him, I wished my *friend* to be different from any individual I had seen. I invested him with a solemn cast of mind, full of poetic feeling, & an idolater of friendship, & possessing a vein of rich sober thought. When I saw [Gay]'s pale but expressive face & large eye, I instantly invested him with the complete character which fancy had formed and though entirely unacquainted with him was pleased to observe the notice which he appeared to take of me. For a year I have entertained towards him the same feelings and should be sorry to lose him altogether."

If a wish to soften feelings of inferiority had been the motive for Emerson's crush on Gay, one would expect Emerson's interest to fade once he discovered Gay was not what he had hoped. Emerson himself believed that as a rule, disappointment detached affection. "Friends should not have infirmities," he wrote in his journal on 5 January 1824. "Friendship will melt like snow if there be anything likely to disgust, between parties." The mature Emerson phrased this even more bluntly: "Men cease to interest us when we find their limitations."[27]

But with Emerson's interest in Gay, this was not the case. The following month, May 1821, Emerson was still fascinated by Gay. "I am more puzzled than ever with [Gay]'s conduct," Emerson wrote, but his own behavior was just as puzzling: "He came out to meet me yesterday and I observing him, just before we met turned another corner and most strangely avoided him. This morning I went out to meet him in a different direction and stopped to speak with a lounger in order to be directly in [Gay]'s way, but [Gay] turned into the first gate and went towards Stoughton. All this baby play persists without any apparent design, and as soberly as if both were intent on some tremendous affair." In matters of the heart, logic can be inappropriate. But it is odd that Gay's dissolution did not dissolve Emerson's interest but rather piqued it. As Emerson himself noted in his journal on 29 November 1822, "To be so agreeably excited by the features of an individual personally unknown to me, and for so long a time, was surely a curious incident in the history of so cold a being, and well worth a second thought. . . . To this day, our glance at meeting, is not that of indifferent persons."[28]

By Occam's razor, the likeliest solution to the mystery is that Emerson was not as cold a being as he thought he was, but merely thought himself cold because he resisted believing he was romantically attracted to men. He resisted admitting where his heart tended because actual, as opposed to "Platonic," homosexuality was taboo in Victorian America. This simple explanation has no high-theoretical glamour to recommend it, but it clears up a number of long-standing paradoxes about Emerson's heart. By itself, the inference is no literary insight, but it will help explain what Emerson hoped literature could do.

An alternative explanation ought to be considered, however: Did Emerson's interest in Gay have to do with power rather than love? As critics and biographers have often noted, Emerson in many ways dodged the competitiveness associated with a traditional masculine identity, with good reason. Emerson's father, William, tyrannized his children with high expectations. As Gay Wilson Allen reports in his biography, "A week before his fourth child's third birthday [William Emerson] wrote a friend: 'Ralph does not read very well yet.' "[29] (Emerson disliked his first name and as an adult asked to be called Waldo.) Those expectations crushed Emerson's brothers. The oldest, William, got off relatively easy: he failed at a religious career after German scholarship had demoralized him, and took quiet and respectable refuge in the law. The hope for a minister in the family passed to Edward, who suffered a nervous breakdown. As Waldo poignantly described Edward's collapse in a letter to William, "There he lay — Edward — the admired learned eloquent thriving boy — a maniac." Edward recovered his sanity only to die young of tuberculosis. The next brother, Robert Bulkeley, was born mentally impaired. Emerson's favorite was Charles, the youngest. After Charles died at age twenty-eight, also of tuberculosis, Emerson found that he could not bear to read the corrosive self-criticism in Charles's journals. "I could not stay to see my noble brother tortured even by himself." One of Emerson's few memories of his father was of how he taught him to swim by shoving him into the ocean.[30]

Like his brothers, Emerson inherited from his father a fierce internal critic. Young Emerson may have survived because he played up his role among the brothers as least likely to succeed. As Emerson himself observed, considering his love of berry picking in light of Edward's breakdown from overwork, "I have so much mixture of *silliness* in my intellectual frame that I think Providence has tempered me against this." The silliness developed into a nonstandard style of masculinity. It was a stance that exasperated the senior Henry James into calling Emerson "an unsexed woman": "Oh you man without a handle!" James once apostrophized him.[31]

The critic Julie Ellison has speculated that "Emerson . . . found a way to stage masculine intimacy as a sentimental drama of differentiation, installing power at the heart of tenderness." Emerson did reverence power, out of an impulse that he called prudence and that is sometimes condemned today as quietism or naïveté. But an interest in power could not have been his motive with Gay; Emerson's desire cannot be explained as a wish to triumph over Gay or to curry his favor by serving him. Emerson's concern with hierarchy in his relationship with Gay was defensive: a camouflage for wishes that do not have to do with power, a propitiatory compliance with norms for male behavior that he was in danger of defying. The unconsummated friendship with Gay is a compromise: Emerson concedes to the fatherly demand for rivalrous achievement that hierarchy still matters. That Gay still matters, after the hierarchy has been established, is what Emerson takes for himself. Gay lingers because Emerson is attached to him by something that disregards triumph or failure. His persistence in Emerson's heart after he has disappointed him speaks of something other than a tenderly administered power, although that is an element of the mix. (After all, of the highest kind of lovers, the celestial, Emerson later wrote, "Power have they for tenderness.")[32]

A modern reader who hopes to see Emerson violate the terms of this compromise will be frustrated. Emerson strictly respected it, and that may justify Ellison's charge that Emerson is complicit with a certain homophobia. In the bargain Emerson struck, the acid of rivalry would not corrode his affection for another man, because Emerson avoided not only competition but intimacy with other men of any sort. As Emerson reflected in a 29 November 1822 journal entry, "From the first, I preferred to preserve the terms which kept alive so much sentiment rather than a more familiar intercourse which I feared would end in indifference." But was Emerson protecting his affection, or was he protecting his obedience to the laws of masculine self-sovereignty? If the two were kept apart, he never had to know. Even Emerson scented the vulnerable logic in his reasoning. "Pish," was his one-word dismissal of the whole topic.[33]

But if Emerson never broke the terms of this compromise, this was in part because he found in literature a way to transcend its terms. Plato's *Phaedrus* suggested to him one path toward what he later called ascension. In that dialogue, Socrates teases the handsome, overearnest young Phaedrus, who has been unduly impressed with a cynical speech by Lysias. Lysias had argued that boys should give their favors to men who do not love them, because nonlovers are less troublesome than lovers. To mock Lysias's cynicism, Socrates exaggerates it. Socrates argues, for example, that "a lover will not willingly put up with a boyfriend who is his equal or superior, but is always working to make the boy he loves weaker and inferior to himself." Envy and competitiveness, Socrates ironically suggests, will always taint love, and so loveless relationships are more up-front and practical.[34]

After he has competed with Lysias in cynicism, Socrates atones for his offense against Cupid with a palinode: he tells a parable that shows why Lysias's romantic pragmatism is more foolish than romantic naïveté. Socrates may not be any less ironic during this second speech. Like all of Socrates's speeches to young men, this one is a seduction, designed to win the heart of the boy in question by playing on his desires and dismissing his fears. After all, Socrates chooses for his parable an epigraph by Stesichorus — "There's no truth to that story: / You never sailed that lovely ship, / You never reached the tower of Troy" — that is delightfully, patently untrue, even if it did mollify Helen. Socrates tells Phaedrus a pretty story that almost (but not quite) takes the sex out of love. The arousal a man feels at the sight of a beautiful boy, Socrates explains, is not mere lust but rather his soul's hunger for the pure forms it once saw beyond heaven. The boy's beauty reminds the man's soul of these nourishing transcendent truths, and as beauty streams in through the man's eyes, his soul begins to resprout its lost wings, a process as itchy and achy as teething. In the course of his parable, Socrates also reconciles anxiety over one's manliness with participation in homosexual love. Because what brings boy and man together is their shared love for the divine principles of which beauty is an emblem, a man who wishes to strengthen his bond with a boy will augment his boy's godliness. Lovers therefore "show no envy, no mean-spirited lack of generosity, toward the boy, but make every possible effort to draw him into being totally like themselves and the god to whom they are devoted."[35]

In Socrates's fairy tale, desire for another man does not lead to sodomy, and love for him does not lead to loss of civic stature. Young Emerson adopted *Phaedrus* into his personal mythology. The dialogue informed the fantasy world of his poem "Initial, Daemonic, and Celestial Love," the trains of thought in his essays "Love" and "Friendship," and even the excuse he gave Lidian Jackson for wooing her so impersonally. But even as early as the episode with Gay, *Phaedrus* offered a model for sublimation and a rationale for believing that interest in Gay's beauty was not vulgar. When Emerson writes that "the discouraging reports which I have gathered of his pursuits and character [are] . . . entirely inconsistent with the indications of his face," he counts not only on the popular discourse of physiognomy to cover his erotic interest but also on Plato's hint that male beauty was the likeliest prospect for a glimpse of transcendent virtue.[36]

In late 1821 or early 1822, Emerson wrote two poems about love he felt for a man, most likely Gay. They are poems of valediction. Emerson had finished with Harvard in August 1821. On a return visit to campus in February 1822, Emerson saw a man — probably Gay — whom in a cryptic Latin journal entry he called an "amicum, etsi veterem, ignorum" ["a (male) friend, though an old one, unknown"]. At the sight of him (and of a woman he also saw that day, "known and to be known"), Emerson felt the "beginnings of love." He hoped, still, that this man (and the woman) would become "a part of life, a part of me." But now that Emerson had graduated, any chance of a real friendship or even acquaintance with Gay was passing, if not already past.[37]

The first of the two poems is only a fragment. Emerson entitled it as if it were a quotation entered in his commonplace book: "From Frodmer's Drama 'The Friends.' " But as the *Journal* editors laconically note, "There is no dramatist named Frodmer." Of the two poems it is the rawer, which may explain why Emerson not only disguised his authorship but also canceled the first four lines. Uncensored, the poem reads as follows:

> Malcolm, I love thee more than women love
> And pure and warm and equal is the feeling
> Which binds us and our destinies forever
> But there are seasons in the change of times
> When strong excitement kindles up the light
> Of ancient memories[38]

If there is any cloak here over Emerson's feelings, the cloth is borrowed from Plato. One hears the reassurances of the *Phaedrus* myth in the assertion that the poet's love is "pure" and "equal." There is an echo of Montaigne as well, who contrasted love's violent, unpredictable fire to the gentler flame of friendship, which "is a general and universal warmth, moderate and even."[39] When Emerson writes that "strong excitement kindles up the light / Of ancient memories," he seems to be referring to Plato's reinterpretation of homosexual desire as a painful itch caused by a boy so beautiful that he awakens a memory of the forms the soul saw when it peered with Zeus over the ridge of heaven. But the costumes that Plato dresses desire in are easily shed, and in these lines Emerson also admits that sometimes his even-tempered affection for Malcolm/Martin flares up into passion. The poem had to remain a fragment because after Emerson had set forth his love, he could not figure out what came next. If these lines did figure in a play called *The Friends,* what would happen in this scene? Would Malcolm return the poet's love? Would Malcolm scorn the poet in disgust? Would the poet lay down his life for Malcolm? There is no happy way to meet the audience's need for a resolution. This love vow is a Chekhovian rifle that Emerson did not know how to fire.

Instead of firing it, Emerson made it a principle to live his life as a loaded gun. In the Platonic dialogue, Socrates winkingly set a rather light punishment for sexual consummation of philosophic boy-love. It was better not to, but if they did, boy and man would live happily ever after nonetheless, and go on to earn their wings in a later reincarnation. Later Emerson learned to wink, but in his poems to Gay, he took his noble abstinence gravely, making his sacrifice the only satisfaction of his desire.

The second poem works by such a dense web of allusions — to Virgil, to Plato, and to Emerson's private history with Gay — that it is advisable to quote it in full:

Dedication.

Quem fugis? Aut quis te nostris complexibus arcet?
Haec memorans, cinerem et sopitos suscitat ignes.

Virgilian lot.

This song to one whose unimproved talents and unattained friendship have interested the writer in his character & fate.

> By the unacknowledged tie
> Which binds us to each other
> By the pride of feeling high
> Which friendship's name can smother

> By the cold encountering eyes
> Whose language deeply thrilling
> Rebelled against the prompt surmise
> Which told the heart was willing;

> By all which you have felt and feel
> My eager gaze returning
> I offer to this silent zeal
> On youthful altars burning,

> All the classic hours which fill
> This little urn of honour;
> Minerva guide & pay the pen
> Your hand conferred upon her.[40]

Appearing at the top of a new page in the original manuscript, the word "Dedication" might refer to the poem's first four lines — the epigraph from Virgil and the lines explaining whom Emerson wrote the poem for. This is how Harold Bloom and Paul Kane have chosen to set the word in their recent edition of Emerson's poetry. But given its placement, "Dedication" might also be the title of the poem as a whole. After all, the body of the poem, as well as its head, is a dedication. It tells the story of the poet's decision to devote to Minerva the energies his friend has aroused in him.

This poem (which I will refer to as "Dedication") and the 7 June 1820 journal entry quoted above seem to be the only two instances of Virgilian lot in Emerson's journal. Perhaps Emerson consulted the *sortes Virgilianae* often, but if so, these are the only two occasions when Virgil and chance answered him so uncannily that he thought the response worth recording. As before, given the response he found apt, Emerson may have been asking about homoerotic feelings. The editors of the *Journal* provide the Loeb translation of the augury: " 'Whom fleest thou, or who bars thee from our embraces?' So speaking, he rouses the embers of the slumbering fires."[41]

At their surface meaning, these lines describe a man reproaching another person for running off. The abandoned man wants to know why the two cannot embrace, and the embers he stirs up seem emblematic of strong but dormant passions between them. Perhaps the embers represent a passion that has died down over time, and the poem that follows is to be read as an attempt to stir the fire back into flame. Alternatively, a more respectable and less sexual gloss might refer to Plato's *Phaedrus*. The slumbering fire might be interpreted as the memory of transcendent forms sleeping in the soul and sparked into life by the sight of beauty. Love for the person fleeing has rekindled the speaker's desire for beauty and the other truths once sighted beyond the ridge of heaven.

The lines could easily speak to a young man wrestling with a love he fears might scare his beloved away — a love that smolders on and on because it is not allowed to flare up and burn out. But when these lines are read in their original context, they take on other, darker meanings. In the *Aeneid,* the lines come after the ghost of Anchises, Aeneas's father, has reminded Aeneas of his divine burden. Aeneas's love for Dido has distracted him from his mission to found Rome, and Anchises' admonition is meant to rededicate him to this task. After Anchises delivers his message, his ghost vanishes, and his son cries out, "Whom fleest thou?" In Virgil's poem, the coals that Aeneas stirs represent his now renewed ambition and a resurgent love for the lost father who brought him this reminder. They refer backward to the fire that consumed Troy, a loss that Rome will avenge, and forward to the fire that will consume Dido, a sacrifice that Rome demands. Aeneas's cry is sadly ambivalent: as Anchises flees from him, he will flee from Dido. Death has taken his father from him, and destiny will take him from Dido. Both removals are mysterious and ineluctable, and by placing these two pains in parallel, Virgil justifies his hero's cruelty to his lover.

Reading the lines with a knowledge of their meaning in the *Aeneid,* one suspects that Emerson hoped to make a kind of emotional sacrifice with his "Dedication." And in the prose sentence that follows the Virgilian lot, Emerson identifies without name the person who will stand as the poem's Dido: "one whose unimproved talents and unattained friendship have interested the writer in his character & fate." This is not quite accurate. What first interested Emerson were Gay's "features": his "pale but expressive face & large eye." The news that Gay failed to improve his talents came later, and the fact that Emerson never attained his friendship came so much later as to be ongoing when Emerson penned these stanzas. But Emerson may be telling a slanted truth here. Emerson chose not just any pretty face, but this man's pretty face, and perhaps what held Emerson's attention was that Gay's beauty was accompanied by indolence — by a provocative lack of haste to realize his ambitions. The Virgilian lot resonates here with Emerson's own Hamlet-like reluctance to take up the duties his father's example imposed upon him. Emerson the berry picker was too silly to be an Aeneas. He managed to become the minister his father wanted him to be, only to cast preaching aside at the first opportunity. Emerson is also at work here picking apart Virgil's logic. Aeneas attained his friendship with Dido by failing to improve his talents; when he improved his talents, he lost Dido. In contrast, Emerson's Gay represents not a choice between love and ambition but a double negative that seems to keep afloat the possibility of both: between unimproved talents and unattained friendship, there is promisingly much to un-undo.

I have elaborated these allusions to Virgil and to Emerson's private history because without their hints, it is difficult to appreciate how much is neatly condensed into the poem proper. "Dedication" is one of the few entries about Gay that Emerson did not try to erase from his journal. That may be because it is a poem not about love but about abdicating love. But it may also be because the poem is so hermetic. It looks clean. Classic in form, the four quatrains are rhymed and in ballad meter, known as long meter when it appears in a hymn (and Emerson does call "Dedication" a "song"). Rhetorically, the poem is a prayer to Minerva. It is a plea for the goddess's blessing, to be spoken, or sung, at the moment of sacrifice.

The anaphora that take up more than half the poem look straightforward at first. "By the . . . tie . . . by the pride . . . by the . . . eyes . . . by all . . . you have felt . . . ," the first two and a half stanzas chant, until by repetition the oathlike structure almost sounds familiar, like a ritual. But these anaphora take away as much as they give, and are in places strangely ambiguous.

In the first stanza, for example, Emerson begins with the same binding affection that was the declaration of the "Frodmer" fragment. But here the tie between the speaker and the "you" he sings to is designated as "unacknowledged" as soon as it is introduced. In lines 3 and 4, the feeling between the two men is high and proud, but in a paradox that became a recurring topos for Emerson, to speak aloud the word *friendship* would smother the emotion it names. "Could we not pay our friend the compliment of truth, of silence, of forbearing?" Emerson asked in his essay "Character." In his poem "Silence," Emerson praised the "Powers above" who "love but name not love."[42]

What the poet swears by, in the second stanza, is just as self-erasing and even more difficult to parse. Emerson ordered his audience to "read the language of these wandering eye-beams" in his essay "Friendship." "Dedication" seems to be Emerson's earliest exercise in what he later called the "ocular dialect." But what are these eyes saying? Emerson describes Gay's eyes as both "cold" and "encountering," much as he would describe the contrary effect of the eyes of his first wife, Ellen, in his poem "To Eva." Ellen/Eva had eyes like "watchful sentinels," Emerson wrote, "Who charm the more their glance forbids, / . . . With fire that draws while it repels." Similarly, Emerson found conversations with Margaret Fuller to be "cold-warm, attractive-repelling." But Gay's were the first pair of eyes to fascinate Emerson with this duality.[43]

The "language deeply thrilling" of Gay's eyes, Emerson continues, "Rebelled against the prompt surmise / Which told the heart was willing." There are two ways to interpret these lines. If the surmise Emerson makes on seeing Gay is that Gay's heart is willing, then the thrill Emerson receives from Gay's glance is that Gay in fact forbids Emerson to approach. According to this interpretation, Gay is strong enough to rebel against a merely sentimental attraction. And this reading conforms to Emerson's later philosophy of friendship, which can sometimes sound like the club that Groucho Marx would only join if it were too snooty to have him for a member. As Emerson wrote in "The Sphinx,"

> Have I a lover
> Who is noble and free? —
> I would he were nobler
> Than to love me.[44]

But according to the *Journal* editors, Emerson originally wrote at line 8 "Confessed the heart was willing." That suggests that the "Which" of the emended line 8 could be understood as referring back to the "eyes" in line 5 rather than the "surmise" in line 7. In that case, the "prompt surmise" would be that Gay's heart is off limits. Gay's eyes would then rebel against this assumption by giving to Emerson the deeply thrilling message that Gay's heart is willing. It is in keeping with the overall direction of the poem that Emerson made a revision that obscures, if not eliminates, this more sentimental reading.

The poem as a whole owes its compactness and unity in part to the fact that its four stanzas comprise only one sentence. At line 11, however, there is a sharp break in grammar. Grammatically, all the things in whose name Emerson swears — the tie, the pride, the eyes, the feelings — have nothing to do with what Emerson swears. If he had replaced the first ten lines with "By Zeus," it would not have disrupted the syntax of the oath that follows. And the emotional disjuncture at this point seems just as great as the grammatical. The tender, unspoken intimacies of the first ten lines give way at line 11 to a formulaic-sounding avowal of ambition:

I offer to this silent zeal
On youthful altars burning,
All the classic hours which fill
This little urn of honour.

It is worth pausing on the non sequitur in Emerson's logic here. In the name of the feelings he silently shares with a man whose indolence has caught his attention, Emerson vows to devote his industry to the principle of zeal. Emerson cannot possibly imagine that he is undertaking this diligence to please Gay, the man of unimproved talents. Perhaps he imagines that industriousness will allow him some vent for feelings he is not able to acknowledge or name — that in the classicism of his classic hours, he will find some Platonic cover for his love. I suspect that much of the emotional and grammatical disconnect here is due to Emerson's significant but puzzling decision to offer his sacrifice not to Gay but instead to zeal. Emerson would have known that *zēlos,* the Greek root of *zeal,* meant "eager rivalry, or emulation." In that ambivalent denotation is the key to Emerson's strange turn. Rather than see the two horns of the dilemma that emulation poses — Dido or Rome, friendship or talent — as distinct and irreconcilable alternatives, Emerson's poem works to transform one into the other. Emerson calls his zeal "this silent zeal." The word "this" directs the reader to what is already present in the reader's mind, suggesting that "this silent zeal" is somehow equivalent to the emotions delicately referred to in the preceding ten lines. (Emerson made a similar substitution in his poem "Etienne de la Boèce." In that poem, to avoid an unmanly, unconditional love, the speaker leads his friend "to my altar," where the two may "worship that world-warming spark / Which dazzles me in midnight dark.")[45]

At line 14 of "Dedication," where the poet's labors are said to fill "This little urn," the word "this" signals that the urn, too, is to be understood as already before the reader's eyes. The poem itself is burning to a cinder inside it. Since the poet's writing contributes to fill an urn, his writing is pictured as under cremation — as a thing on fire. And since the poet places zeal "On youthful altars burning," zeal is also on fire. Finally, since "friendship's name can smother" the feelings between the poet and "you," those feelings, too, are to be understood as on fire. The first flame here is love, but since a sacrifice was traditionally burned on an altar, the trope of fire is able to equate love with the sacrifice of love. What goes up in flames is not only Emerson's love but also the surrender of that love and his labors for its sake. The fire may continue to burn, outshone by the greater fire that engulfs it, in the Platonic ascension that Emerson describes in his essay "Love": "this [higher and impersonal] love extinguishing the base affection, as the sun puts out the fire by shining on the hearth."[46] Sunshine may render a hearth fire less visible, but it does not douse it, and I suspect this flaw in the metaphor is at some level intended.

Ascension, however, does not explain why Emerson felt that a sacrifice was necessary in the first place. To crack that nut, it may help to consider the poem's closing lines: "Minerva guide & pay the pen / Your hand conferred upon her." It is difficult to read these lines without a double take. The lines fool the ear by sounding like a plea directed to the goddess Minerva, and the reader reads them thus, smoothly, until the reader's eye hits the final "her." Since Minerva cannot be both the *you* in "your hand" and the *she* in "her," the jarred reader has to go back to figure out where the initial scan of Emerson's grammar went wrong. It probably went wrong at "Minerva guide & pay," which the reader naturally translates as "O Minerva, please guide and pay," but which Emerson intended to be read as "May Minerva guide and pay." The poem is not sung to Minerva: in the place of the goddess is Martin Gay. Note that Gay also usurps a god's place in that the oath is sworn *by* him — by his eyes and feelings, at any rate — as well as *to* him. The unexpected meaning of the last line is that Martin Gay (represented as a hand) has given Emerson (represented as a mere pen) to Minerva for service. Gay has given Emerson away, like a father bestowing a bride.

The sacrifice of Emerson's love is necessary, then, because Gay has ordained it. In the knotty system of allusions out of which Emerson constructed "Dedication," it turns out that Gay stands not only for Dido but also for Anchises. What Gay the historical individual might have wished for in a friendship with Emerson, neither Emerson nor we ever find out. Gay vanishes behind Virgil's epic mythology and the private demonology of Emerson's own Oedipal complex, reinforced by the plainer interdict of society against homosexual love. With his baffling eyes and reluctance to be named, Emerson's icon of Gay forbids approach, and Emerson's poem treats him — as prayer's auditor and oath's referent — as divine. Gay thus merges with the ghost of Emerson's father — that "somewhat social gentleman, but severe to us children," whose voice the infant Emerson heard with terror, "as Adam that of the Lord God in the garden." This distant but demanding figure, whom Emerson wants to love but who is only to be placated by achievement, is what is represented in the poem's apotheosis of Gay. In Virgil's poem, Anchises told Aeneas to abandon Dido for Rome. Rome symbolized lofty motives for Emerson, as, for example, in this poetic fragment that he wrote when he visited the ancient capital: "ever, in the strife of your own tho'ts, / Obey the nobler impulse. That is Rome." To apply the Virgilian lot to his own life, Emerson changes its terms: in "Dedication," Gay tells Emerson to abandon Gay for literature.[47]

To mistake a lazy but likable classmate for the ultimate patriarch is a rebellious misprision when regarded from a certain angle, but it seems to have been a misprision that Emerson made earnestly, not subversively. "The glance is natural magic," Emerson wrote in "Behavior," adding that this mysterious form of communication was "in the greatest part not subject to the control of the will."[48] First loves often turn out to have been more compulsion than election, and it was not subject to Emerson's control that where he thought he saw a person, he was looking at a ghost. That ghost would continue to haunt Emerson, even though the conclusion to the poem "Dedication" suggests that to resolve his romantic quandary, Emerson will marry writing instead of Gay.

Work may sublimate love, but Emerson's best efforts never quite shook him free of loving men. In discussing a homoerotic reference in one of Emerson's journal entries, Erik Ingvar Thurin observes that "Emerson's works present many problems of this kind, so many, in fact, that they shed a somewhat ironic light on his insistent vindication of the 'innocence' of his ideal self-projection, the Poet." Joel Porte, in a different context, has noted that Emerson as a young preacher "sometimes had a tendency to see sin everywhere" — a dour trait that was "not truly characteristic of Unitarian Christianity in the Boston of the 1820s." Perhaps Thurin's comment and Porte's have a covert relation. In the years following his crush on Gay, several of Emerson's entries about friendship in his journal deteriorated into near rants about the dangers of "vileness." In *The Conduct of Life,* Emerson coolly declared that "there is a pudency about friendship, as about love, and though fine souls never lose sight of it, yet they do not name it." In youth, however, Emerson was not so decorous as to keep quiet about his friendships or the anxieties they brought him. His biographer Robert D. Richardson Jr. believes that Emerson's candor about his feelings for Gay indicates that he was "rather innocent and essentially unembarrassed" about the crush. The journal passages discussed below, however, put paid to the notion that Emerson was innocent of homosexual panic.[49]

"Sympathy is the wine of life," Emerson began one such entry in early 1824. Within a few lines, however, Emerson butted up against friendship's limits. "Words may be free, thought may be free and the heart laid bare to your friend but nevertheless the freedom even of friendship hath a limit & let a man beware how he passes it." (Emerson first wrote, "& beware how you pass it," but switched the phrase to the third person.) It is safe, Emerson suggests, to say "base & vicious words" to your friend if "they come as momentary caprices and not the irrepressible utterance of rooted passions." But no sooner does Emerson suggest this limited license between friends than his rhetoric darkens like an electrical storm.

> To be the slave of a base passion is to be most humbly degraded. He that loosely forgets himself here & lets his friend be privy to the words & acts

which base desires extort from him has forfeited like a fool the love he prized. The waters of affection will soon dry up or disgust will flow in their place. And what is worse, your friend, if he has uprightly disdained to become the accomplice of your vileness, possesses a cruel advantage over you. Whatever tears, whatever bitter remorse the memory of your degradation may cost you, you cannot efface from his mind the scornful recollection. He may expose to the whisper & the scoff of society the secret guilt that lowers you in the scale of moral beings. Give away to your friend the richest treasure God imparts to intelligent creatures — your own self-respect; & then go & eat grass in the field until seventy times be passed over you for the lord of Babylon was less a beast than thou.

It is possible that Emerson is not here describing the shame and disgrace that a young man would risk if he made a sexual overture to a male friend. Perhaps the crime Emerson had in mind when he wrote about the danger of inviting your friend to become "the accomplice of your vileness" was a joint visit to a brothel, a conspiracy to murder, or a bout of heavy drinking. Whatever the crime, it had to have been a grave one, because Emerson multiplied Nebuchadnezzar's sentence by a factor of ten. The context, however, suggests that sodomy is the likeliest candidate. Emerson's language closely echoes Paul's condemnation of homosexuality in Romans 1:26–28.[50]

On 1 March 1824, Emerson took up the topic again. "All human pleasures have their dregs & even Friendship itself hath the bitter lees," Emerson wrote. He proceeded to describe a situation that resembles that of the lovers in *Phaedrus,* who begin with noble intentions but then weakly choose to have sex.

Who is he that thought he might clasp his friend in embraces so tight, in daily intercourse so familiar that they two should be one? They met in equal conversation. I saw their eyes kindle with the common hope that they should climb life's hill together & totter down hand in hand. But the violent flame of youthful affection rapidly wasted itself. They foolishly trusted to each other the last secret of their bosoms, their weakness. Every man has his failing, & these no more than others. But Men prudently cloak up the sore side, & shun to disgust the eye of the multitude. These erred in fancying that friendship would pardon infirmities & that a just confidence demanded that the last door of the heart should be unclosed, and even its secret sensuality revealed. They fell in each other's respect; they slighted, disliked, & ridiculed each other & regret & fear remained at last of the consequences of the implicit confidence of their violent love.

Only heroes (a pair such as Adams and Jefferson, for example) or humble folk may safely have friendships, Emerson continued, presumably because the former are too strong and the latter too weak for their passion to lapse into sex. Emerson ended by noting the "curious" fact that "this violent fondness" is never summoned up by a well-known acquaintance, but only by a stranger. "So James I's propensity to favourites, who successively disgusted him."[51]

Emerson returned to King James's reputation as a sodomite a few weeks later, in an April entry expressly designating "this violent fondness" as a defect that he worried about in himself. In a harsh self-assessment, Emerson lamented the

> want of sufficient *bottom* in my nature, for want of that confidence of manner which springs from an erect mind which is without fear & without reproach. In my frequent humiliation, even before women & children I am compelled to remember the poor boy who cried, "I told you, Father, they would find me out." Even those feelings which are counted noble & generous, take in me the taint of frailty. For my strong propensity to friendship, instead of working out its manly ends, degenerates to a fondness for particular casts of feature perchance not unlike the doting of old King James. Stateliness and silence hang very like Mokannah's suspicious silver veil, only concealing what is best not shewn. What is called a warm heart, I have not.[52]

The last sentence seems to be a peculiar contradiction of everything else in the entry. If Emerson's fault is an overfond doting, it seems odd for him to berate his heart for chilliness. He charged himself with the same paradox two years before, on 13 May 1822, summoning as evidence his fascination with Gay: "I have not the kind affections of a pigeon . . . ," he wrote then. "Have not sufficient feeling to speak a natural hearty welcome to a friend or stranger and yet send abroad wishes & fancies of a friendship with a man I never knew."[53] The warmth of his feelings for Gay do not register on Emerson's thermometer.

This self-accusing self-contradiction returned to vex Emerson when he composed his essays "Friendship" and "Love" in 1839 and 1840. In those years, however, he came to recognize that his coolness was a reflection of the heat of the passions he suppressed. "I cold because I am hot," he wrote on 11 June 1840.[54]

Emerson grieved his whole life that he felt emotionally distant from those around him. To his second wife, Lidian, for example, he apologized that "a photometer cannot be a stove." For years he complained to his journal that marriage was unsatisfying and a trap, although he was too polite ever to mention Lidian by name. And all his life, he craved an imagined friend or teacher. Joking with his brother Charles, Emerson described the figure he longed for as "a decent slovenly gentleman who believes in the resurrection of the dead." In a letter to his aunt, Mary Moody Emerson, written after his first wife's death, his sketch of this figure was almost messianic: "God's greatest gift

is a Teacher & when will he send me one, full of truth of boundless benevolence & heroic sentiments?" Immediately he retracted this hubristic wish, in
a gesture of pious humility undermined by its dazzling simile: "The creature is
never to dawn upon me like a sun-burst." For a time Thomas Carlyle seemed
the fulfillment of prophecy. On 20 November 1834, Emerson wrote that a
letter from Carlyle "for the moment, realizes the hope to which I have clung
with both hands, through each disappointment, that I might converse with a
man whose ear of faith was not stopped, and whose argument I could not
predict."[55]

As my discussion of "Dedication" suggests, Emerson chose a path that led
him to his friend only at moments and only on paper. This is a marked shift in
the relationship of writing to friendship. In the eighteenth century, for John
Fishbourne Mifflin, writing ratified a friendship with another man, gave it
depth, and evened out its emotional vicissitudes. In the nineteenth century, for
Ralph Waldo Emerson — perhaps because of the incursion into consciousness
of anxiety about sexual propriety — writing itself enacted friendship. Before,
writing had smoothed and ordered a private chaos of real feelings. Now,
writing conjured up both the chaos and the order, provoking the sympathy of
the (now anonymous) reader as well as offering to channel it. Emerson's con-
flicted stance toward emotion derives from this new dual role for writing.
Emerson may seem cold because he is secretly hot, but we never misread him;
Emerson's true readers always respond warmly. He always fails to be completely stoic, but that is the nature of his project. He is not really a philosopher
but an essayist — one who tries.

The architect of an impersonalized person, Emerson also takes advantage of
the transition in the social role of literature by writing out his heart's most
poignant moments to a mass audience, all the while protesting that he cannot
bear the intrusion of direct contact with another man's mind. He is not an
exhibitionist, because he reveals not himself but a representative man. And so
he is melancholy. No one will ever have an original relationship with Emerson.
He will always depend on writing, a vehicle that is always breaking down.

This is a strange new burden to ask writing to bear: not just the weight of
recording a relationship but the weight of being a relationship. To preserve
writing's link to men — to keep the torch aflame — Emerson denies that writing
has any value as an end in itself. It is only a self-consuming sign of spirit. "For
we are not pans and barrows, nor even porters of the fire and torch-bearers,
but children of the fire, made of it," Emerson wrote in "The Poet." Place this
fiery soul in a paper boat, and if the paper is inflammable, it must incinerate.
As Emerson explained this principle in "The Over-Soul," the poet's "best
communication to our mind is to teach us to despise all he has done."[56]

When Emerson criticized his brother Charles's valedictory oration, he measured its failure by how little it aroused the listeners. "The vice of his oratory lies here — he is a *spectacle* instead of being an *engine,*" Emerson reproved Charles (in the third person). The axis of his logic here is the reverse of that in his later apology to his wife. He exhorts his brother to be stove, not photometer. He regrets that the most "moving passage passed with no more effect than if the same elegant speaker had said Butterfly butterfly butterfly. . . . He never touched me." Over the years, Emerson upbraided himself for his own performance as a lecturer in similar terms. In August 1837 he wrote of his "hope to arouse young men at Cambridge to a worthier view of their literary duties." In February 1840 he rebuked himself for not rising to his own standards: "I have not once transcended the coldest selfpossession. I said I will agitate others, being agitated myself . . . but no arrows, no axes, no nectar, no growling, no transpiercing, no loving, no enchantment." Always, he felt, he just missed his opportunity "for painting in fire my thought." It is not over-reading to notice the sexual metaphors in Emerson's aspirations for oratory. Emerson himself noticed them when he wrote, "Few men communicate their highest thoughts to any person. . . . Yet are these thoughts as much made for communication as a sex."[57]

As a poem, "Dedication" is clever, like a Chinese puzzle box. But it is not a poetic breakthrough. It does not open the language to new vistas. Its tone is more monumental than exploratory. But "Dedication" may help a reader understand two language effects crucial to the American Renaissance.

The first is Emerson's use in "Dedication" of the second person. This is innovative. The poem is addressed as if to someone the poet knows intimately, but because of the peculiar limbo in which Emerson held Gay, the pronoun calls on an unknown. Emerson surely intended "Dedication" to remain private, but its *you* is kin to the *you* invoked by Emerson's "poet" in the closing lines of *Nature,* a *you* flattered and bullied into godlike greatness. When Emerson addressed a worshiped, intensely personal, and never openly confessed *you* in print, and an anonymous reader took the pronoun personally, the parallax created an illusion of great force. "All that Adam had, all that Caesar could, you have and can do."[58] To read Emerson is like receiving a letter from an anonymous admirer, except that the admirer isn't anonymous; you are. But you forget that detail in the rush of reading the news that God is in you.

Whitman learned his brassy seductions from this Emersonian second person, and in several of Emerson's manuscript poems, the *you* prefigures the bard of Manhattan eerily. In "He must have / Droll fancies," Emerson presumes with Whitmanian egotism to know his reader to be like himself. "I am frank, my friend," Emerson writes, "your eye has found / A gipsy muse that reads your lineaments." In another poem, "Be of good cheer, brave spirit," Emerson not only encourages a shy young male *you*, he also promises a Calamus-like union of "a select family of Sons / Now scattered wide thro' earth" on a day that will "seal the marriage of these minds with thine / Thine everlasting lovers." This son-binding eros, Emerson specified in an earlier draft of this fragment, was "an emulous love." A decade before Whitman burst into song, Emerson was already chanting about "the streets of great New York": "In the city of surfaces / Where I a swain became a surface / I found & worshipped Him."[59]

The second language effect is more particular to Emerson. The ability to respond to it, Joel Porte has written, is what distinguishes an Emersonian reader from a non-Emersonian. In Porte's description, this quintessentially Emersonian resource is "the excited shift of mood and the spontaneous exfoliation of joy out of literally nothing . . . among the best surprises Emerson has to offer." A very early example of it can be found in a journal entry dated late February 1822. Emerson had spotted Gay during a return to the Harvard campus a few days earlier, prompting not only a Latin confession of the "beginnings of love," discussed above, but also several pages of forcefully expressed but cryptically vague pronouncements in English. On one page, beneath the Latin phrase "scripsi nomen, supra" ["I have written the name above"], Emerson burst out with this mysterious joy: "A beautiful thought struck me suddenly, without any connection, which I could trace, with my previous trains of thought and feeling. It had no analogy to any notion I ever remembered to have formed; it surpassed all others by the novelty it bore, and the grasp it laid upon every fibre; for the time, it absorbed all other thoughts; — all the faculties — each in his cell, bowed down and worshipped before this new Star. — Ye who roam among the living and the dead, over flowers or among the cherubims, in real or ideal universes, do not whisper my thought!"[60] About the details of his rapture, Emerson is secretive. This secrecy might have shared a motive with the mild disguise of his feelings in Latin two pages before. Did this unexpected beautiful thought have something to do with the name Emerson had *not* written above — that is, with Gay? It is impossible to say. But the sudden and mysterious showers of pleasure in Emerson's prose, however unmotivated they may seem to the reader and however much Emerson wants us to take them as unmotivated, must have had a long foreground somewhere. A pleasure can be rootless only if it has been cut from its roots, and "Dedication" is a story of holy divorce — of hierotomy, to play on Leslie Fiedler's *hierogamos* and on the Greek *hiera tomia,* the parts cut from a sacrifice and used to swear an oath. In the case at hand, Emerson knows, if not where he plucked his flower, at least the name of the blossom, but he chooses not to reveal even that much.

By the time of his essay "The Poet," Emerson had become so familiar with "*ascension,* or, the passage of the soul into higher forms," that he could reverse its process. In that essay, he tells a parable of a sculptor who "was, as I remember, unable to tell directly, what made him happy, or unhappy, but by wonderful indirections he could tell." Elsewhere Emerson claimed that he preferred to sculpt consciously. In "The Problem," for example, he explained that he would never be the sort of artist who "builded better than he knew." So perhaps Emerson's sculptor is "unable to tell" what pleases him most not because he does not know but because he is not allowed to say. Emerson leaves unclear whether it is us or himself that the sculptor cannot tell. Emerson proceeds, however, to narrate a tale of art remedying both opacities by re-covering through its "wonderful indirections" a lost source of ecstasy: "He rose one day, according to his habit, before the dawn, and saw the morning break, grand as the eternity out of which it came, and, for many days after, he strove to express this tranquillity, and, lo! his chisel had fashioned out of marble the form of a beautiful youth, Phosphorus, whose aspect is such, that, it is said, all persons who look on it become silent." In "Dedication," a hand-some classmate's face passed into a devotion to literary art. In "The Poet," a mysteriously general exhilaration takes shape as an ephebe's beauty. As Thurin has noted, in the journal entry from which the parable of the sculptor originally derives, no sooner does Emerson's joy take a young man's shape than that form must dissolve anew: "Yet is not that figure final or adequate; . . . the thought has already transcended it, is already something else, has taken twenty thousand shapes, whilst poor Hans was hammering at this one." By placing male beauty in the fire circle of art, where "everything tilts and rocks," Emerson surrenders his beloved to the "method of nature," whose "perma-nence is a perpetual inchoation." The beloved is sacrificed to art, to be reborn from art.[61]

# 5

## Too Good to Be Believed: Emerson's "Friendship" and the Samaritans

Two days before Christmas, 1839, Emerson found himself returning to a bundle of letters that upset and discontented him. He confessed to Margaret Fuller that rereading the bundle led to an outburst: "I have read through a second time today the entire contents of the brown paper parcel and startled my mother & my wife when I went into the dining room with the declaration that I wished to live a little while with people who love & hate, who have Muses & Furies, and in a twelvemonth I should write tragedies & romance."[1] No doubt Ruth and Lidian Emerson were startled. It must have been jarring to hear the man in their lives declare that the emotions they aroused in him were pale and unreal compared to emotions he was experiencing vicariously by reading the private correspondence of a circle of young friends to whom Margaret Fuller had introduced him.

As with nearly all of Emerson's many statements of discontent with domestic life, a self-deprecating humor ensured that this blow glanced. Emerson stages himself here as slightly ridiculous. He paints his restlessness as something childlike and excitable, something bound to blow over as soon as he gets supper or a good night's sleep. No one would take seriously the notion of Emerson as playwright or novelist, and he implies in his outburst that the odds that he will act on his emotional distress are as unlikely as a career change. The only consequence of his petulance is to annoy or amuse his wife and his mother.

Although from time to time he may have been able to vent his anxiety in jokes, Emerson brooded for more than a decade on his unhappiness in his marriage to Lidian Jackson. Even in the privacy of his journals, he was too delicate to fault Lidian by name. Instead, he attacked marriage as an institution. A journal entry of 1841 is typically abstract: "It is not in the plan or prospect of the soul, this fast union of one to one." Just as typically, Emerson gave this abstract entry a gruesome heading — "Mezentian marriage" — as if to belie the cool philosophical tone of his complaint. As the *Journal* editors explain, Mezentius was a king in the *Aeneid* who "tied men face to face with corpses and let them die."[2]

Elsewhere Emerson wrote, "Plainly marriage should be a temporary relation."[3] Emerson had wooed his first wife, Ellen Tucker, with heartfelt, even rhapsodical, passion. But Emerson knew when he courted Ellen that their marriage *would* be a temporary relationship, because when he met her, she was already gravely ill with tuberculosis. She succumbed a year and a half after their wedding. Emerson's manuscript poems to Ellen Tucker, before and after her death, have a simple tenderness that is more affecting than most of the verse he published, and there is no reason to doubt the sincerity of his emotions for her. It is nonetheless true that with Ellen Tucker, Emerson lived out what for Charles Brockden Brown had been only a fantasy: an early marriage to a woman who soon died, a scenario that proved his manhood and his romantic nature while leaving him free to write as he pleased, unencumbered by the financial responsibilities that a family would incur. In fact, Ellen, an heiress, bequeathed to her widower a legacy that underwrote his decision to leave the ministry. Emerson surely never schemed for this outcome. But perhaps he felt free to give his heart so completely to Ellen because, at some level, he knew they would not be together long.

The second time he married, Emerson chose a sturdier woman, one who was willing to leave Emerson's emotions largely to himself. It is not clear why Lidian Jackson accepted Emerson's reserve — why she agreed to take as a lover a man who was more photometer than stove. But perhaps it suited her. Her daughter's testimony suggests that Lidian was something of a photometer herself: "The tremendous manner in which she loved Father," Ellen Tucker Emerson wrote in her biography of her mother, "was always as astonishing to me as the coolness with which she treated him." Perhaps Lidian's chronic dyspepsia and malaise should be read as a protest. That was how Margaret Fuller read them. During an 1842 visit to Concord, Fuller speculated in her journal that Lidian "will always have these pains, because she has always a lurking hope that Waldo's character will alter, and that he will be capable of an intimate union." Lidian's bitterness — her ability to "extract poison from the most healthful plants" — in time became a half-joked-about commonplace in the Emerson household.[4] Lidian may have felt that on the question of what kind or degree of emotion she and Emerson would share, she had not been offered much choice.

Even at the very beginning of their relationship, in his written proposal of marriage, Emerson had no passion to give Lidian. Although his letter requesting her hand beseeched her to love him, for his own part he was willing to avow his affection for her only through an extenuation and a double negative: "The strict limits of the intercourse I have enjoyed, have certainly not permitted the manifestation of that tenderness which is the first sentiment in the common kindness between man and woman. But I am not less in love, after a new and higher way." The "higher way" Emerson had in mind was Aristotle's — to be precise, Aristotle's definition of the highest of the three kinds of friendship: "that between good men who are alike in excellence or virtue." "I am persuaded," Emerson wrote Jackson, "that I address one so in love with what I love . . . that an affection founded on such a basis, cannot alter." As Aristotle explains, for two such high-minded individuals "their friendship lasts as long as they are good, and that means it will last for a long time, since goodness or virtue is a thing that lasts."[5]

Mere emotion, in this system, is incidental. As Emerson noted in his journal in 1840, "I marry impersonally."[6] To reinforce his argument, Emerson might have referred to Diotima's speech in the *Symposium,* where as love ascends it purges itself of attachment to any single human being (in Plato's case, of course, the beloved to be transcended was a boy). Emerson did not need to say that he loved Lidian, because if theirs was the highest sort of alliance, what mattered was not that they loved each other, but that they loved virtue. As Socrates observed in the Platonic dialogue *Lysis,* however, a friendship based on this kind of likeness is hardly romantic. "How in the world are the good going to be friends to the good?" Socrates wondered. "They don't yearn for one another when apart, because even then they are sufficient to themselves, and when together they have no need of one another. Is there any way people like that can possibly value each other?"[7] As usual, Socrates' interlocutor was cornered, able to answer only with a sullen and confused "No." And Lidian Jackson seems to have been browbeaten into the same sort of transcendental negative. As Emerson wrote to his brother during the courtship, "This is a very sober joy."[8] Plato's Socrates ended up discarding this definition of *filia* as "virtuous likeness," because it had too little fire in it. After all, in *Lysis,* Socrates was discussing friendship only because he was demonstrating to a crowd of young men that philosophy is a better way to seduce a boy than flattery.

Alikeness in virtue sufficed to achieve Emerson's seduction of the woman whom Fuller somewhat archly dubbed the "sainted Lidian." A few years after he had engineered it, the marriage seems to have felt unsatisfying to Emerson. When Lidian was three months' pregnant with their first son, Waldo, Emerson complained in his journal that "the lover on being accepted, misses the wildest charm of the maid he dared not hope to call his own." And children, Emerson grumbled, were no more than "parricidal fruits." A month later, Emerson's favorite brother, Charles, died of tuberculosis. "In him I have lost all my society," a bereaved Emerson wrote to his aunt Mary. Emerson was lonely; his wife apparently did not keep him company.[9]

And so when her husband invited the saucy-tongued, fearfully well read, emotionally vivid Margaret Fuller to stay with them in Concord for a few weeks in July 1836, Lidian was perhaps wise to have been circumspect. A letter that Lidian wrote to Elizabeth Peabody at the time suggests that before the visit, Lidian made some discreet inquiries about Fuller. The answers that she received apparently calmed her doubts. "I had heard from the best authority that she was sound at *heart*," Lidian wrote, "and I could imagine no peculiarities of intellect or character, that could revolt me or repel my regard — if that was true of her."[10] Lidian's sources assured her that Fuller was morally upstanding. They might have added that she was considered eccentric and homely — and unlikely to pose a threat. Years later, in his contribution to the *Memoirs of Margaret Fuller Ossoli,* Emerson described Fuller's demeanor during her first visit as unappealing to the point of disgust: "Her extreme plainness, — and a trick of incessantly opening and shutting her eyelids, — the nasal tone of her voice, — all repelled; and I said to myself, we shall never get far." They did, however, get quite far. Emerson may have had Fuller in mind years later when he wrote, in his essay "Beauty," that "there are faces so fluid with expression, so flushed and rippled by the play of thought, that we can hardly find what the mere features really are."[11]

Fuller did pose a threat, or more accurately, a challenge: she read Plato differently. As a result of this divergent reading, Fuller conducted her friendships in a style utterly unlike Emerson's. A modern reader of Fuller's correspondence will be charmed by her wit and impressed by her erudition, but awed by the organizational skill, sensitivity of spirit, and linguistic power that Fuller brought to bear on the task of cultivating her romantic friendships. She did not take them up lightly or girlishly (although there were moments of unintellectual fun), nor did she treat them as rehearsals for marriage, but as a way of life. She labored to create around her an environment that would draw out, educate, and fortify her soul and the souls she adopted. In practical terms, this entailed soliciting and respecting a great number of confidences. Fuller educed them adeptly, and as Emerson wrote, she "kept a hundred fine threads in her hand, without crossing or entangling any." So deeply was she trusted that when she died, her orphaned correspondence struck Emerson as a menace to public order—sort of like, later, the nuclear weapons that seemed too potent to be safely left in the hands of the novice, lesser states that survived the Soviet Union. "When I heard that a trunk of her correspondence had been found & opened," Emerson wrote, "I felt what a panic would strike all her friends, for it was as if a clever reporter had got underneath a confessional & agreed to report all that transpired there in Wall street."[12]

Fuller never attempted to displace Lidian with direct sexual competition, but rather to introduce Emerson into the world of her friends. Emerson wrote that Fuller "wore this circle of friends, when I first knew her, as a necklace of diamonds around her neck." Almost immediately, Fuller went to work thread-ing the newest gem, Emerson, onto her chain. Only a month after Fuller's first visit, she had induced Emerson not only to invite her back but also to extend the invitation to "your friend Miss Barker," one of Fuller's protégées. His initiation had begun.[13]

Fuller's was a world heady with emotion, and one Emerson biographer recently tried to approximate his sense of it by writing that "in the early 1840s, Emerson was living emotionally, though not physically, in what would now be called an open marriage."[14] This claim is not quite accurate, because although there were both men and women in Fuller's circle, there was something in it antagonistic to heterosexual love per se. Fuller was elaborating on the codes of love and ritual between women in the late eighteenth and early nineteenth century that have been described by Carroll Smith-Rosenberg. As discussed in Chapter 1, a romance between three male Philadelphia diarists resulted from cross-pollination: after John F. Mifflin learned from Deborah Norris how women conducted their romantic friendships, he and two other upper-class men began to express their love for each other in a similar way. Fuller insti-gated another such cross-pollination. Less permissive about sexual behavior, nineteenth-century society continued to approve of women's romantic friend-ships, no matter how ardently they were expressed, in part because men par-ticipated only as adjuncts. This exclusion of men was a restriction that Fuller, as a feminist, saw no reason not to overrule, but in doing so, she invited men like Emerson to feel for her not what a man would feel, but what a woman would. It may sound like nonsense to assert that Fuller hoped Emerson would respond to her and her friends with emotions that today we would call lesbian. But Fuller did not know in advance how far she could take Romanticism, or, rather, how sharply the world would bring her up short. Odd as it may sound, Fuller hoped for exactly this nonsense, for years.

As Emerson later wrote, Fuller "gave herself to her friendships with an entireness not possible to any but a woman, with a depth possible to few women." And she demanded that womanly depth in reply — from men as well as women. When the young Samuel Gray Ward pulled away from Fuller, she wrote him that she would excuse his loss of love by bearing in mind that she "as you have said 'call up the woman in you.' " Ward could not handle this evocation of his female spirit. Not all men could love as well as women, Fuller discovered, to her chagrin. "Few male natures can long endure a nature as pure, as open, as trusting, above all, as *overflowing* as J[ane]'s," she once counseled a female disciple, alluding to a frustration another of her disciples had recently experienced. "They [i.e., men] want folds to penetrate, dragons to slay, pepper to the cream tart." Fuller saw Emerson as more capacious of a feminine response than most men; in 1842 she wrote of his "sweet girlishness," which came and went and which she wished to see more of. And Emerson recognized the erotic, even homoerotic, strain in Fuller's aggressive search for intimacy, which he admitted he could not satisfy. The tone of her yearning struck him as at once unspeakably carnal and indescribably pure. When he touched on the matter in his memoir of Fuller, he wrote that Fuller's "friendships, as a girl with girls, as a woman with women, were not unmingled with passion, and had passages of romantic sacrifice and of ecstatic fusion, which I have heard with the ear, but could not trust my profane pen to report."[15]

Despite his fears and limitations, Emerson was ripe for an experiment in the late 1830s. He wrote in his journal on 6 May 1837, "Sad is this continual postponement of life. I refuse sympathy & intimacy with people as if in view of some better sympathy & intimacy to come. But whence & when?" To the question If not now, when? Emerson had no good answer, and so he lowered his barriers and let Fuller go to work. She arranged for her choicest friends to meet the Concord sage. The Boston bluestocking and poet Caroline Sturgis visited the Emersons in June 1838, where, Emerson wrote, "twice she engaged my cold pedantic self into a fine surprise of thought & hope." On 3 July 1839, Emerson accompanied Fuller to an exhibition of Washington Allston's paintings in Boston, where he met Samuel Gray Ward, the art-loving scion of a prominent banking family. Emerson met Anna Hazard Barker, a socialite from New York by way of New Orleans, on 4 October 1839 at Jamaica Plain, where Barker had come to visit Fuller. He described Barker to his aunt as "a vision of grace & beauty," and she inspired him to write in his diary a sentence he recycled in his essay "Friendship": "A new person is to me ever a great event."[16]

Barker, Sturgis, and Ward were Fuller's friends long before they were Emerson's. Fuller made him the gift of a posy of intelligent, attractive people. As he joked to Fuller, "For a hermit I begin to think I know several very fine people."[17] The letters Emerson wrote to Barker, Sturgis, and Ward were unlike those he wrote to anyone else. For a hermit, Emerson could gush with sentiment. Although he never altogether let his guard down with Fuller herself, Emerson relaxed with his new young friends, perhaps because they were so young that they were not socially his peers. In 1840, when these friendships climaxed, Sturgis was twenty-one, Ward twenty-three, and Barker twenty-seven. That year Emerson himself was thirty-seven and Fuller turned thirty.

At the peak of these sentimental liaisons, Emerson himself marveled at the change in his emotional habits. He wrote about his new friends with tentative pride to Carlyle: "I have been drawing nearer to a few men & women whose love gives me in these days more happiness than I can write of." With his near sister-in-law Elizabeth Hoar, he was exuberant: "Have I been always a hermit, and unable to approach my fellow men, & do the Social Divinities suddenly offer me a *roomfull* of friends? Please God, I will not be wanting to my fortune but will eat this pomegranate." (In his essay "Of Friendship," Francis Bacon likens the fruit of friendship to "the pomegranate, full of many kernels.") In his portion of the *Memoir of Margaret Fuller Ossoli*, Emerson explained that he and the other editors had considered giving the memoir the title "Margaret and her Friends," so inextricable was Fuller's life from the lives she surrounded herself with. He advised the reader that "the narrative, like a Greek tragedy, should suppose the chorus always on the stage, sympathizing and sympathized with by the queen of the scene." Between the years 1837 and 1841, the same supposition should perhaps be applied to any discussion of Emerson.[18]

Emerson resisted socialization, but Fuller set upon him optimistically. On 21 September 1836, she directed a letter to Emerson with the salutation "My dear friend," explaining that "I may venture to begin so since you have subscribed yourself my friend." A year later, however, she had come to a better appreciation of her subject's intractability. On 14 August 1837, a somewhat dejected Fuller declined to offer any excuses for not having written sooner. "I have not wished to write," she told Emerson. "For I have been in an irreligious state of mind, a little misanthropic & sceptical about the existence of any real communication between human beings. I bear constantly in heart that text of yours 'O *my friends,* there are no friends' but to me it is a paralyzing conviction."[19]

In one of his commonplace books, under the heading "Friendship," Emerson recorded several such grim entries. One Spanish proverb claimed, much like Robert Frost's neighbor in "Mending Wall," that "A wall between both, best preserves friendship." Emerson also transcribed *"Ne cor edito,"* a Pythagorean apothegm he had found in an essay by Francis Bacon, who glossed it thus: *"Eat not the heart.* . . . . Those that want friends to open themselves unto are cannibals of their own hearts." (The same passage impressed Melville, who recorded it along with notes for what would become *Moby-Dick* on the flyleaf of a volume of Shakespeare.) The particular text that stuck in Fuller's throat came from Montaigne's essay "On Friendship." According to Montaigne, high friendships leave no room for doubt, but not all friendships are so lofty. A little mutual suspicion may be "healthy in the practice of ordinary and customary friendships, in regard to which we must use the remark that Aristotle often repeated: 'O my friends, there is no friend.' "[20]

Actually, there is no evidence that Aristotle said any such thing. Aristotle's *Nicomachean Ethics* casts friendship as the sine qua non of the good life. "O my friends, there is no friend" is in fact a mistranslation of a secondhand report on Aristotle.[21] Emerson probably had no inkling of this philological slip, because he no doubt trusted Montaigne's Greek to be better than his own. Nonetheless, it is indicative of Emerson's pessimism that he should have selected what is perhaps the only moment of detraction in Montaigne's paean to friendship. The paradoxical caveat "O my friends, there is no friend" runs counter to the stronger flow of Montaigne's essay, which is a tribute to his friend Etienne de la Boétie and celebrates friendship's ability to merge two souls. But this was the sentence that he took away and that struck Fuller as a "paralyzing conviction." Fuller managed to continue her 14 August 1837 letter by laughing off the nihilism with a bon mot: "However, I must say I feel a desire . . . to see my dear *no friends,* Mr and Mrs Emerson."

Emerson may have quoted the pseudo-Aristotelian proverb in conversation with Fuller. Or she might have read it in an incomplete draft for a lecture on friendship that Emerson cobbled together, sometime between 1834 and 1837, out of a few old sermons and journal entries. This unfinished lecture and the sermons it drew from reveal Emerson's thinking on friendship before he met Fuller. They show the armor of pessimistic philosophy she tried to convince him to remove.

On the surface, Emerson's early sermons were upbeat on the topic of friendship. In sermon 62, delivered on 16 January 1830, Emerson argued that it was not impious to love Christ as a friend. "It seems to me just and becoming not to shut it up in the breast, like a burdensome or sinful secret, but to give it the freest utterance." Emerson looked forward to the advent of universal friendship on earth. Rivalry for "wealth and fame and office" would cease when "instead of money men shall pursue virtue and instead of fame pursue truth." This prophesy of a union of all men as lovers echoed Emerson's manuscript poem "Be of good cheer," in which "God's word brings on the day / To seal the marriage of these minds with thine / Thine everlasting lovers," and it was in turn echoed by the secular vision of "a nation of friends" that concluded his essay "Politics."[22]

In sermon 140, delivered on 8 January 1832, Emerson preached even more rosily of friendship. As Christianity improved morality, widely shared friendships would blossom. "The better men they are, the better friends they will be," Emerson claims, adding, "No man becomes better without becoming more affectionate." But in the middle of the sermon, Emerson notes, more darkly, that friendships in this world are fallen. Quoting Montaigne's "O my friends, there is no friend," Emerson observes that even between intimates, there is no perfect communication between men on earth. "We live with people for years to whom we never impart things we think of every day." Speaking as a minister, Emerson saw the limitations and frustrations that kept mortal men apart as promises not yet fulfilled. "These unsatisfied desires intimate a future state; they promise a gratification yet to come." As if his text were Plato's *Phaedrus* rather than Paul's First Epistle to the Corinthians, Emerson explains that balked friendship in this world causes agitation because it starts us growing our wings for the next. "This restless love, ever seeking its object, points to a future state and to exalted companions, as much as the folded wings of the poor caterpillar indicate that one day it shall cease to creep along the ground and shall rise into the air with new form and increased powers."[23]

In 1834 or slightly thereafter, Emerson, no longer a man of God, recycled the remarks in these sermons for a lecture on friendship. As one might expect, he salvaged the dark middle of sermon 140, repeating his insights about the uncanny solitude a person may feel amid daily companions. Although the lecture as a whole stressed the education that friends offer to the soul — through vicarious experience, stimulation to excellence, and incitement to action — Emerson elaborated on his sense of friendship as disappointing. "There is always something unsaid that is better than any thing that is said," he wrote. "There is always the sense that the communication is not perfect, 'one soul in two bodies' as Aristotle defines friendship."[24]

Again, Emerson was not in fact quoting Aristotle but Montaigne's redaction of Aristotle. And again, Emerson was quoting Montaigne against the grain. In the passage that Emerson pilfered, Montaigne explains that pure friends do not owe each other duties or favors, because they share all. "Everything actually being in common between them — wills, thoughts, judgments, goods, wives, children, honor, and life — and their relationship being that of one soul in two bodies, according to Aristotle's very apt definition, they can neither lend nor give anything to each other." Montaigne was using the idea of one soul in two bodies — which he attributed to Aristotle, although it is not a direct quote — to stress the indivisibility of friends.[25]

With admirable neatness, in this lecture fragment Emerson changed the pious hope of his sermons into pagan skepticism: "The desire of a friend is almost a religion with every pure cultivated mind, and like the religious desires is never satisfied in this world." Emerson still longed for a friend—and still thought this longing admirable—but could no longer keep faith with a religious sublimation of this desire. In sermon 140, Emerson had asked, "Shall these powers go to the grave and perish unknown; and shall these desires remain forever unsatisfied?" As a minister, he was able then to answer "No."[26]

Once he no longer believed in a personal resurrection or a personal divinity, Emerson was forced to admit that desires *could* go to the grave. When Emerson mocked Charles Fourier's utopian optimism in *Representative Men,* he made the French socialist speak in an English borrowed from the young Emerson. "Charles Fourier announced that 'the attractions of man are proportioned to his destinies,'" Emerson wrote, quoting the slogan that hung inscribed on an azure tablet, beside a bust of Fourier, in the common room at Brook Farm. Emerson then translated: "in other words, that every desire predicts its own satisfaction. Yet, all experience exhibits the reverse of this." He was contradicting his early sermon precisely: unsatisfied desires did *not* intimate a future state. They did *not* promise a gratification yet to come.[27]

On the contrary, "each of [the soul's] joys ripens into a new want" Emerson wrote in his essay "Love," in a turn of phrase that sounds cheerful until you think it through. But if this appalled Emerson, it did not dismay Fuller. During the autumn of 1837, while Emerson was revising his notes on friendship yet again, for a lecture to be called "The Heart," Fuller was cajoling Caroline Sturgis to spend three months with her in Providence, Rhode Island, in an arrangement that would resemble a one-on-one live-in tutorial. In eager anticipation, Fuller suggested which books the two women would read together and bargained with the matrons of boardinghouses for lodgings that she and Sturgis could share. Sturgis dithered. She offered excuses, but Fuller knocked them down. When Sturgis complained that she did not feel well, Fuller assured her that Fuller herself would be a better nurse than the Sturgis family could ever be. When Sturgis was particular about her accommodations ("nothing striped diamonded or (above all things) *square*"—stipulations that amused Fuller), Fuller promised to oblige. Finally, Sturgis told Fuller that her father forbade the visit. Fuller was incensed at the hint that Sturgis's father distrusted Fuller's motives, which she defended as "those of disinterested, and uncommon kindness." But Fuller seems to have suspected that Caroline herself was the reluctant party. "If you have dallied with me, I know it is not your fault," Fuller wrote, an avowal of faith in Sturgis's loyalty that sounds as though it was meant to sting. "But at the same time, if you do not come, I shall not write again."[28]

The near ultimatum notwithstanding, the friendship between the two women did not end. Although Sturgis did not go to Providence that winter, Fuller did write again. Fuller appears, here as elsewhere, to have understood vulnerability and frustration as components of passionate love. She knew how to weather its storms: when her affections were rebuffed, she took it as a particular disappointment. Emerson, on the other hand, generalized.

Emerson plunged quickly from the real into the ideal because that was what his own philosophy prescribed. We can be thankful that, he never quite succeeded. He always remained the chimera that James Russell Lowell had identified: "a Plotinus-Montaigne." In Emerson's prose, generalities have the tang of particulars. He puts Plato's ideas into Bacon's English. In a style that shows the recalcitrance of words — the way they pebble up against any attempt to smooth them into a paste of generalization — he phrases and rephrases a single idea: "There is one mind common to all individual men," as he writes in "History"; or, as he puts it, more lyrically, in a manuscript poem, "No heart in all this world is separate / But all are cisterns of one central sea."[29]

According to Emerson's philosophy — a mix of Plato's ideal forms, Coleridge's division of knowledge into subjective and objective, and a Swedenborgian faith in spirit — one soul created the world. All people can withdraw within themselves for access to this soul, where, if they can learn to obey its quiet voice, they will find great power. Sadly, these moments of access are rare, even for the purest. As Joel Porte has noted, Emerson was fond of quoting Wordsworth to describe the "double consciousness" that even the most devoted Transcendentalist experienced while mired in mere Understanding and longing for breakthrough moments of Reason: "And the most difficult of tasks to keep / Heights which the soul is competent to gain." As Emerson put it in "The Over-Soul": "Our faith comes in moments; our vice is habitual."[30]

Although the external world, too, was created by a soul, it is a place of compromise, distraction, and limitation — the province of debased and practical Understanding. The facts of any particular case other than your own are obstacles, until you discern in them the higher pattern of Reason. As Fuller once noted of Emerson, "He does not care for facts, except so far as the immortal essence can be distilled from them." However, if you ignore the particulars in your own case, you risk not hearing the soul speaking softly inside you. Emerson's Transcendentalism, then, is at once a juggernaut determined to crush any individual detail and a paean to the power of any one tack in the road to puncture that juggernaut's tires. Thus Emerson told Caroline

Sturgis that he refused to join Brook Farm because "I will not be generalized," and yet in his chapter on literature in *English Traits,* he found the chief sign of the mental weakness of the modern English to be their "timidity which accumulates mountains of facts." "The English," he wrote disapprovingly, "shrink from a generalization."[31]

Emerson was not contradicting himself here, because the subjective was not the objective. The two spheres could never meet. Emerson knew he was Emerson; no one else could ever know it as well as he. But by the same logic, Emerson could not know who anyone else was, and so, as a general rule, everyone else ought to be generalized into a Neoplatonic soul. Other people ought to be dispatched like Plato's intimates: "If he had lover, wife, or children," Emerson boasted of his hero, "we hear nothing of them. He ground them all into paint." Not to grind them is sentimental timidity.[32]

In "The Heart," a lecture he delivered on 3 January 1838, Emerson confronted the emotional isolation that his Transcendental system caused. The problem had first appeared in *Nature* (1836), without a satisfactory solution. In that book, although human beings were mysteriously attractive to each other, "incomparably the richest informations of the power and order that lie at the heart of things," idealism isolated thinkers from one another. As thinkers moved from Understanding's fetteredness in things toward Reason's freer and superior perception of ideas, they began to discern the boundary between subjective and objective more and more clearly. As "the eye of Reason open[ed]," there was a "reverential withdrawing of nature before its God." Thinkers were left alone with their thoughts, while *realia* — including other people — receded. Idealism, Emerson lamented, "leaves me in the splendid labyrinth of my perceptions, to wander without end. Then the heart resists it, because it balks the affections in denying substantive being to men and women."[33]

This is the American solipsism that Tocqueville had identified as Cartesian. In the conclusion to *Nature,* Emerson looked forward to a mystical state wherein he would see the world as a manifestation of spirit and thus transcend this idealist isolation. What Emerson suggests in "The Heart" is that other human beings are a shortcut to that state. Other people exert their mysterious attraction because they convince you, emotionally, despite the superior logic of Coleridge and Kant, that they represent spirit in the world — that they exist in other subjective spheres, tangent to your own.

Emerson began "The Heart" with a résumé of this problem, locking the soul once more into solitary confinement. "In strictness we ought to say, the soul seems to be insulated. . . . Every man is an infinitely repellent orb, and holds his individual being on that condition." However, linking all people was an ether of affection. This ether was fragile. It "does not admit of being analysed" and "retreats from investigation." The diffused affection resembled electricity in that it was everywhere, and everywhere capable of transmitting a charge — a metaphor that Emerson had first used in a poem written to Ellen Tucker while courting her that described himself as "stricken with the sympathy / That binds the whole world in electric tie." The best proof of the existence of this aura, Emerson suggested, was to be read in the wordless "language of these wandering eye beams." By the eye — the one organ whose loss, even in his highest fit of sublimity, Emerson could not imagine surviving — Emerson could receive conviction. "One of the most wonderful things in nature, where all is wonderful, is, the glance, or meeting of the eyes; this speedy and perfect communication which transcends speech and action also and is in the greatest part not subject to the control of the will. It is the bodily symbol of identity of nature. Here is the whole miracle of our being, made sensible, — the radical unity, the superficial diversity. Strange that any body who ever met another person's eyes, should doubt that all men have one soul." One pair of human eyes could focus another, with a draw as compelling as erotic desire.[34]

A man's gaze had first taught Emerson to believe "in the Indian doctrine of eye-fascination," as discussed in Chapter 4. Almost certainly the memory of that gaze was still with Emerson, but as he composed "The Heart," he was also thinking of a more recent and less rarefied exchange of glances. In 1835, about two weeks before he proposed to Lidian Jackson by letter, Emerson recorded in the thin disguise of the third person an "oeillade" he had shared with a young woman "in a public assembly" — most likely Jackson, attending one of his lectures. After the two participated in a "full, front, searching, not to be mistaken glance," Emerson felt that he and the woman had come uncommonly near, but at the same time he felt he had been "strangely baulked." The classic flirtation by glances aroused sexual disgust in Emerson. When the woman signaled her interest, Emerson "felt the stirring of owls, & bats, & horned hoofs, within him." Her face appeared to be "usurped by a low devil," and when he glimpsed her again as he left the lecture hall, "her form & feet had the strangest resemblance to those of some brute animal."[35]

A year and a half after their marriage, Emerson again remembered this oeillade in his journal. He again recalled the "gnomes" that had repulsed him when they appeared at the window of Lidian's face, but the predominant metaphor now was of a biological process. Attractive glances initiated a series of interactions that ended in sexual union, by a natural law as inexorable as that which determined that "the irritability of the bark & leaf buds" led to "precious fruit." Any affectionate meaning the man or woman invested in the looks they gave each other when they met was illusory. They were caught and governed by a process that was more vegetable than human. "All that at first drew them together was wholly caducous, had merely a prospective end like the scaffolding by which a house is built."[36]

Although Emerson included in "The Heart" the cautions he had learned from his encounter with Lidian (in the form of gnomes, demons, owls, bats, and hoofs), overall he lauds glances. He seems to have fused his experiences with men (i.e., Gay) and his experiences with women (i.e., Jackson) into one narrative of how affection coaxes the self into belief in other selves. It often seems as if Emerson did not distinguish homosexual from heterosexual relationships. As he wrote in his essay "Love," "Thus are we put in training for a love which knows not sex, nor person, nor partiality." With peculiar fairness, Emerson's lecture of 1838 offered his audience a story line that left the human heart free, after a certain amount of experimentation and bruising, to find its harbor in another person either of the opposite sex or of the same — "in the natural Society of Marriage or in the (celestial) Society of Friendship." If anything, as the parallel placement but unequal valences of "natural" and "celestial" in that phrase indicate, Emerson follows Plato in preferring same-sex relationships. When he revised "The Heart" as he prepared his *Essays: First Series,* this unitary narrative underwent meiosis, splitting along the conventional fissure between "Love" (also the topic of a separate lecture) and "Friendship," but even then, his pronouns refused to segregate appropriately. Those two essays seem at times to describe the same androgynous relationship that concerns "The Heart," with this difference: "Love" is about passion after it has waned, and "Friendship" is about a passion not yet, or never to be, consummated.[37]

"The Heart," unlike Emerson's earlier drafts on the topic, allowed Montaigne to speak unedited his praise of friendship. Emerson's reservations about friendship appeared as his own, not fathered onto a misquoted Aristotle. But these reservations were severe. "It turns the stomach, blots the light," Emerson wrote, "where I looked for a manly furtherance or at least a manly resistance to find a mush of concession. Better be a nettle in the side of your companion than be his echo."[38] These strictures have been called homophobic, and they do seem designed to restrain Emerson from any male friendship so indulgent as not to be "manly." But Fuller came to feel that they were directed at her.

Within Emerson's philosophy, emotional reticence was not a personal defect but a prudent measure that any Transcendentalist might choose to take. If another person attracts you by representing spirit, and if the fact of that person's incarnation reassures you that your soul is not alone in the world, nevertheless to yield even one jot of your will to this attraction is to compromise your self. "Let the parties be so related that they shall not need to accommodate too much," Emerson advised. Gender is not meant to be an issue here.

But as Emerson discovered through his conversations with Fuller, given the narrower choices available to women in Victorian America, this rule of self-sufficiency was harder on women than on men. As Emerson reported one of their conversations, "There is no society say I; there can be none. 'Very true but very mournful,' replies my friend; we talk of courses of action. But to women my paths are shut up."[39]

How to achieve the human connection that the glance promises and that Emerson fears is no small problem. To balance the heart's extremes — whether an isolated integrity or a swamping of the self in others — Emerson recommends in his lecture education of the soul. A conversation with the traditions of humane knowledge both rejuvenates and protects. Culture teaches the heart both to "trust its instincts" and to "discriminate between a capricious liking and a love that is natural and necessary." Whereas mere experience isolates the heart by traumatizing it, culture insulates the heart with intellectual play, which paradoxically enables the heart to open and renovate its faith.[40]

Culture achieves this by interpolating a third in any encounter between two: "the reverence for moral beauty." Emerson never springs the soul free from its cell. In fact, he ends by declaring that "friends such as we desire are dreams, fables, but a sublime hope cheers ever the faithful heart that elsewhere in other kingdoms of the universal power souls are now acting, enduring, and daring which can love us and which we can love." Actual congress of hearts is not to be had; there are only fictions, which may convey sympathy — a dream, a fable, a hope. Emerson sometimes spoke of this middle term, where alone union was possible, as if it were all that remained of divinity in the world. As he would elaborate in his essay "The Over-Soul," "In all conversation between two persons, tacit reference is made, as to a third party, to a common nature. That third party or common nature is not social; it is impersonal; is God."[41]

In "The Heart," to those who still longed for contact, Emerson offered only a millennial vision of a "society of heroes," much like the resurrection of loving brothers projected in his sermons, and the cold comfort that until that infinitely postponed day, men's and women's infirmities could not be exposed. In this world, meanwhile, there were only forms of fantasy. Like dreams, fables, and hopes, a lecture or an essay might convey a spark of spirit from one person to another. It was not that Emerson did not want a direct merging. "Could any man conduct into me the pure stream of that which he pretends to be!" he cried in his essay "Nominalist and Realist"; he yearned for a greater man to flow into him. But Emerson did not believe such flows were possible. The promise of eros to dissolve the boundary between self and other was a delusion. "Marriage . . . is impossible," he wrote in "Experience," "because of the inequality between every subject and every object. . . . Never can love make consciousness and ascription equal in force."[42]

Emerson's pessimism about friendship, which Fuller and her friends confronted, is thus deeply enmeshed with Emerson's literary style — with his pessimism about language. "Truly speaking, it is not instruction, but provocation, that I can receive from another soul," he explained in the Divinity School Address.[43] The Eurydice-like message of Emerson's prose is that you the reader have lost him by hoping to see him; by turning toward him, you have turned away from the only path that might have brought you to him; you glimpse only his ghost, receding.

The difficulty of writing is cognate with the difficulty of people. In "The Heart," Emerson described every person as "an infinitely repellent orb." A few months later, when he gave Carlyle a sketch of his daily routine for writing, he used the same phrase to describe the contumacy of the English language. "Here I sit & read & write with very little system & . . . with the most fragmentary result: paragraphs incompressible, each sentence an infinitely repellent particle."[44] It was as hard to combine sentences into essays as to combine friends into society. Merely to place them next to each other did not join them; they could be linked only by threading them on a single idea.

Emerson applied his pessimism about human relationships to his friendships with both sexes. Henry Thoreau and Ellery Channing came to feel at least as much anger and resentment as Fuller did at Emerson's pattern of seduction, adoption, and rebuff.[45] Nonetheless, his tone of voice with each gender was distinct.

As an example of the tone he took with women, there are the apologies he made to Lidian, discussed above, and as Fuller began to woo him, there are the near putdowns in his journal that he would never have dared voice to Fuller. In 1836, after her first visit, he had been irked by her need to know what he thought of her: " 'I know not what you think of me,' said my friend. Are you sure? . . . You know all which can be of any use to you." In February 1838, in his journal he again reproved her for her emotional demands: "You must love me as I am," he wrote. "Do not tell me how much I should love you." By contrast, the same month, when Carlyle wrote that *Nature* had given the English poet John Sterling a wish to know Emerson personally, Emerson confided in his journal that "I am not a sickly sentimentalist though the name of a friend warms my heart & makes me feel as a girl."[46]

The letters that Emerson actually sent to Fuller could be effusive. On 28 June 1838, for example, he thanked Fuller for sharing a manuscript with him and then exclaimed, "Can I see it again? & again as it grows? So shall I have presence in two places"—an echo of Bacon, who had praised friendship as extending a person's powers beyond the site of the body, which is "confined to a place." "Friends on any high footing," Emerson continued, "are surely very noble possessions and make the earth & the starred night, as you walk alone, more divine." But a few months later, a September journal entry harshly rebuked a "young maiden"—either Fuller or her protégée Sturgis—for letting eros taint their friendship. "Not to be lovely but to be courted, not to be mistress of yourself but to be mistress of me, is your desire," Emerson wrote. "I hear . . . an ugly harlot sound in the recesses of your song, in the niceties of your speech, in the lusciousness (forgive the horrid word) of your manners." As he later wrote in his essay on Swedenborg, "I am repelled, if you fix your eye on me, and demand love."[47]

Compare these strictures on intimacy with women to a sensuous daydream about intimacy with a man that Emerson inscribed in his journal on 7 June 1838, shortly before Sturgis came to Concord for her first visit. In a wistful tone, Emerson imagined being "shut up in a little schooner bound on a voyage of three or four weeks with a man—an entire stranger—of a great & regular mind of vast resources in his nature." The two men would delay any meeting between them and loll together separately on the open sea, in monastic ecstasy. "I would not speak to him, I would not look at him; . . . so sure should I be of him, so luxuriously should I husband my joys that I should steadily hold back all the time, make no advances, leaving altogether to Fortune for hours, for days, for weeks even, the manner & degrees of intercourse." With no exchange of caresses or even words, Emerson and the stranger would open to each other silently, laved by the calming ocean of each other's presence. What thrilled Emerson about the fantasy was the prospective sense that "here close by me, was grandeur of mind, grandeur of character; that here was element wherein all I am, & more than I am yet, could bathe & dilate, that here by me was my greater self; he is me, & I am him." Emerson never admitted to Fuller or in print that he longed for selfhood to be so transitive. In his public statements, he never relented on the "gulf between every me and thee."[48]

It was a technique of Fuller's to transfer confidences from one of her intimates to another. In January 1839, for example, Fuller mailed to Sturgis a packet of James Freeman Clarke's letters, containing "allusions to the 3 love affairs which formed him into manhood." This remarkable sharing (or breach) of confidence seems to have had several ends: to inspire Sturgis to make similar confidences in Fuller, to bind her into the group's web of overlapping trusts, to serve as an informal textbook for Sturgis's sentimental education, and to demonstrate Fuller's place at the center of her network—"like the queen of some parliament of love," as Emerson said. To surrender to Fuller's discretion was a condition of friendship with her. As Fuller explained to Sturgis, "I know he [Clarke] would entirely confide in my judgment as to the propriety of showing them." Fuller did not show everyone everything, but in deciding whom to show what, sometimes it was her own sensitivity rather than that of her original correspondent that she consulted. On 21 February 1839, she apologized to Sturgis for not having sent any of Anna Barker's letters, because "to get at any one which it would be right to show, I should have to read over what would disturb my feelings exceedingly."[49]

Perhaps as early as July 1838, Fuller began to share with Emerson "pictures" of her friends, including their letters. "I send some of Cary's letters but they must be kept for your own reading *exclusively* and returned when I see you next," Fuller wrote. Emerson responded cautiously in September 1838. "I contemplate with joy the meeting & relation of all the parties you name, without the least desire of nearer participation." He was grateful for what amounted to tickets to the theater, but he declined to step on stage himself. On 12 October 1838, Emerson again thanked Fuller for forwarding letters she had received from another woman. "What a brave healthy susceptible soul!" Emerson sang. But even though he was pleased to have been let in on this young woman's personal history, Emerson bucked a little against what he perceived as Fuller's attempt at seduction — at her insinuation that he, too, might want to swim out to these deeper, more turbulent waters. He acknowledged their attraction but resisted:

> Such pictures as you have sent me now & before exalt our interest in individual characters & suggest ideas of society — oh how lofty & refined! but not now to be realized. We are armed all over with these subtle antagonisms which as soon as we meet begin to play, & translate all poetry into such stale prose! It seems to me that almost all people *descend* somewhat into society. All association must be a compromise; and, what is worst, the very flower & aroma of the flower of each of the beautiful natures disappears as they approach each other. What a perpetual disappointment is actual society even of the virtuous & gifted.

This passage pleased Emerson so well that he copied it into his journal. He repeated the central insight, more pithily, in the same pages a few weeks later: "Men descend to meet." Both formulations worked their way into his *Essays: First Series*, in "Friendship" and "The Over-Soul." Neither turn of phrase sat well with Fuller, who several years later, in an essay for *The Dial*, referred to the idea of "descend[ing] to meet" with scorn.[50]

Fuller did not see how intimacy could be construed as compromise. As a matter of fact, neither did Emerson's favorite essayists. Bacon thought men who avoided society were by and large beastly. Bacon admitted the possible exception "of a love and desire to sequester a man's self for a higher conversation"—that is, conversation with the gods—but he hinted that most people who justified their wish for solitude on these grounds were frauds. Montaigne wrote that "enjoyment destroys [love], as having a fleshly end, subject to satiety." But in Montaigne's opinion, friends, unlike lovers, had no need to ration themselves to each other. "Friendship, on the contrary, is enjoyed according as it is desired; it is bred, nourished, and increased only in enjoyment, since it is spiritual."[51] But as I suggested above, the most striking disagreement between Fuller and Emerson was in how they read yet another traditional authority on friendship—Plato.

Fuller was capable of persuading herself that a person could be transsubstantiated into an idea, along the lines set forth by Diotima in her doctrine of the "rising stairs" in Plato's *Symposium*. In a 21 October 1838 letter to her pupil Jane Tuckerman, Fuller recounted her painful recovery seven years earlier from a heartbreak, a case of "deceived friendship, domestic discontent, and bootless love." On Thanksgiving Day, 1831, Fuller recalled, she had gone for a long walk, until she found herself alone "in the meditative woods, by the choked-up fountain." There, after much thought, she reached a state of Platonic resignation. "I saw then how idle were my griefs; that I had acquired *the thought* of each object which had been taken from me, that more extended personal relations would only have given me pleasures which then seemed not worth my care, and which surely have dimmed my sense of the spiritual meaning of all which had passed." Thus far, Fuller has not diverged from Emerson; we can almost hear the wording he used for the same Platonic idea in *Nature*: "When [a friend] has, moreover, become an object of thought. . . it is a sign to us that his office is closing." But Fuller continues, as Emerson did not: "I felt . . . that if separation could be, real intimacy had never been. All the films seemed to drop from my existence, and I was sure that I should never starve in this desert world, but that manna would drop from heaven, if I would but rise with every rising sun to gather it."[52]

Fuller's recourse to idealism was only for recuperation, in preparation for a further assault on reality. To appreciate how far this reading of Plato is from Emerson's, it helps to turn to another letter by Fuller, written to Caroline Sturgis a few months later, on 27 January 1839. The letter is a masterpiece of gossip, social advice, and a highly personal form of literary criticism. Fuller knew it was good. She opened by bragging about its merit: "I pay you a compliment in [writing to you] for I have just been reading Plato's Phaedrus, and last night I banqueted with him, — so I think I must be tuned up to concert pitch." (Fuller read Plato in French translation, and her joke about "banqueting" referred to the French title of the *Symposium*.)

"I have many feelings in reading Plato, perhaps not orthodox," Fuller began. Her first departure from orthodoxy was in her very experience of reading Plato. She refused to feel that his loftiness was uncommon. "Plato's thoughts have, indeed, so passed into our intellectual life that I feel as if only returning to my native mountain air while with these philosophers and cannot be quite enough of a disciple. It is true it is like the banquets of the Gods after our common life, but I never, never, never have lived in the actual and find here my own aspirations in golden letters."[53] Mountain air is rarer than the air of plain or valley, but Fuller asserts that she is native to it. She claims, a little grandly, that it is the actual that feels unfamiliar to her. Plato's ideas are Fuller's reality; they are where she lives and breathes.

Although Emerson appreciated the tension between ideal and real in Plato's writing, and between the ascetic and the erotic, he was always more taken by the side of Plato that he called "the broadest generalizer." Now, in her letter to Sturgis, Fuller resisted this Plato. She chose the naughty humor of *Phaedrus* and the *Symposium* over the abstemiousness of the *Laws,* in terms that suggest an impatience with what she was hearing from Emerson:

> Socrates does not soar, he does not look up, he sees all around him, the light wells out from him, every object round assumes its proper hue. He is a man, not an angel. For my part I should be ashamed to be an angel before I have been truly man. But these Greeks no more merged the human in the divine, than the divine in the human, the wise charioteer managed both his steeds; he needed not to unyoke either but chose rather to remember their several natures. The mere Idealist vexes me more than the mere Realist, because he seems to me never to have lived. He might as well have been a butterfly; he does not know the human element.

Line by line, there is nothing here that Emerson would have disagreed with. In fact, Fuller's reproach of the Idealist closely resembles Emerson's reproach of a formalist preacher in his Divinity School Address the year before: "If he had ever lived and acted, we were none the wiser for it." By accident, Fuller even echoes the critique Emerson had written of his brother Charles's college valedictory speech, in which a "moving passage passed with no more effect than if the same elegant speaker had said Butterfly, butterfly butterfly." But these congruences only sharpen the edge of Fuller's argument with Emerson: How could he, of all people, avoid friendship with such a pale excuse as that "actual society" is a "perpetual disappointment"? Even Plato's myth of love in

*Phaedrus* — whose principle of "ascension" was the touchstone for Emerson's emotional continence — had given the soul two horses. And it was the bad horse, the disappointing one, that made you human.[54]

Gnomes, wings, and hoofs might have frightened Emerson into isolation, but in her letter, Fuller went on to embrace the monstrous, in all its unregenerate particularity:

> I love the stern Titanic part, I love the crag, even the Drachenfels[55] of life — I love its roaring sea that dashes against the crag — I love its sounding cataract, its lava rush, its whirlwind, its rivers generating the lotus and the crocodile, its hot sands with their white bones, patient camels, and majestic columns toppling to the sky in all the might of dust. I love its dens and silvery gleaming caverns, its gnomes, its serpents, and the tiger's sudden spring. Nay! I would not be without what I know better, its ghostly northern firs, haggard with ice, its solitary tarns, tearful eyes of the lone forest, its trembling lizards and its wounded snakes dragging to secretest recesses their slow length along.[56]

The real, including the indelicacy and pain of human relationships, was not a thing to be overcome. That was not how Fuller understood transcendence. Rather, the antagonism between real and ideal had to be fully lived. In her journal, in 1840, Fuller revisited the mystic insight she had come to in the woods on Thanksgiving Day, 1831. Enlightenment, she wrote in 1840, had come when her sorrow gave way to a sense of strangeness: "I remembered how, a little child, I had stopped myself one day on the stairs, and asked, how came I here? How is it that I seem to be this Margaret Fuller? What does it mean? What shall I do about it? I remembered all the times and ways in which the same thought had returned. I saw how long it must be before the soul can learn to act under these limitations of time and space, and human nature; but I saw, also, that it MUST do it, — that it must make all this false true, — and sow new and immortal plants in the garden of God, before it could return again."[57] In Elizabeth Bishop's poem "In the Waiting Room," a seven-year-old girl felt a similar unease as she leafed through a copy of *National Geographic* while a dentist operated on her aunt. Identity came to the girl as a sort of dislodging:

> . . . I felt: you are an *I*,
> you are an *Elizabeth*,
> you are one of *them*.
> . . . I knew that nothing stranger
> had ever happened, that nothing
> stranger could ever happen.[58]

To insist on the purity of the pronoun *I* was not a solution. Nor was it a solution to capitulate to the mere fact of being Margaret Fuller. The soul's task, Fuller decided, was to "make all this false true." According to Fuller's Plato, a soul could not return to the ideal until it had been fully real, and that experience included the madness of love. Emerson's premature turn to the general was a hesitation "to act under these limitations of time and space, and human nature," to use Fuller's words. It was a resistance to being Waldo Emerson.

In 1842, while Fuller was visiting Concord, she and Emerson fell into one of their debates "on Man and Woman, and Marriage," which by then had become habitual. "W[aldo] took his usual ground," Fuller wrote. "Love is only phenomenal." She reported that Emerson ended his side of the argument by stating, rather snidely, that a woman might claim she wanted "to further the genius of her husband . . . but her conduct will always be to claim a devotion day by day that will be injurious to him, if he yields." By 1842, Fuller and Emerson had already harrowed hell in pursuit of a resolution to this disagreement, and she no longer tried to answer him. "I made no reply, for it is not worthwhile to, in such cases, by *words*." Only practice could show up her friend's pessimism.[59]

But in 1839 both Emerson and Fuller were still hopeful for a more amicable result. One optimistic sign was the enthusiasm with which Emerson read Elizabeth Brentano von Arnim's *Goethe's Correspondence with a Child* in July. Posing as a Lolita-like ingenue with the nickname Bettina, von Arnim presented a series of fictional letters as authentic — as if they were a sentimental, heterosexual complement to the conversations between Goethe and Eckermann. The book told the story of a sexually charged but apparently unconsummated romance between Goethe and Bettina, and its plot — elder sage versus winsome, erotic girl — set the tone for the friendships to come between Emerson and Fuller's circle of youths. Emerson wrote of von Arnim that "it seems to me she is the only formidable test that was applied to Goethe's genius." It was a test that Goethe did not seem to have passed. Goethe's response to Bettina was timorous. It showed he was "too discreet and cowardly to be great," Emerson noted. Emerson aspired to be equal to any Bettina who challenged him, but he was far from sure of himself. Twice that year he expressed his worry in his journal: "How can I hope for a friend to me who have never been one?"[60]

During 1839 and 1840, even as Fuller bestowed her friends on Emerson, she herself was losing her hold on them. Like Emily Dickinson, whose beloved brother, Austin, married her best friend, Susan Gilbert, Fuller had the bad luck of losing two loves at once, to each other.

The first of Fuller's loves was Anna Hazard Barker. A beautiful socialite,

Barker was raised in New York City, although her family relocated to New Orleans in 1834, when she was twenty-one. Adopting a genteel southern custom, Jacob Barker sent the family women north during the summers, away from the heat and the danger of plague, to stay with relatives in Philadelphia, New York City, Newport, and Cambridge. Barker was staying with her cousin Eliza Rotch Farrar, a sophisticated Quaker who had written a popular book of etiquette for young women, when she first met Fuller, who was Farrar's Cambridge neighbor and confidante. Fuller mentioned Barker in her correspondence as early as 1834. By all accounts, Barker was a graceful woman, at ease with her femininity. It would have been easy for someone like Fuller to react to Barker's poise and beauty with envy, but she didn't. Instead, she fell in love. Writing about the two women years later, William Henry Channing thought it was as though Fuller had wanted to merge with her young friend — as if Fuller were one of Aristophanes' split people and had recognized in Barker her complement. "Margaret seemed to long, as it were, to transfuse with her force this nymph-like form, and to fill her to glowing with her own lyric fire," Channing wrote. "She sought by genial sympathy thus to live in another's experience." Between 1835 and 1837, Fuller wrote more than half a dozen poems about her feelings for Barker.[61]

In "To A.H.B.," which Fuller composed in 1836, Barker boards the ship that has brought Fuller back to Boston, in order to greet Fuller on her return from a holiday in New York State. That holiday in 1835 soon turned out to have been a brief respite of pleasure in Fuller's life, because the death of Fuller's father a couple of months later plunged her and her immediate family into poverty. When the two young women embrace on deck, as yet ignorant of this tragedy but "full of fears / For future days," Fuller daydreams of launching the ship back out to sea, of whisking Barker away to "some isle far from the haunts of men," where she would be spared "treachery's pestilence, and passion's strife." But then Fuller thinks better of her impulse to flee, because it would be wrong to deprive Barker of the chance to struggle with the world herself. "For thee as me," Fuller concludes, "fire the gold should test." The tests Barker faced would never be as severe as those that confronted Fuller, but something in Fuller reached out to the young beauty in a tender wish to protect her.[62]

Another poem describes Barker nursing Fuller through a fever. She appeared almost as an angel in Fuller's dreams, prompting Fuller to observe in her journal that "as I have masculine traits, I am naturally often relieved by the women in my imaginary distresses." Looking back in 1842, Fuller admitted that "I loved Anna for a time I think with as much passion as I was then strong enough to feel." Fuller often compared her love for Anna with Madame de Staël's love for Madame de Récamier, and made no secret of the comparison.

*Portrait of Samuel Gray Ward,* by an unidentified photographer. Circa 1850–1855. Boston Athenaeum.

Within Fuller's circle, Récamier became Barker's cognomen: "Shall you introduce me to your Recamier this summer?" Emerson asked Fuller on 18 June 1839. Fuller defended her love for another woman in her journal, writing, "It is so true that a woman may be in love with a woman, and a man with a man. It is so pleasant to be sure of it because undoubtedly it is the same love that we shall feel when we are angels." She stipulated carefully that her passion was "purely intellectual and spiritual, unprofaned by any mixture of lower instincts," but as a reader of Plato, she felt that the mystery of her attraction to Anna had the same solution as the question "Why did Socrates love Alcibiades?"[63]

The second of Fuller's two loves was Samuel Gray Ward. Like Barker, Ward was from a wealthy family, who, in his case, hoped he would follow his father into banking. Eventually he did, but when Fuller met him, in July 1835, Ward was in college and "looked upon myself as a student and literary man," as he later explained to his father. They met on the same New York trip to Trenton Falls that figures in Fuller's "To A.H.B." Fuller's impression of Ward at the time was not favorable. "Did not like him much," she wrote in her journal. But a few months before her death, she wrote Ward from Italy that she looked back on their vacation upstate as "the last period of tranquillity in my life." Ward contributed poems to *The Dial*, and during an 1836–38 trip to Europe — a trip which Fuller was invited to share but which her father's death prevented — Ward collected reproductions of famous paintings and sculptures and found himself gravitating to the fine arts. Today his name is engraved in marble in the foyer of the Metropolitan Museum of Art, which he helped to found, years after he left Transcendentalism for the world of finance.[64]

In the *Memoirs of Margaret Fuller Ossoli*, Emerson wrote that Ward was Fuller's "companion, and, though much younger, her guide in the study of art." Emerson explained, as delicately as he could, that Fuller's art-historical interest in Ward was accompanied by a romantic one. The affinities they shared, "though sincere, were only veils and occasions to beguile the time, so profound was her interest in the character and fortunes of her friend." Fuller's correspondence is more blunt and revealing. A letter she wrote to Ward on 20 April 1836 compares the undulations of a pool of water to "the heaving of the bosom," in highly sensuous prose. "Oh! what wild work makes a female pen," Fuller flirtatiously exclaimed. In February 1839, Fuller thanked Sturgis for a hand-decorated box and asked her to make another with a pale blue lining, to "hold all I have had and shall have from my friend Raphael; Letters verses sketches all. I will keep it devoted to him while I live." "Raphael" was the cognomen Ward had earned, for the interest he took in that artist. Unfortunately, by the time summer came, in July 1839, Fuller was reproaching Raphael-Ward for keeping her at a distance. "If you love me as I deserve to be loved, you cannot dispense with seeing me." From the start, age and social status had placed them in two different circles. "Nothing but love bound us together," she explained, "and it must not be *my* love alone that binds us."[65]

As Ward drifted away from Fuller, Emerson took him up. In July, the same month that Fuller complained of Ward's neglect, Emerson met Ward for the first time, during a group visit to Washington Allston's Boston gallery. Ward invited Emerson to come back to Boston soon, to see the casts that Horatio Greenough had made of Michelangelo's *Day* and *Night*. Emerson could not accept Ward's invitation until November, but in August the two ran into each by chance while hiking in the White Mountains. That autumn, they began to correspond regularly.[66]

At the end of July, Emerson received a poem from Henry David Thoreau that struck a chord. Titled "Sympathy," the poem described Thoreau's infatuation with eleven-year-old Edmund Sewall. "I might have loved him had I loved him less," Thoreau wrote. The boy's beauty had caused Thoreau pain and left him lonely, and Thoreau laid the blame for this on his own inability to achieve a *Phaedrus*-like vision of the principle shining through Sewall's good looks. "If I but love that virtue which he is," Thoreau concluded, skipping over Plato's fascination with male bodies to Plato's transcendence of them, "Still shall we be truest acquaintances." In Emerson's opinion, Thoreau's poem was "the purest strain & the loftiest, I think, that has yet pealed from this unpoetic American forest."[67]

On the page immediately following this acclamation of Thoreau, Emerson wrote a short monologue warning off a young would-be friend. "I have no right of nomination in the choice of my friends," Emerson wrote sternly. "Sir, I should be happy to oblige you, but my friends must elect themselves." Emerson was accustomed to resolving his erotic attractions by means of Platonic abnegation, as Thoreau had in "Sympathy." The experiment of weaving these attractions into friendships made him uneasy. At first Emerson seems to have resisted Ward, but this resistance was not rejection. In a September 24 journal entry, Emerson took issue with Fuller for misunderstanding his slowness. " 'If you do not like my friend at first sight you will never like him.' Indeed! I had not thought so. I did not, I remember, like you at first sight, yet we manage to converse now without disgust." Emerson found Ward attractive, but he had reservations. "Who is rich, who is fashionable, who is high bred, has great hindrances to success" if he hopes to befriend me, Emerson wrote. Ward would have to prove himself. "Whom have I rejected? whom have I not admired?" Emerson wrote to Fuller when she accused him of a sour unwillingness to open his heart. "The utmost of my offence is the sluggishness of my perceptions."[68]

Meanwhile, Fuller was losing patience with the polite stratagems by which Ward kept her at bay. "You love me no more," she wrote him in September. She remembered with anguish that in earlier days, "how did you pray me to draw near to you!" Ward put her off a little longer, explaining that he was "not yet a man" and that intimacy with her felt threatening to his fragile manhood.

Although he desired "the gush of mingling souls" as fervently as any Romantic, he feared that any wish of his "to cast myself into the arms of some other nature" was "womanish." By manhood, Ward meant in part the respectable banking career that his father wanted for him. Fuller accepted this excuse, as if it were only natural that she should be associated in his mind with rebellion from a correctly gendered future. "I will bear in mind that my presence is like to recal all you have need to forget and will try to believe that you would not be with me lest I 'spoil you for your part on life's dull scene,' or as you have said 'call up the woman in you.'" Ward seems, however, to have been telling Fuller only a partial truth. Soon, with a flood of emotions, the full truth about his affections emerged.[69]

In early October 1839, Anna Barker came to stay with Fuller at her home in Jamaica Plain, outside Boston. In "the very first days of Anna," to adopt the regnal chronology used by Fuller, the two women renewed their romance. Fuller was "so intoxicated" and "so uplifted by that eldest and divinest love" that her health was overwhelmed, and she took to bed. There she wrote to Caroline Sturgis, whose rebuffs had recently wounded her. In her bliss, Fuller now forgave Sturgis, but she hinted that Barker's return demoted Sturgis to an understudy — much in the way that Mifflin had demoted Gibson when Norris returned from Europe.[70]

On Friday, October 4, Emerson went to Jamaica Plain, where for the first time he met the woman he had been calling "the beautiful Anna" for years. During his two-day visit, Emerson was charmed to share "the frank & generous confidence of a being so lovely, so fortunate, & so remote from my own experiences." In his journal, he paid Barker the high compliment of calling her "a unit & whole." Although the bias of her nature was "not thought but emotion or sympathy," Emerson found, to his puzzlement, that she "does not distance me as I believe all others of that cast of character do." In Emerson's essay "Manners," Barker became a "Persian Lilla" who acted as "a solvent powerful to reconcile all heterogeneous persons into one society."[71]

In fact, Barker's erotic power divided rather than united this small society of Transcendentalists. On October 15, Fuller wrote to Ward that at last she knew the truth. Ward and Barker, the two children of wealth and privilege, had fallen in love. They had been in love since the autumn of 1837, since the European tour Fuller had not been able to afford. In Switzerland they had spent two months admiring the mountain landscapes together. When Ward bought a Saint Bernard, Barker named it Alp. Between December 1838 and March 1839, Ward had visited Barker again, in New Orleans. As Ward wrote to his father on 4 March 1839, he did not then become engaged, but he had no doubt that his father "should find in her all that you could desire or wish for in your daughter and your son's wife." During Barker's return to Massachusetts in October 1839 — the same visit that "so intoxicated" Fuller — the couple's feelings for each other deepened, although as Ward was careful to observe to his father, "My relation to Miss Anna Barker has not changed" — that is, there was still no formal engagement. Nonetheless, someone, probably Barker, thought it was time to disillusion Fuller. "I understand all perfectly," Fuller wrote to Ward on October 15 in a spirit of resignation. She reproached Ward for underestimating her; he should have told her sooner; she wished only to further his happiness. "Do you not feel how I should grieve to be the ghost to cross the path of true communion in the Elysian grove[?] Live without me now."[72]

In her journal, Fuller was not so accepting. "The son of the Gods has sold his birthright," she wrote. "He has received therefor one, not merely the fairest, but the sweetest and holiest of earth's daughters. Yet it is not a fit exchange."[73] Fuller may have been suffering from jealousy and heartache, but her comments reflect an accurate understanding of the practical compromises that the union of Ward and Barker would demand. If they married, Ward and Barker would no longer be able to depend on their parents for financial support. If they wanted to live the way they were both accustomed to living, they would have to give up the intellectual life. Ward would be expected to take up a traditional career in order to earn enough money to satisfy Barker's expensive tastes. For her part, Barker would cultivate those tastes instead of learning to think or fend for herself. Marriage would stunt the development of both the man and the woman.

In *Woman in the Nineteenth Century,* Fuller elaborated her disappointment with Ward and Barker into a feminist critique, writing, "Now there is no woman, only an overgrown child." Since marriage was often to blame, Fuller found herself in that book telling stories against marriage as commonly understood: of an Indian maiden who became betrothed to the sun, of a German man and woman who fulfilled their love by joining a monastery and a convent, of lovers who resided on different continents. Paraphrasing a "wise contemporary," Fuller wrote that "union is only possible to those who are units." The wise contemporary was almost certainly Emerson, who wrote in "Friendship" that "there must be very two, before there can be very one." In Fuller's hands, Emerson's eschewal of too much intimacy with other men became an argument against heterosexual marriage. Emerson's hierotomy had preserved both his arousal and his innocence with men; it was the impetus, the always postponed reward, and the condition of his literary work. In a fascinating twist, Fuller adapted this hierotomy to feminist ends. If its effect in Emerson's thinking had been somewhat homophobic, its effect in Fuller's was heterophobic.

Men and women should not marry, because marriage made permanent a set of bad habits that crippled male sensibility and undermined female strength. "Celibacy," she wrote, is "the great fact of the time. It is one from which no vow, no arrangement, can at present save a thinking mind."[74]

For a time, in Fuller's circle celibacy prevailed. Ward and Barker had given Fuller and Emerson a bad scare, but there was as yet no proposal of marriage. As Ward himself later recalled, "There was very little probability of such a connexion unless my plans of a scholar's life gave place to some lucrative profession." And Ward was not ready to give up his literary and artistic ambitions. On 21 October 1839, Emerson wrote in his journal that Fuller had privately told him "a chronicle of sweet romance, of love & nobleness which have inspired the beautiful & brave." Two pages later, Emerson reconsidered Fuller's version of their story, somewhat more ambivalently. "I heard with joy that which thou toldest me O eloquent lady, of thy friends & mine, yet with my joy mingled a shade of discontent. Things must not be too fine. Parian marble will not stand exposure to our New England weather. . . . I dare not believe that a mood so delicate can be relied on like a principle for the wear & tear of years." If Fuller had told Emerson the simple story of Barker and Ward's courtship, he would perhaps have been disappointed by Ward's defection to money-making if Ward had defected (he hadn't yet), but there would have been no occasion for him to doubt that a relationship between these two wealthy, gifted, and lovestruck people would endure. It is more likely that Fuller told Emerson that Barker and Ward had exchanged vows of love but decided to forgo their enjoyment of each other in order to pursue more lofty goals. This more complicated story would have both elated Emerson and caused him to wonder if it could last.[75]

Emerson was right to be skeptical of what Fuller told him. Fuller seems to have projected her own wishes and concerns onto the Barker-Ward relationship. News of the romance set Fuller weighing the pros and cons of her own romantic state: on the one hand, "No one loves me," but on the other, "I have no fetter on me," as she wrote in her journal. Perhaps to console herself, Fuller began to formulate the idea that reached its fullest expression in *Woman in the Nineteenth Century*, that marriage as it was then practiced impeded personal fulfillment. In her journal in the fall of 1839, she speculated that great spirits could never marry, because either marriage would shackle the spirit, or greatness would throw off the bridle of marriage as it would any other constricting sham. "Social wedlock," she wrote, "is ordinarily mere subterfuge and simulacrum: it could not check a powerful woman or a powerful man." Lonely and let down, Fuller seems to have persuaded herself that these insights about marriage were as true for Ward and Barker as they were for herself.[76]

With careful archival work, the scholar Eleanor Tilton has rectified most of Fuller's misconstructions and corrected the story and chronology that Fuller, out of wishful thinking, somewhat garbled in her poems and in her correspondence. As Tilton points out, somewhat harshly, Fuller got a number of the facts wrong, for the simple reason that no one told them to her: they were none of her business. Fuller's misconstructions seem to have irritated Tilton, but I would like to pay some attention to them here. Emerson's initial skepticism of Fuller soon gave way to complicity.

Perhaps the key thing to understand is that Fuller (and later Emerson) took as permanent a state of affairs that Ward and Barker no doubt understood to be a stopgap. The two lovers were in conflict: Barker wanted financial security, and Ward wanted a life of the mind. In 1839 they thought they should not marry until they could resolve this conflict. In 1840 they married anyway, and they resolved their conflict by living it out. They tried both ways of life. After their marriage, Ward worked for three years in Boston as a broker, and then the couple spent five years as Transcendental-Jeffersonian farmers in the Berkshires. When, in the end, Ward accepted the position his father had once held as the American representative of the British investment bank Baring Brothers, it was not so much a compromise of his true self as a recognition that in his half-decade of sketching and independent study he had not accomplished much. As the banker he finally chose to become, Ward was an outstanding success. If Barker and Ward gave each other up in 1839, they must have sensed in their hearts that the surrender was temporary. Fuller, however, convinced herself otherwise.[77]

It was against this background that Emerson's friendship with Ward burgeoned. After the two men met in July and August, Ward seems to have courted Emerson with a series of gifts. Early in the fall, he forwarded to Emerson the florid and ungrammatical poems of his friend Ellery Channing. Emerson responded on 3 October in measured tones. He gave the poems qualified praise, and he agreed—almost grudgingly—to meet the poet. Emerson spent 4 and 5 October with Ward's beloved, Barker. Then, on 8 October, Emerson received from Ward a "rich pacquet": Ward's portfolio of copy sketches of paintings and sculpture by European masters, along with a commentary by Fuller. What Emerson was glimpsing of Ward's world impressed him. "Two persons lately, very young children of the most high God," Emerson wrote in his journal in mid-October 1839, "have admonished me by their silent being. It seemed as if each answered to my heart's inquiry Whence is your power? 'From my nonconformity.' "[78]

Emerson had seen some of the images in Ward's portfolio a year before, when Fuller brought them to Concord. But in the autumn of 1839, Emerson held on to the sketches for two months. He wrote about them repeatedly in his journal, and in December, when he returned the portfolio to Ward, he summed up his impressions in a six-page commentary. Emerson's comments are revealing of the different desires that male and female beauty aroused in him. He described the female figures as beautiful in their inattention. They are "pensive," "unconscious," "thinking of something else," and "stony inscrutable." He described male beauty, on the other hand, as natural power. The face of a Raphael angel "intimates authority impossible to dispute." Guido's *Aurora* has "the most masculine force" with "no convulsion, no straining, no ado, no foam, but flowing grace & ease." Michelangelo is "always colossal even in boys & cupids." And a Roman relief of Endymion displays "the beauty & greatness of one to whom the senses suffice."[79]

On 27 October, Emerson wrote to thank Ward for a second gift of Ellery Channing's poetry. He liked the new batch better than the first — better, apparently, than Ward himself liked them. "There was no progress" in Channing's verses, Ward objected when he and Emerson met in early November.[80] Emerson also acknowledged that he liked Ward's attentions. "I am very happy in the new relations to which you invite me by your persevering kindness." A few days later, Emerson at last went to the Boston Athenaeum to see the casts of Michelangelo's *Night* and *Day* that Ward had recommended. He also saw Ward. When Emerson reported the visit to Elizabeth Hoar, he bestowed on his new young friend a cognomen even more extravagant than the one Fuller had given him: "I have also seen the Prince-of-the-Purple-Island himself at some leisure & advantage not here but twice in Boston and we have got on farther but not yet farthest." Emerson had earlier written to Ward that "there are fewer painters than poets." But after an evening's and a morning's tutelage from Ward in Boston, artists jumped to the top of Emerson's list of world geniuses. "I had told [Bronson] Alcott that my First Class stood for today perhaps thus; Phidias, Jesus, [Michel] Angelo, Shakspeare."[81]

Emerson's ranking of the arts was not the only prejudice of his that Ward was altering. Emerson's thoughts on friendship were also in flux. Back in June, his opinion of friends was the doctrinal paradox he had laid out in "The Heart": "though I prize my friends I cannot afford to talk with them and study their visions lest I lose my own." In October, however, when Emerson confided his thoughts on friendship to his journal, they were no longer so aloof. Where before he had presented himself as waving his friends off, now he imagined himself pining for them. "What needs greater magnanimity than the waiting for a friend; a lover, for years?" A few days after his trip with Ward to the Athenaeum, Emerson was counseling himself, rather than his importunate friends, to observe a reticent silence. "Why dare you to intermeddle in so sacred a formation as Friendship? . . . for *you* to say aught, is to be frivolous. Wait until the necessary & everlasting overpowers you, until day & night avail themselves of your lips."[82]

By "day & night" Emerson no doubt meant a metonymy of nature's force. But he may also have been alluding to the twinned Michelangelo statues he and Ward had seen at the Athenaeum, monuments of the body's power and confinement in itself: *Day* a man in middle age, weighted down by his musculature, his face still half-unshapen in marble; *Night* a woman, also heavy with strength, writhing, one breast jutting almost angrily forward. In their ripeness, the couple suggest time as an irresistible force — "the necessary & everlasting," in Emerson's words — that moves, by the alternation of day and night and by the opposition of male and female, toward death.

During his Athenaeum visit, Emerson probably also saw Bertel Thorvaldsen's *Ganymede,* first exhibited in Boston in 1839. He made no comment on this statue in his correspondence or journal — although another work by Thorvaldsen, *The Triumphant Entry of Alexander into Babylon,* appeared in Ward's portfolio. Fuller, however, mentioned the *Ganymede* in her *Dial* review of the exhibition, and several years later, in 1843, she wrote "Ganymede to His Eagle," a poem inspired by it. Fuller imagined the cupbearer as waiting anxiously, "a willing servant to sweet love's command," pleading for Zeus's eagle to return and carry him again to Olympus. In Fuller's version, the eagle is not an incarnation of Zeus himself but an intermediary: the bird is the god's "messenger" and the boy's "destined brother friend." (The bird is also, of course, the emblem of the sovereignty of the United States, as Fuller's anecdote about a chained eagle, a few chapters earlier, makes clear.) In the eagle's company, the boy can ascend. But in the moment of the poem, Ganymede is alone, not sure that the eagle cares for him anymore. He longs to be united again with his equal/eagle so that he can rise to his ministry, the dispensing of drinks from a spring which, like the forms the gods feast on in *Phaedrus,* seems to be both nourishment and truth to the poets who sip from it.[83]

Fuller elides sex in her retelling of the Ganymede myth, although her Ganymede does address as "O bliss" the eagle who will "upbear / My earthlier form into the realms of air." Here as everywhere in the Fuller-Emerson circle, Plato's *Phaedrus* is the model for introducing and then overcoming a same-sex erotic charge. The passion that Ganymede feels for union with the eagle is to be understood as a passion for poetic inspiration, not (or not only) as a carnal desire. Thorvaldsen sculpted Ganymede in several versions. One of them stands alone, and in the other two, Zeus appears as an eagle, not a human figure. Thorvaldsen thus avoided presenting two men as lovers, circumventing the sort of reaction that Fuller recorded in her journal in September 1839, when she discussed "the great difficulty of bringing two male faces any where near each other without exciting extreme disgust." "When people embrace on the stage I am ready to die of shame and disgust at the sight," Fuller wrote. "How can they endure to get so near one another, I feel." Fuller in 1839 seems to have been far from her 1842 rhapsodizing over love between two men or between two women as "the same love that we shall feel when we are angels." As an exception to her disgust, Fuller cited Raphael's painting of Jupiter embracing Cupid, in the Villa Farnesina, where the closeness of the two male figures for some reason did not repel her.[84]

Raphael's *Jupiter and Cupid* must have been reproduced in either Fuller's or Ward's portfolio because it was referred to again, a year later, in a dreamy letter that Fuller's protégée Sturgis wrote to Emerson. Sturgis's letter is worth quoting at length as another example of how Emerson's intimates were using same-sex images from European art to eroticize and etherealize the psychodynamics of their friendships:

> Yesterday the reflection of the sunset so concentrated itself into a golden column that did not seem to lie upon the river, but rose high in the air. The base was hidden by long grass, the capital stood fairly forth. With my eye I carved it into a Jupiter & placed an Amore Greco beside it, then asked myself which I would be. Now will you not wonder that I chose to be the Amore, because I said, then I can admire that golden Jupiter, but if I were the Jupiter I should be alone & have nothing to admire. But when I saw how noble he was, how he glowed within himself, & evolved light, I chose to be the Jupiter, & saw I could admire the being beside me, pale, passionate, & pure, because his beauty would differ from mine. Thus for the hundredth time did I learn that which is around is of worth as well as that above.[85]

There was meant to be a lesson in Sturgis's conclusion, a little jab at Emerson, who, in Fuller's and Sturgis's opinion, insisted on acting like a Jupiter disdainful of his Ganymedes.

In Concord, the myths painted by Europe's Old Masters could easily take on personal meanings. And in Emerson's case, I believe, these images may have served to channel a resurgence of the feelings he had experienced in college. As a boy, Emerson had rationalized his attraction to Martin Gay into a puzzled interest in gazes. In a similar way, a middle-aged Emerson transposed the feelings that Samuel Gray Ward stirred in him into an attachment to the visual arts. Ward was, after all, Raphael to Fuller and her friends. (His other nickname was Michelangelo.) "I have identified your collection with the collector," Emerson confessed to Ward on 26 November 1839. When he admitted to Fuller that it saddened him to have to return the portfolio to Ward, he wrote in a style that echoed the *Phaedrus*-like passage in *Nature*. "I shall part with it,"

Emerson wrote of an image of Raphael's "Cumaean sibyl," "with a like feeling to that which arose when beautiful persons have passed out of my sight. The Endymion too—I did not know that drawing had been so perfect." The arts gave Emerson a new vocabulary, one in which, perhaps, the heavy, fated heterosexual couple of Michelangelo's *Day* and *Night* might be contrasted with the smooth, airy homosexual communion of boy and eagle in Thorvaldsen's *Ganymede*.[86]

In "Ode to Beauty," Emerson wrote of turning the pages of

> . . . the proud portfolios
> Which hold the grand designs
> Of Salvator, of Guercino,
> And Piranesi's lines.

The reference is to a portfolio of art reproductions that Fuller brought him on 8 June 1838, a few months before she brought him Ward's. Emerson's ode apostrophizes Beauty as a goddess ("Queen of things!") who has enslaved Emerson. But the manner of the enslavement recalls Emerson's teenage "eye-fascination" with Gay:

> When first my eyes saw thee,
> I found me thy thrall,
> By magical drawings,
> Sweet tyrant of all!

In Emerson's pun, artists' drawings are magically able to "draw" Emerson because ideal Beauty peeps out through artwork, as it peeped out through ephebes in the *Phaedrus*, luring and intoxicating the viewer. "Thy dangerous glances / Make women of men," Emerson writes. As in Plato, to love this beauty philosophically is to understand that the people and things it shines through should neither be owned nor touched. Beauty, when glimpsed here on earth, is "Somewhat not to be possessed / Somewhat not to be caressed."[87]

On 24 November 1839, Fuller sent Emerson a parcel of letters and poems she and Sturgis had exchanged, as well as passages from her private journal. Fuller probably also sent—either in this parcel or in a supplement that followed it—letters by (or at least concerning) Ward. The parcel added rich detail to the story of Ward, Barker, and Fuller that Fuller had confided to Emerson in outline in October. As Fuller explained, "All the verses, even the transl[atio]ns bear some reference to Anna, W[ard] and myself." One poem rather cryptically turned the three protagonists into flowers—a dahlia, a rose, and a heliotrope. It was this parcel that caused Emerson to startle his wife and mother with his wish "to live a little while with people who love & hate."[88]

Two days later, on 26 November, Emerson received another gift. "Ward has given me the Endymion with friendliest letter," Emerson reported in his journal. "It shall hang by Carlyle's Guido." Guido's *Aurora* was the token of Carlyle's friendship with the Emersons, and the place beside it was a place of high honor. No doubt Ward had selected the *Endymion* as a gift because Fuller had relayed to him Emerson's liking for the image. Emerson was strongly affected. "I confess I have difficulty in accepting the superb drawing which you ask me to keep," he wrote to Ward, the same day. In Emerson's letter, it sounds as though Ward had shown Emerson a bouquet and plucked out the prettiest rose just for him. But Emerson thought the copy sketches more intimate and more revealing than flowers would have been. "Your mute friends," as Emerson dubbed the images, "tell me very eloquently what you love, & a portfolio seems to me a more expressive vehicle of taste & character than a bunch of flowers. This beautiful Endymion deserves to be looked on by instructed eyes, and I like to think of you surrounded by such objects. But I shall not resist your generosity, and indeed am warmed at heart by your good will to me."[89]

To match Ward's gift, Emerson copied out Thoreau's poem "Sympathy." Ward must have liked it, because on 3 December, Emerson wrote to him that "I see it will be vain for me to resist you, if you like Bettina so well, & my young poet too." (Years later, Emerson sent another homoerotic masterpiece to Ward: even before he found time to write back to Walter Whitman, Emerson forwarded Ward his copy of *Leaves of Grass*.)[90]

Responding to a note of melancholy in Ward's letter, Emerson's 26 November thank-you letter went on to offer a dose of cheerful Transcendental boilerplate, which probably depressed Ward further. "What space can be allowed you for a moment's despondency? The free & the true, the few who conceive of a better life, are always the soul of the world." Ward was hoping to find a way to marry the girl of his dreams *and* satisfy his intellectual ambitions. Unhelpfully, Emerson waved the carrot of high-minded purity and brandished as a stick "the general mediocrity of thought produced by the arts of gain." By now this gesture of wishful, unworldly thinking should be familiar — comparable to Mifflin's wish for Gibson to go into some other field than law, or Brown's attempt to dissuade Wilkins from passing the bar. To the extent that Emerson was thinking of Ward as if he were a work of art that Emerson had fallen in love with, there was a temptation to play Pygmalion — a sort of Transcendental Professor Higgins, snootily refashioning Ward after the Emersonian ideal.

The next day, 27 November, Emerson wrote to Fuller with the good news about the *Endymion*. "I delight much in what I dreamed not of in my first acquaintance with you — my new relations to your friends," he told her. As he

*Drawing of Endymion, After the Original in the Capitoline Museum.* Gift of Samuel Gray Ward to Ralph Waldo Emerson. 1830s. By permission of the Ralph Waldo Emerson Memorial Association and of Houghton Library, Harvard University. Photo by John Kennard.

described to her what it felt like to read the parcel of letters and poems she had sent, he chose a curious metaphor. In *Nature,* Emerson had felt during a moment of ecstasy as if he were "a transparent eye-ball." Now, reading about the passions of his new friends, he felt as though he were *inside* an eyeball — in fact, swimming in it. The experience in *Nature* had been one of isolation and removal from the world he perceived. But inside an eyeball, Emerson imagined, perception would be as dangerously near and concrete as the flotsam of a wrecked ship to a swimmer in a storm:

> I plunge with eagerness into this pleasant element of affection with its haps & harms. It seems to me swimming in an Iris where I am rudely knocked ever & anon by a ray of fiercer red, or even dazzled into momentary blindness by a casual beam of white light. . . . How fine these letters are! I do not know whether they contented or discontented me most. They make me a little impatient of my honourable prison — of my quarantine of temperament wherefrom I deal courteously with all comers, but through cold water . . . I should like once in my life to be pommelled black & blue with sincere words.

Ward's gift and the story of Ward and Barker's romance had sparked a confession and a wish not typical of Emerson — an almost masochistic wish for emotional contact. They also sparked a series of highly self-critical journal entries. The same day he wrote to Fuller rejoicing at Ward's gift, Emerson wrote in his journal that he felt unworthy of an overture like Ward's. "When once & again the regard & friendship of the nobleminded is offered me, I am made sensible of my disunion with myself." One or two days later, he wrote a brooding entry that hearkened back to the sort he had written while an aspiring clergyman, about the shame that awaited any man who invited his friend to become the "accomplice of your vileness." "There is at least this satisfaction in crime," he wrote on 28 or 29 November 1839, " 'Crimen quos inquinat aequat' [Crime makes equal those whom it taints]. You can speak to your accomplice on even terms. To those whom we admire & love we cannot." The passage, which he used in "Friendship," leads to a rather perverse inference: Emerson would be able to relate to Ward more easily if, instead of loving the young man, he were to sin with him.[91]

The following week, just before returning Ward's portfolio to its owner, Emerson recorded in his journal a parable that went far toward explaining his chronic emotional chilliness: "Rob was tender & timid as a fawn in his affections, yet he passed for a man of calculation & cold heart. He assumed coldness only to hide his *woman's heart*. There is a play in which the sister is enamoured of her brother & when they embrace, she exclaims, 'J'ai froid.' " It is impossible to know for sure whether these or any other entries from the winter of 1839–40 are responses to Ward rather than to some other intimate. No proper names attach to the three entries cited in the previous paragraph. Another candidate might be John Sterling, Carlyle's friend and Emerson's admirer from afar, whom Emerson did write about by name during this season. But Sterling and Emerson had not met in person, and Emerson did not get around to writing a response to Sterling's September 1839 letter until May 1840. It is hard to imagine an expostulation to Sterling such as "O friend! you have given me that sign which high friendship demands, namely, ability to do without it" as other than a screen for the strong feelings he felt for friends who were closer to him and who might, like Fuller, read his journal. Indeed, the sentences following the address to Sterling quickly shift to the broader topic of "my friends, the old & the new." Emerson often diffuses the force of his new feelings by ascribing them to friends in the plural, rather than to any singular friend. "I have had such fine fancies about two or three persons lately," he writes in his journal in December 1839, the same month he tells Carlyle that "I am very happy lately in adding one or two new friends to my little circle." The task of discerning whom Emerson loves is not helped by his own philosophy on the matter. "A lover does not willingly name his mistress," Emerson wrote in his journal in June 1840; "he speaks of all persons & things beside; for she is sacred. So will the friend respect the name of his friend."[92]

There are, however, several reasons to think Emerson had Ward, more than any other person, in mind as he wrote the journal passages that became the raw material for his essay on "Friendship." First, there is Emerson's direct testimony. Ward was the first person Emerson sent the essay to when he finished it. He told Ward that "I have written nothing with more pleasure, and the piece is already indebted to you and I wish to swell my obligations" by asking for Ward's commentary. By contrast, whenever Emerson mentioned this essay to Fuller, his tone was workaday, and his mind turned to friendship's obstacles rather than its ecstasies. On 17 January 1840, for example, he told Fuller that his writing of "Friendship" was stalled by "a droll experience of limitation as if our faculties set a limit on our affections." On 8 July, he wrote to ask her to return his 1838 letter to her asserting that "all association must be a compromise," because he intended to recycle it in his near-finished essay "to fill up a bad hole in a paragraph."[93]

Second, there is indirect testimony from the same source. Emerson's letters to Ward are warmer and more cajoling than those he wrote to anyone else. Not long after Emerson wrote to Ward that "I see it will be vain for me to resist you," the shoe seems to have switched to the other foot. Henceforth Emerson pursued Ward. On 10 January 1840, he invited Ward to visit Concord on "some summer's day," declaring that "I am very dogmatical about Poetry, but you shall be dogmatical on Art. We will stand each on his stool of glass, each insulated & each positively charged. I wish the summer were come." Electromagnetic repulsion has never sounded so much like elective affinity. A week later, Emerson told Ward that friendship was "to me the most attractive of all topics, and, I doubt not, whenever I get your full confession of faith, we shall be at one on the matter." When he found himself Emersonizing on the subject, he broke the letter off with a piece of flirty self-deprecation: "as I wish you to like me, I will not add another word." On 25 January, Emerson flattered and wooed Ward more ardently than he ever had Lidian: "Who are you that wrote me this letter — & how came you to know all this? I thought you were younger. I love you very much." And on 1 March 1840, he teased Ward by describing him with the same words he had used to describe beauty in his lecture "Love": "Our friend M[argaret] F[uller] insists menacingly on your elfin properties — You are magical opaline evanescent. — It is all in vain. I think I may defy you to get quite away from me who am born the lover of genius & honor."[94]

"I love you very much" is a remarkable sentence, coming from Emerson.[95] He was probably as candid in his lost letters to Ellen Tucker, but he was rarely so explicit about his affections after his first wife's death.

The third sort of evidence pointing to Ward is reached by process of elimination. Consider the 22 December 1839 journal entry: "It has seemed to me lately more possible than I knew to carry a friendship greatly *on one side*, without due correspondence on the other." This entry became the capstone of "Friendship" as a finished essay. It was written a day before Emerson declared to Fuller that he "wished to live a little while with people who love & hate." (Fuller replied, a bit crabbily, "If you could look into my mind just now, you would send far from you those who love and hate.") Thus its subject is almost certainly one of Fuller's circle. As I noted above, Emerson named no names in this passage. However, no candidate is as likely as Ward. The gender of the pronoun points to him, and, as I have already mentioned, Emerson's letters to Ward during this period have a tone of affectionate longing.[96]

No other candidate makes as much sense. The next most likely one is Caroline Sturgis. But although Emerson and Sturgis wrote to and visited each other during the 1839–40 winter, their friendship and correspondence did not really begin in earnest until after the marriage of Ward and Barker in October 1840. The tone of Emerson's letters to Sturgis in this earlier period is familiar, but not deeply affectionate. By Emerson's own description, the two were not yet quite friends. In a letter to Fuller dated 7 and 8 June 1840, Emerson wrote that he and Sturgis were "beginning to be acquainted and by the century after next shall be the best friends."[97] In August 1840, Emerson began a draft of a letter to Sturgis by writing, "My dear friend, I should gladly make this fine style [i.e., of calling her a friend] a fact, but a friend is not made in a day nor by our will. You & I should only be friends on imperial terms." As was the case with Fuller, Emerson enjoyed Sturgis's attention but kept her at arm's length. In late summer, Fuller reproached Emerson with "a certain inhospitality of soul" on her own and Sturgis's behalf. The next few years often found Emerson putting Sturgis off with his trusty Montaigne–pseudo-Aristotle paradox that there were no friends. "Who is fit for friendship? Not one," he told her on 15 March 1841.[98]

As for Fuller herself, she was far too generous with her affections to have been the longed-for figure in the 22 December entry. In the passage under examination, Emerson was giving himself permission to love unrequitedly. That contrasts sharply with a 22 October 1840 letter of his to Fuller, in which he granted himself a quite different permission: "Can one be glad of an affection which he knows not how to return? I am."[99]

The final and least likely candidate would be Anna Hazard Barker. Although she held a prominent place in Emerson's imagination that winter, they had met only for one weekend and did not yet even correspond. For Emerson she was more a fictional character than a person. "She is the very heroine of your dreamed romance which you related to Charles & me at Elm Vale once," he wrote to his aunt Mary.[100]

Nearly all of the brilliant sentences in "Friendship" were written in Emerson's journal during the winter of 1839–40. For example, he wrote, "Are you the friend of your friend's buttons, or of his thought?" in late December 1839. "Thou art to me a delicious torment," ran the letter to a "Dear Friend," composed on 3 February 1840. If these passages were written with Ward in mind, as I suggest, then they read as if Emerson were coaching himself in restraint. Socrates might have made similar entries if he had kept a private notebook of his struggle to construct the façade of aloof, desireless poise that Alcibiades was to find so intriguing. Emerson was moderately less discreet in his journal than in print. In his journal, for instance, he wrote that he felt a "wild delicate throbbing property in his [friend's] virtues," but in the published version of "Friendship," all Emerson felt was "property," tout court.[101]

In spring 1840, as he was completing "Friendship," Emerson went to some pains to frame the print of Endymion that Ward had given him. It may also be significant that a few days after the original gift, Emerson copied passages from Keats into his journal. Although none of the lines he copied were from "Endymion" itself, perhaps an association of the image given to him by Ward with that masterpiece of Romantic poetry had led Emerson to thumb through his Keats.[102] Endymion's was a myth remarkably suitable to stand as an emblem of Emerson's love for Ward. Apollodorus gives a straightforward précis:

"As [Endymion] was of surpassing beauty, the Moon fell in love with him, and Zeus allowed him to choose what he would, and he chose to sleep for ever, remaining deathless and ageless." As one of the chaste goddesses, Diana could not actually have Endymion. She could visit him only in his sleep. Like the infamous painting by Girodet-Trioson, Keats's poem presents a male beauty who remains passive while he is admired, unconscious of (though mysteriously aroused by) the caresses bestowed upon him. Both Girodet-Trioson and Keats also treated Endymion's dream as a type of Neoplatonic ecstasy: union with a god's love while dreaming brought poetic inspiration and knowledge from a higher plane. "I would rather be struck dumb," Keats's Endymion told his sister, "Than speak against this ardent listlessness." Fuller and Emerson hoped that Ward would remain in a similar state of ardent listlessness — a sort of erotic suspended animation — where he would continue to have access to Transcendental truths, and they could continue to love him with a shame-straitened pleasure.[103]

That spring, the sleeper roused himself. According to Tilton, Ward left for New Orleans on 24 March 1840, and when he arrived in early April, he proposed marriage. Barker refused him. Her father had warned her not to expect any inheritance, and so she could not marry Ward until he was able to satisfy "not only her feelings but her tastes," as Ward delicately phrased it some time later. On 1 May 1840, Ward wrote to his father, "I no longer have any expectation of making Anna Barker my wife." Despite the lovers' discretion, word traveled quickly. While Ward was traveling home by a scenic route through the West, Fuller and Emerson alluded to the affair in their letters. By 8 July, Emerson was calling "the fact that Anna & her lover had parted — that she was not engaged — a fact which belongs to the world." The venal motive for Barker's rejection seems to have caused a minor scandal among Transcendentalists. Ellery Channing was still ranting about it two years later.[104]

When Ward returned to his father's Boston home, he took to bed with an ague. Emerson wrote the feverish man a series of concerned letters — on 16 June, 22 June, 3 July, 7 July, and 14 July. Illness had given John F. Mifflin an opportunity (nearly a pretext) for closer intimacy with his friends, and Charles Brockden Brown's heroes responded to disease with counterphobic thrill. Emerson seems usually to have regarded illness the way Auden did: as a sign of psychic confusion, to be reprimanded rather than indulged. As Fuller observed in her 1842 journal, Emerson studiously failed to respond to Lidian's fits of indisposition; her neurotic character was probably worsened by the opium she was given. In Lidian's satire, "The Transcendental Bible," she took revenge on her husband's indifference. Under the heading "Duty to your Neighbour," she placed the commandment "Loathe and shun the sick." "They are in bad taste,"

Lidian wrote, "and may untune us for writing the poem floating through our mind."[105]

The solicitous letters that Emerson wrote to Ward in quick succession seem to belie somewhat Emerson's standard position on illness, which was to "impart . . . truth and health in rough electric shocks" rather than to "weep foolishly" beside a sickbed. Emerson did not, however, leave Concord to nurse Ward. He stuck to his desk, where he was finishing "Friendship." The last journal entries that he used as raw material for the essay were written between 29 June and 10 July. While Ward was still convalescing, Emerson asked if Ward would read the essay when it was finished. "I would gladly provoke a commentary from so illuminated a doctor of the sweet science as yourself." He mailed Ward a finished draft on 14 July. But before "Friendship" was ready, Emerson was eager for Ward to read another document, Augustine's *Confessions*.[106]

At first glance, it may seem odd that Emerson would present Augustine's *Confessions* and his own essay on friendship as parallel, even equivalent, documents. "I will keep the paper & send the Book," he wrote Ward on 7 July, as if the two were interchangeable. As Andrew Sullivan has noted, Augustine's book testifies eloquently to the beauty of friendship. The church father described friendship as "sweet to me beyond all the sweetnesses of life," and the death by fever of a young friend left Augustine in despair. In his 1843 *Dial* notice of a reprint of the *Confessions,* it was this elegiac passage that Emerson quoted, explaining that he had chosen it by "opening the book at random": " 'O madness, which knowest not how to love men like men!' " Perhaps Emerson urged the book on Ward because he identified with the strong feelings Augustine expressed for his dying friend, but if so, the identification must have been less than fully conscious. To send a sick man a book about death and bereavement would have been a highly ambiguous gesture. Emerson himself gave a different reason. He cited his "gratitude to some golden words I read in [the *Confessions*] last summer" as his motive for recommending the book.[107]

Emerson's journals show that he had been reading the *Confessions* in April 1839. (Not in the summer: in the summer of 1839 he met Ward.) Unlike Ward, the modern reader can turn to those journal entries to discover which of Augustine's "golden words" had so impressed Emerson. On 6 April 1839, Emerson copied out this passage from a 1620 translation: "The learning to write & to read was better than the Latin lessons in poetry whereby I was constrained to lay up the follies of I know not what Aeneas whilst I forgot mine own, & to bewail Dido dead because she killed herself for love, whilst in the meantime I, most miserable creature, did endure myself with dry eyes to depart & die from thee O my God, & my life." Perhaps, like Augustine,

Emerson in middle age repented of his youthful misuse of literature — his decision to praise Aeneas and weep for Dido when it would have been wiser to look to his own soul's needs. As I discussed in Chapter 4, in his manuscript poem "Dedication," a teenage Emerson had patterned the sacrifice of his feelings for his classmate Martin Gay after the literary model of Aeneas's sacrifice of his love for Dido. With "silent zeal," young Emerson had given up his "unattained friendship" with Gay in favor of a literary vocation. The mature Emerson, however, bore a message somewhat at odds with this early sacrifice. Life, the adult Emerson maintained, should never be sacrificed to literature: "The student is . . . to esteem his own life the text, and books the commentary." The literature of the past consists of the stories of others, which distract and damage young minds. "Biographies, histories, and criticism" are only "the sepulchres of the fathers." What's Hecuba — or Dido and Aeneas, for that matter — to a young American?[108]

In his letter to Ward, Emerson did not cite chapter or verse, but the paragraph quoted above was almost certainly the passage in Augustine that he had in mind, because his letter continues, "But do not read. Why should you read this book or any book? It is a foolish conformity & does well for dead people."[109] If Emerson thought Augustine's *Confessions* and his own "Friendship" were parallel texts, perhaps it was because both works directed themselves toward life rather than toward other works of literature. Both aspired to bring the soul in right relation to itself and other souls. The somewhat melancholy paradox is that Emerson's behavior with Ward differed little from his behavior with Gay. In both cases, he channeled his feelings into a work of literature, imbuing that work with a special energy and asking it to justify his renunciation. There is only this small, important difference: Emerson never sent "Dedication" to Gay, but he mailed "Friendship" to Ward as soon as it was finished.

Assessing the Transcendentalist reaction to the eventual marriage of Ward and Barker, Eleanor Tilton observed with some asperity that "apparently even Emerson could entertain 'a mere imagination' and an absurd one: that his four friends Miss Fuller, Miss Sturgis, Miss Barker, and Mr. Ward would remain forever celibate, devotees of 'Celestial Love,' perhaps." Subtracting Tilton's scorn, the observation is correct. By the spring of 1840, this fond hope was Emerson's as well as Fuller's, as Emerson's journal entry of 11 June 1840 makes clear. The entry begins with the insight "I cold because I am hot, — cold at the surface only as a sort of guard & compensation for the fluid tenderness of the core." He goes on to assert that "a better & holier society will mend this selfish cowardice and we shall have brave ties of affection not petrified by law, not dated or ordained by law to last for one year, for five years, or for life; but drawing their date like all friendship from itself only; brave as I said because innocent & religiously abstinent from the connubial endearments, being a higher league on a purely spiritual basis. This nobody believes possible who is not good. The good know it is possible. Cows & bulls & peacocks think it nonsense." Emerson believed that "innocent & religiously abstinent" love could triumph over the "connubial endearments." The only doubters were those who were "not good" — those who could not imagine living without sex: the cows whose docility would never question it, the bulls who raged with it, and the peacocks who lived for display and attraction. As late as 16 August, Emerson could write "how joyfully would I form permanent relations with the three or four wise & beautiful whom I hold so dear, and dwell under the same roof or in a strict neighborhood. That would at once ennoble life. And it is practicable." Sexual coolness would bring Emerson emotional heat; chastity would license intimacy. Thus when Emerson wrote in his journal on 21 June, in what would become one of "Friendship's" most famous lines, "Let him be to thee forever a sort of beautiful Enemy," he followed this invitation to brotherly sparring with a touch of sisterly wistfulness: "And yet, as Elizabeth Hoar said, though I do not wish my friend to visit me, I wish to live with him."[110]

   Emerson and his circle of "Samaritans" (as he once called them) interacted on terms more emotional than rational, and correspondingly, the sense to be made of the essay "Friendship" is not philosophic but dramatic. Emerson mines the literary tradition of the philosophy of friendship, including Aristotle, Plato, Cicero, Bacon, and Montaigne, but he perverted many of the received wisdoms. Porte has hypothesized that Emerson, as a former preacher, structured his lectures and essays as demonic sermons — as commentaries on a scriptural text that he deformed and then submerged. In "Friendship," Emerson seems to have written according to the process that Porte describes, but with secular texts.[111]

   For example, Emerson counsels, "Treat your friend as a spectacle." Emerson seems to mean, Look but don't touch. Take in all the pleasure you like through your eyes, but "stand aside" from your friend so as not to inhibit or interfere with his growth. The apothegm probably derives from Bacon's essay "On Love," where Bacon quotes Epicurus: "*Satis magnum alter alteri theatrum sumus* [We are a sufficiently large theater to each other]." Bacon, however, calls the Latin text a "poor saying," because the notion strikes him as a dismal compromise, "as if man, made for the contemplation of heaven and all noble objects, should do nothing but kneel before a little idol, and make himself a subject, though not of the mouth (as beasts are), yet of the eye, which was given him for higher purposes." Bacon disapproves of treating your beloved as a spectacle — of making the object of your affection into an idol of the eye. Emerson has stolen the Epicurus quote from Bacon and put it to a contrary use. It may also be telling that Emerson took it from Bacon's essay on love rather than his essay on friendship.[112]

Although another sentence from Emerson falls in "Circles" rather than in "Friendship," let us consider it here. "The love of me accuses the other party" expresses one of Emerson's most peculiar ideas, but one that recurs often, in places as disparate as his poem "The Sphinx" and his lecture "New England Reformers." Emerson prefers his friend to be better than he is, so that emulation will spur Emerson to higher achievements. Any friend who cares for Emerson triggers skepticism of the friend's merit.[113]

Here Emerson appears to be misconstruing an Aristotelian concept. In the *Nicomachean Ethics,* Aristotle proposed that in a friendship between unequal men, their unequal merit should be counterbalanced by unequal affection. "The better and more useful partner should receive more affection than he gives," Aristotle decreed, "for when the affection is proportionate to the merit of each partner, there is in some sense equality between them."[114] Aristotle suggested the rule of "proportionate affection" in order to preserve the feeling of equality that friendship demanded, even in an extreme case such as between a commoner and a king. Because the king would have more wealth and power to give, Aristotle suggested that the commoner could restore balance and dignity to their relationship by giving the king in return a greater amount of affection. Emerson twists this notion into a caricature of itself. He turns unequal affection into the index rather than the compensation for unequal merit. In Emerson's version, if Henry loves Waldo more than Waldo loves Henry, then perhaps Waldo is more kinglike than Henry and should look around to see if he can do better.

For a third example, there is Emerson's famous paradox "Let [thy friend] be to thee for ever a sort of beautiful enemy." As George Kateb has observed, this idea has "no partisans" and "seems to lack precedents." An old Greek proverb advised that "we ought to love as if we are one day going to hate." The proverb warned against trusting imprudently, but Emerson is arguing that even a friendship in no danger of betrayal will be improved if both parties "guard their strangeness." However, nothing else in Emerson's sources even approximates this idea, and so it is noteworthy that nearly all his sources refute the proverb, sometimes angrily. Cicero regards it "with particular distaste" and instructs his reader that "we must *never* make a friend whom we might some day come to hate." Montaigne writes that the proverb might be prudent and appropriate in common, lowly friendship but that it is "abominable in this sovereign and masterful friendship." Montaigne also writes that although a surfeit of intimacy may deaden love, friendship can never be sated. Similarly, Bacon advises men to keep love in check, if possible, but he advises no such restraint with friendship, which seems to be all boon. In Plato's *Phaedrus,* Socrates mockingly improves on Lysias's cynical claim that nonlovers make better friends than lovers do, only to set in high relief the praise of love that follows. The Emerson who laments that "almost all people descend to meet" — the Emerson whom Kateb calls "the advocate of more distance" — has no one to second him.[115]

There is, in other words, nothing like Emerson's essay in the literature of friendship. Straying so far from orthodoxy has a cost. Emerson's distortions of his precursors yield fascinating paradoxes, but poor philosophy and even poorer advice about relationships. As a literary essay, however, "Friendship" succeeds. Its closest relative is the work of Plato. In his dialogues, Plato plays with the question of eros in friendship while pretending to answer it. Plato toys with the arousal and the shame that the possibility of sex brings to a relationship between men, but rather than force a reconciliation or showdown between these two emotional responses, Plato stages a drama where the tension can be acted out. The audience is never certain of the nature of the relationship discussed. The audience is also never certain of the nature of the relationship dramatized. What is going on between Socrates and Phaedrus, or between Socrates and Alcibiades? Why does what Socrates means by *filia* become more ambiguous the more he stickles over its definition? The same drama exists in Emerson's text, though less explicitly. The reader is provoked to wonder what is going on between Emerson and his unnamed friend, or between Emerson and the reader himself. The game hinges on not being able to say for sure.

"We have a great deal more kindness than is ever spoken," Emerson begins. As with his lecture "The Heart," Emerson starts in a mist, "bathed with an element of love like a fine ether" (341).[116] There is as yet no friend, but the ether is charged. It energizes the people who swim in it; it enhances their powers of communication and amplifies their loving impulses. If "Friendship" were a play, then in its opening scene, Emerson is alone, but he and his audience are expectant. There is something in the air, Emerson says. We in the audience wait for it to manifest.

As he describes this air of expectation, Emerson gives details of what it is that we expect. And as he does, the ether condenses into a human figure: the "commended stranger." "He stands to us for humanity," Emerson writes. "He is what we wish." Before the commended stranger comes, he raises hopes and spirits. "An uneasiness betwixt pleasure and pain invades all the hearts of a household" (341). He seems not so much to arrive as to be conjured out of the anxieties and wishes of those who expect him. But almost as soon as he appears, this new figure tumbles into a cascade of perceptions and emotions — misrecognition, exhilaration, recognition, disappointment, and exhilaration again — that will run through the essay the way a major theme runs through a sonata.

At first, while we still mistake our fancy of the stranger for the stranger, "we talk better than we are wont. We have the nimblest fancy, a richer memory." But then, awfully and irrevocably, the stranger himself mars the illusion. The mood of exaltation is interrupted. We get to know him. "He is no stranger now. Vulgarity, ignorance, misapprehension are old acquaintances." If the cascade were to end here, the essay it informs would be little more than misanthropic complaint. Emerson, however, goes further. After the disappointment — after "the throbbing of the heart, and the communications of the soul" will come no more — Emerson exults: "What is so pleasant as these jets of affection which make a young world for me again?" (342).

This is startling. Readers who pause here must wonder what this essay is about. They have heard a character named Emerson say that living in the world of affections is something like living in a thundercloud. A charge builds up, tingling on your skin; the cloud darkens into a shape; and then the energies in the air draw themselves together into a single bolt of lightning, beautiful in its force. Once the lightning strikes, though, it dissipates. It turns out to have been only a little brightness in the air, perhaps not even real. But the letdown afterward does not much compromise the beauty and pleasure of the experience. However brief or illusory, the "jets of affection" make Emerson's world seem young again. He is immediately ready for another "delicious . . . just and firm encounter of two" (342). Is Emerson describing the growth of a friendship or an act of lovemaking?

Readers may also wonder whether Emerson has any friends. He says he does. "I awoke this morning with devout thanksgiving for my friends, the old and the new" (342). But he launched his essay by vividly explaining that the attractions friends exert are illusory. And he has been careful to call his friends beautiful only "on their approach to this beating heart." Once they reach the beating heart, apparently, the heart relapses to its regular pulse. When Emerson offers up a "devout thanksgiving" for his friends, he describes them as "pass[ing] my gate" rather than entering it. And he ends his paragraph of thanks by asserting that he is indifferent to the question "Will these, too, separate themselves from me again?" The indifference sounds so lofty as to be inhuman.

However, just after claiming that he is above worrying whether his friends will leave him — "I know not, but I fear it not" — he confesses "to an extreme tenderness of nature" (343). "It is almost dangerous to me to 'crush the sweet poison of misused wine' of the affections." But if Emerson does not care whether his friends leave him, how could his affection for them be "dangerous"? Here an ungenerous reader might question Emerson's good faith. But most readers will respond by treating Emerson as a character rather than a philosopher. They will supply an explanation on Emerson's behalf: his loftiness is defensive. He pretends to be invulnerable because he is exceptionally vulnerable. He doubts the reality of his friendly feelings not because there is anything particularly unreal about friendship but because the stakes are higher than he is letting on. Emerson is in love, although he is telling himself it is only friendship. He colds because he is hot.

Emerson himself never offers this explanation. But as if to encourage it, his next paragraph indulges his "fine fancies about persons" (343). They give him a pleasure that "yields no fruit." In fact, he admits, they distort his perceptions. "We over-estimate the conscience of our friend. His goodness seems better than our goodness, his nature finer, his temptations less." This is all fiction, Emerson suggests, but he hints that although he knows it to be fiction, he is not able, or even willing, to resist it. But why would Emerson, the champion of painful truths, rhapsodize about sentimental self-deception?

Next, however, Emerson becomes as stern as he has just been indulgent: "Friendship, like the immortality of the soul, is too good to be believed" (343). It is as if Emerson suspects that the reader is on to him, as if he calculates that the reader has begun to wonder whether Emerson himself fully understands why he treats his friends so warily. No sooner do we suspect him of softness than he displays his philosophical rigor. Emerson does not deny that his wariness is a psychological defense or a quirk of his personal temperament. But he presents it now as an appropriate response to metaphysical fact. His doubt proceeds from the distinction that Transcendental philosophy makes between the subjective and objective modes of experience. "I cannot make your consciousness tantamount to mine," he explains. "I cannot deny it, O friend, that the vast shadow of the Phenomenal includes thee also in its pied and painted immensity" (344).

At this point, if "Friendship" were being staged as a Platonic dialogue, Emerson would again have changed his role. He would have switched from a happy gull in love to a realist disillusioning a suitor as politely as possible. "Shall we fear to cool our love by mining for the metaphysical foundation of this Elysian temple?" (344). There has been an abrupt turning of tables. If the reader imagines "Friendship" as a conversation, the friend is now the one who is reluctant to face facts. The Emerson character is merely being reasonable and perhaps a little condescending. The friend has asked for more than it is fair to expect. After all, another person's subjectivity can only be experienced objectively.

This is a sloppy moment in Emerson's logic. The subjective and the objective may indeed be modes of perception that never intersect. But what has that got to do with our feelings for other people? We cannot get inside another person's subjectivity, but that does not prevent us from recognizing that other people have subjectivities. And it is not clear that loving another person in any way betrays our own subjective experience. Aristotle, for instance, readily admits that there can be no friendship for others without a primary friendship with oneself: one does not compromise the other; they make each other possible. "Thou art not my soul," Emerson says to the suppliant friend. But that is not the real stumbling block. The real stumbling block is much humbler. The trouble is not that other people are "Phenomenal," as Emerson puts it, but that one may lose them. Disarmingly, Emerson admits this, though in a defensively grand peroration: "Is it not that the soul puts forth friends as the tree puts forth leaves, and presently, by the germination of new buds, extrudes the old leaf?" (344). Emerson does not want to be shed like an old leaf, nor does he want to feel guilty if he sheds someone else. Any sympathetic reader who fails to follow Emerson's pseudo-Coleridgean logic here — which most readers will fail to do, because it does not quite add up — will instead make sense of the passage by intuiting that the character Emerson has just revealed to the audience a human weakness. Emerson has observed that people often discard those whom they once loved, and he is holding himself aloof to protect himself from this potential hurt.

And yet, he does not hold himself aloof for long. As he closes his harangue on the impossibility (or at least, the impermanence) of souls' meeting, he acknowledges that what he has been discussing must be deeper and stronger than what most people refer to as friendship. He is addressing, he admits, a "candidate for his love" (344). The dynamics of the scene are again in flux. By "candidate," does Emerson mean someone who wants Emerson's love or someone whom Emerson wants to love, or both? Before the reader can decide, Emerson reproduces in its entirety an extraordinary "letter" he wrote in his journal on 3 February 1840.

> DEAR FRIEND: —
> If I was sure of thee, sure of thy capacity, sure to match my mood with thine, I should never think again of trifles in relation to thy comings and goings. I am not very wise; my moods are quite attainable; and I respect thy genius; it is to me as yet unfathomed; yet dare I not presume in thee a perfect intelligence of me, and so thou art to me a delicious torment. Thine ever, or never. (345)

This letter captures in miniature the spirit of the essay as a whole. Like the essay, it is an attempt to state the nature of a relationship that is not static. And like the essay, it is unevenly opaque. In any communication, the most semantically loaded zones are the beginning and the end. They appear to be remarkably transparent in this letter. Most readers would know what to make of a letter that began by wondering what would happen "If I was sure of thee" and ended by declaring that "thou art to me a delicious torment." If the start and the end of it were all we had, we would not hesitate to say that this is a love letter, from a passionate but somewhat flirty supplicant. "Thine ever, or never," indeed. But we have the middle of the letter, too, and that middle is tortuous. Once we move past the first phrase, it turns out that it is not the friend's heart that Emerson wants to be sure of but his "capacity." Emerson might mean "capacity to love," but if so, he does not spell this out. Explicitly, his concern is only whether the friend has "a perfect intelligence of me." Yet Emerson is also careful to say that neither his wisdom nor his moods are out of his friend's reach ("I am not very wise; my moods are quite attainable"), as if to indicate that his doubt of his friend's "intelligence" is not a doubt of his friend's intellectual capacity. He must therefore mean some other kind of intelligence. Also, although he says it somewhat elliptically, Emerson seems to be worried about losing his friend or not holding his attention. The implication of the first sentence is that since Emerson is *not* sure of his friend, he thinks of "thy comings and goings" as anything *but* "trifles."

Emerson's one-paragraph letter is deliberately incomplete. It fails to give the reader enough information to assemble an adequate paraphrase of its denotative meaning. It is, however, rich with tones and nuances that the reader could use while imagining a relationship between the character Emerson and the character of his friend. Moving from atom to molecule, consider the essay "Friendship" as a whole. Like the small letter it contains, the larger letter of "Friendship" seems deceptively clear if you look only at its extremities. The first sentences of its first and last paragraphs read as follows: "We have a great deal more kindness than is ever spoken" and "It has seemed to me lately more possible than I knew, to carry a friendship greatly, on one side, without due correspondence on the other" (341, 354). From this line of sight, the letter's intent could not be more plain. Suppose you received a letter that began and ended with these confessions, but whose middle protested with great ingenuity that its author was not in love, because he did not believe love was anything more than an illusion, and that for a number of reasons, it was inadvisable anyway for two people to get very close to each other. You would know what the writer, despite himself, meant. And perhaps more than any other American writer, Emerson writes despite himself.

Much of what a reader understands from a text is inferred. Even with essayistic prose, the reader imagines a scene, with characters and a setting. Whenever Emerson mentions "friendship," the reader imagines a character named Emerson and a character who is Emerson's friend, and the reader imagines a narrative, however skeletal, that puts their relationship in context. The essay "Friendship" dazzles its readers in part because, sentence by sentence, there are drastic shifts in the background narrative that the reader must construct to make sense of what Emerson is saying. It was Emerson's method of composition to patch together pithy and stylistically elegant observations that he had condensed from life experiences. By the time the observations appeared in his published essays, the details of the life behind them had been omitted long ago. The sentences that compose "Friendship" are clipped from many moments in many relationships, with various people and at various times. In Chapter 4, I called this method of cutting an emotion or an insight away from the circumstances that generated it "hierotomy," a holy divorce that is as typical of American literature as Fiedler's holy marriage is. Hierotomy gives Emerson's prose its distinctive flavor—at once highly abstract and revealingly personal. It hides Emerson's actual experience by dividing it into pieces and then jumbling those pieces. But it also makes the reader especially curious about that actual experience. Each sentence seems to give a glimpse into Emerson's heart that, though brief, is altogether unobstructed. And by causing rapid contradictions and shifts in the background story that the reader is building and remodeling while reading, hierotomy forces the reader to spend more energy speculating about this background story than would a text whose mode of composition was more organic and straightforward. By the effort it requires, so similar to the effort of interpretation and explanation that is the chief mental labor of an intimate relationship, hierotomy may even give the reader the feeling of being in a personal relationship with Emerson. Repeatedly, the reader must extend sympathy into the prose to make sense of it. The character of the friend is the easiest character for the reader to play. After all, Emerson has defined friendship according to terms that are accurate and appropriate for a relationship between writer and reader, however inaccurate or needlessly confining they may be between friends or lovers in real life.

In the summer of 1840, Anna Barker's annual sojourn in the north was impatiently awaited. She delayed it, not arriving until early August, when she came to stay with Fuller in Jamaica Plain. After ten days with Fuller, Barker moved to Mrs. Farrar's, nearby in Cambridge. On Friday, 14 August, Emerson saw Barker, probably in Cambridge, and then shared a ride with Fuller as far as Jamaica Plain, on his way back to Concord. Although neither Emerson nor

Fuller knew about it for two more weeks, Barker had changed her mind and accepted Ward's proposal of marriage on or around this date. Ignorant of Barker and Ward's defection, Emerson and Fuller spent their ride together renegotiating the terms of their celestial friendships. As Emerson confided in his journal, Fuller "taxed me as often before so now more explicitly with inhospitality of soul. She & Caroline would gladly be my friends, yet our intercourse is not friendship, but literary gossip." As he wrote to Sturgis in a letter he never mailed, "I confess to the fact of cold & imperfect intercourse, but not to the impeachment of my will, and not to the deficiency of my affection." In that unsent letter, Emerson suggested that he was reluctant to open himself more deeply to Sturgis because he was protecting himself against the danger that she might find a husband and leave him in the lurch.[117]

As Emerson asserted, his affections were not deficient. On the contrary, as he wrote in his journal on 18 August, the attraction with which these young people drew him was so great as to make them his "tyrants." "Two or three men and three or four women rule the life of every mortal. . . . Unable to escape from these tyrants, he scuds behind a grave-stone at last, and if you go there to look, you shall find a tuft of fresher grass." Emerson later turned this journal entry into the poem "Manners," where he gives the character based on his addled, love-oppressed self the name Endymion. The name strangely muddles the poem. In the myth as most readers know it, it is Diana, not Endymion, whose painful need to gaze on her beloved puts her at a loss.[118]

The weekend of 22–24 August, Emerson hosted Barker, Fuller, and Sturgis in Concord. "My three golden days," Emerson called their time together; "these flying days." The four seem to have reached a new level of spiritual closeness. In high Swedenborgian style, they vowed to address each other as brother and sister. "I shall never quite go back to my old arctic habits," Emerson wrote to Fuller afterward. "I shall believe that nobleness is loving, & delights in sharing itself."[119] Emerson's letters describe this interlude in a tone so exalted as to be cloying, perhaps because by the time the letters were written, only a few days later, that exaltation had already met with disappointment. He was asserting the glories of a moment he knew had already passed.

His hopes were dashed on 27 August, at the Phi Beta Kappa ceremonies of the Harvard commencement. There, Barker let Emerson know that she and Ward were engaged. Emerson's first reaction was "a certain terror." It stunned him to discover that Barker's engagement antedated the "three golden days" she had spent with Emerson, Fuller, and Sturgis. As he explained to Sturgis, "I thought that the whole spirit of our intercourse at Concord implied another resolution. I thought she had looked the world through for a man as universal as herself & finding none, had said 'I will compensate myself for my great renunciation as a woman by establishing ideal relations: Not only Raphael [Ward] shall be my brother, but that Puritan at Concord [Emerson] who is reputed at some time to have seen the mighty Gods, I will elect him also.'" What most baffled Emerson was that neither Barker nor Ward appeared to show any signs of guilt for what he regarded as a betrayal. "She does not feel any fall. There is no compunction written on either of their brows." When Emerson wrote to Fuller about his disappointment, he seemed to forget that he himself was already married, and complained that "the fragment of confidence that a wife can give to an old friend is not worth picking up after this invitation to Elysian tables."[120]

The marriage of Ward and Barker destroyed Emerson's dream of realizing chaste fellowship here on earth. "A flash of lightning shivers my castle in the air," he wrote to Fuller. As Carl F. Strauch has noted, Emerson repeated this metaphor in his poem "Initial, Daemonic, and Celestial Love," where he asserted that the pride and selfishness inherent in "Daemonic" love would, in the end, "shiver the palaces of glass." Emerson had mistakenly believed that Ward and Barker's love rose above the "Daemonic" to the "Celestial" level, which was governed by the principle set forth in his couplet "When each the other shall avoid, / Shall each by each be most enjoyed." To Emerson's chagrin, Barker and Ward turned out not to be the "shining examples of Denial" he had hoped they were.[121]

"Celestial" was also the word that Lidian, with one of her customary sideswipes, used to describe Emerson's letter of congratulation to Barker and Ward. "Mr. Emerson," Lidian wrote to her sister-in-law on 2 September 1840, "has written Anna a *celestial* letter on the occasion. This expression must not be repeated. I don't want it talked about and made ridiculous as it easily might be." "Celestial" was how Emerson described the sincerity with which Barker and Ward would henceforth be able to address their "high prisoner," Emerson. Lidian was correct that the letter might easily be made ridiculous, but incorrect in claiming that it was written to Barker. It was studiously addressed to both husband- and wife-to-be. Its *you*s cannot be sorted. Consider the following passage:

> Certainly I have never yet got so far with *you*, my dear brother, (for so today at least I will joyfully call you;) we have halted hitherto on the precincts of speech with whatever confidence we have both augured our final relation— And Anna for the most of the time has quite overpowered all my talents And yet I must say in some moments your angel has appeared at all the doors melted my reserves & prepared me to say things never before spoken. But if you grow so fast on my love & reverence that I can dare believe that this dear style we are learning to use to each other is to become very fact then we can

drop our words-of-course & can afford the luxury of sincerity. There are many degrees of sincerity, & persons like us three who know the elegance of truth may yet be far without their own highest mark of simple intercourse.

Emerson begins by addressing Ward as "*you,* my dear brother." Then he refers to Barker in the third person as "Anna." By the end of the section, he is discussing "us three" — Emerson, Ward, and Barker. Whose angel appeared at all the doors? Deliberately and perhaps appropriately — since two flesh are to be made one — it is impossible to say for sure.[122]

Like Emerson, Fuller, too, experienced the marriage as both a personal loss and a philosophical letdown. For years afterward, her journals memorialized 3 October — Ward's birthday and the date of Barker and Ward's wedding — as a sad anniversary. She recorded 3 October 1844, for example, as an "Anniversary of the most moving event of my life, when the Ideal seemed nearest an earthly realization — alas!" Just as Emerson wrote "Initial, Daemonic, and Celestial Love" to work through his disappointment, Fuller composed in January 1841 a long poem about the mystic union of an angel of music named Melodia (representing Fuller) and a man conjured from white marble named Paria (representing Ward).[123]

Whereas Emerson settled on the ancient Roman relief of Endymion as his emblem of chaste love, Fuller chose a painting by Raphael of the Virgin Mary and Christ Crucified. Fuller saw the bond between Christ and his mother as the paragon for nonsexual relationships of great strength and intensity. In a woundingly frank letter that Ward wrote to Fuller, probably during this period of final revelations, Ward referred to Fuller's belief "that an attachment subsisted between Jesus and Mary sufficient to suggest to the spotless son of God the existence of a new, vast, and tumultuous class of human emotions." Fuller had evidently accused Ward of turning his back on this new class of emotions. His angry response came very close to reminding her that as a virgin she had no way of knowing for sure that sexual love was a lesser thing than Platonic love. "*I,* too, once knew and recognized the possibility of Platonic affection. It is possible to those who have never passed the line X X X X. Before that, all the higher class of emotion all the nobler views of life exist; but in a shape that seems sublimated and idealized to the more experienced: to those who *have* passed that line, the higher emotions and the passions are apt to be always afterward inextricably commingled."[124]

Emerson relapsed easily into his former Transcendental isolation. Fuller took the blow harder. Her identification with Raphael's Madonna formed part of a larger religious crisis. To Sturgis, she wrote of "mighty changes in my spiritual life." Emerson did not think much of these changes. When news of the engagement had broken, he had warned Fuller that "*you* must be generous beyond even the strain of heroism . . . & resign without a sigh two Friends." In Emerson's opinion, Fuller's new piety indicated that the strain had been too much for her. In his section of the *Memoirs of Margaret Fuller Ossoli,* years later, Emerson recalled that "in the summer of 1840, she passed into certain religious states, which did not impress me as quite healthy, or likely to be permanent."[125]

No doubt Fuller's loss of Barker and Ward was aggravated by her sense that Emerson, too, had begun to withdraw. In the aftermath of Ward and Barker's engagement, Emerson's relationships with Fuller and Sturgis changed quickly. At first, Sturgis advanced, as if by default, from her role as sentimental backup. She and Emerson exchanged a series of letters whose maudlin vows escalated dangerously. Sturgis assured him that she would continue to love him even if she married; he wrote that "you shall be my saint & purify me wholly." She explained that "I loved you so much, that I could easily see how I could love you & others also"; he wrote that "you shame my little faith by your large-ness." But then, as quickly as their friendship had overheated, it crashed. By 13 October, Emerson seems to have wearied of Sturgis's melodramatic rap-tures. "And you have found out that you are alone, & only now, and only for yourself," he wrote her, once again in the style of no-friend to no-friend. "I am alone, and will you please to tell me of any friend of yours whom you know or have read of, who is not." On 18 October, he reproved her sharply for her credulous interest in animal magnetism and for using too many superlatives. "I have written you down in my books & in my heart for my sister because you are a user of the positive degree," he warned her. She was free to love him with others, if necessary, but not to abuse her adjectives.[126]

As with Sturgis, so with Fuller, but more sourly. Fuller must have hoped that the sympathy of a shared loss would bring Emerson closer to her. It did not. The two did not experience even the brief surge of unreal, friendly hyperbole that Sturgis and Emerson exchanged. Instead, Fuller turned to Emerson with the full burden of her emotional needs, exacerbated by her recent losses. Emer-son retreated. On 13 September, in a half-apology for not answering her letters promptly, he explained that he was rationing his correspondence. "A letter for a letter & not for a billet, especially, if, as in late instances, that billet be a dun." Fuller's billets, however *doux,* struck Emerson as accounts payable. On 26 September, he complained in his journal, "You would have me love you. What shall I love? Your body? The supposition disgusts you." While he strug-gled to reestablish the walls that had formerly distanced them, she struggled to tear them down. Emerson alleged that there was "a certain willfulness" in her claim that "I am yours & yours shall be." He maintained that in fact "we meet & treat like foreign states."[127]

"But did not you ask for a 'foe' in your friend?" Fuller urged Emerson, quoting "Friendship" back to him. "Did not you ask for a 'large formidable nature'? But a beautiful foe, I am not yet to you." The strictures that Emerson had set on himself to enable him to approach Ward now did double duty as barriers that kept Fuller at bay. After a month of Fuller's recriminations and Emerson's regrets—rendered especially awkward when Emerson was invited to Ward and Barker's wedding and Fuller apparently was not—Emerson shut the door firmly. "Ice has its uses," he told her on 22 October. On 24 October, he wrote that "I ought never to have suffered you to lead me into any conversation or writing on our relation." By repeatedly analyzing their friendship, Fuller had violated the "pudency" that, in Emerson's opinion, ought to insulate friendship from language.[128]

Fuller and Sturgis consoled each other by sharing notes on the rejections each had received from Emerson. After Fuller read over one of Emerson's scolding letters to Sturgis, she wrote Sturgis that "Waldo is . . . secluded by a doubt, secluded by a sneer." "O these tedious, tedious attempts to learn the universe by thought alone. Love, Love, my Father, thou hast given me.—I thank thee for its pains." But Emerson wanted no more of its pains. Although they protested, the two women had to accept the new limits Emerson set to their intimacies with him. They continued to write and see him often. But the experiment in celestial love was over.[129]

One night near New Year's, 1841, Emerson dreamed of a convention assembled to discuss the institution of marriage, where "grave & alarming objections [were] stated on all hands to the usage." But this reformist debate took a strange turn:

> One speaker at last rose & began to reply to the arguments, but suddenly extended his hand & turned on the audience the spout of an engine which was copiously supplied from within the wall with water & whisking it vigorously about, up, down, right, & left, he drove all the company in crowds hither & thither & out of the house. Whilst I stood watching astonished & amused at the malice & vigor of the orator, I saw the spout lengthened by a supply of hose behind, & the man suddenly brought it round a corner & drenched me as I gazed. I woke up relieved to find myself quite dry, and well convinced that the Institution of Marriage was safe for tonight.

This dream has been much interpreted. Christopher Newfield has read it as if the reformers' objections to marriage stemmed from an opposition to patriarchy and as if the dream was Emerson's way of using passivity to identify himself with a restored patriarchal power. Joel Porte has read it as if the reformers' objections were to the failure of marriage to give sufficient vent to sexuality and as if the dream offered Emerson "an alternative way to express his drives," which were not being satisfied with Lidian.[130]

Dreams can accomplish a number of contradictory purposes and usually do. But it is likely that the dream reformers' objections were the same objections that Emerson and Fuller had offered to the marriage of Ward and Barker over the course of the previous year. That is, marriage, with its proprietary claims, impeded the exchange of emotions that celestial friendships left free and clear. Marriage would bring Ward financial burdens that would have bad "consequences to the history of his genius," just as it would put Barker in a state of financial dependence that would infantilize *her* genius. The vigorous firehose, then, corresponds not to the force of patriarchy or to the force of Emerson's sexual drive but to what had thwarted Fuller and Emerson: Ward's sexual drive. Transcendental rationales could not contain it. In his dream, Emerson takes a vicarious pleasure in the dousing — he is "astonished & amused" — because it confirms Ward's erotic power. This power always fascinated Emerson. "What a master in life!" he wrote to Sturgis about Ward several years later. "I compared this man, who is a performance, with others who seem to me only prayers."[131] At the end of his dream, Emerson also takes a firsthand pleasure in the dousing when the speaker hoses him, too. The dream thus assuages Emerson: even as Ward is lost to marriage, the eruption of his sexual energy includes Emerson in its shower.

"Ward I shall not lose," Emerson vowed shortly after he learned that Ward would marry. And he never did lose him. Emerson wrote to Ward until the end of his life. It was hard for Emerson to reconcile himself to Ward's marriage and what this meant for Ward's "genius." A year after the wedding, Emerson praised Ward to Carlyle as "a beautiful & noble youth of a most subtle & magnetic nature" while still regretting that Ward had "sacrificed [his art] to Despair." And Ward is probably behind an enigmatic entry in Emerson's 1843 journal: "A soft lovely child always truer & better, unhurt amidst the noxious influences of wealth & ultra whiggism, & can resist everything unless it were the vitriolic acid of marriage." But despite his bitterness over Ward's choice of life, Emerson continued to love him. A tone of longing persists through all Emerson's letters to Ward. In 1848, on board a steamship returning from England, Emerson wrote to Ward as if he were at last realizing the fantasy of his 1838 journal, of being "shut up in a little schooner . . . with a man" and "husband[ing] my joys" by thinking of but not speaking to this beloved fellow passenger: "What is it or can it be to you that through the long mottled trivial years a dreaming brother cherishes in a corner some picture of you as a type or nucleus of happier visions & a freer life. I am so safe in my iron limits from intrusion or extravagance, that I can well afford to indulge my humour with the figures that pass my dungeon window, without incurring any risk of a ridiculous shock from coming hand to hand with my Ariels & Gabriels." "Your loving fellow film," Emerson signed this letter. As he explained in one of his last letters to Ward, "I . . . only desire to know that there is a mind with me in the car or the ship."[132]

Emerson's hierotomy completes a movement that the diaries of Leander and Lorenzo began. The essay "Friendship" has cut itself off from the desire that generated it, its author's wish to reach another man. It bloomed from this situation, which gives it its aroma. But although Emerson once asserted that "the root of the plant is not unsightly to science, though for chaplets and festoons we cut the stem short," it was in fact his technique to cut the flower from its root.[133] In the genteel, wealthy beau monde of eighteenth-century America, it was the connection of a work of art to its author that counted. But in the public, democratic marketplace of nineteenth-century literature, the work had to be cut from its author so that any purchaser of the text could find meaning and pleasure there.

Emerson is crucial to American literature because he resists this demand even as he accommodates himself to it. His style brings forward the cruelty that the marketplace inflicts on the personal, in a way that the marketplace can appreciate. By making hierotomy central to his style, Emerson draws attention to the cut. Again and again, Emerson intimates to us that he has suffered a loss that grief will never quite heal. "The only thing grief has taught me, is to know how shallow it is," he writes in "Experience." Emerson respects the cut he has made, and he never connects with what he has lost. Even his son's death "does not touch me."[134] The reader is thus able to substitute private losses for Emerson's, who has, as it were, cut his losses to make this possible.

Emerson resists moving forward from this moment of sacrifice. He knows that his strength is in transition. "Power . . . resides in the moment of transition from a past to a new state," he writes in "Self-Reliance"; and in his essay on Plato, Emerson recommends that transitions "be adroitly managed to present as much transitional surface as possible." Emerson's moment fell in what Tocqueville called a "period of glory as well as of ferment, when the conditions of men are not sufficiently settled for the mind to be lulled in torpor, when they are sufficiently unequal for men to exercise a vast power on the minds of one another." The sacrifice of the personal held the greatest poignancy when literature had not yet finished its migration from the drawing room to the bookstore.[135]

Emerson managed his own literary career to maximize this transitional surface. Lyceum lecturing was a livelihood that locomotives made possible just as newspapers threatened to render it obsolete. Throughout his career, Emerson had to bully and sweet-talk newspaper editors out of printing transcripts of his lectures, because newspapers threatened to deliver his message to the masses too well. For lectures to support him, Emerson had to deliver them in person, which was not as efficient as the existing technology permitted. Emerson's lectures perpetuated an authorial presence that was increasingly archaic, the hallmark of an earlier literary mode.

Emerson's sortie into magazine publishing also attempted to exploit a transition. In his late career, Charles Brockden Brown had struggled to make a commercial success out of an American magazine. By contrast, Emerson's magazine *The Dial* was designed at the outset to be something other than a commercial success. It was not necessary for *The Dial* to fail in the marketplace, but to succeed there was not its goal. Emerson and Fuller intended *The Dial* to perform a kind of literary arbitrage, to take advantage of the disparity in prestige between belles lettres and the marketplace. They did not look beyond their social circle for contributors. *The Dial* was a liminal form — a printed, mass-circulation vehicle for the writings of an elite accustomed to exchanging their work privately. "It serves as a sort of portfolio," Emerson explained to Carlyle, "to carry about a few poems or sentences which would otherwise be transcribed and circulated."[136]

Corresponding to this ambition, one theme of *The Dial* was the value (and difficulty) of romantic friendships, the relationships that composed belletristic circles. The tone of etherealized homosexual libido that pervaded the correspondence of the Fuller-Emerson circle also infused *The Dial*. Thoreau, for example, contributed his poems "Sympathy" and "Friendship," as well as his elegant translations of Anacreontic verse, which muted but did not altogether suppress their frequent homoeroticism.[137] *The Dial* published Charles King Newcomb's one and only literary work, a story entitled "The First Dolon," whose bewildering mix of sadism, pedophilia, and religiosity went unmatched for half a century.[138]

In *The Dial*, Fuller was able to continue the homilies on friendship that Emerson no longer wanted to hear. On the last page of the first issue, she admonished any reader who was overprudent in offering affection, "Wise man, you never knew what it is to love." In her essay on "Romaic and Rhine Ballads," she jabbed at Emerson by quoting his intimacy-averse couplets from "The Sphinx,"

> Have I a lover
> Who is noble and free?
> I would he were nobler
> Than to love me

and alleging that they would have nonplussed the Norse hero Siegfried, who was as fearless of friendship as of dragons. In her essay "Bettine Brentano and

Her Friend Günderode," Fuller again took Emerson to task with another disparaging quotation. Fuller noted that although Goethe had failed Bettina, Bettina had been able to save her faith in romantic friendship by turning to a female friend, the canoness Günderode. An individual failure like Goethe's, Fuller observed, ought not to discourage faith in friendship itself. "Happy the survivor if in losing his friend, he loses not the idea of friendship." In the same-sex relationship of Bettina and Günderode, friendship's ideal was realized without compromise. "We feel of these two that they were enough to one another to be led to indicate their best thoughts, their fairest visions, and therefore theirs was a true friendship. They needed not 'descend to meet.' " [139]

But for the story this chapter tells, perhaps the most provocative example in this vein was a poem Ward gave to *The Dial*. "The Twin Loves" fused the Platonic myths of *Phaedrus* and the *Symposium* to the Choice of Hercules that Ward faced in his personal life. In the poem, the narrator descends from the starry sphere to earth, forgetting all but "a faint dim belief" in heaven as he falls. Once on earth, he meets two gods of love, both male, each of whom beckons to the narrator to follow. The first god, "like the *Grecian Eros*," stands silent at first, "so statue-like, so earnest, so severe." The second god prattles amiably and seductively about earthly pleasures. The first god interrupts the second god sternly, and the narrator knows which alternative he must choose. "My soul was strengthened, so that the proud tone / Answered to power within me like its own." The narrator chooses to follow the austere first god up the "rocky path" toward virtue. Intriguingly, the narrator brings the second, softer love-god with him, and whenever the rocky path's "roughness the boy's feet offend, / In my strong arms I bear the sorrowing child." In crude biographical terms, no doubt the first love-god represents Ward's mentor, Emerson, and the second love-god represents his wife. Emerson once averred that American literature was "optative"; nonetheless, "both" is not really a satisfactory resolution to the Choice of Hercules. It was a pleasant fiction on Ward's part, written perhaps for Emerson's benefit. In the event, Ward let the stern angel tread his rocky path alone.[140]

As these items suggest, *The Dial* would well repay a literary critic who examined it from the angle of gay studies. So would another of Emerson's long-running interests, the Persian poet Hafiz, whom Emerson first mentioned in his journal in 1841. " 'Tis easy out of the soul to banish lust / Not easy the friend from the soul to thrust," ran one of Emerson's manuscript translations of a Hafiz *ghazal*. The couplet captures Emerson's own ambivalent attitude toward love and friendship almost too well. More often, Hafiz's interest in friendship ran to the ecstatic, unabashedly. Emerson filled hundreds of journal pages with his translations of Hafiz, made not from Persian texts but from two books of German versions prepared by Joseph von Hammer-Purgstall.[141]

Emerson found in Hafiz, as he had not found in Fuller or among her circle, a bad horse naughty enough to match his good horse Plato. In his first collection, the *Poems* of 1847, Emerson published two of his secondhand translations of Hafiz. The Persian title of one of the poems was *Sakiname,* or "The Book of the Cupbearer." Emerson modestly retitled it "From the Persian of Hafiz." But as the original title suggests, this and many of Hafiz's poems were addressed to young men. Emerson knew this. In the essay "Persian Poetry," Emerson translated with unrectified gender the compliment that Hafiz once paid to a youth he liked: "Take my heart in thy hand, O beautiful boy of Shiraz! / I would give for the mole on thy cheek Samarcand and Buchara." Aside from his infamous 1860 advice to Whitman to tone down the sexual content of *Leaves of Grass,* Emerson almost never felt shame when other writers expressed loves he would have sternly censured in himself. In *Representative Men,* he grandly proclaimed, "Let none presume to measure the irregularities of Michel Angelo and Socrates by village scales." And in the case of Hafiz, too, Emerson asserted that "this boundless charter is the right of genius."[142]

Emerson never published any but those first two of his translations of Hafiz, and he omitted even these from the second and all later editions of his poetry. Still, the energy he privately poured into his translations of Hafiz during the next decade suggests that he was thinking about sex, love, friendship, and literary art long after his experiment in intimacy with Fuller, Ward, Barker, and Sturgis had collapsed. Perhaps Hafiz appealed so strongly because Emerson had learned to distinguish Plato's austere conclusions from Plato's more playful methods; perhaps he had learned to read Plato more as Fuller read him. After all, as Ward's poem intimated, Emerson himself was a sort of love-god—a Cupid-Socrates whose arrows were all the sharper for teaching that desires were never meant to be satisfied. "I do not drink wine," Emerson wrote in his journal in 1849, "but would have the name of drinking wine." Or, as he put it, even more ambiguously, in a stanza he adapted from Hafiz:

> To a wink sacrificed I
> My virtue
> Ah therein is all my store
> Of good works.[143]

# 6

## *The Heart Ruled Out: Melville's Palinode*

"Each man kills the thing he loves," Oscar Wilde wrote in "The Ballad of Reading Gaol."[1] It is easy to pardon the sentimentality. Wilde's impulse, after all, was generous. He was forgiving all killers whose crimes were of passion — an absolution that no doubt included Wilde's own "killer," his lover Alfred Douglas, who in pushing Wilde into the courts may have been more concerned with spiting his father than with Wilde's well-being. The self-pity of the line was hyperbolic, but the hyperbole is excusable, considering that Great Britain committed a much worse offense, injustice, when it jailed Wilde for his homosexuality.

Nevertheless, the line is untrue. Typically, Wilde was making his case by overstating it. Wilde had not killed anyone, nor had Douglas. Guardsmen who love their girlfriends do not as a rule murder them, and a knife stab is not kinder than a bitter look, despite what Wilde's ballad claimed. In the twentieth century, however, to which Wilde precociously belonged, this kind of emotional self-indulgence was appealing, especially to homosexual readers. It appealed partly because it helped to disguise a dark fact about homosexual life: society often asked them to betray their lovers, and sometimes homosexuals found reasons — cowardice, ambition, revenge, whim, social aspiration — to oblige. Wilde's wish, in proclaiming that "each man kills the thing he loves," is that the destruction of love might testify, on the lower frequencies, to the strength of the passion destroyed.

Wilde made a poem out of this wish, but the poem is maudlin, and the wish is self-deceiving. It is a wish for belief in something that is not true. First of all, the destruction of love is not inevitable, although in a despair like Wilde's there may be a carrion comfort in believing, perversely, that it is. Second, although the destruction of a love may acquire something of the aura of what it kills, a destroyed love cannot say what a living love would say. And third, most people who destroy a love are not psychotic or criminal. Their actions are not compelled. They choose to rank something else higher than affection. Wilde's sentimentality obscures these people's power and responsibility. It would have been too easy for Alfred Douglas to read "The Ballad of Reading Gaol" and cry over it without remorse.

The later Wilde's sentimentality has also obscured the nature of a very different literary work — *Billy Budd,* the novel that Herman Melville left in manuscript at his death. "Each man kills the thing he loves" is not the moral of *Billy Budd,* but many critics, gay and straight, have been tempted to read Melville's novel as if it were. "The Ballad of Reading Gaol" was written a few years after *Billy Budd,* but it was published a quarter-century sooner, so the paths of Melville's and Wilde's writings crossed in their reception. No reader ever came to *Billy Budd* innocent of Wilde's scandal and fall, although Melville was innocent of them when he wrote it. The embrace of Melville's novel by twentieth-century gay sentimentality was spontaneous and deeply felt. However, I would like to disentangle the two, at least briefly, in order to show that *Billy Budd* also fits well as the capstone to the earlier sentimental configuration that this book has been describing — that is, as a text written to convey the feelings of one man for another, replacing a more direct union between the two individuals, such that the author finds in this indirection a wider scope for artistic experiment, self-knowledge, and emotional license while remaining sensitive to the violence and sacrifice this substitution may entail.

The crossing of Melville's and Wilde's literary paths may account for a curious fact about the reception of *Billy Budd:* early readers alert to the homosexual suggestions in the novel often idealized Captain Vere's decision to hang the sailor Budd. They seemed to read through the same sentimental haze that had befogged Wilde in jail. For example, E. L. Grant Watson, the first critic to point out the "suggestive shadows of primal, sexual simplicities" in *Billy Budd,* famously described the novel as "Melville's testament of acceptance." "Melville is no longer a rebel," Watson claimed in his *New England Quarterly* essay of 1933, thereby launching a debate about the political implications of the book that continues to this day. It was no coincidence that Watson was among the first to celebrate both the homoeroticism and the submissiveness of its tone: Watson saw the two phenomena as linked.[2]

"In so conscious a symbolist as Melville," Watson wrote, "it would be surprising if there should be no meaning or half-meaning in the spilling of Billy's soup towards the homosexually-disposed Claggart, in the impotence of Billy's speech in the presence of his accuser, in his swift and deadly answer, or the likening of Claggart's limp, dead body to that of a snake." Watson characterized the novels *Pierre* and *Clarel* as Melville's Freudian-style self-analyses. He then suggested that *Billy Budd* contained "a further, deeper wisdom. And as the philosophy in it has grown from that of rebellion to that of acceptance, as the symbolic figures of unconscious forces have become always more concrete and objective, so we may assume that these hints are intentional, and that Melville was particularly conscious of what he was doing." Watson argued that Melville had become "particularly conscious" of his homosexual imagery because his investigations of his own psyche in *Pierre* and *Clarel* had led him to change his philosophic stance from "that of rebellion to that of acceptance." In the coy language of an earlier era, Watson was claiming Melville as a writer who had come to terms with his homosexuality.[3]

To claim Melville as a self-aware homosexual without stating his case explicitly, Watson had to make a strange, unfortunate conflation. Watson had to confuse a personal acceptance of homosexuality (the plot that Watson implied was latent in *Billy Budd*) with eroticized submission to worldly authority (the plot he saw as manifest in *Billy Budd*). To blur these two plots into one, the haze had to be rather thick.

In fact, it was so thick that almost no one seems to have understood what Watson was up to. Later critics set Watson's hints about homosexuality to one side, as if these hints had nothing to do with what Watson thought *Billy Budd* affirmed. Instead, Watson's colleagues focused on what Watson had said about affirmation per se. Watson became the whipping boy of critics who, unencumbered with sexual concerns, were able to explore Melville's political ironies more fully than Watson had.

Watson's strong (and perhaps strategic) misreading was repeated and aggravated in what is still the most famous rendering of *Billy Budd*—the 1951 opera by Benjamin Britten, with a libretto by E. M. Forster and Eric Crozier. Melville warns his readers that Billy Budd "is not presented as a conventional hero" and that "the story in which he is the main figure is no romance" (53).[4] Unfortunately, Forster and Crozier heeded this warning by setting up another character as the main figure—Captain Vere—and by doctoring the plot to ensure that Vere came off as a hero. As if to ratify their decision, Britten cast his lover, Peter Pears, in the role of Vere.[5]

Forster, Crozier, and Britten fill a number of the novel's silences and decide many of its ambiguities. For example, in the opera, Captain Vere appears at the start and the finish, framing the action as his own reminiscence. He thus occupies the place held in the novel by the narrator, whose relation to the action was much more ambiguous. When Britten's Billy Budd joins the man-of-war as a freshly impressed sailor, his new crewmates salute him with a jingoistic, unpleasantly "hearty" song ("Starry Vere we call him") announcing how much they love their captain.[6] By contrast, Melville was conspicuously silent about what "people" thought of Vere, noting only that his colleagues "found him lacking in the companionable quality, a dry and bookish gentleman" (63). In fact, in Melville's long digressions about Horatio Nelson, the implied comparison slighted Vere, "the most undemonstrative of men," who lacked Nelson's showy love of glory and risk and thus had none of Nelson's natural charisma (60).

When a French ship is sighted and Captain Vere orders a chase, Britten's score sweetens into a hunting anthem that might have been composed by John Williams to convey Luke Skywalker's excitement in pursuit of Imperial storm-troopers. But Melville never wrote anything to suggest that the *Bellipotent*'s sailors cared about the war they had been conscripted to fight. Melville's Vere even admitted that "in His Majesty's service — in this ship, indeed — there are Englishmen forced to fight for the King against their will. Against their conscience, for aught we know" (112). Britten's musical politics are reactionary. (A genuine John Williams score would have signaled that Vere was piloting an eighteenth-century version of the Death Star.)

Having pumped up Captain Vere's charm and the crew's attachment to him, Forster and Crozier proceed to eliminate the ambiguities of Vere's behavior in the "trial" of Budd. In the novel, it was Vere who advocated the death penalty for Budd and pressed his "jurors" into consenting to it. In the opera, however, Vere showily refuses to give his personal opinion as to the verdict. Forster and Crozier's libretto reassigns Vere's insistence on punishment to the sailing master. In the novel, the sailing master had hoped to "mitigate the penalty," but in the opera he is made to sing of his lust for "revenge, revenge." The opera accommodates Vere's sentimental posturing so obligingly that Vere is allowed to sing of Budd's ordeal, "It is not his trial, it is mine, mine."[7]

It is odd that Forster should have misread *Billy Budd* so grotesquely, for its setup resembles that of *Howards End*. In Forster's novel, the Schlegels may have all the charisma, but the Wilcoxes own the house. Similarly, in Melville's novel, Budd may have all the beauty and inspire all the love, but Captain Vere commands the ship. But perhaps this is *why* Forster gets it wrong: he is tempted to treat Vere's hanging of Budd as if it were a marriage.[8] Yet contra Forster, as contra Wilde, killing is not an expression of love. Melville's imagery sometimes compares the consummation of love between men to a murderous embrace, as in the battle between the *Serapis* and the *Bon Homme Richard* in *Israel Potter,* or as in the metaphors and threats of cannibalism throughout his novels.[9] But Melville never claimed a murder could be an act of love. That is a distortion of Forster's imagination, not Melville's.

Melville would never have eroticized one man killing another in order to represent a personal or general acceptance of sexual love between men, because it would not have occurred to Melville that male sexual desire for men was something that needed to be affirmed (or denied). It was a fact of shipboard life, sometimes to be celebrated, sometimes to be regretted — much like sexual desire on land, which, however, tended to be heterosexual and which Melville found he could not write about as convincingly. Men who stayed at sea for any length of time began to think of each other romantically and sometimes erotically. "History, and here cited without comment," as Melville wrote of the *Somers* mutiny hangings (114). Melville was so far behind Watson's and Forster's concerns as to be ahead of them. He did not think of male-male sexual desire as good or bad; it was merely one of the engines available to drive a plot.

Since Stonewall, gay readers have become suspicious of Captain Vere. He is nowadays the villain, where before he was the hero. "If Vere loves Billy," Robert K. Martin has written, in his groundbreaking study of homoeroticism in Melville's novels, "it is a love that kills in the name of discipline." Where Watson found a "testament of acceptance," Martin finds a "testament of despair," but the disparity of these critics' responses reflects changes in gay political self-understanding rather than conflicting assessments of what Melville wrote. In fact, Watson and Martin pronounce their different judgments on similar readings of the text. Both identify an erotic charge investing the execution of Budd. It seems to have heartened Watson to find homosexual suggestions in a text fast becoming classic, but the same suggestions dismay Martin because, as Martin correctly observes, "the sexuality of *Billy Budd* is a sexuality divested of its subversive power." Martin sees *Billy Budd* as the cri de coeur of a homosexual Melville lamenting a world that systematically represses love between men in order to rechannel that libidinal energy into the maintenance of governmental authority. In Martin's narrative of Melville's career, *Moby-Dick* was the acme of Melville's erotic optimism, and *Billy Budd* was his act of mourning — the sharp finale to a long, cruel disillusionment. Martin writes that in Melville's last novel, "male friendship, once a potent force to counteract the arbitrary authority of the Captain, has now gone underground."[10]

Unlike Watson, Martin is appalled by the quality of eros in *Billy Budd*. Like Watson, however, Martin thinks Melville intended his novel to be a final verdict about the nature of love on earth. And like Watson, Martin comes close to saying that this verdict is not only more mature than Melville's younger statements but also somehow more true. Thus Martin, too, though with a profound regret, puts Wilde's moral to Melville's story. " 'Each man kills the thing he loves,' " Martin quotes, and then explains: "So in Melville's darkest mood he recognized the intricate relationship between love and hatred and what seemed like the inevitable destruction of love by a system that needed to make chiefs of police out of its greatest villains."[11]

As this passage suggests, Martin's Melville is somewhat Foucauldian. Foucauldian insights abound in Melville — for example, in his frequent sarcasm about the veneer that separates civilization from so-called barbarism. But like most novelists, Melville did not think systematically, and Martin confuses fiction with philosophy when he suggests that Melville intended for *Billy Budd* to pose the question "Can the good person serve the state?" It is not true, as Martin claims, that "every Captain in Melville is corrupt, a tyrant, or a madman." In *Israel Potter,* Melville's affection for Captain John Paul Jones is unforced. Paul Jones is not a madman: he is vain and half-civilized, childishly pleased with his Scotch cap and his half-hidden cannibal tattoos. He is not corrupt: at great expense he buys back the silver plate that his officers plundered from Lady Selkirk. And he is not a tyrant: "I'm a democratic sort of sea-king," Paul Jones tells Israel, and Melville's narrative supports his claim. There is nothing devious about Paul Jones. He is "intrepid, unprincipled, reckless, predatory, with boundless ambition, civilized in externals but a savage at heart" — like America, Melville boasts. His boldness comes from his hunger for fame.[12] In this he resembles Nelson, whom Melville wryly describes in *Billy Budd* as motivated by "an excessive love of glory, impassioning a less burning impulse, the honest sense of duty" (58).

Martin claims that Melville meant Nelson to be "a doubly ironic foil for Vere" — that is, that Melville believed "Vere can never be Nelson, but then Nelson is not worth being anyway." This is unlikely. Melville disliked the formalism of Vere's authority, but he could and did admire authority where it was passionately earned. In *White-Jacket,* Melville's narrator credits Mad Jack's dictatorial streak with having saved his life. "Mad Jack was a bit of a tyrant — they *say* all good officers are," White-Jacket admits, unresentfully. The charismatic Paul Jones leads men naturally. "Captain Paul is the devil for putting men up to be tigers," one of his sailors brags. As the characters Mad

Jack and Paul Jones demonstrate, Melville could imagine a man who could lead without cauterizing or distorting his emotions. In *Billy Budd,* Nelson is a sympathetic — not an ironic — emblem of this type. Vere lectures against yielding to the "feminine in man" (111), but Melville and many of his readers probably knew the anecdote that Emerson had retold, in *English Traits,* to illustrate what Emerson called the "hermaphrodism" of England's best heroes: "Nelson, dying at Trafalgar, sends his love to Lord Collingwood, and, like an innocent schoolboy that goes to bed, says, 'Kiss me, Hardy,' and turns to sleep."[13]

Two recent critics — Eve Kosofsky Sedgwick in *Epistemology of the Closet* and James Creech in *Closet Writing / Gay Reading* — have followed in the footsteps of Martin's gay-inflected reading of *Billy Budd,* though somewhat anxiously. Sedgwick offers a series of questions rather than a settled hypothesis about *Billy Budd,* but a repeated theme in her analysis is that the kind of understanding that Melville's text solicits is typical of the rhetoric that used to shroud homosexuality. According to Sedgwick, Melville sets readers up to doubt what they know, thus inducing a kind of paranoid recognition (feeling sure that they know what is going on, precisely because they have not been allowed to know for sure) that is typical of how homosexuality was understood, or carefully not understood, in Melville's day and later. Sedgwick foregrounds this paranoid way of knowing, which she calls the "epistemology of the closet," to defend against a danger that she identifies and that Creech explores in detail: the risk of being dismissed as kitsch.

Most gay readings depend in part on a sentimental identification with the text. Readers sense, more strongly than with other texts, that Melville is talking about someone like them. The readings are therefore vulnerable to disparagement as emotional impressions rather than critical facts. Modernists may accuse a reader like Martin of having artificially and unnecessarily limited what Melville, as an ironist, meant by what he did not say. And poststructuralists (such as, most famously, Barbara Johnson) may take this accusation to a more metaphysical level and fault gay readers for a vulgar sentimentalization of meaning itself. By repackaging it as an epistemology, Sedgwick moves gay reading to what seems to be higher, safer ground.

If you believe that Melville intentionally referred to homosexual desire in *Billy Budd,* and I do, you might at first welcome Sedgwick's and Creech's defense. It saves homosexual specificity from being generalized away into "irony" or "undecidability" — a maneuver usually accompanied by a heterosexual "whoosh of relief," as Sedgwick writes, in a neat description of the intellectual escape hatch that most gay critics have seen their colleagues take.[14] But there is a flaw in Sedgwick and Creech's logic: if you accept its terms, it is unanswerable. Worse, it is a balloon that can be blown up to any size.

By their own admission, the way Sedgwick and Creech perceive a reference to homosexuality is paranoid. Their logic runs in a circle. It might be (somewhat unfairly) caricatured thus: whenever Melville fails to say something, in a way that reminds a gay critic of the way that homosexuality used to be not spoken about, it would be homophobic to deny that what Melville fails to refer to on such an occasion is homosexuality. Unfortunately, under this hermeneutic dispensation, the only point of entry for new evidence is through the gay critic's judgment of what constitutes "the way that homosexuality used to be not spoken about." As a negative, this is a category that historical research cannot refine.

In practice, lesbian and gay studies has investigated this category as if it were a positive. Most researchers have taken it to mean "the way that homosexuality was hinted at" or "the contexts in which homosexuality was most often discussed." When they examine textual detail, Sedgwick and Creech are themselves among the most acute readers of this sort. These categories can be refined by research, which may contest or confirm them. They are also open to empirical challenge, unlike Sedgwick's "epistemology" or its recent, even more metaphysical spinoff, queer theory. For the lesbian and gay researcher in the archive, sentimental identification remains an indispensable tool, but proof must consist of a documented history of patterns and associations. Pruned of metaphysics, lesbian and gay studies may also reengage the middle ground. It is possible, for instance, that Melville intended to suggest that Claggart was homosexual without intending for homosexuality to occupy all of the ground covered by his ambiguous definition of "natural depravity." This nonhomophobic but moderate opinion seems to have been Auden's, when he observed that "the motive for Claggart's behaviour, half-stated only to be withdrawn because no motive will really do, is homosexual desire."[15]

With a fierceness that may have impeded critical dialogue, then, post-Stonewall gay critics have defended a new sentimental reading of *Billy Budd*. This reading mirrors the gay sentimental reading of the early twentieth century, reversing its value judgments. Claggart now wins sympathy, though not quite approval, for his impossible position as "the homosexual in this text." Like Martin, Sedgwick savages Captain Vere. She diagnoses his agony over Budd's death sentence as Nixonian — he "suffers in private in public." And she finds nothing redemptive in the sexual charge running between the captain and the doomed sailor: "Vere's condemnation of Billy is scarcely the antithesis but, rather, the ground of their embrace, and certainly of its assumed poignancy for any reader."[16]

Post-Stonewall gay critics have arrived at their dislike of Captain Vere with such unanimity perhaps because they have followed the arrow's flight of desire in the text: they have read with their hearts, and they have self-consciously rebellious hearts. Melville may have been gay, they assert, but he did not kiss the rod. Their indignation outpaces that of the Cold War readers, hoodwinked by Melvile's slippery tone, who decided that the message of the book was authority, and also the formalist readers, including the poststructuralists, who were so pleased with their knowing identification of Melville's slipperiness that they decided that the slipperiness was the message, under the name irony or *différance*. Like their precursors, the new gay sentimentalists have concerns that are congruent with but not identical to Melville's. But T. S. Eliot's description of Henry James's mind — "so fine that no idea could violate it" — could probably be applied to Melville's heart. Vere is a figure that the narrative teaches us to distrust, not because he is untrue to a particular idea of love, but because he is untrue to the love that happens to be offered to him. My dissent from the new gay consensus on *Billy Budd* is not a radical one. It could be phrased by stressing a caveat that Segwick herself offers: "This is a dangerous book to come to with questions about the *essential nature* of men's desire for men."[17]

"Each man kills the thing he loves," whether said with regret or with a naughty thrill, dissolves particular, conflicting emotions into a general idea. It is also quietist. Any reader willing to believe it true — or, as in Martin's carefully argued case, to believe it was true for the world Captain Vere lived in — ought to be willing to side with Vere. Perhaps the new gay sentimentalists have not been sentimental enough; they have not followed their hearts into full revolt. Although they have paid long-overdue attention to Melville's references to homosexual desire, they have not been as careful with his references to feeling, which, in a book with only male characters, must also be homosexual. "Each man kills the thing he loves" obscures an insight that Melville's novel hinges on: it is easy to take a sexual interest in someone you do not care for.

What light does the American literary tradition of sympathy and friendship throw on *Billy Budd?*

The likeliest place to start to answer this question is the book's dedication.

DEDICATED

TO

JACK CHASE

ENGLISHMAN

Wherever that great heart may now be
Here on Earth or harbored in Paradise

Captain of the Maintop
in the year 1843
in the U.S. Frigate
*United States*

In 1851, Melville inscribed *Moby-Dick* to Nathaniel Hawthorne, but after the collapse of their friendship, Melville's dedications turned ironic. He dedicated *Pierre* to Mount Greylock and *Israel Potter* to the Bunker Hill Monument. Melville's dedication of *Billy Budd,* however, appears to be sincere.

Jack Chase figured as a character in *White-Jacket,* Melville's 1850 novel based on his experiences as an ordinary seaman in the man-of-war *United States.* Chase was "a Briton, and a true-blue; tall and well-knit, with a clear open eye, a fine broad brow, and an abounding nut-brown beard," Melville recorded. Richard Henry Dana Jr. had rhapsodized over a similar "handsome sailor" from Britain in *Two Years Before the Mast,* and Chase appears so much larger than life—a rugged sailor who quotes Shakespeare and Camoëns extempore and who is beloved and obeyed by all the crew—that it is a surprise to find him not a piece of Melvillean embroidery.[18]

There was a John J. Chase, aged fifty-three, muster number 513, on board the *United States* while Melville served in 1843. At least one of Melville's boasts on his behalf is factual. On 18 November 1840, Chase deserted the American navy for the Peruvian. In *White-Jacket,* Melville credited Chase with the highest motives for his desertion. Because he was "a stickler for the Rights of Man, and the liberties of the world," Chase left his post as boatswain's mate on the USS *St. Louis* "to draw a partisan blade in the civil commotions of Peru." Thanks to the intervention of a Peruvian admiral, Chase was able to return to the American navy on 29 May 1842 without suffering any corporal punishment for his interlude of freedom-fighting. Just six weeks after his return, Chase was promoted to the captaincy of the maintop, the petty office with the grand name in which Melville would find him the following year. *White-Jacket* bore no dedication, but its narrator addressed Chase directly: "Wherever you may be now rolling over the blue billows, dear Jack! take my best love along with you; and God bless you, wherever you go!"[19]

But although Melville's dedication of *Billy Budd* looks straightforward, Melville probably did not expect Chase to read his book. If Chase had still been alive in 1891, he would have been one hundred one years old. The sentiment was almost certain not to reach its designated reader.

Furthermore, when the earnestness of the dedication is set beside the ironies of the novel dedicated, the juxtaposition may unsettle those readers whom the book has managed to reach. *Billy Budd* tells the story of three men who end unhappily: the naive sailor Billy Budd, the envious master-at-arms John Claggart, and the bookish Captain Edward Fairfax Vere. In outline, the plot has the violent symmetry of a fairy tale. Budd's youth and beauty inspire a mysterious hatred in Claggart, who spuriously charges Budd with mutiny. When Vere asks Budd to respond to the charge, Budd's righteous indignation worsens his stammer, and he can say nothing. In his mute anger, Budd strikes Claggart,

who dies instantly. "In the jugglery of circumstances," Melville writes, "innocence and guilt personified in Claggart and Budd in effect changed places"
(103). On the grounds that Budd's insubordination might inspire the crew to
mutiny, Vere improvises a trial for Budd, ensures a conviction, and has him
hanged. Vere later dies from a battle injury, repeating Budd's name as his
last words.

Why should this story be addressed to a man like Jack Chase? It is hardly a
fair return for the one piece of art that Chase offered to Melville. In *White-
Jacket,* Chase performed for the crew of the *Neversink* the role of Percy Royal-
Mast, in the play *The Old Wagon Paid Off.* The scene in which Percy "rescues
fifteen oppressed sailors from the watch-house, in the teeth of a posse of
constables," thrilled the audience, and the disruption of military discipline by
dramatic spectacle gave White-Jacket a brief hope that goodwill might prevail
between officers and crew.[20] By contrast, there is no give in the ties binding
performance to reality in *Billy Budd.* On the contrary, the more disorder is
feared, the more scrupulously naval ritual is adhered to. "If possible, not to let
the men so much as surmise that their officers anticipate aught amiss from
them is the tacit rule in a military ship" (117). There are no orders to skylark
aboard the HMS *Bellipotent.* Though a work of art, *Billy Budd* offers no
respite from reality.

While Melville was writing *Billy Budd,* he kept pasted to the side of his
makeshift desk a motto he had found in Schiller: "Keep true to the dreams of
thy youth!"[21] This motto and the dedication to Jack Chase raise similar questions: How did a story with such a dismal ending remain true to the dreams of
Melville's youth? How did a tale of hatred and murder send Jack Chase more
of the love sent in *White-Jacket?* Both questions must have answers if Melville
believed that his last book was faithful to the dreams and love of his youth.

Here a sentimental nihilism would suggest that Melville kept his faith by
giving voice to despair. His last novel was dark because he realized at the end
of his life that dreams and love are doomed. They can only be saved the way
James Dean saved his good looks — with a pretty corpse. It is hard to resist this
nihilism. Melville probably wrote *Billy Budd* ironically; the clues we have of
his intent fail to point to the novel he in fact wrote. But once the reader admits
even a seed of irony, it and the reader's suspicion of it metastasize. If *Billy Budd*
expresses faith through a vision of despair, perhaps Melville no longer believed in what he wished he could stay faithful to. After all, how can irony
express any kind of faith? It is hard to keep from slipping into an interpretive
abyss.

While discussing *Hamlet* with another swindler, the hero of *The Confidence-
Man* complains, "I don't exactly see how Shakespeare meant the words he puts

*Portrait of Captain John Chase (1790–1890?)*, by an unidentified painter. Circa 1830–40. Maryland Historical Society, Baltimore, Maryland.

in Polonius' mouth." To borrow the language of espionage professionals, the confidence-man was unable to figure out whether Shakespeare was "doubling" or "tripling": he could not tell whether Shakespeare was lying in order to mislead his readers or telling the truth in order to mislead readers who expected him to lie. Picking a way through the maze of ironies, readers of *Billy Budd* may also feel like confidence-men out of their depth. They might take a clue from the character who holds his ground most honorably in *The Confidence-Man,* the barber. The barber loses only the price of a shave, because he keeps "one foot on confidence and the other on suspicion." If readers accept Melville's dedication to Jack Chase confidently, as a kind of sentimental reference point, then they are less likely to lose their way in the doubling and tripling ironies of the story that follows.[22]

With one foot on confidence and the other on suspicion, then, consider Jack Chase and *Billy Budd.* Although the novel may be dedicated to Jack Chase, Jack Chase is not in it. Like Chase, Billy Budd is a handsome sailor, may have been the "by-blow" of a nobleman, and inspires love in nearly all who meet him. The scholar Charles Anderson has noted yet another resemblance between the two: "In both cases their masculine beauty [is] marred by a single defect, Chase by the loss of a finger, Budd by a tendency to stammer."[23] The comparison that these parallels invite, however, is not to Budd's advantage. As Melville explains, a genuine Handsome Sailor draws attention with not only beauty but also strength — physical, intellectual, and moral. Budd is "such a cynosure, at least in aspect, and something such too in nature, though with important variations made apparent as the story proceeds" (44). The narrator's qualifying phrases take away as much as the designation "Handsome Sailor" grants. Budd does not measure up. A page after he is introduced, he is unjustly taken from the merchant ship *Rights of Man,* and his "uncomplaining acquiescence" to authority on this occasion contrasts sharply with the rebellious spirit of Chase, who deserted the navy *for* the rights of man (45). Unlike Chase, Budd has "an incapacity of plumply saying *no*" (81).

Although Budd is not Chase, the two are linked. Melville wrote in *The Confidence-Man* that "it is with fiction as with religion: it should present another world, yet one to which we feel the tie."[24] In Budd, Melville invents a younger version of Chase, imagined without the intellectual defenses and moral wisdom of middle age. If Chase had read *Billy Budd,* he would have recognized that Budd was not him, but he would have felt the tie nonetheless. Reading sympathetically, Chase would have wished to protect this other, more vulnerable self.

This wish Melville frustrates. The author introduces Budd, the child-man who cannot say no, into a community whose threats he is unable even to recognize. To attentive readers, Melville signals the nature of these threats with metaphors that switch Budd's gender. Budd's face, for example, is "all but feminine in purity of natural complexion" (50). His new "position aboard the seventy-four was something analogous to that of a rustic beauty transplanted from the provinces and brought into competition with the highborn dames of the court" (50–51). His stutter is like the "blemish" of "the beautiful woman in one of Hawthorne's minor tales" (53). During his confrontation with Claggart, Budd becomes "a condemned vestal priestess" (99).

As *Billy Budd*'s narrator in his roundabout way explains, a British man-of-war during the Napoleonic wars had the social dynamic of a British prison, and much the same population (65–66). Budd, whose nicknames are Baby and Beauty, has become an object of desire. Although Budd may not understand this, the other sailors do. "Something about him provoked an ambiguous smile in one or two harder faces among the bluejackets," Melville writes (51). Before extending his limited sympathy to Budd, the Dansker indulges in "equivocal merriment" at Budd's expense (70). A word like *equivocal* may mean almost anything, but in *White-Jacket* it described a certain kind of stain on a midshipman's hammock. "What do you call that, sir?" the captain asked the midshipman. "Captain Claret, . . . you know what that is, sir, as well as I do."[25]

The narrator of *White-Jacket* instinctively dodged the kind of attention Budd attracts. By custom, the earlier novel explained, "the Commodore's Barge and the Captain's Gig are manned by gentlemanly youths, who may do credit to their country, and form agreeable objects for the eyes of the Commodore or Captain to repose upon as he tranquilly sits in the stern." Although these duties were light, White-Jacket had no desire to be on display. When appointed a gig-man by chance, he passed the assignment off to another sailor at the first opportunity.[26]

The *Bellipotent*'s atmosphere of sexual threat takes concrete form in the person of John Claggart. In his first description of the master-at-arms, Melville likens Claggart's chin to that of Titus Oates. As the *Dictionary of National Biography* recounts, Oates was one of the chief fabricators of the Popish Plots. By falsely accusing Roman Catholics of planning regicide, Oates caused the "judicial murder" of nearly thirty innocent men. What the *Dictionary* does not recount—except by the sort of periphrases, conventionally ominous and vague, that created the market for Sedgwick's epistemology of the closet—is that Oates was nearly as notorious for sodomy as for manufacturing charges of treason.[27] From E. L. Grant Watson to Robert K. Martin, critics have seen a reference to homosexual desire in Claggart's reaction to the soup Budd spills, the playful tap "from behind with his rattan" that Claggart gives to Budd, and

Melville's statement that "Claggart could even have loved Billy but for fate and ban" (72, 88). To explain what is the matter with Claggart, Melville alludes to Ann Radcliffe's Gothic novel *The Mysteries of Udolpho,* much as in *White-Jacket* he explained the "Gomorrahs of the deep" by alluding to Horace Walpole's Gothic play *The Mysterious Mother* (74).[28]

Claggart's lust for Budd is nearly explicit. But even Captain Vere, "a bachelor of forty or thereabouts," may have a sexual interest in Budd (60). The captain appreciates the *Bellipotent*'s newest recruit with the sort of metaphoric excess that Melville mocked in *Typee* when missionaries and naturalists bestowed it on Polynesian men: "Though in general not very demonstrative to his officers, [Vere] had congratulated Lieutenant Ratcliffe upon his good fortune in lighting on such a fine specimen of the *genus homo,* who in the nude might have posed for a statue of young Adam before the Fall" (94). As Sedgwick has noted, so attractive is Budd that Vere considers promoting him to captain of the mizzentop, a transfer that "would more frequently bring him under [Vere's] own observation" and would replace "a man not so young whom partly for that reason [Vere] deemed less fitted for the post" (95). Sedgwick has speculated, too, on the erotic potential in Vere's private interview with Budd after Budd is found guilty and in the dying Vere's repetition of Budd's name. As Sedgwick admits, these last two hints must remain no more than hints, because Melville's narrator, aficionado of conditionals and negatives, tells the reader only what might have happened in Vere's private interview with Budd and only what the accents of Vere's dying words were not.[29]

There is another hint, in part sexual, in Captain Vere's name. Charles Anderson has identified a historical Sir William George Fairfax whose career in the British navy may have served as the model for the fictional Captain the Honorable Edward Fairfax Vere. Like Captain Vere, Sir William had served under Lord Rodney in the West Indies during the American Revolution and for his success had been promoted to the rank of post captain.[30]

That accounts for Fairfax but not for Vere. The captain's surname has often been read in light of its etymon, the Latin word for "truth." However, Melville himself provides a rather different clue when he tells the story behind Vere's nickname.

> In the navy he was popularly known by the appellation "Starry Vere." How such a designation happened to fall upon one who whatever his sterling qualities was without any brilliant ones, was in this wise: A favorite kinsman, Lord Denton, a freehearted fellow, had been the first to meet and congratulate him upon his return to England from his West Indian cruise; and but the day previous turning over a copy of Andrew Marvell's poems had lighted, not for the first time, however, upon the lines entitled "Appleton House," the name of

one of the seats of their common ancestor, a hero in the German wars of the seventeenth century, in which poem occur the lines:

> This 'tis to have been from the first
> In a domestic heaven nursed,
> Under the discipline severe
> Of Fairfax and the starry Vere.

And so, upon embracing his cousin fresh from Rodney's great victory wherein he had played so gallant a part, brimming over with just family pride in the sailor of their house, he exuberantly exclaimed, "Give ye joy, Ed; give ye joy, my starry Vere!" This got currency. (61)

With his peculiar voice — sidewinding and orbicular — the narrator has led the reader down a garden path. Authors are allowed to give their characters arbitrary names, but nicknames given within a fiction ought to be motivated. If Vere is in no way starry — if he has no "brilliant" qualities — then the narrator's digression must link the word *starry* to some other aspect of Vere's character, if it intends to explain how the nickname "got currency." A chance phrase, stumbled upon by a kinsman, which happens to contain two elements of Vere's name is a coincidence unlikely to have caught the naval community's imagination, unless the text that contained the phrase was extremely familiar. It was not. Perhaps the reader is meant to infer that Vere is called Starry because of his occasional "dreaminess of mood," described one paragraph prior to this quotation. But if so, then the excursus about Lord Denton was not altogether necessary. The whole passage has the air of an explanation too ponderous for the thing explained, and the reader begins to suspect that Melville is commenting not within the story but upon it. Perhaps Melville's narrator has bungled his account of the motivation behind Vere's nickname because Melville the author wanted to give the motivation behind Vere's name.

Marvell's poem "Upon Appleton House: To My Lord Fairfax" praises Nun Appleton, one of the smaller estates owned by his patron, Thomas Lord Fairfax. (Another Fairfax estate mentioned in Marvell's poem, Denton, supplies the name of Captain Vere's kinsman.) The poem also praises Lord Fairfax's only child, his daughter Mary. Two things immediately strike the reader whom *Billy Budd* has led to "Appleton House." First, in Marvell's poem, "starry Vere" refers to a woman — Fairfax's wife. Thomas Paine once gibed that an aristocratic title, like a nickname, "renders man into the diminutive of man in things which are great, and the counterfeit of woman in things which are little."[31] In naming Captain Vere, Melville seems to have taken Paine's gibe literally.

Second, the four lines quoted by Melville do not speak to *Billy Budd* as tellingly as does the stanza containing them. The complete stanza reads as follows:

> This 'tis to have been from the first
> In a domestic heaven nursed,
> Under the discipline severe
> Of Fairfax, and the starry Vere;
> Where not one object can come nigh
> But pure, and spotless as the eye;
> And goodness doth itself entail
> On females, if there want a male.[32]

Perhaps Melville hoped that some would read his quotation metonymically. Marvell's lines could easily be applied to the remarkable innocence and the feminine beauty of Billy Budd.

In the context of "Appleton House," the lines describe young Mary Fairfax, whom Marvell tutored. The girl's education was so rigorous and strict, Marvell writes, that she was spared even the sight of evil. Marvell explains that Mary, though female, will inherit the Fairfax estate, for Lord Fairfax had no sons. And in this stanza, as throughout the poem, Marvell makes much of Mary's virginity. Appleton was built on the ruins of a nunnery, and Marvell imagines that a century and a half earlier, Mary's ancestor Isabel Thwaites took refuge in this nunnery from her betrothed, Sir William Fairfax. Marvell further imagines that, eager for Isabel's inheritance, the nuns at that time tried to seduce Isabel with man-hating blandishments. " 'Twere sacrilege a man t' admit / To holy things, for heaven fit," the nuns said, and then enticed her with a vision of happy sisters who sing, make jam, arrange flowers, scent themselves with ambergris, eat pâté, and sleep with a different virgin bedmate every night. This is a rather ambiguous picture of virginity — no surprise, since Marvell is the poet who famously conceived of virginity, in his address to his coy mistress, as something it would be nice to take. In the end, Isabel's is taken when Sir William storms the nunnery. Marvell views this rape as a fortunate fall, and hints that his young pupil's virginity will come to a similar happy conclusion. At the moment of the poem, however, in the stanza quoted above, Marvell lauds Mary for her somewhat unlikely achievement of virtue: although she has been educated in a kind of Eden, sheltered by her parents from worldly evil, she is nonetheless armed against sin. She is impervious to any attack a swain might launch, including

> Tears (wat'ry shot that pierce the mind);
> And sighs (Love's cannon charged with wind);
> True praise (that breaks through all defence);
> And feigned complying innocence.[33]

These are the attacks that Captain Vere resists, and urges the judges of his drumhead court to resist, in the trial of Budd. "Ashore in a criminal case, will an upright judge allow himself off the bench to be waylaid by some tender kinswoman of the accused seeking to touch him with her tearful plea?" Vere asks the court when they are reluctant to convict. "Well, the heart here, sometimes the feminine in man, is as that piteous woman, and hard though it be, she must here be ruled out" (111). In Marvell's poem, a woman resists a man's sentimental siege. In Melville's novel, the genders are reversed and then doubled: Vere is not merely a man resisting feminine sentiment; he is a man who conceives of his heart as a woman, resisting the sentimental appeal that a woman might make on behalf of a man.

Marvell only pretends that Mary Fairfax is invulnerable. His hymn to virginity is provisional: "Till Fate her worthily translates, / And find a Fairfax for our Thwaites."[34] To wall out sympathy forever is the siren song of the nuns — in Marvell's view, happily defeated. In fact, according to sentimental convention, for a man to rule out his feminine heart leads, in this world, to sin.

This was the moral dramatized in Salomon Gessner's *The Death of Abel*. Translated from the German, Gessner's novel was a sentimental best-seller in America in the late eighteenth century. Melville may have owned a copy as an adult, but he is also likely to have encountered the book as a child. In Gessner's retelling of the world's first murder, Cain's motives are much like Captain Vere's. "While I breathe," Cain warns his father, "my firm soul will never be dissolved to that effeminate weakness that so endears [Abel] to you, and makes your eyes run over with transport." In Cain's self-justification is lodged an icy reproach: he steels himself against effeminacy because Adam, at a critical moment, did not. "To a softness like this we all owe the curse denounced against us, when, in paradise, you weakly suffered yourself to be overcome by a woman's tears." When Gessner's Cain smites Abel — who personifies complying innocence — Cain's outburst reads to a modern eye as homophobic rage. Abel begs, "Receive my embraces." Cain cries out, "Ah, thou serpent! Wouldest thou twine thyself about me!" and swings his club. In its dramatic elements, the scene prefigures the death of Claggart; and in its insult to sentiment, it prefigures the courtroom peroration of Vere.[35]

These allusions and literary antecedents suggest that Vere's ideas of discipline, guilt, innocence, and sympathy are not those of a righteous and worldly man. Rather, Vere is like a virgin not ready to surrender to marriage, or like a sinner shutting up his heart in order to confirm himself in wickedness. He does not yet know and trust his heart. Vere's antecedents have taught themselves to resist their own feelings — Marvell's Mary comically and Gessner's Cain tragically. Faced with the feminine sentiment of a man's overtures, Mary Fairfax, Cain, and Captain Vere retreat behind the anxiously defended idea that virtue consists in the suppression of feeling.

Like Marvell's Mary Fairfax, Captain Vere reacts to Budd's sexual appeal

THE

# DEATH OF ABEL.

IN

FIVE BOOKS,

ATTEMPTED

FROM THE GERMAN

OF

*MR. GESSNER.*

First Baltimore Edition.

Baltimore:
PRINTED AND SOLD BY WARNER & HANNA, AT THE
BIBLE AND HEART PRINTING OFFICE.

1807.

Title page of Salomon Gessner's *Death of Abel*, translated by Mary Collyer, with a wood engraving by Alexander Anderson. 1807. Print Collection, Miriam and Ira D. Walllach Division of Art, Prints and Photographs, New York Public Library, Astor, Lenox and Tilden Foundations. Photo by Robert D. Rubic.

with a prudish hardness of heart. Like Gessner's Cain, Vere becomes violent when a man's offer of affection threatens the integrity of his manhood. To the extent that Vere is responding to Budd erotically, his response is violently ambivalent. When these hints about Vere's response are placed beside Melville's hints about Claggart's desire and Budd's appeal, the portrait of homosexual eros that emerges is not a pleasant one.

The sexual innuendos may interfere with a reader's feelings for Budd. Almost every reader's heart goes out to Budd at the start of the novel. But then Melville's narrator insinuates that not a few people have felt their hearts go out to Budd — or rather, what they might prefer to call their hearts. Readers unsure of the purity of their generous impulses — readers less confident of their love than Jack Chase was — will begin to suspect the nature of their feelings for Budd. These feelings may catch in a reader's throat (particularly so if the reader is a straight male). As Budd finds himself tripped up by desires he does not understand, the reader may be tempted to limit his own interest in the sailor, because Melville has made almost any kind of interest in Budd look compromised. It is difficult to feel compassion for a man (or a woman) in trouble because he attracted sexual attention he could not handle. The contemporary reader, self-consciously enlightened about sex, might underestimate Melville's appreciation of this difficulty. But Melville understood acutely the discomfort that Budd's plight would provoke. "More than once," Melville wrote in *White-Jacket,* "complaints were made at the mast in the *Neversink,* from which the deck officer would turn away with loathing, refuse to hear them, and command the complainant out of his sight."[36] As Melville knew, people are tempted, in a case like Budd's, to protect their virtue by committing the injustice of not extending Budd sympathy. They are tempted, that is, to identify with Vere.

Melville could imagine a sexual interest coinciding happily with a sympathetic one. This was the case with the "fellow-feeling" that White-Jacket felt while "killing time" aboard the *Neversink* and likewise with Ishmael's marriage to Queequeg in *Moby-Dick.* Something like this may also have been the case in Melville's real-life relationship with Jack Chase. But in *Billy Budd,* Melville intended for the sexualization of sympathy to appall. At the climax, Melville interrupts the sublime pageant of Budd's death with grotesque speculation about the lack of an orgasm in Budd's corpse. Like the purser and the surgeon who discuss it, critics have often been distracted by their interest in orgasms. But this distraction, rather than the meaning of orgasm, is the point of the passage. Melville wanted to turn the reader's stomach by showing how willing the reader was to drop from an exalted tone to one that was, as he put it in *White-Jacket,* "slightly physiological in . . . nature." Behind the apparently transcendent beauty of Budd's sacrifice — Melville breaks in to say, as rudely as he can — there is a sexual fascination, the same kind of base sexual fascination you thought you had disowned, or at least sacrificed to principles that were morally and aesthetically higher, when you agreed that Budd must hang.[37]

Melville uses sex to make a sentimental point. However, sex is not the only force distorting sympathy in *Billy Budd,* nor is it necessarily the most important. To discern another, it may help to consider what a reader like Jack Chase would have thought of Captain Vere. But unlike Captain Vere (whose "honesty prescribes to [him] directness") and like Melville's narrator (who found that "bypaths have an enticement not readily to be withstood"), I am going to consider this via a digression (63, 56).

In choosing to name the captain of the *Bellipotent* after a matron in charge of a sanctuary from sin, Melville may have had in mind a famous experiment in nautical education designed to produce sailors free of vice. Religious-minded Americans had long worried about the virtue of boys sent to sea. As the Quaker John Woolman observed in 1772, "A pious father whose mind is exercised for the everlasting welfare of his child may not with a peaceable mind place him out to an employment among a people whose common course of life is manifestly corrupt and profane." To address this problem, a captain in the U.S. navy named Alexander Slidell Mackenzie decided as an experiment to train boys in isolation from the depraving influence of men. As Mackenzie's wife recalled, "His wish was that some of the smaller vessels might be used as school ships and worked only by boys." Mackenzie's first experiment took place on the USS *Somers.* He chose boys from the country rather than the city, because he believed rural boys had "a higher moral tone." In a crew of 120 sailors, 96 aboard the *Somers* were minors, and only two officers — the captain and the first lieutenant — were over twenty-one.[38]

"Boyhood is a natural state of rascality," the irascible Pitch had claimed in *The Confidence-Man,* and "as all boys are rascals, so are all men."[39] The *Somers* experiment proved Pitch right.

On 26 November 1842, as the brig was sailing home from Africa, the first lieutenant brought Captain Mackenzie bad news. According to the purser's steward, nineteen-year-old acting midshipman Philip Spencer was plotting to "get possession of the vessel; murder the commander and officers; choose, from among those of the crew who were willing to join him, such as would be useful, and murder the rest; and commence pirating." Captain Mackenzie responded by taking justice into his own hands. Less than a week later, on 1 December 1842, midshipman Spencer and two petty officers — boatswain's mate Samuel Cromwell and captain of the maintop Elisha Small — were hanged as mutineers.[40]

Cromwell died protesting his innocence. Small felt that he was guilty, although he admitted only to talking about mutiny. "See what a word will do," Small told his fellow sailors, just before he was hanged. Small also told Captain Mackenzie, "You are doing your duty, and I honor you for it; God bless that flag and prosper it!" — probably the inspiration for Billy Budd's final salute, "God bless Captain Vere!" By all accounts, Spencer's head had been turned by the fantasy of commanding a pirate ship, but it was not clear that the boy ever acted on his fantasy. He seems to have gone no further than idle talk and a list of potential fellow pirates, scribbled in Greek letters (like Roderick Random's diary, which was mistaken for evidence of conspiracy in Tobias Smollett's novel). Only four names on Spencer's list were marked "Certain"; of these four, one was Spencer's own, and another was the name of the purser's steward who turned him in. Cromwell's name appeared nowhere on the list. Small was marked as "Doubtful." As such critics as James Fenimore Cooper later pointed out, the only evidence of a mutiny, apart from Spencer's list and wild talk, was a sullen mood that Mackenzie perceived among the crew and a series of mishaps and coincidences that Mackenzie construed as a pattern of resistance.[41]

When the *Somers* arrived in New York Harbor on 14 December, scandal erupted — not least because Spencer's father was President Tyler's secretary of war. Mackenzie had had no legal authority to try a capital case aboard the *Somers*. As Mackenzie's attorney conceded when Mackenzie himself was tried later on, "It is admitted, that under ordinary circumstances it would have been his duty to . . . bring them home to be tried." "In the necessities of my position I found my law," Mackenzie wrote in his report, "and in them I must trust to find my justification." To defend himself at his court-martial, Mackenzie had to convince the navy that he was correct in his belief that he would have lost his ship if he had waited to hang Spencer, Cromwell, and Small. It weakened his argument that the *Somers* reached a safe haven, the island of Saint Thomas, only three days after the hangings. Mackenzie was acquitted. But as Melville remarked in *White-Jacket*, "To this day the question . . . is socially discussed."[42]

The first lieutenant on board the *Somers* was Melville's cousin Guert Gansevoort. When the scandal broke, Melville was in the Pacific, where he had joined a nonviolent mutiny aboard the whaler *Lucy Ann* only three months earlier, an episode he fictionalized in *Omoo*. The following year, Melville enlisted as a common seaman aboard a man-of-war and experienced American military discipline firsthand. The *Somers* mutiny must have commanded Melville's attention, for it involved his family, his personal experience, and the subject matter of his future art.[43]

In an autobiography, published in 1883, the politician Thurlow Weed revealed a confidence that Lieutenant Guert Gansevoort had made to his cousin

Hunn Gansevoort, who in turn had confided it to Weed. According to this thirdhand story, the council of *Somers* officers that Captain Mackenzie had assembled were extremely reluctant to hang Spencer, Cromwell, and Small. They "did not attach much importance" to the evidence that Mackenzie found so decisive, and even after Mackenzie ordered the officers to reexamine the witnesses, "the court was not prepared to convict the accused." Only when Captain Mackenzie demanded that the officers' council consider the question a third time, did they deliver a "reluctant conviction." Recall that none of these officers was yet twenty-one. The day after relaying this story to Weed, Hunn Gansevoort embarked, in the *Grampus,* on a voyage that ended at the bottom of the sea. Several years later, Weed took Lieutenant Guert Gansevoort to dinner and told him what he knew from Hunn. "Whereupon [Gansevoort] looked thoughtfully a moment, then drank off his champagne, seized or raised the bottle, again filled his glass and emptied it, and, without further remark, left the table."[44]

Melville knew this story, either directly from Guert or from Weed's memoir. In his poem "Bridegroom Dick," Melville portrayed Guert as the "boozing" Tom Tight, who had been "lieutenant in the brig-o'-war famed / When an officer was hung for an arch-mutineer" but who refused to talk about the affair, even in his cups.[45]

"The circumstances on board the *Somers* were different from those on board the *Bellipotent,*" as Melville himself observed (114). The *Somers* case had occurred while the United States was at peace, and the alleged mutiny had been suppressed before any violence had been attempted. By shifting the action to wartime and by having Budd strike and kill an officer, Melville made it more likely that a duly convened court-martial would have convicted Budd. As Hayford and Sealts note in their preface to *Billy Budd,* during an 1846 blockade of the Mexican coast, the navy abridged none of its legal procedures and nonetheless hanged a seaman for hitting a lieutenant (30–31).

What Melville rendered more ambiguous was not the final verdict on Budd but Captain Vere's rough handling of the law, whose "measured forms" one would expect Vere to reverence (128). Melville is careful to place the *Bellipotent* "almost at her furthest remove from the fleet" — the only condition that might extenuate — although the law still would not approve — a captain who convened a court-martial (90). Like Mackenzie, however, Vere could defend his arrogation of judicial power only by arguing necessity. And here, Vere's case is worse than Mackenzie's. Inaccurately but nonetheless honestly, Mackenzie believed that a mutiny was afoot and had already spread to twenty men. Vere, on the other hand, is certain that Claggart invented the charge of mutiny against Budd and does not believe there are any current plans for mutiny among the crew (106). The *Somers* was only a ten-gun brig, and in his defense, Mackenzie argued that its small size made it impossible to hold twenty men prisoner. The *Bellipotent* is a seventy-four-gun brig, and Vere needs to keep only one man in irons. Although Mackenzie was accused of acting in haste, he did not hang the alleged mutineers until day five. Vere hangs Budd in less than twenty-four hours. Vere may be accurate when he exclaims that "the angel must hang!" (101). But he is strangely eager to be the one to hang him. He breaks the law to do so.[46]

Why? There may be a sexual component to Captain Vere's arousal. But Vere may also be seduced by the pathos of the role he has an opportunity to play.

To understand the nature of this temptation, consider one more aspect of the *Somers* case. Alexander Slidell Mackenzie was an author as well as a captain. He had written two travelogues, two biographies, and a book of essays. As he composed his official report of the *Somers* affair, Mackenzie must have suspected that it would have a wider readership than any of his books. In the event, newspapers reprinted the report as soon as it was made public at the court of inquiry on 29–30 December 1842. As the merchant Philip Hone observed in his diary, when Mackenzie's report came out, it reeked of the "pride of authorship."[47]

Captain Mackenzie was eager to appear as the hero of the story he told—a man of action, virtue, and feeling. He was also eager to appear as an author who knew the sentimental value of novelistic details. He indulged in self-consciously literary touches that did not serve him well. For example, when he reported the condemned Spencer's lament, "This will kill my poor mother," he paused for what moviemakers today call a reaction shot: "I was not before aware that he had a mother; when recovered from the pain of this announcement, I asked him if it would not have been still more dreadful had he succeeded in his attempt."[48]

"Instead of a concise, manly statement," Hone complained,

> we have a long rigmarole story about private letters discovered on the person of young Spencer, orders to blow out the brains of "refractory men," religious ceremonies, cheers for the American flag, and conversations with the accused, in one of which he said to Spencer that "he hung him, because if he took him to the United States he would escape punishment, for everybody got clear who had money and friends," . . . . In the name of all that is wonderful, why should he stigmatize himself by relating such a conversation in a document which will be carried on the wings of the wind to the most distant part of the earth?[49]

In the court of public opinion, Captain Mackenzie's report backfired because it was apparent to readers that he was grandstanding. Like Amasa Delano's *Narrative,* Mackenzie's report offered Melville a story of nautical pride that contained its own ironic comeuppance. Mackenzie's eagerness was the eagerness of a writer who knows he has a great story on his hands, although he himself is in it. As any journalist with the mildest self-awareness knows, few things can be more corrupting.

Captain Vere is not a writer. But Melville put into Vere not a little of his writerly self. Like Melville, Vere refuses to compromise his lofty language, even when addressing an audience who cannot appreciate it (63). Vere's dreaminess and his authoritarian irritation when his daydreams are interrupted correspond to what some critics have speculated were Melville's writing habits. Vere "loved books," including one of Melville's favorites, Montaigne's *Essays* (62). This single detail, more than any other, seems to make it difficult for professional students of Melville to believe that Vere is not a sympathetic character. But consider Thoreau's attack on the burghers who thought John Brown had overreacted to slavery: "So they proceed to live their sane, and wise, and altogether admirable lives, reading their Plutarch a little." Yet Thoreau loved Plutarch.[50]

After Budd is hanged, Vere makes a strange, pleased outburst in praise of "measured forms." He claims that the power of forms is the "import couched in the story of Orpheus" (128). Vere seems to think that his ambition — to order the sympathies of his audience by executing a pathetic scene with formal perfection — is consonant with the ambition of an artist. Vere is wrong. But he could hardly be expected to know this, for he does not read novels or poems. As Melville explains, Vere has "nothing of that literary taste which less heeds the thing conveyed than the vehicle" (62). It may take the reader some time to appreciate Vere's mistake, because in the climactic scenes, Melville loans to Vere's performance his own style — one of the most beautiful and powerful vehicles in English prose.

In contrast to Captain Vere, Jack Chase was not shy of imaginative writing. He "had read all the verses of Byron, and all the romances of Scott. He talked of Rob Roy, Don Juan, and Pelham; Macbeth and Ulysses," Melville reported in *White-Jacket.* "Noble Jack, with his native-born good sense, taste, and humanity, was not ill qualified to play the true part of a *Quarterly Review.*" Anyone who could quote *Macbeth* to thank his superior officers for their condescension must have had a fine sense of literary irony. In Jack Chase, Melville knew a reader with his heart in the right place, who understood that a text may mean something other than what it appears to say.[51]

But there is another, still more vital way that Chase's understanding of literature differs from Captain Vere's. Vere's literary interests detach him from sympathetic interaction with his officers and men. With Vere, literature is a mark of class status, the sign of an education and leisure activity that few could afford. His allusions distance him from those he speaks with, who respect Vere but find him "pedantic," "dry and bookish." Literature is Vere's impressive personal possession; he never goes to sea "without a newly replenished library" (62–63).

A common sailor like Chase, however, could not travel with books, and so he memorized them. "We Homers who happen to be captains of tops must write our odes in our hearts," Chase told White-Jacket. Chase loved literature in a way that brought him closer to his fellow men. He shared his favorite passages by quoting them aloud, used his literary knowledge to charm favors from the captain for the crew, and praised and critiqued the apprentice writing of the aspiring sailor-poet Lemsford. By treating it as a thing of common interest, Chase forged from literature a sympathetic community.[52]

Melville set *Billy Budd* in the last decade of the eighteenth century. That era seemed momentous to Melville for much the same reasons that it had felt momentous to Charles Brockden Brown and Elihu Hubbard Smith: a new idea, promising either freedom or anarchy, had then been unleashed in the world. The New York Friendly Club had heralded William Godwin as the apostle of this novelty, but Melville's more dialectic mind preferred to cast it as a debate: Edmund Burke versus Thomas Paine.

On the side of Paine was Jack Chase — "a stickler for the Rights of Man."[53] As Melville explains in *Billy Budd, The Rights of Man* was the title of Paine's "book in rejoinder to Burke's arraignment of the French Revolution [that] had . . . gone everywhere." It was also, of course, the name of the merchant ship from which Budd was impressed (48). On the other hand, Captain Vere's high-minded disapproval of the new social ideas coming from France is a patent echo of Paine's foe, Burke: "Vere disinterestedly opposed [the new ideas] not alone because they seemed to him insusceptible of embodiment in lasting institutions, but at war with the peace of the world and the true welfare of mankind" (63).

In 1797, the bloody excesses of the French Revolution seemed to have given the lie to Paine's optimistic rebuke to Burke. Burke seemed to have won the argument; the doctrine of human rights had brought France anarchy, not liberation. This was not, however, the end of the story. As Melville explained almost a century later, in a chapter of *Billy Budd* that he later discarded, "During those years . . . the wisest [could not] have foreseen that the outcome of all would be what apparently it has turned out to be, a political advance along nearly the whole line for Europeans."[54] Perhaps Melville discarded this passage because it showed his hand too clearly. In his final manuscript, Melville left no statement with such a clear political affiliation. He gave the novel to Burke's Vere and the dedication to Paine's Chase. But if Chase had read the novel, he might well have applied to Vere a reproach that Paine made of Burke: "He pities the plumage, but forgets the dying bird."[55]

Nothing of Burke's had galled Paine quite so sharply as Burke's lament for the vanishing beauties of the aristocracy. "The age of chivalry is gone," Burke had mourned.[56] It angered Paine that Burke rated his own aesthetic impression of aristocratic society more highly than the longings and sufferings of the people that society had oppressed. And it incensed Paine that Burke's rhetoric, with Quixotic appeal, tugged at the heartstrings even of those who ought to have rejoiced in the extinction of chivalry. To puncture this appeal, Paine reminded his readers, over and over, that the pathos of Burke's lament ran counter to their interests as individuals and as a class. Paine felt he had to prevent the people from being seduced into a sublime sacrifice when they ought to be attending to their exploited, oppressed, hungry selves, which were not sublime and were not as pleasant to contemplate.

In Mackenzie, Melville found a model for bringing Burke to sea. By separating captain from author, Melville improved on Mackenzie's narrative, rendering its moral challenge more subtle. Vere may stage-manage Budd's hanging, but Melville produces the pathetic, Burkean effects of the narrative. But even though Vere is not a writer, he nonetheless, like Mackenzie, commits Burke's literary sin. He thinks the aesthetic forms discernible in society have a value in and of themselves. He believes them to be beneficent and potent. He believes in forms so blindly that for him the aesthetic pleasure of sympathy may be distinguished from the fate of the human beings who trigger it.

"Of all insults, the temporary condescension of a master to a slave is the most outrageous and galling," Melville wrote in *White-Jacket*. He was indicting "the facility with which a sea-officer falls back upon all the severity of his dignity, after a temporary suspension of it" — a practice known among old man-of-war men as the "shipping of the quarter-deck face."[57]

The practice distressed Melville because it allowed an officer to indulge in the pleasure of sympathizing with the men he commanded but to revoke that sympathy before it could moderate the cruelty of the actual relationship that obtained between them. A brief fantasy of concord cost an officer nothing; but each time it was indulged, the men suffered another disillusionment. "How can they have the heart?" Melville asked.[58]

The most repugnant moments in Captain Mackenzie's report to the navy were his interviews with the men he had sentenced to death. He sought for a sentimental release with each. Cromwell thwarted him, by doggedly insisting on his innocence. Spencer and Small complied. In Gessner's *Death of Abel,* Abel had plaintively asked Cain, just before Cain struck, "Have I offended thee my brother? — Unknowingly have I offended thee?" As if in parody of Abel's words, Mackenzie asked Spencer "if I had ever done anything to him to make him seek my life." "It was only a fancy," Spencer reassured his captain, and he granted Mackenzie his forgiveness. Mackenzie also asked Small if he had ever done him any harm. "What have you done to me, Captain Mackenzie?" Small replied, echoing the captain's question; "what have you done to me, sir? — nothing, but treat me like a man." At the court of inquiry, Lieutenant Gansevoort also reported this exchange with Small, though with a slight difference. According to Gansevoort, "The Commander said to him 'Small, what have *I* done to you that you won't bid me good-bye?' Small replied 'I did not know that you would bid a poor *bugger* like me good-bye sir.' "[59]

If Melville ever read his cousin's testimony, it may have occurred to him that no shipping of the quarterdeck face could be managed with as much impunity as one coinciding with a sentence of death. With a sailor about to be hanged, an officer may be as familiar as he likes. Since the sailor will not live, he need never be disillusioned. He may go to the next world thinking his captain's condescension is genuine. Melville's fury that men could allow themselves to be thus duped — that sympathy could undergo this perversion — is the one chord he strikes in *The Confidence-Man* over and over again. "Who betrays a fool with a kiss," Melville wrote in that book, "the charitable fool has the charity to believe is in love with him, and the charitable knave on the stand gives charitable testimony for his comrade in the box."[60]

The charitable reader who is not a fool — that is, a reader like Jack Chase — would understand at once the meaning of the gesture Captain Vere makes as he recovers his equilibrium after Budd kills Claggart. "Slowly he uncovered his face," Melville writes, "and the effect was as if the moon emerging from eclipse should reappear with quite another aspect than that which had gone into hiding. The father in him, manifested towards Billy thus far in the scene, was replaced by the military disciplinarian" (99–100). Beneath the tone of what Paine would have called "astrological mysterious importance," Captain Vere is shipping his quarter-deck face.[61]

Nor would Chase have been fooled by the narrator's assertion that Captain Vere was "very far . . . from embracing opportunities for monopolizing to himself the perils of moral responsibility." To a reader familiar with and attentive to details of protocol and usage, it would be clear that Vere plays his drumhead court like a puppet show. As I suggested above, and as Melville suggests in the text, Vere ought to have held Budd until reaching either England or a commodore, and he almost certainly could have held him safely. Vere further defies usage, the narrator tells us, by inviting a marine to judge "a case having to do with a sailor." As Melville had explained in *White-Jacket,* captains knew that marines could be relied on for their prejudice against sailors.[62] This particular marine, however, Vere is not quite sure of, because he is "extremely good-natured" and therefore "might not prove altogether reliable in a moral dilemma involving aught of the tragic"—that is, he might be of too equable a temper to accept Vere's invitation to moral panic. The trial itself is a sham. (Unlike Vere, Mackenzie knew better than to call his proceedings a "court"; he was careful to refer to the men he summoned as a "council.") As a witness, Vere is said to "sink . . . his rank," but he does so while standing on the ship's weather side, which is higher ground. When the marine suggests that the court ought to call witnesses, Vere puts him off. He invokes the "mystery of iniquity." This is more "astrological mysterious importance." Like Budd's lack of an orgasm, it is another of Melville's diversions, and it has succeeded in seducing critics into speculation about its meaning, when they ought to focus on its effect within the plot: it prevents the court from investigating the case. If the afterguardsman had testified, would Budd have hanged? Vere's "thoughtful" reference to the debates of "psychologic theologians" forecloses this possibility.

The members of Vere's court soon realize that any exercise of independent judgment is discouraged. It disturbs the marine when Vere's words signal "prejudgment," but the marine does not call Vere's bluff. Nor does the first lieutenant, who allows himself to be "overrulingly instructed by [Vere's] glance." In his closing arguments, Vere explicitly asks the members of his court to deny their hearts and their consciences. As Melville's wily narrator allows the reader to know, Vere fails to persuade the officers, although he frames his speech for the prosecution in a high Burkean style. "At bottom, they dissented," Melville writes. The dissent remains submerged. The officers do not resist Vere; none of them are Jack Chase. But the narrator is careful to specify that Vere gets his drumhead court to convict *not* by the force of his starry reason but with a low appeal to fear. He panics them by suggesting the crew will mutiny unless Budd is punished harshly (104–14).

Since Vere intends early on to hang Budd, it would be no surprise to a Jack Chase that Captain Vere ships his quarter-deck face. But it would be an outrage that he unships and reships it at will. Vere switches between paternal kindness and implacable authority with heartbreaking ease. One moment his voice cracks with pity, and the next, he directs the judges not to bother considering Budd's motives. Vere allows himself all of sentiment's pleasures and all of authority's power, sometimes without waiting for a change of scene. His private conference with Budd, where "the austere devotee of military duty . . .

may in end have caught Billy to his heart" (115), could not have been meant without irony by the author who wrote, in *The Confidence-Man,* that "geniality has invaded each department and profession. We have genial senators, genial authors, genial lecturers, genial doctors, genial clergymen, genial surgeons, and the next thing we shall have genial hangmen."[63]

Melville intended for *Billy Budd* to boomerang on the reader, as Captain Mackenzie's report had. Melville overwhelms the reader with interested sentimental prompting while providing details that can be assembled into a counter case. He provokes and arms the reader to revolt against the narrator. (A live vaccine, Melville's inoculation unintentionally finished off many of its readers.) *Billy Budd* raises its voice against no one, but it implies a critique of anyone who, like Captain Vere, detaches feelings from the object of those feelings.

Vere's Burkean style of sympathy—his pity for the plumage but not the dying bird—bears a striking resemblance to the literary treatment of sympathy between men that I called hierotomy in my chapters on Emerson. From the *Phaedrus,* Emerson had learned that he could preserve the sense of energy and purpose that love for a man gave him if, rather than simply kill this love as forbidden and sinful, he cut the love from the man, like a flower from its roots. If he kept Martin Gay or Samuel Gray Ward at a fond distance, Emerson could enjoy the feelings they inspired and transform the feelings into a literary ecstasy, which he presented in his prose as if it were abstract. In his satire of Emerson in *The Confidence-Man,* Melville hit the weak spot in this neurotic defense. Hierotomy protected Emerson too well: it protected him from the men he thought he loved. It was, as Melville put it when he caricatured Emerson's physical appearance, "the color of warmth preserved by the virtue of chill."[64]

Melville had studied Emerson carefully. He may even have caught the drift of Emerson's interest in Persian poetry. In *The Confidence-Man,* Mark Winsome (Melville's version of Emerson) boasts, "I quaff immense draughts of wine from the page of Hafiz, but wine from a cup I seldom as much as sip." In *The Confidence-Man,* an allegoric satire, money stood for all the dangerous needs and desires that men try to extract from or deny one another—all the desires that hierotomy sets apart when it sets apart the man. These may in some cases be sexual, Melville hinted. When Winsome's disciple Egbert (Thoreau) disavows any friend base enough to ask for a loan, Egbert in his indignation changes the metaphoric currency from cash to sex: "He is no true friend that, in platonic love to demand love-rites." (When the confidence-man affects to be hurt by Egbert's severity, Egbert exclaims, "Fie! you're a girl.") In Emerson's philosophy, as Melville joked, there are only "hypothetical friends."[65]

It was one thing for Emerson to etherealize a love, like Ward's, that he knew he would never have, although he wished Ward well. It was quite another thing for Captain Mackenzie to appear to be writing down at dictation Philip Spencer's last letter to his parents when in fact he was scribbling a rough draft of the report he hoped would make him a hero. But this is the corruption that hierotomy is liable to. Once the artist has discovered that art becomes more touching if the artist's sentiments fail to reach their object, then it is highly dangerous to be the object of an artist's love. Humanity may be sacrificed to aesthetic form; a noble, wistful tone may conceal self-interested cruelty. This is what Paine condemned in Burke. "He is not affected by the reality of distress touching upon his heart," Paine wrote, "but by the showy resemblance of it striking his imagination. . . . He degenerates into a composition of art."[66]

Melville is not here damning the art of writing. As I noted above, Vere "had nothing of that literary taste which less heeds the thing conveyed than the vehicle" (61). Vere dislikes language that is aware of itself as a vehicle. This is a sign of Vere's tyranny, just as it was the sign of the confidence-man's deceit that he found irony "so unjust."[67] Like the writer who dislikes irony, the writer who affects not to care about literary style wants to believe that words are adequate representations of things. That writer wants the link between life and art to be unbreakable, hoping that an adequate control of words will lead to control over life. A pretended art is the mask of this writer's sadism. Language meant for communication, however, invites doubleness. Real sympathy cannot occur without a fiction. A work of art that makes no distinction between itself and what it describes is not a work of art but an exercise in control.

In Chapter 3, in my discussion of Charles Brockden Brown's *Wieland*, I suggested that Theodore Wieland represents a negative model of the sympathetic author, whom I called the copyist. The copyist identifies with his father's authority as if his father were only an embodiment of law — as if his father had not also lived out a struggle between his own humanity and law. At first glance, Captain Vere may appear to be a copyist. The agony of his condemnation of Budd may appear to be like Wieland's strangulation of his wife as he pities her. The reader can almost sympathize with Wieland. After all, Wieland truly believes that God wants each man to kill the thing he loves.

But this belief is how we know Wieland is insane. Captain Vere is not insane. And he is not a copyist: repeatedly he bends the law that he affects to submit himself to. Vere is something more diabolical: he is a ventriloquist, playing that he is a copyist. At the drumhead court, Vere throws his voice into others, as artfully as Carwin ever did. He contrives it that the officers serving on the drumhead court consent in voice to what they dissent from in their hearts.

The proper reaction to Captain Vere is anger, which Melville does not express. No one rises to anger in *Billy Budd*. Melville gives only Budd's stammer and punished blow and the three stifled murmurs of the crew. "Madness, to be mad with anything," was the confidence-man's consistent advice, because anger would break the sympathetic bond that holds his victim. As Melville might have read in Adam Smith's *Theory of Moral Sentiments,* the expression of anger arouses no sympathy in the beholder. "The furious behaviour of an angry man is more likely to exasperate us against himself than against his enemies," Smith explained. The artistic problem that Melville solves in *Billy Budd* is how to anger readers without repelling them. Melville does not let so much as a whisper of his fury escape. Instead he provokes, by trying to dupe readers with the pacifying ruse that has infuriated him. *Billy Budd* remains true to the dreams of Melville's youth because he wrote it in the faith that it would find readers like Jack Chase. To borrow yet another phrase from Paine, the book's imagined reader is one with "virtue enough to be angry."[68]

The story told in *Billy Budd* is thus a strong negative example of the configuration of literature and sentiment described in these pages. But *Billy Budd* itself is a strong positive example of the same configuration. To write such a pessimistic story, Melville must have been an optimist about the genre. He could have written *Billy Budd* only if he believed in readers who could see through him.

*Billy Budd* concludes with the ballad "Billy in the Darbies." Critics have often called the poem a false ending because its Billy is not the novel's Budd. In the ballad, Billy is able to deal in double meanings. "O, 'tis me, not the sentence they'll suspend," he puns, and "Ay, ay, all is up; and I must up too" (132). But in irony Melville finds the only honest representation: any author who refuses to allow for the possibility that his sentimental message might miscarry has already sacrificed the mess of reality to some trim idea.

By not writing about Jack Chase, Melville has written a work that is true to Jack Chase. Like Leander's diary, Brown's novels, or Emerson's essay on friendship, *Billy Budd* is a work written by one man for another man, loved and absent, and is meant to convey feelings that would otherwise be lost. But it does not answer for Chase. That would be to substitute a literary proxy for a human response — more ventriloquism. Instead, it awaits his anger. This reticence can be hard to distinguish from despair, but Melville may have hinted at his hope in the name he gave his nonhero. On the last page of *The Rights of Man,* Paine wrote about plucking a twig from an English tree in February. "By chance [I] might observe, that a *single bud* on that twig had begun to swell. I should reason very unnaturally, or rather not reason at all, to suppose *this* was the *only* bud in England which had this appearance. . . . What pace the political summer may keep with the natural, no human foresight can determine."[69] What this Budd stammers, the flower of man might say.

In the meantime, *Billy Budd* says nothing. It unsays. It tells the truth by palinode — setting out all the lies that love must take back. "There's no truth to that story," Melville might as well have written to Jack Chase, as Stesichorus wrote to Helen. "You never sailed that lovely ship, / You never reached the tower of Troy."[70]

# Notes

| | |
|---|---|
| *Leander* 1 | Journal of Leander [John Fishbourne Mifflin]. 12 May 1786–11 November 1786. Private collection. |
| *Leander* 2 | Journal of Leander [John Fishbourne Mifflin]. 12 November 1786–11 May 1787. Historical Society of Pennsylvania. (Bound with *Lorenzo* and catalogued as James Gibson, "Journal of Lorenzo and Leander," Am. 069.) |
| *Lorenzo* | Journal of Lorenzo [James Gibson]. 6 February 1786–1 October 1786. Historical Society of Pennsylvania. (Bound with *Leander* 2 and catalogued as James Gibson, "Journal of Lorenzo and Leander," Am .069.) |
| MME | Mary Moody Emerson |
| RWE | Ralph Waldo Emerson |
| RWEL | *The Letters of Ralph Waldo Emerson.* Ed. Ralph L. Rusk and Eleanor M. Tilton. 10 vols. 1939; reprint, New York: Columbia University Press, 1990–95. |
| SGW | Samuel Gray Ward |
| SMF | [Sarah] Margaret Fuller |
| SMFL | *The Letters of Margaret Fuller.* Ed. Robert N. Hudspeth. 6 vols. Ithaca: Cornell University Press, 1983–1994. |
| *SMFJ* 1839 | "Margaret Fuller's 1839 Journal: Trip to Bristol." Ed. Robert N. Hudspeth. *Harvard Library Bulletin* 27 (1979): 445–70. |
| *SMFJ* 1842–1 | "Margaret Fuller's 1842 Journal: At Concord with the Emersons." Ed. Joel Myerson. *Harvard Library Bulletin* 21 (1973): 320–40. |
| *SMFJ* 1842–2 | "Margaret Fuller's Journal for October 1842." Ed. Robert D. Habich. *Harvard Library Bulletin* 33 (1985): 280–91. |
| *SMFJ* 1844 | " 'The Impulses of Human Nature': Margaret Fuller's Journal from June Through October 1844." Ed. Martha L. Berg and Alice de V. Perry. *Proceedings of the Massachusetts Historical Society* 102 (1990): 38–126. |
| WD | William Dunlap |
| WWW | William Wood Wilkins |

### Introduction: The Ghost of André

1. Washington Irving, *History, Tales and Sketches* (New York: Library of America, 1983), 1081.

2. Adam Smith, *The Theory of Moral Sentiments*, ed. D. D. Raphael and A. L. Macfie (Indianapolis: Liberty Fund, 1984), 9–10.

3. Henry David Thoreau, *A Week on the Concord and Merrimack Rivers* (Princeton: Princeton University Press, 1980), 270; *E&L,* 479.

4. Anthony Ashley Cooper, Third Earl of Shaftesbury, "Sensus Communis, an Essay on the Freedom of Wit and Humour in a Letter to a Friend," in *Characteristics of Men, Manners, Opinions, Times,* ed. Lawrence E. Klein (New York: Cambridge University Press, 1999), 29–69; Aristotle, *Nicomachean Ethics,* trans. Martin Ostwald (Indianapolis: Bobbs-Merrill, 1962), 215.

5. Francis Hutcheson, *Philosophical Writings,* ed. R. S. Downie (London: J. M. Dent, 1994), 72.

6. Thomas Paine, *Collected Writings* (New York: Library of America, 1995), 124.

7. Shaftesbury, *Characteristics,* 52; AH to JL, 11 October 1780, *AHP,* 2:461.

8. Arnold A. Rogow, *A Fatal Friendship: Alexander Hamilton and Aaron Burr* (New York: Hill and Wang, 1998), 45; AH to JL, April 1779, *AHP,* 2:34–35. To preserve the flavor of older texts, I have not modernized or corrected their spelling when quoting. In a few cases, however, I have silently inserted a comma or dash to spare the reader unnecessary confusion.

9. AH to JL, April 1779, *AHP,* 2:37–38; AH to JL, 11 September 1779, *AHP,* 2:165.

10. AH to JL, 11 September 1779, *AHP,* 2:169; AH to JL, 12 September 1780, *AHP,* 2:428; AH to JL, 8 January 1780, *AHP,* 2:255; AH to JL, 16 September 1780, *AHP,* 2:431; Rogow, *Fatal Friendship,* 57.

11. AH to JL, 11 October 1780, *AHP,* 2:462.

12. Winthrop Sargent, *The Life of Major John André, Adjutant-General of the British Army in America* (New York: D. Appleton, 1871), 150, 302, 298. See also Carl Van Doren, *Secret History of the American Revolution* (New York: Viking, 1941).

13. "By a strange chance," André's biographer observes, this tree "was scathed with lightning on the very day that the news of [André's] execution came to Tarrytown" (Sargent, *André,* 314).

14. AH to ES, 25 September 1780, *AHP,* 2:442.

15. AH to ES, 2 October 1780, *AHP,* 2:449.

16. AH to JL, 11 October 1780, *AHP,* 2:466, 468.

17. Sargent, *André,* 369; AH to ES, 2 October 1780, *AHP,* 2:448.

18. AH to JL, 11 October 1780, *AHP,* 2:468; Sargent, *André,* 399.

19. Sargent, *André,* 348; AH to JL, 11 October 1780, *AHP,* 2:469; *E&L,* 473.

20. "Carolina Exile," 6 September 1781, *Pennsylvania Packet,* in *Diary of the American Revolution: From Newspapers and Original Documents,* ed. Frank Moore (New York: Charles Scribner, 1860), 2:484. For more on popular reaction to Washington's sentence, see Kenneth Silverman, *A Cultural History of the American Revolution* (New York: Thomas Y. Crowell, 1976), 377–82; and Jay Fliegelman, *Prodigals and Pilgrims: The American Revolution Against Patriarchal Authority, 1750–1800* (New York: Cambridge University Press, 1984), 215–19.

21. Thomas Pym Cope, *Philadelphia Merchant: The Diary of Thomas P. Cope, 1800–1851,* ed. Eliza Cope Harrison (South Bend: Gateway Editions,1978), 68.

22. Sargent, *André,* 89; Cope, *Philadelphia Merchant,* pl. 1.

23. Cope, *Philadelphia Merchant,* 141, 142.

24. Cope, *Philadelphia Merchant,* 142; Sargent, *André,* 89.

25. Sargent, *André,* 90, 93, 95–96, 96 n.

26. Sargent, *André,* 165–77; Randall Fuller, "Theaters of the American Revolution: The Valley Forge *Cato* and the Meschianza in Their Transcultural Contexts," *Early American Literature,* 34 (1999): 126–46; Catherine La Courreye Blecki and Karin A. Wulf, eds., *Milcah Martha Moore's Book: A Commonplace Book from Revolutionary America* (University Park: Pennsylvania State University Press, 1997), 52; Van Doren, *Secret History,* 440.

27. Cope, *Philadelphia Merchant,* 142, 144.

28. The last few years have seen the publication of Elizabeth Barnes's *States of Sympathy: Seduction and Democracy in the American Novel* (New York: Columbia University Press, 1997); Bruce Burgett's *Sentimental Bodies: Sex, Gender, and Citizenship in the Early Republic* (Princeton: Princeton University Press, 1998); Andrew Burstein's *Sentimental Democracy: The Evolution of America's Romantic Self-Image* (New York: Hill and Wang, 1999); Mary Chapman and Glenn Hendler's anthology *Sentimental Men: Masculinity and the Politics of Affect in American Culture* (Berkeley: University of California Press, 1999); Julie Ellison's *Cato's Tears and the Making of Anglo-American Emotion* (Chicago: University of Chicago, 1999); and Julia A. Stern's *The Plight of Feeling: Sympathy and Dissent in the Early American Novel* (Chicago: University of Chicago, 1997).

29. Sargent, *André,* 326.

30. In the *London Public Advertiser* of 14 March 1781, a British defender of André explicitly argued that André's social status ought to have exempted him from hanging. "A peasant, a low-lived mercentary, taken as a spy . . . actuated merely by the promise or prospect of a sordid fee" deserved punishment, but "generals or commissioned officers, though taken in the very attempt at such a service," did not (*Diary of the American Revolution,* 2:394).

31. William Dunlap, *André, a Tragedy in Five Acts* (New York: Dunlap Society, 1887), xxx.

32. Sargent, *André,* 347; Van Doren, *Secret History,* 476, pl. following p. 366.

33. Henry D. Thoreau, *Journal,* ed. John C. Broderick et al. (Princeton: Princeton University Press, 1981), 1:105; A. Smith, *Theory of Moral Sentiments,* 38.


Chapter 1. In the Pear Grove:
The Romance of Leander, Lorenzo, and Castalio

1. *Lorenzo,* 58.

2. Henry D. Thoreau, *A Week on the Concord and Merrimack Rivers* (Princeton: Princeton University Press, 1980), 155.

3. Sarah Cadbury, "Extracts from the Diary of Ann Warder," *Pennsylvania Magazine of History and Biography* 18 (1894): 54; Deborah Norris Logan, *The Norris House* (Philadelphia: Fair-Hill Press, 1867), 1.

4. Logan, *Norris House,* 3–11.

5. Once, while admiring a painting in a pretty young widow's collection, Mifflin lectured about its color scheme sententiously and at length, gesticulating with his umbrella, until the woman's embarrassment became so obvious that he squinted again at the

painting in question and discovered that unawares he had been repeatedly calling her attention to a female nude in a "lascivious" position; *Leander* 1:106. For Mifflin's age and genealogy, see John Houston Merrill, *Memoranda Relating to the Mifflin Family* (Printed for private distribution 24 April 1890); and Frank Willing Leach, *The Mifflin Family* (Philadelphia: Historical Publication Society, 1932). For his trust fund, see Elizabeth Bordley Gibson, *Biographical Sketches of the Bordley Family, of Maryland, for Their Descendants* (Philadelphia: Henry B. Ashmead, 1865), 1:110. The American Philosophical Society holds one of the receipt books that Mifflin took with him on his dunning errands (16 January 1800–10 March 1813). Other details are from *Leander* as follows: weight (1:226 and 1:246), cane (2:142), hair style (2:124), snowball (2:154), and near-sightedness (1:106).

6. Richard L. Bushman, *The Refinement of America: Persons, Houses, Cities* (New York: Knopf, 1992), 130. *Leander* 1:3, 47; 2:211; 1:8.

7. Royall Tyler, *The Contrast* (1790), in *The Heath Anthology of American Literature,* ed. Paul Lauter et al. (New York: Houghton Mifflin, 1998), 1:1149. For an overview of the social transformations of the period, see Jay Fliegelman, *Prodigals and Pilgrims: The American Revolution Against Patriarchal Authority, 1750–1800* (New York: Cambridge University Press, 1984); and Gordon S. Wood, *The Radicalism of the American Revolution* (New York: Knopf, 1992).

8. Charles-Louis de Secondat, baron de Montesquieu, *De l'esprit des lois* (Paris: Editions Garnier Frères, 1961), 1:342; *Leander,* 1:44. For the interaction of politeness with Whig ideology, see J. G. A. Pocock, "The mobility of property and the rise of eighteenth-century sociology," in *Virtue, Commerce, and History* (New York: Cambridge University Press, 1985); and Lawrence Klein, "The Third Earl of Shaftesbury and the Progress of Politeness," *Eighteenth-Century Studies* 18 (1984–85): 186–214.

9. Edward Young, *The Complaint; or, Night Thoughts* (Hartford: S. Andrus and Son, 1847), 43; Henry Mackenzie, *The Man of Feeling* (New York: Norton, 1958), 4.

10. Fliegelman, *Prodigals,* 24; Wood, *Radicalism,* 224–25. For an overview of the philosophy of sympathy, see G. J. Barker-Benfield, *The Culture of Sensibility: Sex and Society in Eighteenth-Century Britain* (Chicago: University of Chicago Press, 1992); R. S. Crane, "Suggestions Toward a Genealogy of the 'Man of Feeling,' " *ELH* 1 (1934): 205–30; Norman S. Fiering, "Irresistible Compassion: An Aspect of Eighteenth-Century Sympathy and Humanitarianism," *Journal of the History of Ideas* 37 (1976): 195–218; and John B. Radner, "The Art of Sympathy in Eighteenth-Century British Moral Thought," *Studies in Eighteenth-Century Culture* 9 (1979): 189–210. For a provocative reading of Thomas Jefferson as a sentimentalist, see Garry Wills, *Inventing America: Jefferson's Declaration of Independence* (New York: Vintage, 1979), which is strongly contested by Ronald Hamowy, "Jefferson and the Scottish Enlightenment: A Critique of Garry Wills's *Inventing America,*" *William and Mary Quarterly* 36 (1979): 503–23. Hamowy accuses Wills of exaggerating the extent and garbling most of the details of Scottish influence on Jefferson, but he agrees that Jefferson followed sentimental theory in believing that "all men possessed a moral sense . . . not reducible to reason" (522).

11. Qtd. in Wood, *Radicalism,* 71.

12. Allan Silver, "Friendship in Commercial Society: Eighteenth-Century Social Theory and Modern Sociology," *American Journal of Sociology* 95 (1990): 1474–1504.

13. William Wordsworth, *The Prelude, 1799, 1805, 1850* (New York: Norton, 1979), 428, 432.

14. *Leander,* 2:213. Moyes's blindness and the size of audience are mentioned in an unsigned letter to SE [Samuel Emlen?], 4 March 1785, Miscellaneous items, Bringhurst Manuscripts (J), Friends Historical Library, Swarthmore College.

15. *Leander,* 1:13, 184; James Gibson to "Mama," typescript, 28 December 1785, Class of 1787, Undergraduate alumni records, Seeley G. Mudd Manuscript Library, Princeton University; "John Gibson, Mayor of Philadelphia, 1771–1772," in *Genealogies of Pennsylvania Families: From the Pennsylvania Genealogical Magazine* (Baltimore: Genealogical Publishing Co., 1982), 1:652–53. For Gibson's weight, see *Leander* 2:226 and 2:246; for age at puberty, see Joseph F. Kett, *Rites of Passage: Adolescence in America, 1790 to the Present* (New York: Basic Books, 1977), 44; for Gibson's hair, see *Leander* 2:124 and *Lorenzo* 20; for the bargain with Barlowe, see *Lorenzo* 31.

16. *Lorenzo* 90. For an overview of Gibson at Princeton, see Ruth L. Woodward and Wesley Frank Craven, eds., *Princetonians, 1784–1790: A Biographical Dictionary* (Princeton: Princeton University Press, 1991), 187–91; for Gibson's class rank, see *Leander* 2:136.

17. *Leander* 1:185; Diary of John Rhea Smith ["Diary of an Anonymous Student"], 1 January 1786–22 September 1786, Bound photostat, General Mss. Bound, Firestone Rare Books and Manuscripts Library, Princeton University; *Lorenzo* 59. Selections from Smith's diary have been published as Ruth L. Woodward, ed., "Journal at Nassau Hall: The Diary of John Rhea Smith, 1786," *Princeton University Library Chronicle* 46 (1985): 269–91; and ibid., 47 (1985): 48–70. For more on the Cliosophic Society, see James McLachlan, "The *Choice of Hercules:* American Student Societies in the Early Nineteenth Century," in *The University in Society,* ed. Lawrence Stone (Princeton: Princeton University Press, 1974), 2:449–94; J. Jefferson Looney, *Nurseries of Letters and Republicanism: A Brief History of the American Whig-Cliosophic Society and Its Predecessors, 1765–1941* (Princeton: Trustees of the American Whig-Cliosophic Society, 1996).

18. *Leander* 2:141–43.

19. David S. Shields, *Civil Tongues & Polite Letters in British America* (Chapel Hill: University of North Carolina Press, 1997), 263–64. For the examples of cognomens given here, see Kathryn Zabelle Derounian, "'A Dear Dear Friend': Six Letters from Deborah Norris to Sally Wister, 1778–1779," *Pennsylvania Magazine of History and Biography* 108 (1984): 487–516; John A. H. Sweeney, "The Norris-Fisher Correspondence: A Circle of Friends, 1779–82," *Delaware History* 6 (1955): 187–232; Deborah Norris Logan to Sally Fisher, 10 November 1779, Charles Smith Ogden Papers, Scrapbooks, Friends Historical Library, Swarthmore College; Philander [Joshua Fisher] to Cleora [Hannah Pemberton], 24 November 1781 and 1 June 1783, Pemberton Papers, HSP.

20. "An Address to the Inhabitants of Latonia," "Amusement for the Circle," "Letters to the Thompsonians," and "The Universal Magazine and Literary Museum," Norris of Fairhill Manuscript Books, HSP. This collection would be an excellent source for a study of children's and adolescents' reactions to the Revolution.

21. Ethel Armes, ed., *Nancy Shippen; Her Journal Book* (New York: Benjamin Blom,

1968), 29, 32. Otto signed his love letters not as Leander but as Lewis, Maria, John-Wait-Too-Long, Damon, Mr. Venoni, J Wait-Patiently, Mr. Runaway, Lewis Scriblerius, and Mr. Reciprocity.

22. Ardelia [Deborah Norris] to Sally Fisher, 16 November 1779, in Sweeney, "Norris-Fisher Correspondence," 196.

23. *Leander* 1:223; Young, *Complaint*, 29.

24. *Leander* 2:15–18, 100, 119, 57–58.

25. *Leander* 2:127.

26. Young, *Complaint*, 34.

27. Woodward, "Journal at Nassau Hall," 46:273.

28. *Lorenzo* 1, 22.

29. *Leander* 1:1.

30. *Leander* 1:195. For trips, see Mary Parker Norris to Isaac Norris III, 28 October 1785, Norris Papers, Family Letters, HSP; *Leander* 2:87.

31. "S Rhoads is amost agreeable friend & neighbor, I am sorry she meets with the difficultys she has to encounter settling her affairs. — I have another excellent neighbour, the Widow Gibson" (Mary Parker Norris to Mary Dickinson, 4–6 March [1786?], Loudoun Papers, HSP). For genealogical information on the Norris family, see *The Norris Family, Reprinted from the Provincial Councillors of Pennsylvania* (Trenton: Wm. S. Sharp, 1882), 2–13; and John W. Jordan, ed., *Colonial and Revolutionary Families of Pennsylvania: Genealogical and Personal Memoirs* (Baltimore: Genealogical Publishing Co., 1978), 1:88–89. For proof that Castalio is Isaac Norris III, see Mary Parker Norris to Isaac Norris III, 22 December 1785, Norris Papers, Family Letters, HSP, which includes a postscript from "J M Jr" to "my dear Castalio" in Mifflin's hand. For the Rhoads family, see S. Castner Jr., *The Rhoads Family of Pennsylvania* (Philadelphia: George H. Buchanan, 1901), 9–13. The identification of the Rhoads children as Maria, Eliza, and Ascanius is based on comparison of details in Leander's diary with two letters: Elizabeth Rhoads to Samuel Rhoads, 29 August 1786, and Mary Rhoads to Samuel Rhoads, 9 September 1786, Rhoads Family Manuscripts, E-95, HSP. Also see Sarah Rhoads, "Account of my beloved Daughters," Manuscript Commonplace Books, HSP, which includes poems commemorating the deceased "Eliza" and "Maria." For thumbnail biographies of many of the people mentioned in Mifflin's diary, including servants, see [Joseph Parker Norris,] "Register of Deaths in the Lloyd & Norris Families, with some of their near & particular Friends," *Extracts from the Letter Books of Isaac Norris,* Norris of Fairhill Manuscript Books, HSP, 3:249–72. Leonora might be Clementina Ross, Mifflin's future wife, and Eugenius might be Jabez Maud Fisher (see Sweeney, "Norris-Fisher Correspondence," 200 n. 27), but there is no firm evidence for either guess. Eugenius is the name Laurence Sterne gave to his friend John Hall-Stevenson in his fiction.

32. *Leander* 1:1, 7. Cicero, *Selected Letters,* trans. D. R. Shackleton Bailey (New York: Penguin, 1986), 49.

33. *Leander* 1:2, 6, 7; 2:7–8.

34. *Leander* 1:25; 2:129.

35. *Lorenzo* 4, 25, 26.

36. *Leander* 2:122.

37. *Leander* 1:15, 169; 2:180.

38. Delia [Deborah Norris Logan], "Again the sun recalls the vernal year," April 1780, Maria Dickinson Logan Papers, HSP; Shields, *Civil Tongues,* 130; Deborah Norris Logan to Isaac Norris, 7 August [1783?], Norris Papers, Family Letters, HSP.

39. Deborah Norris to Sally Fisher, n.d., in Sweeney, "Norris-Fisher Correspondence," 215; Deborah Norris to Sarah Wister, 2 August 1779, in Derounian, "'A Dear Dear Friend,'" 513; Ardelia [Deborah Norris] to Sally Fisher, 16 November 1779, in Sweeney, "Norris-Fisher Correspondence," 197.

40. *Leander* 2:208.

41. Carroll Smith-Rosenberg, "The Female World of Love and Ritual: Relations Between Women in Nineteenth-Century America," in *Disorderly Conduct: Visions of Gender in Victorian America* (New York: Oxford University Press, 1985), 53. In *Home Fronts: Domesticity and Its Critics in the Antebellum United States* (Durham: Duke University Press, 1997), Lora Romero has explored this overlap between men's and women's worlds in the young republic. For an overview of the evolution of the trope of "separate spheres" in the past three decades of women's history, see Linda K. Kerber, "Separate Spheres, Female Worlds, Woman's Place: The Rhetoric of Women's History," in *Toward an Intellectual History of Women* (Chapel Hill: University of North Carolina Press, 1997), 159–99. The romantic friendships in the Norris circle took place in an eighteenth-century beau monde that was not yet the exclusive province of either gender. Like the European court that was its ultimate model, the American beau monde gave special place to women but until well into the Federalist era welcomed both sexes (Shields, *Civil Tongues,* 11–14, 99–122). Mifflin and Gibson may have slipped through a closing door; men who thrived in the beau monde were becoming suspect. John Adams registered the emerging distrust when he found suspicious the attention that his daughter's cosmopolitan suitor Royall Tyler paid to Mrs. Adams: "I don't like this method of Courting Mothers"; Adams to Abigail Adams, 22 January 1783, in *The Book of Abigail and John: Selected Letters of the Adams Family, 1762–1784,* ed. L. H. Butterfield, Marc Friedlander, and Mary-Jo Kline (Cambridge: Harvard University Press, 1975), 336–39.

42. Mary Dickinson to Isaac Norris III, 16 March [178?] and n.d. [1:82], Norris Papers, Family Letters, HSP.

43. Smith-Rosenberg, "Female World," 55.

44. Fliegelman, *Prodigals and Pilgrims,* 41; Toby L. Ditz, "Shipwrecked; or, Masculinity Imperiled: Mercantile Representations of Failure and the Gendered Self in Eighteenth-Century Philadelphia," *Journal of American History* 81 (1994): 51–80.

45. James Boswell, *Boswell's London Journal, 1762–63,* ed. Frederick A. Pottle (New Haven: Yale University Press, 1992), 40. The Hamilton-Laurens friendship is discussed in Jonathan Ned Katz, *Gay American History: Lesbians and Gay Men in the U.S.A.* (New York: Thomas Y. Crowell, 1976), 451–56; the Webster-Bingham friendship is discussed in E. Anthony Rotundo, *American Manhood: Transformations in Masculinity from the Revolution to the Modern Era* (New York: Basic Books, 1993), 77–80.

46. Diary of John Rhea Smith, 19 January 1786. According to Smith's diary, tutor Gilbert Snowden winked at a similar episode of goofing off on 25 Saturday 1786: "this evening also Gilbert comes & finds the lads in my room & says Oh! Gentlemen, Gentlemen, & then smiling withdraws." Mifflin did find the other boys' presence undesirable:

"his [Gibson's] roommate Mr Smith was there, & some awkward chums who soon disappeared & then Mr S. & I had some *solid* conversation" (*Leander* 1:125).

47. *Leander* 2:145; Robert V. Wells, "Quaker Marriage Patterns in a Colonial Perspective," *William and Mary Quarterly,* third series, 23 (1972): 420, 429; *Leander* 2:74, 217.

48. *Lorenzo* 40; James Gibson to "Mama," 28 December 1785, Seeley G. Mudd Manuscript Library, Princeton; Mary Parker Norris to Hannah Thomson, 18 October 1786, Maria Dickinson Logan Papers, HSP; Mary Parker Norris to Isaac Norris III, 28 October 1785, Norris Papers, Family Letters, HSP; Mary Parker Norris to Charles Thomson, 16 May 1786, Maria Dickinson Logan Papers, HSP; Mary Parker Norris to Isaac Norris III, 17 June 1785, Norris Papers, Family Letters, HSP; Joseph Parker Norris to Deborah Norris Logan, 11 September 1785, Robert R. Logan Collection, HSP; Mary Parker Norris to Isaac Norris III, 9 September 1785, Norris Papers, Family Letters, HSP.

49. Smith-Rosenberg, "Female World," 59; Søren Kierkegaard, *The Sickness unto Death: A Christian Psychological Exposition for Upbuilding and Awakening,* trans. H. Hong and E. Hong (Princeton: Princeton University Press, 1980), 119.

50. *Leander* 2:214; 1:1–2.

51. *Leander* 1:8, 17, 20.

52. *Leander* 2:154; 1:30, 42, 110–11; 2:183.

53. Fliegelman, *Prodigals and Pilgrims,* 174–80; *Leander* 2:5, 3.

54. Sweeney, "Norris-Fisher Correspondence," 200 n. 27.

55. *Lorenzo* 52, 60; *Leander* 1:89; *Lorenzo* 70, 73.

56. Francis White's *Philadelphia Directory* (Young, Stewart & McCulloch, 1785) lists a "Mifflin John, Esq; counsellor at law, Second b. Walnut & Spruce-streets," which corresponds to the address on the verso of H. Thomson to Mifflin, 15 September 1785, Manuscript Collection, Library Company of Philadelphia.

57. *Leander* 2:92; Deborah Norris to Sarah Wister, 2 August 1779, in Derounian, " 'Dear Dear Friend,' " 511.

58. Deborah Norris to Sarah Wister, 27 July 1779, in Derounian, " 'Dear Dear Friend,' " 509; "Amusement for the Circle," No. 2, 19 August 1780; Boswell, *London Journal,* 136. See Laurence Sterne, *A Sentimental Journey* (New York: Penguin, 1986), 85, for a mention of Castalia that the Norris circle would have been familiar with. Charlotte Cibber Charke put Otway's play to a gender-deviant use in her 1756 novel, *The History of Henry Dumont, Esq.* When the sodomite Billy Loveman makes a pass at the hero Henry, Billy dresses up "in a female rich dishabille" and cries out to Henry, "I come, I fly to my adored Castalio's arms! my wishes lord! . . . Do my angel, call me your Monimia!" Qtd. in *Pages Passed from Hand to Hand: The Hidden Tradition of Homosexual Literature in English from 1748 to 1914,* ed. Mark Mitchell and David Leavitt (New York: Houghton Mifflin, 1998), 20.

59. The figure labeled "I Norris," in "A Party to Virginia," watercolor sketch, *Rhoads Family Manuscripts,* E-95, 1:60, HSP. This fanciful watercolor portrays many of the young people in the Norris circle, including Becky Jones, Sarah Drinker (1761–1807), Joseph Parker Norris (1763–1841), Nancy Emlen (1755–1815), Charles Logan (1754–94), Polly Jackson, Nancy Drinker (1764–1830), Polly Fishbourne (1760–1842), Thomas Lloyd, Mary Pleasants (17??–1794), Captain Alexander Spotswood Dandridge

(1753–85), Sally Jones (1760–?), Deborah Norris (1761–1839, Betsy Wister (1764–1812), Jonathan Jones (1762–1822), Sally Wister (1761–1804), Colonel James Wood (1750–1813), Mrs. Wood, and the Woods' daughter.

60. Mary Dickinson to Deborah Norris Logan, 18 April 1789, Robert R. Logan Collection, HSP.

61. Mary Dickinson to Isaac Norris, not dated [1:82], Norris Papers, Family Letters, HSP; Mary Dickinson to Isaac Norris III, 28 March 1791, Norris Papers, Family Letters, HSP; Isaac Norris, "Poem ['Say what is Life if Frenzy clouds the Mind']," Logan Papers, HSP.

62. Mary Dickinson to Isaac Norris III, 28 March 1791, Norris Papers, Family Letters, HSP; Mary Dickinson to Isaac Norris III, 2 February 1790, Norris Papers, Family Letters, HSP; Erik Erikson, *Identity and the Life Cycle* (New York: Norton, 1980), 32–33.

63. Richard Steele, "Spectator No. 364," in *The Spectator,* ed. Donald F. Bond (London: Oxford, 1965), 3:368; Deborah Norris Logan to Isaac Norris, 7 August [1783?], Norris Papers, Family Letters, HSP.

64. Charles Thomson to Isaac Norris, 19 June 1784, in Lewis R. Harley, *The Life of Charles Thomson, Secretary of the Continental Congress and Translator of the Bible from the Greek* (Philadelphia: George W. Jacobs, 1900), 200; John Adams to Abigail Adams, 14 August 1776, *Book of Abigail and John,* 156.

65. Charles Thomson to Thomas Jefferson, 18 June 1784, in *The Papers of Thomas Jefferson,* ed. Julian P. Boyd (Princeton: Princeton University Press, 1953), 7:305–6; Jefferson to Thomson, 11 November 1784, in *Papers of Thomas Jefferson,* 7:518–19.

66. Mary Parker Norris to Isaac Norris, 15 May 1784, Norris Papers, Family Letters, HSP; *Philadelphia Monthly Meeting (Arch Street) Minutes, 1782–1789,* microfilm, Friends Historical Library, Swarthmore College, 308–9 (30 March 1787), 295 (29 December 1786), and 320 (25 May 1787).

67. Robert Morton to to John Pemberton, 21 November 1783, Pemberton Papers, HSP; Mary Parker Norris to Isaac Norris, 30 October 1784, Norris Papers, Family Letters, HSP.

68. Isaac Norris to Deborah Norris Logan, 29 July 1783, Robert R. Logan Collection, HSP; Isaac Norris to Deborah Norris Logan, 4 February 1784, Robert R. Logan Collection, HSP; Isaac Norris to Deborah Norris Logan, 18 April 1784, Robert R. Logan Collection, HSP; Erikson, *Identity,* 119–20.

69. Hannah Thomson to John Mifflin, 12 May 1785 and 12 December 1786, Manuscript Collection, Library Company of Philadelphia; Joseph Parker Norris to Deborah Norris Logan, 4 February 1786, Robert R. Logan Collection, HSP; Isaac Norris to Deborah Norris Logan, 12 March 1786, Robert R. Logan Collection, HSP; Joseph Parker Norris to Deborah Norris Logan, 4 February 1786, Robert R. Logan Collection, HSP.

70. *Leander* 1:150–151.

71. Mary Parker Norris to Isaac Norris, 23 April 1784, Norris Papers, Family Letters, HSP; *Leander* 2:148; Mary Parker Norris to Isaac Norris, 7 August 1784, Norris Papers, Family Letters, HSP; *Leander* 1:152, 50.

72. *Leander* 1:150.

73. *Leander* 1:50; *Lorenzo* 51. A separate essay could be written on the timing of Mifflin's illnesses. He himself admitted that "my complaints are not constitutional—they

are adventitious & have arisen out of the inauspicious turns of my fate" (*Leander* 1:218). They seem to coincide often with Mifflin's displeasure at the kind or degree of attention he is receiving from one of his friends.

74. *Leander* 1:58; *Lorenzo* 55–56.

75. *Leander* 1:59.

76. *Leander* 1:59–60.

77. *Lorenzo* 59.

78. *Leander* 1:137; Robert Morris to John Nicholson, 14 December 1797, in "Original Letters and Documents," no. 3, *Pennsylvania Magazine of History and Biography* 6 (1882): 112.

79. *Leander* 1:153, 156–58.

80. *Leander* 2:249; 1:184; 2:73, 75, 93–94, 125, 192; Mary Parker Norris to Charles Thomson, 15 November 1787, Maria Dickinson Logan Papers, HSP; *Leander* 2:120, 17.

81. *Leander* 1:218, 214, 223.

82. *Leander* 1:95; *Lorenzo* 79; *Leander* 1:121, 239, 241.

83. *Leander* 1:85; 2:41, 35.

84. *Leander* 2:30. Discussing eighteenth-century romantic friendships between British women, Lillian Faderman found that to focus on the sexual act led her to an interpretive dead end. About the famous Ladies of Llangollen, she wrote, "We do not know whether or not their relationship was genital, but they were 'married' in every other sense." Lillian Faderman, *Surpassing the Love of Men: Romantic Friendship and Love Between Women from the Renaissance to the Present* (New York: William Morrow, 1981), 125.

85. *Leander* 1:84; 2:66; 1:210; 2:288; and an unnumbered page following 2:52.

86. Mary Dickinson to Isaac Norris, 4 December 1787, Norris Papers, Family Letters, HSP; Isaac Norris to Mary Dickinson, 22 January 1790, Norris Papers, Family Letters, HSP; Mary Dickinson to Isaac Norris, 6 May 1790, Norris Papers, Family Letters, HSP; Isaac Norris to Deborah Norris Logan, 13 May 1790, Robert R. Logan Collection, HSP; Mary Dickinson to Isaac Norris, 14 March 1791, Norris Papers, Family Letters, HSP; Mary Parker Norris to Deborah Norris Logan, 15 March 1793, Maria Dickinson Logan Papers, HSP; Mary Parker Norris to Deborah Norris Logan, 29 August 1793, Maria Dickinson Logan Papers, HSP.

87. This passage was heavily crossed out by a later hand.

88. Mary Parker Norris to Deborah Norris Logan, 9 March 1796, Maria Dickinson Logan Papers, HSP; Mary Parker Norris to Deborah Norris Logan, 18 December 1798, Robert R. Logan Collection, HSP; Mary Dickinson to Isaac Norris, 8 July 1798, Norris Papers, Family Letters, HSP; Mary Dickinson to Isaac Norris, not dated [1:82], Norris Papers, Family Letters, HSP; Mary Parker Norris to Hannah Griffitts, 3 November 1799, Maria Dickinson Logan Papers, HSP; Joseph Parker Norris, "Register," 267; *Federal Gazette,* 9 October 1802.

89. Elizabeth Mifflin, "Memoir of John Ross, Merchant, of Philadelphia," *Pennsylvania Magazine of History and Biography* 23 (1899): 77–85; Merrill, *Memoranda,* 56; Elizabeth Mifflin, "John Mifflin Genealogical Data," Society Collection, HSP; John Fishbourne Mifflin, "John F. Mifflin to Mrs. Anne Penn. Letter Book No. 1," 17 November 1788–4 March 1802, HSP.

90. Woodward and Craven, *Princetonians,* 189–91; "The Erie Triangle and North-

western Pennsylvania Land Titles," *Pennsylvania Magazine of History and Biography* 11 (1887): 358–61; R. Nelson Hale, "The Pennsylvania Population Company," *Pennsylvania History* 16 (1949): 122–30; *Genealogies of Pennsylvania Families,* 1:653.

91. *Early Proceedings of the American Philosophical Society for the Promotion of Useful Knowledge, Compiled by One of the Secretaries, from the Manuscript Minutes of Its Meetings from 1744 to 1838* (Philadelphia: McCalla and Stavely, 1884), 236, 396; Francis James Dallett, *Guide to the Archives of the University of Pennsylvania from 1740 to 1820* (Philadelphia: University of Pennsylvania Archives, 1978); "Sons of Washington," *Pennsylvania Magazine of History and Biography* 24 (1900): 127–28; Olive Moore Gambrill, "John Beale Bordley and the Early Years of the Philadelphia Agricultural Society," *Pennsylvania Magazine of History and Biography* 66 (1942): 410–39.

92. Woodward and Craven, *Princetonians,* 190; James Gibson to "my dear sister," typescript, 9 June 1817, Class of 1787, Undergraduate alumni records, Seeley G. Mudd Manuscripts Library, Princeton University. For Gibson's obituary, see *Philadelphia Public Ledger* 41, no. 93 (10 July 1856). For more on Elizabeth Bordley Gibson, see Patricia Brady, ed., *George Washington's Beautiful Nelly: The Letters of Eleanor Parke Custis Lewis to Elizabeth Bordley Gibson, 1794–1851* (University of South Carolina Press, 1991); Elizabeth Bordley Gibson, *Biographical Sketches of the Bordley Family, of Maryland, for Their Descendants* (Philadelphia: Henry B. Ashmead, 1865).

93. Years after Isaac's death, his sister wrote that "the tender blossoms of the Sassafras riminds me of my dear Isaac, and of our walk in the Spring to gather them for tea." Diary of Deborah Norris Logan, 15 February 1815, HSP.

94. Isaac Norris to Mary Dickinson, 23 April 1788, Norris Papers, Family Letters, HSP.

## Chapter 2. The Decomposition of Charles Brockden Brown: Sympathy in Brown's Letters

1. Paul Allen, *The Life of Charles Brockden Brown* (Delmar, N.Y.: Scholars' Facsimiles and Reprints, 1975), 11–12; Peter Kafer, "The Browns; or, The Transformation: A Pennsylvania Quaker Tale" (paper presented at "Revising Charles Brockden Brown," a conference at the University of Pennsylvania, Philadelphia, 24 October 1998).

2. P. Allen, *Life of Charles Brockden Brown,* 12, 15; Leslie Fiedler, *Love and Death in the American Novel* (New York: Anchor, 1992), 145.

3. P. Allen, *Life of Charles Brockden Brown,* 49.

4. P. Allen, *Life of Charles Brockden Brown,* 12; CBB to JBJr, 20 May 1792 (Bennett #21) and 30 May 1792 (Bennett #23), Charles Brockden Brown Papers, Special Collections and Archives, Bowdoin College Library (hereafter cited as Bowdoin CBB Papers). All my quotations of Brown's letters derive from an edition of his correspondence prepared by John R. Holmes, Edwin J. Saeger, and Alfred Weber, which they shared with me in an early electronic form. For clarity of reference, I have cited the original manuscripts of the letters, although in most cases I have not personally consulted these manuscripts. Letters are further identified by the numbering system in Charles E. Bennett, "The Letters of Charles Brockden Brown: An Annotated Census," *Resources for American Literary Study* 6, no. 2 (1976): 164–90.

5. Robert Hemenway, "Charles Brockden Brown's Law Study: Some New Documents," *American Literature* 39 (1967): 201; John R. Holmes, "Charles Brockden Brown's Earliest Letter," *Early American Literature* 30 (1995): 74.

6. CBB, "Aretas" ["By C. B. Brown. my Son. at 15 years Old. his first Essay On some of his School fellows, members of the Philological Society"], Charles Brockden Brown Papers, 1742–1810, HSP; David Lee Clark, *Charles Brockden Brown: Pioneer Voice of America* (Durham: Duke University Press, 1952), 49.

7. P. Allen, *Life of Charles Brockden Brown*, 14, 18.

8. P. Allen, *Life of Charles Brockden Brown*, 17, 21.

9. CBB to JBJr, 20 May 1792 (Bennett #21).

10. Clark, *Charles Brockden Brown*, 53–107; Eleanor M. Tilton, "'The Sorrows' of Charles Brockden Brown," *PMLA* 69 (1954): 1304–8.

11. Clark, *Charles Brockden Brown*, 63, 101.

12. Clark, *Charles Brockden Brown*, 74.

13. For genealogical information on Bringhurst, see "Miscellaneous Papers Collected by Henry Carvill Lewis Preparatory to a History of the Bringhurst, Claypoole, DeVeaux, Evans, Foulke, Parker, and Allied Families," Collections of the Genealogical Society of Pennsylvania, HSP. Somewhat confusingly, Joseph Bringhurst Jr. was the son of James Bringhurst Sr. (1730–1810), and James Sr.'s brother Joseph Sr. was the father of James Bringhurst Jr. For a count of known Brown letters, see Charles E. Bennett's census and the preface to Holmes, Saeger, and Weber's forthcoming edition of Brown's correspondence.

14. CBB to JBJr, n.d. (Bennett #20 and #8), Bowdoin CBB Papers; Charles E. Bennett, "A Poetical Correspondence Among Elihu Hubbard Smith, Joseph Bringhurst, Jr., and Charles Brockden Brown in *The Gazette of the United States*," *Early American Literature* 11 (1977–8): 279; Thomas Pyn Cope, *Philadelphia Merchant: The Diary of Thomas P. Cope, 1800–1851*, ed. Eliza Cope Harrison (South Bend: Gateway Editions, 1978), 44; Elihu Hubbard Smith, *The Diary of Elihu Hubbard Smith (1771–1798)*, ed. James E. Cronin (Philadelphia: American Philosophical Society, 1973), 166.

15. James Bringhurst to Job Scott, 16 December 1793, Bringhurst Mss. (T), Friends Historical Library, Swarthmore College; CBB to JBJr, December 1792 and 29 December 1795 (Bennett #34 and #67), Bowdoin CBB Papers; EHS, *Diary*, 166; John R. Holmes and Edwin J. Saeger, "Charles Brockden Brown and the 'Laura-Petrarch' Letters," *Early American Literature* 25 (1990): 183–86; Charles E. Bennett, "Poetical Correspondence"; William Dunlap, "Charles Brockden Brown," in *The National Portrait Gallery of Distinguished Americans*, ed. James B. Longacre and James Herring (Philadelphia: Henry Perkins, 1836); Joseph Bringhurst Jr., "A Sketch of the Life of William Wood Wilkins Esq.," Charles Brockden Brown Papers, 1715–1827, HSP.

16. CBB to JBJr, 5 May 1792 (Bennett #12), Bowdoin CBB Papers.

17. CBB to JBJr, 7 May 1792 (Bennett #14), Bowdoin CBB Papers.

18. CBB to JBJr, n.d. (Bennett #9) and 15 May 1792 (Bennett #18), Bowdoin CBB Papers.

19. CBB to JBJr, n.d. (Bennett #20).

20. P. Allen, *Life of Charles Brockden Brown*, 16, 55–56; CBB to JBJr, 5 May 1792 (Bennett #12).

21. CBB to JBJr, n.d. (Bennett #9), 20 March 1792 (Bennett #5), and n.d. (Bennett

#20), Bowdoin CBB Papers; CBB to WWW, n.d. (Bennett #6), Harry Ransom Humanities Research Center, University of Texas at Austin (hereafter cited as Ransom Center).

22. CBB to JBJr, n.d. (Bennett #29), Bowdoin CBB Papers; Charles Brockden Brown, *Arthur Mervyn; or, Memoirs of the Year 1793, First and Second Parts* (Kent, Ohio: Kent State University Press, 1980), 340.

23. CBB to JBJr, n.d. (Bennett #9).

24. Jean-Jacques Rousseau, *Les Confessions* (Paris: Bibliothèque de la Pléiade, 1933), 5; CBB to JBJr, 20 May 1792 (Bennett #21).

25. CBB to JBJr, 9 August 1792 (Bennett #30), 22 April 1793 (Bennett #40), and n.d. (Bennett #42), Bowdoin CBB Papers. In the matter of Brown's truths and lies, it does not pay a scholar to be overconfident. Peter Kafer has recently verified as true a story that critics had long believed was one of Brown's most egregious fictions. In a letter to Bringhurst, Brown had claimed that at "eleven or twelve years of age I spent twelve hours in each day, that is, . . . I passed the night, for 8 months together in a *Jail*" (n.d., Bennett #9). He drew a prose sketch of himself, sitting on a bench, ears stuffed with cotton, practicing shorthand in a corner, surrounded by inmates. Brown scholars used to feel certain that this episode was a figment of Brown's imagination, but Kafer has located family letters in the Waln Collection of Haverford College that prove that Elijah Brown was in fact imprisoned for debt in 1784 for a "considerable amount." See Kafer, "The Browns; or, The Transformation."

26. CBB to JBJr, 20 May 1792 (Bennett #21) and 9 May 1792 (Bennett #16), Bowdoin CBB Papers; Clark, *Charles Brockden Brown*, 105.

27. For the eighteenth-century literary debate over whether to admire, weep over, or disdain Cato's example, see Ian Donaldson, "Cato in Tears: Stoical Guises of the Man of Feeling," in *Studies in the Eighteenth Century,* ed. R. F. Brissenden (Toronto: University of Toronto Press, 1973), 377–95.

28. CBB to JBJr, n.d. (Bennett #8) and 5 May 1792 (Bennett #12).

29. Joseph Addison, "The Spectator, No. 1 [Mr Spectator introduces himself]," in *Selections from the Tatler and the Spectator* (New York: Penguin, 1982), 199; CBB, *The Rhapsodist and Other Uncollected Writings,* ed. Harry R. Warfel (New York: Scholars' Facsimiles and Reprints, 1943), 1, 2.

30. Herbert Brown, "Charles Brockden Brown's 'The Story of Julius': Rousseau and Richardson 'Improved,'" in *Essays Mostly on Periodical Publishing in America,* ed. James Woodress (Durham: Duke University Press, 1973), 39, 42.

31. H. Brown, "Brown's 'Story,'" 49, 40.

32. When Brown joined a poetical correspondence published in the *Gazette of the United States* two years later, he wrote as "Henry" — perhaps the twin of Henrietta, as Julius was the twin of Julietta? The other two men in the correspondence wrote under the female cognomens Ella and Birtha. Bennett, "A Poetical Correspondence."

33. CBB to JBJr, 20 May 1792 (Bennett #21); JBJr, "Life of William Wood Wilkins," 12, 1, 12–13; P. Allen, *Life of Charles Brockden Brown,* 11.

34. William Dunlap, *The Life of Charles Brockden Brown: Together with Selections from the Rarest of His Printed Works, from His Original Letters, and from His Manuscripts Before Unpublished* (Philadelphia: James P. Parke, 1815), 1:46; JBJr, "Life of William Wood Wilkins," 15; CBB to JBJr, 20 May 1792 (Bennett #21); P. Allen, *Life of Charles Brockden Brown,* 42.

35. WWW to Robert Schenk, December 1785, qtd. in JBJr, "Life of William Wood Wilkins," 7; CBB to WWW, n.d. (Bennett #11), Papers of Charles Brockden Brown (MSS 6439), Clifton Waller Barrett Library of American Literature, Special Collections Department, University of Virginia Library (hereafter cited as Virginia CBB Papers); WWW to CBB, 1 May 1792, in David Lee Clark, "Unpublished Letters of Charles Brockden Brown and W. W. Wilkins," *Texas Studies in English* 27 (June 1948): 83–85; CBB to JBJr, 20 May 1792 (Bennett #22); JBJr, "Life of William Wood Wilkins," 48.

36. CBB to WWW, n.d. (Bennett #4), Virginia CBB Papers; WWW to CBB, 4–8 May 1793, in Clark, "Unpublished Letters of Brown and Wilkins," 105–6; CBB to WWW, n.d. (Bennett #17), qtd. in Clark, "Unpublished Letters," 79–82; CBB to WWW, November 1792 (Bennett #33), qtd. in P. Allen, *Life,* 61–67; WWW to CBB, 1 May 1792.

37. WWW to CBB, n.d., in Clark, "Unpublished Letters," 85; CBB to JBJr, 20 May 1792 (Bennett #21); WWW to CBB, n.d., in Clark, "Unpublished Letters," 86–87.

38. WWW to CBB, 27 November 1792, in Clark, "Unpublished Letters," 95–100; CBB to WWW, 31 December 1792 (Bennett #37), in Clark, "Unpublished Letters," 101–3.

39. CBB to JBJr, 7 May 1792 (Bennett #13), 9 June 1792 (Bennett #26), 1 June 1792 (Bennett #24), and n.d. (Bennett #29), Bowdoin CBB Papers.

40. JBJr, "Life of William Wood Wilkins," 17, 32, 19.

41. JBJr, "Life of William Wood Wilkins," 24, 34–35, 29; WWW to CBB, 27 November 1792.

42. Hemenway, "Brown's Law Study," 202 n. 13; CBB to WWW, 3 November 1792 (Bennett #31), in Clark, "Unpublished Letters," 93–95.

43. CBB to WWW, n.d. (Bennett #7), in P. Allen, *Life of Charles Brockden Brown,* 57–60; CBB, *Alcuin: A Dialogue; Memoirs of Stephen Calvert* (Kent, Ohio: Kent State University Press, 1987), 192; CBB to JBJr, 20 March 1792 (Bennett #5); P. Allen, *Life of Charles Brockden Brown,* 40.

44. CBB to JBJr, 20 December 1793–8 January 1794 (Bennett #50), Bowdoin CBB Papers; CBB to WWW, 3 November 1792 (Bennett #31); CBB to WWW, November 1792 (Bennett #33), in P. Allen, *Life of Charles Brockden Brown,* 61–67.

45. WWW to CBB, 27 November 1792. See similar allusions to Brown's slow progress in WWW to CBB, 24 October 1792, and WWW to CBB, 4 November 1792, in Clark, "Unpublished Letters," 92, 95.

46. JBJr, "Life of William Wood Wilkins," 34; CBB to JBJr, 20 December 1793–8 January 1794 (Bennett #50).

47. CBB to JBJr, n.d. (Bennett #25), Bowdoin CBB Papers.

48. Donaldson, "Cato in Tears," 379.

49. CBB to JBJr, 20 May 1792 (Bennett #21); WWW to CBB, 1 May 1792; CBB to JBJr, 9 June 1792 (Bennett #26); CBB to JBJr, 10 June 1792 (Bennett #27), Bowdoin CBB Papers.

50. CBB to WWW, n.d. (Bennett #28), in P. Allen, *Life of Charles Brockden Brown,* 50–55.

51. P. Allen, *Life of Charles Brockden Brown,* 43; CBB to WWW, n.d. (Bennett #28); CBB to James Brown, 14 April 1795 (Bennett #56), Virginia CBB Papers.

52. CBB to JBJr, 5 May 1792 (Bennett #12).

53. CBB to JBJr, December 1792 (Bennett #34); Cope, *Philadelphia Merchant,* 248; CBB to JBJr, 9 December 1792 (Bennett #35) and 21 December 1792 (Bennett #36, 44,

and 46), Bowdoin CBB Papers. For more on Brown's vocational anxiety, see Robert A. Ferguson, *Law and Letters in American Culture* (Cambridge: Harvard University Press, 1984), 129–34.

54. Phyllis Greenacre, *Emotional Growth: Psychoanalytic Studies of the Gifted and a Great Variety of Other Individuals* (New York: International Universities Press, 1971), 1:93; Helene Deutsch, *Neuroses and Character Types: Clinical Psychoanalytic Studies* (New York: International Universities Press, 1965), 337; Lucy LaFarge, "Transferences of Deception," *Journal of the American Psychoanalytic Association* 43, no. 3 (1995): 766.

55. Thomas Pim Cope, "Notes Taken on a Journey to Soho and N York, 1800," Quaker Collection, Haverford College, 25.

56. LaFarge, "Transferences," 766.

57. CBB to WWW, n.d. (Bennett #4); CBB to JBJr, 20 May 1792 (Bennett #21).

58. Greenacre, *Emotional Growth*, 2:542.

59. John Bernard, *Retrospections of America, 1797–1811* (1887; reprint, New York: Benjamin Blom, 1969), 252–53.

60. CBB to WWW, n.d. (Bennett #32), Virginia CBB Papers; CBB to JBJr, 9 December 1792 (Bennett #35); CBB to JBJr, 21 December 1792 (Bennett #36, 44, and 46).

61. CBB to WWW, 22 January 1793 (Bennett #39), Ransom Center; CBB to JBJr, 9 December 1792 (Bennett #35).

62. EHS, *Diary*, 37.

63. Robert A. Ferguson, "Yellow Fever and Charles Brockden Brown: The Context of the Emerging Novelist," *Early American Literature* 14 (1979–80): 296–97; WD, *Life of Charles Brockden Brown*, 1:56.

64. James E. Cronin, "Elihu Hubbard Smith and the New York Friendly Club, 1795–1798," *PMLA* 64 (June 1949): 471–79; Harry R. Warfel, *Charles Brockden Brown: American Gothic Novelist* (Gainesville: University of Florida Press, 1949), 40.

65. EHS, *Diary*, 209, 305.

66. CBB to JBJr, 22 April 1793 (Bennett #40).

67. CBB to JBJr, n.d. (Bennett #42).

68. CBB to JBJr, 22 May 1793 (Bennett #43), 11 June 1793 (Bennett #44 and 46), and July 1793 (Bennett #45), Bowdoin CBB Papers.

69. CBB to JBJr, July 1793 (Bennett #45).

70. CBB to JBJr, 22 May 1793 (Bennett #43).

71. CBB to JBJr, 25 July 1793 (Bennett #47), Bowdoin CBB Papers.

72. CBB to JBJr, 25 July 1793 (Bennett #47) and 29 July 1793 (Bennett #48), Bowdoin CBB Papers.

73. CBB to JBJr, 16 August 1793 (Bennett #49), Bowdoin CBB Papers; Cope, *Philadelphia Merchant*, 248; CBB to James Brown, 14 April 1795 (Bennett #56); CBB to JBJr, 25 July 1793 (Bennett #47).

74. Clark, *Charles Brockden Brown*, 109; William Godwin, *Enquiry Concerning Political Justice and Its Influence on Modern Morals and Happiness* (New York: Penguin, 1985), 529, 248.

75. Godwin, *Political Justice*, 218; CBB to Susan Godolphin, 2 July 1793, HSP.

76. Godwin, *Political Justice*, 317, 312; CBB to William C., 29–31 August 1793, Ransom Center.

77. Steven Watts, *The Romance of Real Life: Charles Brockden Brown and the Origins of American Culture* (Baltimore: Johns Hopkins University Press, 1994), 57.

78. Godwin, *Political Justice*, 222.

79. Cope, *Philadelphia Merchant*, 192.

80. Godwin, *Political Justice* 316, 311. Godwin seems to have been counting on the pleasure of true confession outweighing the pleasure of crime. As a utopian, he was too hopeful about human nature to imagine that the two pleasures could be reconciled and combined or that a confession of crime to the right media outlet would one day turn a profit as well as be fun.

81. Godwin, *Political Justice*, 556.

82. *Leander* 1:193, 208, 219, 231.

83. John Woolman, *The Journal of John Woolman* (New York: Corinth Books, 1961), 23; Godwin, *Political Justice*, 314; Woolman, *Journal*, 151.

84. EHS, *Diary*, 258.

85. EHS, *Diary*, 261, 330, 46, 69–70, 143; Cope, *Philadelphia* 248; William Godwin to WD, n.d., Dreer Collection of English Prose Writers, HSP.

86. Cope, *Philadelphia Merchant*, 248.

87. EHS, *Diary*, 164.

88. EHS, *Diary*, 171. Smith "never sent the letter which I wrote, on the 27th of May, to Charles B. Brown. To-day I composed a new one — in which part of the former was incorporated" (EHS, *Diary*, 184). The revised letter does not survive; these quotations come from the 27 May 1796 first draft. The wording Brown actually saw may have been less brusque.

89. EHS, *Diary*, 171, 163, 164, 171.

90. WD, *Life of Charles Brockden Brown*, 2:12.

91. Fiedler, *Love and Death*, 148; WD, *Life of Charles Brockden Brown*, 2:47; Ferguson, *Law and Letters*.

92. See Peter Kafer, "Charles Brockden Brown and Revolutionary Philadelphia: An Imagination in Context," *Pennsylvania Magazine of History and Biography* 116 (1992): 487 n. 42. Kafer notes that *pace* most of the criticism, "the yellow fever epidemic broke out *after* Brown began his writing binge."

93. Smith received the first two parts of *Alcuin* in the mail on 7 August 1797 (EHS, *Diary*, 342). Smith read the rest of *Alcuin* and "Sky-Walk" on 17–19 April 1798 (EHS, *Diary*, 438). Dunlap listened to Brown read from the beginning of *Wieland* on 12 April 1798 (William Dunlap, *Diary of W⸺m Dunlap (1766–1839): The Memoirs of a Dramatist, Theatrical Manager, Painter, Critic, Novelist, and Historian* [New York: New-York Historical Society, 1930], 1:242), and Smith recorded that he read the end of it on 5 August 1798 (EHS, *Diary*, 459). "A Series of Original Letters" appeared in the *Weekly Magazine* of 21 April–2 June 1798 (CBB, *Rhapsodist*, x). The final installment of *The Man at Home* was published on 28 April 1798 (CBB, *Arthur Mervyn*, 451; see also CBB, *Rhapsodist*). Norman S. Grabo believes Brown had written at least twelve chapters of *Arthur Mervyn* before the yellow fever plague hit New York in August 1798 and forced the suspension of its serial publication (CBB, *Arthur Mervyn*, 453). On 8 August 1798, Smith recorded reading "Brown's 'Carwin,' as far as he has written it" (EHS, *Diary*, 460). On 4 September 1798, Smith read more of Carwin and the "new-begun 'Stephen Cal-

vert'" (EHS, *Diary,* 463). Smith died of yellow fever on 19 September 1798 (EHS, *Diary,* 464; WD, *Diary,* 1:340).

94. *Ormond* was published in January 1799 (CBB, *Ormond; or, The Secret Witness* [Kent, Ohio: Kent State University Press, 1982], 307). *Arthur Mervyn, First Part* was published between March and May 1799 (CBB, *Arthur Mervyn,* 457). A fragment of *Edgar Huntly* appeared in the *Monthly Magazine* in May 1799; the book was published in August 1799 (CBB, *Edgar Huntly; or, Memoirs of a Sleep-Walker* [Kent, Ohio: Kent State University Press, 1984], 299, 301).

95. Brown met Elizabeth Linn in March 1800 (CBB to EL, 23 March 1801 [Bennett #131], Ransom Center). *Arthur Mervyn, Second Part* was published in September 1800 (CBB, *Arthur Mervyn,* 460). *Clara Howard* was published in June 1801 (CBB, *Clara Howard in a Series of Letters and Jane Talbot: A Novel* [Kent, Ohio: Kent State University Press, 1986], 442). *Jane Talbot* was published in December 1801 (CBB, *Clara Howard and Jane Talbot,* 449).

96. EHS, *Diary,* 163; CBB to JBJr, 11 May 1796 (Bennett #73), Bowdoin CBB Papers; Godwin, *Political Justice,* 313, 321.

97. EHS, *Diary,* 186.

98. EHS, *Diary,* 186.

99. CBB to JBJr, 7 May 1792 (Bennett #13); Clark, *Charles Brockden Brown,* 58; CBB to JBJr, 21 April 1793[?] (Bennett #41), Bowdoin CBB Papers.

100. Godwin, *Political Justice,* 493–505; CBB to JBJr, 24 October 1795 (Bennett #62 and #63) and 20 July 1796 (Bennett #77), Bowdoin CBB Papers; EHS, *Diary,* 164.

101. CBB to William C., 29–31 August 1793.

102. CBB to William C., 29–31 August 1793.

103. CBB to William C., 29–31 August 1793; J. H. Powell, *Bring Out Your Dead: The Great Plague of Yellow Fever in Philadelphia in 1793* (Philadelphia: University of Pennsylvania Press, 1993), 63.

104. EHS, *Diary,* 272; CBB to WD, September 1795 (Bennett #59), qtd. in WD, "Charles Brockden Brown."

105. EHS, *Diary,* 61, 290; CBB, *Arthur Mervyn,* 450.

106. EHS, *Diary,* 74, 417; WD, *Life of Charles Brockden Brown,* 1:56.

107. EHS, *Diary,* 199.

### Chapter 3. The Transformation, the Self Devoted, and the Dead Recalled: Sympathy in Brown's Fiction

1. Dunlap, *Life of Charles Brockden Brown,* 1:107; EHS, *Diary,* 364, 395.

2. Dunlap, *Life of Charles Brockden Brown,* 1:107. It is not clear which novel Brown finished on 31 December 1797. In his biography of Brown, William Dunlap presented a story fragment, "Jessica," as an excerpt of this lost first novel (Dunlap, *Life of Charles Brockden Brown,* 1:108). The twentieth-century biographer David Lee Clark believed that Dunlap was mistaken and that the first novel Brown finished was the first novel he showed to his friends, "Sky Walk," also lost (Clark, *Charles Brockden Brown,* 159). Most modern critics have agreed with Clark. However, the earliest mention of "Sky Walk" by name was on 17 March 1798, when a prospectus for it appeared in the *Weekly*

*Magazine* (CBB, *Rhapsodist*). Between 31 December 1797 and 17 March 1798 there would have been enough time for Brown to launch a new novel; it is possible, then, that Dunlap was correct in representing "Jessica" as Brown's first complete romance.

3. EHS, *Diary,* 208, 300; CBB to WD, 1 January 1798 (Bennett #90), Dreer Collection, HSP.

4. WD, *Diary,* 1:133; CBB to WD, 1 January 1798 (Bennett #90).

5. CBB to WD, 1 January 1798; EHS, *Diary,* 163.

6. WD, *Life of Charles Brockden Brown,* 1:56–57; EHS, *Diary,* 231, 233, 238, 272, 289, 290, 297, 336.

7. CBB to WD, 1 January 1798; WD, *Diary,* 1:201.

8. Warfel, *Charles Brockden Brown,* 44; Lewis Leary, "John Blair Linn, 1777–1805," *William and Mary Quarterly,* third series, 4 (1947): 148–76; EHS, *Diary* 417; WD, *Diary,* 1:236.

9. Sigmund Freud, *The Ego and the Id* (New York: Norton, 1989), 30.

10. Brown probably knew Shakespeare's play. It was staged in Philadelphia in 1787 under the title *Filial Piety,* and in 1788, Brown's future friend and roommate Dunlap painted a self-portrait, *The Artist Showing a Picture from "Hamlet" to His Parents,* that contained a visual quote from it (Fliegelman, *Prodigals and Pilgrims,* 220–21). In *Wieland,* Brown quotes *Macbeth* directly (203) and structures scenes that closely resemble Othello's strangling of Desdemona and Macduff's reaction to the news of his wife's and children's deaths. Alexander Cowie, "Historical Essay" in CBB, *Wieland; or, The Transformation; An American Tale; and Memoirs of Carwin, the Biloquist* (Kent, Ohio: Kent State University Press, 1977), 316 n. 11.

11. In this section, page numbers in parentheses refer to CBB, *Wieland.*

12. Stephen Burroughs, *Memoirs of Stephen Burroughs* (Boston: Northeastern University Press, 1988), 367; Greenacre, *Emotional Growth,* 1:104.

13. Sigmund Freud, *Group Psychology and the Analysis of the Ego* (New York: Norton, 1989), 48.

14. EHS, *Diary,* 336; WD, *Life of Charles Brockden Brown,* 2:123.

15. Warfel, *Charles Brockden Brown,* 21; Benjamin Franklin, *Writings* (New York: Library of America, 1987), 1340; Elijah Brown, Commonplace Books, Brown Papers (Am 03398), HSP, vols. 7 and 9.

16. Kafer, "Browns," 8–14.

17. Cf. Jay Fliegelman, "Introduction," in *Wieland and Memoirs of Carwin the Biloquist* (New York: Penguin, 1991), xxiv.

18. Brown might have found a model for the contrast between Carwin's clothes and his sensibility when he and Dunlap visited William Bartram in his garden on 9 May 1797. Bartram's "hat was old and flapped over his face, his coarse shirt was seen near his neck, as he wore no cravat or kerchief; his waistcoat and breeches were both of leather, and his shoes were tied with leather strings." At first Brown and Dunlap did not realize that "this was the botanist, traveller, and philosopher we had come to see." WD, *Diary,* qtd. in William Bartram, *Travels and Other Writings* (New York: Library of America, 1996), 604.

19. A. Smith, *Theory of Moral Sentiments,* 1.

20. A. Smith, *Theory of Moral Sentiments,* 10.

21. Isaiah 53:3.

22. Cf. Nina Baym, "A Minority Reading of *Wieland*," in *Critical Essays on Charles Brockden Brown,* ed. Bernard Rosenthal (Boston: G. K. Hall, 1981), 102 n. 7; Cowie, "Historical Essay," 323.

23. Fliegelman, "Introduction," xxix.

24. There was a precedent for this kind of demise in the family history. Clara's maternal grandfather had followed off a cliff voices that only he could hear (179). Horatio feared that Hamlet would meet the same end if he followed his father's ghost: "What if it tempt you toward the flood, my lord, / Or to the dreadful summit of the cliff / . . . And draw you into madness?" (1.4.69–74).

25. A. Smith, *Theory of Moral Sentiments,* 9, 12.

26. WD, *Diary,* 1:319; WD, *Life of Charles Brockden Brown,* 1:56; EHS, *Diary,* 457.

27. Cope, *Philadelphia Merchant,* 79; CBB, Notebook, Brown Papers (Am. 03399), HSP, vol. 14.

28. EHS, *Diary,* 290; CBB to James Brown, 25 October 1796 (Bennett #81), Rush Papers, Library Company of Philadelphia; Ferguson, "Yellow Fever and Charles Brockden Brown," 299.

29. WD, *Diary,* 1:335. Medical opinion about yellow fever was split, and Smith and Rush shared the same controversial opinion. Both men were climatists rather than contagionists — that is, they believed that the yellow fever was caused by local conditions of the air rather than spread through direct contact with infected individuals. No one at the time suspected the role of the mosquito, but a document such as Smith's 9 September 1796 letter to Rush, where he explains how the diversion of a stream to eliminate marshland succeeded in reducing infection, suggests that climatists were paying close attention to the evidence (EHS, *Diary,* 214–18). Less fortuitously, Smith and Rush also shared a belief in what Smith called the "depleting system," Rush favoring cathartics, Smith favoring induced salivation. EHS to Benjamin Rush, 19 November 1795, Rush Papers, Library Company of Philadelphia; EHS, *Diary,* 464 n. 62; Powell, *Bring Out Your Dead,* 14 ff.

30. WD, *Life of Charles Brockden Brown,* 2:3–4; EHS, *Diary,* 462; CBB to James Brown, 4 September 1798 (Bennett #103), qtd. in WD, *Life of Charles Brockden Brown,* 2:4–5.

31. EHS, *Diary,* 420, 464; CBB to James Brown, 16 September 1798 (Bennett #107), qtd. in WD, *Life of Charles Brockden Brown,* 2:7–8; EHS to Benjamin Rush, 13 September 1798, Rush Papers, Library Company of Philadelphia.

32. WD, *Life of Charles Brockden Brown,* 2:5–6; EHS, *Diary,* 464; WD, *Diary,* 1:341; CBB to James Brown, 16 September 1798 (Bennett #107), qtd. in WD, *Life,* 2:7–8.

33. WD, *Diary,* 1:340; WD, *Life,* 2:8; CBB to James Brown, 18–20 September 1798 (Bennett #109), qtd. in WD, *Life,* 2:9–10.

34. WD, *Diary,* 1:340.

35. WD, *Life,* 2:10; WD, *Diary,* 1:336, 343.

36. In this section, page numbers in parentheses refer to CBB, *Arthur Mervyn.*

37. WD, *Life of Charles Brockden Brown,* 2:29, 40; Elizabeth Drinker, *The Diary of Elizabeth Drinker,* ed. Elaine Forman Crane (Boston: Northeastern University Press, 1991), 2:1256. Although it diminishes my punchline, I ought to admit that Drinker made her comment after reading only the first of *Arthur Mervyn*'s two parts.

38. Sigmund Freud, "Fragment of an Analysis of a Case of Hysteria," in Freud, *Collected Papers* (New York: Basic Books, 1960), 3:24.

39. Francis Hutcheson, *A System of Moral Philosophy* (New York: Georg Olms, 1990), 1:9; A. Ferguson qtd. in Fliegelman, *Prodigals and Pilgrims*, 104; A. Smith, *Theory of Moral Sentiments*, 317, qtd. in Fiering, "Irresistible Compassion," 211.

40. Benjamin Rush, *Letters of Benjamin Rush*, ed. L. H. Butterfield (Princeton: American Philosophical Society, 1951), 2:641, 655, 667; cf. 2:664, 669.

41. Hutcheson, *System*, 1:20.

42. Mathew Carey, *A Short Account of the Malignant Fever, Lately Prevalent in Philadelphia: With a Statement of the Proceedings That Took Place on the Subject, in Different Parts of the United States. To Which Are Added, Accounts of the Plague in London and Marseilles; and a List of the Dead, from August 1, to the Middle of December, 1793*, 4th ed. (Philadelphia: Carey, 1794), 21–22; Susanna Dillwyn to William Dillwyn, 9 September 1793, Dillwyn Manuscripts, Library Company of Philadelphia; John Welsh to Robert Ralston, 13 September 1793, Society Miscellaneous Collection, HSP; Rush qtd. in William Bradford to Rachel Bradford, 17 September 1793, Wallace Papers, HSP.

43. Joseph Price, 1 September 1793, Diary, HSP; Drinker, *Diary*, 1:514, 500; Caspar Wistar Haines to Hannah Haines, 1793, Wyck Papers, American Philosophical Society (10:22, Ms. Coll. No. 52).

44. Not only was such risky benevolence rarely volunteered; it was actively discouraged. In an anecdote recorded by Brown's friend Thomas P. Cope, a police officer intervened to prevent an uninfected citizen from assisting a "well dressed, genteel looking man" whose illness had caused him to stagger and fall in the street. The policeman "forbid, in a peremtory manner, their being together, threatening the healty person, with all the rigours of the law, if he dared to touch the other, & did not instantly depart, reminding him of the hazard he exposed himself & his fellow citizens to, by thus running into danger." Thomas Pym Cope, "A brief acct of the Yellow Fever that prevailed in Philada. in 1793, communicated in a Letter to Joshua & Joseph Pim," Thomas P. Cope Collection, Miscellaneous Documents, Uncatalogued, HSP.

45. Godwin, *Political Justice*, 169–70.

46. CBB to James Brown, 4 September 1798 (Bennett #103); Carey, *Short Account of the Malignant Fever*, 72; EHS to Benjamin Rush, 10 September 1798, Rush Papers, Library Company of Philadelphia.

47. William Cobbett, *Peter Porcupine in America: Pamphlets on Republicanism and Revolution*, ed. David A. Wilson (Ithaca: Cornell University Press, 1994), 229; Rush, *Letters*, 2:1214, 1215.

48. Cobbett, *Peter Porcupine*, 113, 198.

49. CBB, *Arthur Mervyn*, 426.

50. In this section, page numbers in parentheses refer to CBB, *Alcuin: A Dialogue; Memoirs of Stephen Calvert* (Kent, Ohio: Kent State University Press, 1987).

51. WD, *Life of Charles Brockden Brown*, 2:11, 12; CBB to Armit Brown, 20 December 1798 (Bennett #114), qtd. in WD, *Life of Charles Brockden Brown*, 2:93–94; Warfel, *Charles Brockden Brown*, 169; Ferguson, *Law and Literature*, 143.

52. CBB, *Literary Essays and Reviews*, ed. Alfred Weber, Wolfgang Schäfer, and

John R. Holmes (New York: Peter Lang, 1992), 116; CBB to Armit Brown, 1 January 1799 (Bennett #116), qtd. in WD, *Life of Charles Brockden Brown,* 2:94–95.

53. Sydney J. Krause, "Historical Essay," in CBB, *Edgar Huntly; or, Memoirs of a Sleep-Walker* (Kent, Ohio: Kent State University Press, 1984), 303–6; WD, *Life of Charles Brockden Brown,* 1:259; CBB to James Brown, April 1800 (Bennett #120), qtd. in WD, *Life of Charles Brockden Brown,* 2:99–100; CBB to James, 26 July 1799 (Bennett #118), qtd. in WD, *Life of Charles Brockden Brown,* 2:95–97.

54. Cicero, "Laelius: On Friendship," trans. Michael Grant, in *Cicero on the Good Life* (New York: Penguin, 1971), 180, 181.

55. A. Smith, *Theory of Moral Sentiments,* 71, 12.

56. Sigmund Freud, "Mourning and Melancholia," in *Collected Papers* (New York: Basic Books, 1960), 4:154.

57. Cicero, "Laelius: On Friendship," 226.

58. In this section, page numbers in parentheses refer to CBB, *Edgar Huntly.*

59. CBB to Samuel Miller, 20 June 1803 (Bennett #171), Manuscripts Division, Department of Rare Books and Special Collections, Princeton University Library; EHS, *Diary,* 119, 213, 251; CBB, *Clara Howard in a Series of Letters; Jane Talbot: A Novel* (Kent, Ohio: Kent State University Press, 1986), 227; CBB, *Literary Essays and Reviews,* 126, 128.

60. CBB, "Somnambulism, a Fragment," in *Somnambulism and Other Stories,* ed. Alfred Weber (New York: Peter Lang, 1987), 5–24; Krause, "Historical Essay," 303–17.

61. This denouement may have come from an anecdote Bartram related in his *Travels,* of a mistreated Indian who vowed "he would kill the first white man he met," but relented when that man turned out to be the harmless Bartram. Bartram, *Travels,* 43–44.

62. W. H. Auden, "In Praise of Limestone," in *Selected Poems,* new ed., ed. Edward Mendelson (New York: Vintage, 1989), 184–87.

63. It resembles the scrub forest outside town where R. H. Dana Sr.'s Paul Felton befriends the mad, starving boy Abel, whom Felton later blames for corrupting his mind to murder. Richard Henry Dana Sr., "Paul Felton," in *Poems and Prose Writings* (Philadelphia: Marshall, Clark, 1833), 271–377.

64. Melanie Klein, "Mourning and Manic-Depressive States," in *The Selected Melanie Klein* (New York: Free Press, 1986), 148.

65. Klein, "Mourning," 162, 158.

66. Cicero, "Laelius: On Friendship," 226–27.

67. CBB to James Brown, April 2000 (Bennett #120); CBB to EL, n.d. (Bennett #149), n.d. (Bennett #155), and 17–18 March 1801 (Bennett #129 and 130), Ransom Center; John R. Holmes, Edwin J. Saeger, and Alfred Weber, Annotation of CBB to EL, 17–18 March 1801 (Bennett #129 and 130); Clark, *Charles Brockden Brown,* 319–29; Christopher Looby, *Voicing America: Language, Literary Form, and the Origins of the United States* (Chicago: University of Chicago Press, 1996), 193–202; Charles C. Cole Jr., "Brockden Brown and the Jefferson Administration" *Pennsylvania Magazine of History and Biography* 72 (1948): 253–63; CBB, *Literary Essays and Reviews,* 62. Consider Brown's praise of how Fuseli painted the ghost of Hamlet's father: "the picture of a man *flead alive,* and who continues alive notwithstanding the loss of his cutaneous vesture" (CBB, *Literary Essays and Reviews,* 112).

68. CBB, *Literary Essays and Reviews,* 130, 131. There is a similar knowing disapproval in Brown's review of the poetry of Hafiz, in the hands of whose translators "the 'angel-faced cup-bearer' and 'infidel boy' are converted into damsels and nymphs of paradise" (150).

69. S. W. Reid, "Textual Essay," in CBB, *Edgar Huntly,* 401–49; CBB, *Somnambulism and Other Stories,* 257–58.

70. CBB, *Rhapsodist,* 151, 149.

71. In this section, page numbers in parentheses refer to CBB, "The Death of Cicero," in *Sonnambulism and Other Stories,* 117–33.

72. Plutarch, *Lives,* trans. Bernadotte Perrin (Cambridge: Harvard University Press, 1971), 7:205; Elder Seneca, *Declamations,* trans. M. Winterbottom (Cambridge: Harvard University Press, 1974), 2:579, 575.

73. Plutarch, *Lives,* 7:207.

74. Paine, *Collected Writings,* 50, 124; Cicero, "Laelius: On Friendship," 187.

## Chapter 4. The Unacknowledged Tie: Young Emerson and the Love of Men

1. Alexis de Tocqueville, *Democracy in America,* trans. Henry Reeve, Francis Bowen, and Phillips Bradley (New York: Vintage, 1990), 2:4; *E&L* 32, 694.

2. Tocqueville, *Democracy,* 2:99, 324, 165.

3. Tocqueville, *Democracy,* 2:99.

4. Tocqueville, *Democracy,* 2:56, 111.

5. Tocqueville, *Democracy,* 2:59, 111.

6. Tocqueville, *Democracy,* 2:60, 73.

7. "Plato," *E&L* 641; *E&L* 119; RWE to A. D. Woodbridge, 6 July 1841, *RWEL* 2:414–15.

8. RWE to MME, 18 October 1842, *RWEL* 7:513; RWE to SMF, 18 & 19 October 1843, *RWEL* 3:215.

9. *E&L* 58; James Creech, *Closet Writing / Gay Reading: The Case of Melville's Pierre* (Chicago: University of Chicago Press, 1993), 51; *E&L* 97.

10. Jan Mukařovský, "Standard Language and Poetic Language" in *The Critical Tradition: Classic Texts and Contemporary Trends,* ed. David H. Richter (New York: St. Martin's, 1989), 861.

11. Creech phrased thus the puzzle this rule poses to gay-inflected criticism: "At a time [the mid-twentieth century] when homophobia was as unquestioned a touchstone of American culture as virtually any other defining feature, it is a literary-historical problem of significant proportions to discern precisely how *Billy Budd* or *Moby-Dick,* like *Leaves of Grass,* could have become staples of high school and college English courses" (Creech, *Closet Writing / Gay Reading,* 78). Or, as Leslie Fiedler asked, a generation earlier, "How could Antinoüs come to preside over the literature of the nineteenth century United States, which is to say, at a time and in a place where homosexuality was regarded with a horror perhaps unmatched elsewhere and ever?" (Fiedler, *Love and Death,* 350).

12. *E&L* 240.

13. *JMN* 1:55. All quotes from Emerson's journal given here are reading texts. For the *literatim* genetic texts, with full details about erasures and insertions, see *JMN*.

14. *JMN* 1:133 n. 34.

15. *JMN* 1:130.

16. *JMN* 1:22.

17. *JMN* 1:22 n. 41.

18. *JMN* 1:17. The journal editors supply the Loeb translation of the lines from Virgil.

19. *JMN* 1:39.

20. *JMN* 1:39–40.

21. Henry Adams, *Novels, Mont Saint Michel, The Education,* ed. Ernest Samuels and Jayne N. Samuels (New York: Library of America, 1983), 772; *EIHJ* 170.

22. *E&L* 971, 497; *JMN* 7:439; "Culture," *E&L* 1016; *EIHJ* 186.

23. *JMN* 3:25.

24. *JMN* 3:25.

25. A. Smith, *Theory of Moral Sentiments,* 114.

26. *JMN* 1:52–53.

27. *JMN* 1:52–53; *EIHJ* 40; "Circles," *E&L* 406.

28. *JMN* 1:54; 2:59.

29. Gay Wilson Allen, *Waldo Emerson: A Biography* (New York: Viking, 1981), 4. Children were educated sooner in those days. Margaret Fuller was taught to read and write at age three and a half. Thomas Wentworth Higginson received a birthday note from a friend that read, "I am glad you are six years old. I shall be four in March" (qtd. in Joan von Mehren, *Minerva and the Muse: A Life of Margaret Fuller* [Amherst: University of Massachusetts Press, 1994], 12–13). The Reverend Emerson was more demanding than the parents of Fuller and of Higginson's friend, but only by an interval of six months to a year.

30. Robert D. Richardson Jr., *Emerson: The Mind on Fire* (Berkeley: University of California Press, 1995), 35–36; RWE to William Emerson, 3 July 1828, *RWEL* 7:172; *EIHJ* 158; RWE to William Emerson, 10 February 1850, *RWEL* 4:179.

31. *EIHJ* 67; Henry James qtd. in David Leverenz, *Manhood and the American Renaissance* (Ithaca: Cornell University Press, 1989), 46.

32. Julie Ellison, "The Gender of Transparency: Masculinity and the Conduct of Life," *American Literary History* 4:597; RWE, *Collected Poems and Translations,* ed. Harold Bloom and Paul Kane (New York: Library of America, 1994), 89.

33. *JMN* 2:59.

34. *E&L* 458; Plato, *Complete Works,* ed. John M. Cooper (Indianapolis: Hackett, 1997), 518.

35. Plato, *Works,* 528, 530.

36. RWE to Lidian Jackson, 24 January 1835, *RWEL* 7:232–33; *JMN* 2:59.

37. *JMN* 1:94–95, 99.

38. *JMN* 1:292.

39. Michel de Montaigne, *Complete Works,* trans. Donald M. Frame (Stanford: Stanford University Press, 1958), 137.

40. *JMN* 1:321–22.

41. *Aeneid* 5.742–43, qtd. in *JMN* 1:321 n. 82.

42. *E&L* 507; RWE, *Collected Poems,* 243.

43. *E&L* 341; "Behavior," *E&L* 1042; RWE, *Collected Poems,* 75; *EIHJ* 264.

44. RWE, *Collected Poems,* 7.

45. RWE, *Collected Poems,* 66.

46. *E&L* 334.

47. RWE to William Emerson, 10 February 1850, *RWEL* 4:179; RWE, *Collected Poems,* 346.

48. *E&L* 1042.

49. Erik Ingvar Thurin, *Emerson as Priest of Pan: A Study in the Metaphysics of Sex* (Lawrence: Regents Press of Kansas, 1981), 53; Joel Porte, *Representative Man: Ralph Waldo Emerson in His Time* (New York: Columbia University Press, 1988), 182; *E&L* 1094; Richardson, *Emerson,* 34.

50. *JMN* 2:203–4.

51. *JMN* 2:227–28.

52. *JMN* 2:240–41.

53. *JMN* 1:134.

54. *EIHJ* 240.

55. RWE to Lidian Jackson, 8 and 10 March 1848, *RWEL* 4:33; RWE to Charles C. Emerson, 1 January 1828, *RWEL* 1:225; RWE to MME, 18 April & 17? May 1833, *RWEL* 1:376; RWE to Thomas Carlyle, 20 November 1834, *The Correspondence of Emerson and Carlyle,* ed. Joseph Slater (New York: Columbia University Press, 1964), 106.

56. *E&L* 447, 397.

57. RWE to Charles C. Emerson, 15 July 1828, *RWEL* 1:239; *EIHJ* 166, 235, 321; *JMN* 3:272. Emerson bowdlerized this metaphor when he used it in a sermon on friendship: "Thus it happens that the best part of our nature is not known or shared. Yet were these thoughts made for communication as much as light for the eye or air for the lungs." RWE, *The Complete Sermons of Ralph Waldo Emerson,* ed. Albert J. von Frank, Teresa Toulouse, Andrew Delbanco, Ronald A. Bosco, and Wesley T. Mott (Columbia: University of Missouri Press, 1989–1992), 4:52.

58. *E&L* 48.

59. RWE, *Collected Poems,* 312, 318, 605, 373–74.

60. Porte, *Representative Man,* 209; *JMN* 1:96.

61. RWE, *Collected Poems,* 11; *E&L* 458; Thurin, *Emerson as Priest of Pan,* 59; *JMN* 8:316; *E&L* 116, 119.

### Chapter 5. Too Good to Be Believed: Emerson's "Friendship" and the Samaritans

1. RWE to SMF, 23 December 1839, *RWEL* 2:245.

2. *JMN* 8:34. "One to one, married & chained through the eternity of Ages, is frightful beyond the binding of dead & living together" (*JMN* 7:532).

3. *JMN* 8:95.

4. Ellen Tucker Emerson, *The Life of Lidian Jackson Emerson,* ed. Delores Bird Carpenter (Boston: Twayne, 1980), 48; *SMFJ* 1842–2:331–32; *SMFJ* 1844:109. Cf. *RWEL* 2:117; and Lidian's "Transcendental Bible," in E. T. Emerson, *Lidian Jackson Emerson,* 81–83.

5. RWE to Lidian Jackson, 24 January 1835, *RWEL* 7:232; Aristotle, *Nicomachean Ethics,* 219.

6. *EIHJ* 235.

7. Plato, *Works,* 691.

8. RWE to William Emerson, 5 February 1835, *RWEL* 1:436.

9. *SMFL* 1:269; *EIHJ* 160; RWE to MME, 12 May 1836, *RWEL* 7:259.

10. Lidian Jackson Emerson to Elizabeth Peabody, July 1836, *The Selected Letters of Lidian Jackson Emerson,* ed. Delores Bird Carpenter (Columbia: University of Missouri Press, 1987), 49. It is intriguing that when Sarah Clarke first met Lydia Jackson in February 1835, she thought that the independent mind and fine sensibility of Emerson's fiancée reminded her of no one so much as Margaret Fuller (E. T. Emerson, *Lidian Jackson Emerson,* 49).

11. *Memoirs of Margaret Fuller Ossoli,* ed. William Henry Channing, James Freeman Clarke, and Ralph Waldo Emerson (Boston: Phillips, Sampson, 1852), 1:202; *E&L* 1109.

12. *Memoirs of Margaret Fuller Ossoli,* 1:214; *JMN* 11:258, qtd. in *SMFL* 1:60.

13. *Memoirs of Margaret Fuller Ossoli,* 1:213; RWE to SMF, 20 September 1836, *RWEL* 2:35–37.

14. Richardson, *Emerson,* 329.

15. *Memoirs of Margaret Fuller Ossoli,* 1:281; *SMFL* 2:91, 41; *SMFJ* 1842–1:333; *Memoirs of Margaret Fuller Ossoli,* 1:281–82.

16. *EIHJ* 161; *JMN* 7:15, 221; RWE to MME, 22 December 1839, *RWEL* 2:244; *JMN* 7:259.

17. RWE to SMF, 28 June 1838, *RWEL* 2:143.

18. RWE to Thomas Carlyle, 30 August 1840, *Correspondence of Emerson and Carlyle,* 277; RWE to Elizabeth Hoar, 12 September 1840, *RWEL* 2:330; Francis Bacon, *A Selection of His Works,* ed. Sidney Warhaft (Indianapolis: Bobbs-Merrill, 1965), 118; *Memoirs of Margaret Fuller Ossoli,* 1:205.

19. SMF to RWE, 21 September 1836, *SMFL* 1:260; SMF to RWE, 14 August 1837, *SMFL* 1:294.

20. *JMN* 6:160–62; Bacon, *Selection,* 115; Montaigne, *Works,* 140.

21. In his *Lives and Opinions,* Diogenes Laertius attributed to Aristotle the saying ō *filoi, oudeis filos* (1:465, qtd. in *SMFL* 1:296). For corroboration, Diogenes Laertius referred to a passage in the *Eudemian Ethics* where Aristotle posited that since human attention and intimacy were finite, the fewer friends one had, the truer those friends were likely to be.

If breathings, accents, and iota subscripts are garbled or not marked — and these are the sort of details that medieval scribes most often fumbled — then the text is open to two interpretations. Either the initial word may be read as the third-person-singular dative of the relative pronoun *who,* or it may be read as the vocative particle O. Montaigne chose the latter reading, a defensible mistake — perhaps a justifiable one, depending on the edition he was working with — and translated the sentence "O friends, no one is a friend." But given Diogenes Laertius's reference to the *Eudemian Ethics* and given the uniformly positive estimation of friendship in texts that are known to be Aristotle's, it is much likelier that the correct translation would be "To him who has [many] friends, no one is a friend." It is not a rare thought in ancient Greek ethics. An injunction against having too many friends is also the burden of Plutarch's essay "On Having Many Friends," in his *Moralia*.

22. RWE, *Complete Sermons*, 2:119; RWE, *Collected Poems*, 318; *E&L* 570.

23. RWE, *Complete Sermons*, 4:50–52.

24. Karen Kalinevitch, "Emerson on Friendship: An Unpublished Manuscript," *Studies in the American Renaissance, 1985,* ed. Joel Myerson (Charlottesville: University Press of Virginia, 1985), 56–57.

25. Montaigne, *Works,* 141. In *Nicomachean Ethics,* Aristotle quotes a Greek proverb that held that "[friends have] one soul" (p. 260).

26. Kalinevitch, "Emerson on Friendship," 56; RWE, *Complete Sermons,* 4:52.

27. Barbara L. Packer, "The Transcendentalists," *Cambridge History of American Literature,* ed. Sacvan Bercovitch (New York: Cambridge University Press, 1995), 2:488; *E&L* 708.

28. *E&L* 327; SMF to CS, 2 November 1837, *SMFL* 1:311; SMF to CS, 16 November 1837, *SMFL* 1:315.

29. James Russell Lowell qtd. in F. O. Matthiessen, *American Renaissance: Art and Expression in the Age of Emerson and Whitman* (New York: Oxford University Press, 1941), 4; *E&L* 237; RWE, *Collected Poems,* 344).

30. *E&L* 205; *JMN* 8:242 qtd. in Porte, *Representative Man,* 188; *E&L* 385.

31. *SMFJ* 1842–1:330; RWE to CS, 11? November 1840, *RWEL* 7:429; *E&L* 899.

32. *E&L* 635. Although when Emerson condemned the constitutional reluctance of the English to accept ideas in place of things, the Montaigne in him could make his condemnation sound like praise: the English, he wrote, "must be treated with sincerity and reality, with muffins, and not the promise of muffins" (*E&L* 893). Bully for the English.

33. *E&L* 31, 33, 41.

34. RWE, *The Early Lectures of Ralph Waldo Emerson,* ed. Stephen E. Whicher, Robert E. Spiller, and Wallace E. Williams (Cambridge: Harvard University Press, 1959–72), 2:279, 281; RWE, *Collected Poems,* 321; RWE, *Early Lectures,* 2:282, 283.

35. *EIHJ* 6; *JMN* 5:8.

36. *JMN* 5:297–98.

37. *E&L* 337; RWE, *Early Lectures,* 2:288.

38. RWE, *Early Lectures,* 2:289.

39. RWE, *Early Lectures,* 2:289; *EIHJ* 173.

40. RWE, *Early Lectures,* 2:293, 294.

41. RWE, *Early Lectures,* 2:294; *E&L* 390.

42. *E&L* 575, 488.

43. *E&L* 79.

44. RWE, *Early Lectures,* 2:279; RWE to Thomas Carlyle, 10 May 1838, in *Correspondence of Emerson and Carlyle,* 185.

45. In 1856, Channing wrote to Elizabeth Hoar, "How strange it seemed to hear W[aldo] lecturing on friendship. If he knew all the hearts he has frozen, he might better read something on the fall of human hopes" (qtd. in Kathryn B. McKee, "'A Fearful Price I Have Had to Pay for Loving Him': Ellery Channing's Troubled Relationship with Ralph

Waldo Emerson," in *Studies in the American Renaissance, 1994,* ed. Joel Myerson [Charlottesville: University Press of Virginia, 1994], 262). See also Robert Sattelmeyer, " 'When He Became My Enemy': Emerson and Thoreau, 1848–49," *New England Quarterly* 62 (1989): 187–204; Carl F. Strauch, "Hatred's Swift Repulsions: Emerson, Margaret Fuller, and Others," *Studies in Romanticism* 7 (1968): 65–103.

46. *JMN* 5:187; *EIHJ* 180; *JMN* 5:449.

47. RWE to SMF, 28 June 1838, *RWEL* 2:142–43; Bacon, *Selections,* 118; *JMN* 7:77; *E&L* 680.

48. *JMN* 7:6; "Experience," *E&L* 488. In "Spiritual Laws," Emerson did write that a teacher and student could achieve a pronoun-erasing union, but only by means of a third term — a "state or principle" that both rose into. "There is no teaching until the pupil is brought into the same state or principle in which you are; a transfusion takes place; he is you, and you are he; then is a teaching" (*E&L* 316). What makes this journal fantasy provocative is that the third term is not pedagogical purpose but shipboard reverie.

49. SMF to CS, 10 January 1839, *SMFL* 2:35; W. H. Channing, in *Memoirs of Margaret Fuller Ossoli,* 1:213; SMF to CS, 21 February 1839, *SMFL* 2:50.

50. SMF to RWE, July? 1838?, *SMFL* 1:337; RWE to SMF, 28 & 29 September 1838, *RWEL* 2:163–64; RWE to SMF, 12 October 1838, *RWEL* 2:168; *JMN* 7:106–7, 141; *E&L* 345, 391; SMF, *The Essential Margaret Fuller,* ed. Jeffrey Steele (New Brunswick: Rutgers University Press, 1992), 66.

51. Bacon, *Selections,* 112–13; Montaigne, *Works,* 137.

52. Plato, *Works,* 493; SMF to Jane Tuckerman, 21 October 1838, *SMFL* 1:347–48; *E&L* 31.

53. SMF to CS, 27 January 1839, *SMFL* 2:40.

54. *E&L* 633; SMF to CS, 27 January 1839; *E&L* 85.

55. By "Drachenfels" Fuller seems to have meant a painful, wild experience of passion. Literally, the Drachenfels were "the high cliffs where maidens were exposed to dragons in German legend." Jeffrey Steele, "Freeing the 'Prisoned Queen': The Development of Margaret Fuller's Poetry," in *Studies in the American Renaissance, 1992,* ed. Joel Myerson (Charlottesville: University Press of Virgnia, 1992), 142.

56. SMF to CS, 27 January 1839.

57. SMF, *Essential Margaret Fuller,* 11.

58. Elizabeth Bishop, *The Complete Poems, 1927–1979* (New York: Farrar, Straus and Giroux, 1994), 160.

59. *SMFJ* 1842–1:330–31.

60. Richardson, *Emerson,* 327–28; RWE to SMF, 31 July 1839, *RWEL* 2:210; *JMN* 7:204; *EIHJ* 229. Von Arnim's book was probably also responsible for Louisa May Alcott's odd novel *Moods,* where Emerson and Thoreau are cast as eligible bachelors of a certain age. Cf. Richardson, *Emerson,* 627 n. 10.

61. David Baldwin, "The Emerson-Ward Friendship: Ideals and Realities," in *Studies in the American Renaissance, 1984,* ed. Joel Myerson (Charlottesville: University Press of Virginia, 1984), 307; Charles Capper, *Margaret Fuller: An American Romantic Life,* vol. 1: *The Private Years* (New York: Oxford University Press, 1992), 279; Eleanor M. Tilton, "The True Romance of Anna Hazard Barker and Samuel Gray Ward," *Studies in the American Renaissance, 1987,* ed. Joel Myerson (Charlottesville: University Press of Vir-

ginia, 1987), 54–55; Joan von Mehren, *Minerva and the Muse: A Life of Margaret Fuller* (Amherst: University of Massachusetts Press, 1994), 35; *SMFL* 1:203; *Memoirs of Margaret Fuller Ossoli*, 2:9; J. Steele, "Freeing the 'Prisoned Queen,' " 138.

62. *SMFL* 1:232–36; SMF, *Essential Margaret Fuller, 1*.

63. SMF, *Essential Margaret Fuller*, 2, 7; *SMFJ* 1842–2:287; RWE to SMF, 18 June 1839, *RWEL* 2:205; *SMFJ* 1842–2:286, 287.

64. SGW qtd. in Baldwin, "Emerson-Ward Friendship," 305; SMF qtd. in *JMN* 11:484; SMF to SGW, 24 February 1850, *SMFL* 6:67; Baldwin, "The Emerson-Ward Friendship," 301–6. Ward also backed the *Nation* at its start (Capper, *Margaret Fuller*, 283).

65. *Memoirs of Margaret Fuller Ossoli*, 1:208–9; SMF to SGW, 20 April 1836, *SMFL* 1:249–50; SMF to CS, February 1839, *SMFL* 2:49; SMF to SGW, July 1839, *SMFL* 2:81.

66. *JMN* 7:221; *RWEL* 7:350–51; *RWEL* 2:220.

67. Walter Harding, *The Days of Henry Thoreau* (New York: Knopf, 1965), 81–82; Thoreau, *A Week*, 260–61; *JMN* 7:230–31.

68. *JMN* 7:231; *JMN* 7:244; RWE to SMF, 1 October 1839, *RWEL* 2:226.

69. SMF to SGW, September 1839, *SMFL* 2:90–91; SGW qtd. in Capper, *Margaret Fuller*, 283; *SMFL* 2:91.

70. SMF to CS, 7 October 1839, *SMFL* 2:93.

71. *RWEL* 2:76; *JMN* 7:259, 260; *E&L* 530.

72. Tilton, "True Romance," 57–65; SMF to SGW, 15 October 1839, *SMFL* 2:95–96.

73. SMF, *Essential Margaret Fuller, 5*.

74. SMF, *Essential Margaret Fuller*, 347, 301, 275, 334, 312; *E&L* 350.

75. SGW qtd. in Capper, *Margaret Fuller*, 283; *JMN* 7:273–74.

76. SMF qtd. in Capper, *Margaret Fuller*, 288–89.

77. Baldwin, "Emerson-Ward Friendship," 304–5.

78. RWE to SGW, 3 October 1839, *RWEL* 7:354–56; *JMN* 7:261.

79. Capper, *Margaret Fuller*, 246–47; *JMN* 7:46, 62; *RWEL* 7:313–14; *JMN* 7:231, 278, 314–15, 321; *RWEL* 7:360–62; *RWEL* 10:230–32. According to the evidence in Fuller's and Emerson's journals and letters, the following seem to have been among the works of art reproduced in Ward's portfolio: outlines of a Pietà, a head of Aspasia, and two Cupids in the Vatican Museum; Raphael's red chalk sketch of a sibyl, his painting of the *Expulsion of Heliodorus from the Temple* in the Vatican, his painting of *Jupiter and Cupid* in the Villa Farnesina, Rome, and his painting of *Four Sibyls* in the Church of Santa Maria della Pace, Rome; Bertel Thorvaldsen's frieze of *The Triumphant Entry of Alexander into Babylon*; Guido Reni's *Aurora*; Michelangelo's *Joel*; and a Hellenistic relief of *Endymion*, seated, from the Capitoline Museum. The *Aurora* may, however, have been the reproduction that Carlyle gave to Lidian (*Correspondence of Carlyle and Emerson*, 220 n. 1).

80. *JMN* 7:293. Tilton believes the verses in question are Thoreau's rather than Channing's, but this is one of her few missteps. Emerson did not send Thoreau's poem to Ward until 26 November 1839. Cf. *RWEL* 7:360 n. 101.

81. RWE to SGW, 27 October 1839, *RWEL* 7:357; RWE to Elizabeth Hoar, 4 November 1839, *RWEL* 2:230; RWE to SGW, 27 October 1839; *JMN* 7:284.

82. *JMN* 7:215, 269, 286.

83. SMF, *Essential Margaret Fuller,* 101–3; *SMFJ* 1844:71 n. 62.

84. SMF qtd. in Capper, *Margaret Fuller,* 259.

85. CS to RWE, 22 September 1840, *RWEL* 7:408–9 n. 145.

86. *SMFL* 2:121; RWE to SGW, 26 November 1839, *RWEL* 7:359; RWE to SMF, 14 November 1839, *RWEL* 2:235.

87. RWE, *Collected Poems,* 69–71; *JMN* 7:6; RWE, *The Poetry Notebooks of Ralph Waldo Emerson,* ed. Ralph H. Orth, Albert J. von Frank, Linda Allardt, and David W. Hill (Columbia: University of Missouri Press, 1986), 882.

88. SMF to RWE, 24 November 1839, *SMFL* 2:98–100; J. Steele, "Freeing the 'Prisoned Queen,'" 144–45.

89. *JMN* 7:315; RWE to SGW, 26 November 1839, *RWEL* 7:359.

90. RWE to SGW, 3 December 1839, *RWEL* 7:361; *RWEL* 8:442–43.

91. RWE to SMF, 27 November 1839, *RWEL* 2:240; *RWEL* 2:239–40; *JMN* 7:315; *JMN* 2:204; *JMN* 7:317.

92. *JMN* 7:321, 324, 325; RWE, *Correspondence of Emerson and Carlyle,* 254; *JMN* 7:371.

93. *RWEL* 7:392; RWE to SMF, 17 January 1840, *RWEL* 2:250; RWE to SMF, 8 July 1840, *RWEL* 2:314.

94. RWE to SGW, 10 January 1840, *RWEL* 7:366–67; RWE to SGW, 17 January 1840, *RWEL* 7:367; RWE to SGW, 25 January 1840, *RWEL* 7:368; RWE to SGW, 1 March 1840, *RWEL* 7:370. "We cannot get at beauty," Emerson wrote in his lecture on on love. "Its nature is like opaline dovesneck lustres, hovering and evanescent" (RWE, *Early Lectures,* 3:60). The same sentence also appears in the essay version of "Love" (*E&L* 332).

95. To Ellery Channing, Emerson wrote on 30 January 1840 of "your friend Samuel G. Ward, whom though I have known but a little while I love much" (*RWEL* 2:252). On 7 July 1840, Emerson again ended a letter to Ward by noting that "I . . . wish you to love me" (*RWEL* 7:394).

96. *JMN* 7:325; *SMFL* 2:104–5.

97. RWE to SMF, 7 and 8 June 1840, *RWEL* 2:304. Emerson went on to say he would not earn Ward's friendship "until one century later," which on the face of it would put Sturgis closer to Emerson than Ward was. The grandeur of the hyperbole, however, suggests that the flourish about Ward should not be taken literally. In Emerson's economy of libidinal frustration, the most distant is almost always the most prized.

98. RWE to CS, August 1840, *RWEL* 2:324–25; RWE to CS, 15 March 1841, *RWEL* 7:447; RWE to CS, 1 October 1845, *RWEL* 8:55–56.

99. RWE to SMF, 22 October 1840, *RWEL* 2:351.

100. RWE to MME, 22 December 1839, *RWEL* 2:244.

101. *JMN* 7:333, 337, 327; "Friendship," *E&L* 343.

102. *RWEL* 7:383–84, 390, 395; *JMN* 7:319. Fuller was tutor to Keats's niece Emma, and Keats's brother George gave Barker the original manuscript of Keats's "To Autumn" on 15 November 1839 (von Mehren, *Minerva and the Muse,* 102; Tilton, "True Romance," 66).

103. Apollodorus, *The Library,* trans. Sir James George Frazer (Cambridge: Harvard University Press, 1976), 1:61; James Henry Rubin, "Endymion's Dream as a Myth of

Romantic Inspiration," *Art Quarterly* 1 (1978): 47–84; John Keats, *Keats: Poetical Works,* ed. H. W. Garrod (New York: Oxford University Press, 1973), 75.

104. Tilton, "True Romance," 68; SGW qtd. in Capper, *Margaret Fuller,* 283; SGW qtd. in Tilton, "True Romance," 67; RWE to SMF, 27–29 May 1840, *RWEL* 2:297–98; SMF to RWE, 31 May 1840, *SMFL* 2:135; RWE to SMF, 8 July 1840, *RWEL* 2:313; *SMFJ* 1842–1:327.

105. *SMFJ* 1842–1:331–32; E. Emerson, *Life of Lidian Jackson Emerson,* 82.

106. "Self-Reliance," *E&L* 276; *RWEL* 7:392, 394–95.

107. RWE to SGW, 7 July 1840, *RWEL* 7:393; Andrew Sullivan, *Love Undetectable: Notes on Friendship, Sex, and Survival* (New York: Knopf, 1998), 174–75; Augustine, *Confessions,* trans. Henry Chadwick (New York: Oxford University Press, 1998), 57; *The Dial: A Magazine for Literature, Philosophy, and Religion* (New York: Russell and Russell, 1961), 3:414–15; *RWEL* 7:393.

108. *JMN* 7:182; *E&L* 239, 7.

109. RWE to SGW, 7 July 1840.

110. Tilton, "True Romance," 69; *JMN* 7:368, 510, 370–71; *RWEL* 2:324.

111. RWE to SMF, 31 July 1841, *RWEL* 2:438; Porte, *Representative Man,* 90.

112. *E&L* 350; Bacon, *Selections,* 69.

113. *E&L* 406; RWE, *Collected Poems,* 7; *E&L* 604.

114. Aristotle, *Nicomachean Ethics,* 227.

115. *E&L* 351; George Kateb, *Emerson and Self-Reliance* (Thousand Oaks: Sage, 1995), 109–12; Cicero, "Laelius: On Friendship," trans. Michael Grant, in *Cicero on the Good Life* (New York: Penguin, 1971), 207; "Manners," *E&L* 522; Montaigne, *Works,* 140, 137; *E&L* 345.

116. In this section, numbers in parentheses refer to RWE, "Friendship," *E&L,* 339–54.

117. Tilton, "True Romance," 69; *SMFL* 2:157; *JMN* 7:509; RWE to CS, 16 August 1840, *RWEL* 2:325.

118. *JMN* 7:510; RWE, *Collected Poems,* 203.

119. *RWEL* 7:400; *SMFL* 2:157; *RWEL* 7:402; *RWEL* 2:327.

120. RWE to CS, 6 September 1840, *RWEL* 7:404; RWE to SMF, 29 August 1840, *RWEL* 2:327.

121. RWE to SMF, 29 August 1840; RWE, *Collected Poems* 87, 89; Strauch, "Hatred's Swift Repulsions," 84–87; *RWEL* 7:404.

122. L. J. Emerson, *Selected Letters,* 89; RWE to SGW and Anna Hazard Barker, September 1840, *RWEL* 2:339.

123. *JMN* 11:460; *SMFJ* 1844:121; SMF, *Essential Margaret Fuller,* 15–18.

124. *SMFJ* 1844:63, 69; Capper, *Margaret Fuller,* 259; J. Steele, "Freeing the 'Prisoned Queen,'" 156; SGW qtd. in *SMFJ* 1844:77.

125. SMF to CS, 26 September 1840, *SMFL* 2:158; RWE to SMF, 29 August 1840, *RWEL* 2:327–28; *Memoirs of Margaret Fuller Ossoli,* 1:289.

126. *RWEL* 7:403 n. 131, 404, 405 n. 138, 406, 420, 422.

127. RWE to SMF, 13 September 1840, *RWEL* 2:332; *JMN* 7:400; RWE to SMF, 25 September 1840, *RWEL* 2:336–37.

128. SMF to RWE, 29 September 1840, *SMFL* 2:160; *RWEL* 2:340; RWE to SMF, 24 October 1840, *RWEL* 2:352; "Considerations," *E&L,* 1094.

129. SMF to CS, 25 October 1840, *SMFL* 2:170.

130. *JMN* 7:544; Christopher Newfield, *The Emerson Effect: Individualism and Submission in America* (Chicago: University of Chicago Press, 1996), 144; Porte, *Representative Man*, 226.

131. RWE to SMF, 29 August 1840, *RWEL* 2:327; RWE to CS, February 1845, *RWEL* 3:278, qtd. in Baldwin, "Emerson-Ward Friendship," 310.

132. RWE to SMF, 29 August 1840, *RWEL* 2:327; RWE to Thomas Carlyle, 14 November 1841, *Correspondence of Emerson and Carlyle*, 310; *JMN* 8:411; *JMN* 7:7; RWE to SGW, 22 July 1848, *RWEL* 8:183; RWE to SGW, 29 November 1872, *RWEL* 10:97.

133. *E&L* 344.

134. *E&L* 472.

135. *E&L* 271, 641; Tocqueville, *Democracy in America*, 2:259–60.

136. RWE to Thomas Carlyle, 1 July 1842, *Correspondence of Emerson and Carlyle*, 323.

137. *Dial* 1:71–72; 2:204–5; 3:484–90.

138. Charles King Newcomb, "The Two Dolons," *Dial* 3:112–23. In Newcomb's story, a boy named Dolon, who has a mystical understanding of nature, beatifically allows himself to be murdered by a madman who has read somewhat too much ancient Greek literature. Dolon seems to be partly an idealization of Emerson's son Waldo, recently dead of scarlet fever, and partly the fantasy pupil of A. Bronson Alcott's pedagogical theories. Newcomb meant to write a "Second Dolon," but — we can be thankful — never did. In 1894, however, an Oxford undergraduate named John Francis Bloxam as good as wrote it for him when he penned "The Priest and the Acolyte," whose heroes drink poisoned communion wine together in the same spirit of woozy passivity. Oscar Wilde contributed a set of aphorisms to the magazine (edited by Bloxam himself) that published "The Priest and the Acolyte." The propinquity helped send Wilde to jail.

139. *Dial* 1:136; RWE, *Collected Poems*, 7; *Dial* 3:152–53; *Dial* 2:322.

140. *Dial* 4:455–57.

141. RWE, *The Complete Works of Ralph Waldo Emerson*, Centenary Edition, ed. Edward W. Emerson (Boston: Houghton Mifflin, 1903–4), 8:413; RWE, *Collected Poems* 469; J. D. Yohannan, "Emerson's Translations of Persian Poetry from German Sources," *American Literature* 14 (1943): 407.

142. J. D. Yohannan, "The Influence of Persian Poetry upon Emerson's Work," *American Literature* 15 (1943): 26; RWE, *Complete Works*, 8:251; *E&L* 660; RWE, *Complete Works*, 8:249.

143. *JMN* 11:124; RWE, *Collected Poems* 476.


### Chapter 6. The Heart Ruled Out: Melville's Palinode

1. Oscar Wilde, *The Ballad of Reading Gaol, by C.3.3.* (London: Journeyman Press, 1978), 14.

2. E. L. Grant Watson, "Melville's Testament of Acceptance," *New England Quarterly* 6 (1933): 324.

3. Watson, "Melville's Testament," 324–25.

4. In this chapter, page numbers in parentheses refer to Herman Melville, *Billy Budd, Sailor (An Inside Narrative),* ed. Harrison Hayford and Merton M. Sealts Jr. (Chicago: University of Chicago Press, 1962).

5. E. M. Forster and Eric Crozier, libretto to *Billy Budd,* an opera by Benjamin Britten (London Symphony Orchestra, Decca, 1989).

6. Forster and Crozier, libretto to *Billy Budd,* 42.

7. Forster and Crozier, libretto to *Billy Budd,* 67, 65, 6 .

8. Perhaps this explains the inadvertent silliness of the de th of Leonard Bast.

9. "The belligerents were no l.....,., in the ordinary sense of things, an English ship, and an American ship. It was a co-partnership and joint-stock combustion-company of both ships; yet divided, even in participation." Herman Melville, *Israel Potter: His Fifty Years of Exile* (Evanston: Northwestern University Press; Chicago, Newberry Library, 1982), 126. For the parallels between homosexuality and cannibalism, see Caleb Crain, "Lovers of Human Flesh: Homosexuality and Cannibalism in Melville's Novels," *American Literature* 66 (1993):25–53.

10. Robert K. Martin, *Hero, Captain, and Stranger: Male Friendship, Social Critique, and Literary Form in the Sea Novels of Herman Melville* (Chapel Hill: University of North Carolina Press, 1986), 113, 122, 108, 124.

11. Martin, *Hero, Captian, and Stranger,* 113.

12. Martin, *Hero, Captain, and Stranger,* 113, 114; Melville, *Israel Potter,* 90, 120.

13. Martin, *Hero, Captain, and Stranger,* 120; Melville, *White-Jacket; or, The World in a Man-of-War* (Evanston: Northwestern University Press; Chicago: Newberry Library, 1970), 106, 34; Melville, *Israel Potter,* 89; *E&L* 802.

14. Eve Kosofsky Sedgwick, *Epistemology of the Closet* (Berkeley: University of California Press, 1990), 247; James Creech, *Closet Writing / Gay Reading: The Case of Melville's Pierre* (Chicago: University of Chicago Press, 1993).

15. W. H. Auden, "The Passion of Billy Budd," in *The Enchafèd Flood,* reprinted in *Twentieth Century Interpretations of Billy Budd,* ed. Howard P. Vincent (Englewood Cliffs: Prentice-Hall, 1971), 87.

16. Sedgwick, *Epistemology of the Closet,* 109, 116, 119 n. 20. Claire Denis recently made sympathy for Claggart the organizing principle of her film *Beau Travail,* which retold *Billy Budd* from Claggart's point of view and granted him a disco-dancing solo in the closing scene.

17. Sedgwick, *Epistemology of the Closet,* 94.

18. Melville, *White-Jacket,* 13; Richard Henry Dana Jr., *Two Years Before the Mast: A Personal Narrative of Life at Sea* (New York: Penguin, 1986), 135, 164.

19. Melville, *White-Jacket,* 17; Charles Roberts Anderson, *Melville in the South Seas* (New York: Columbia University Press, 1967), 366, 381–85; Hershel Parker, *Herman Melville: A Biography,* vol. 1: *1819–1851* (Baltimore: Johns Hopkins University Press, 1996), 271–73; Melville, *White-Jacket,* 14.

20. Melville, *White-Jacket,* 94.

21. Eleanor Melville Metcalf, *Herman Melville: Cycle and Epicycle* (Cambridge, Harvard University Press, 1953), 284.

22. Herman Melville, *The Confidence-Man: His Masquerade* (Evanston: Northwestern University Press; Chicago: Newberry Library, 1984), 171, 229.

23. Charles Roberts Anderson, "The Genesis of *Billy Budd*," *American Literature* 12 (1940):344.

24. Melville, *Confidence-Man*, 183.

25. Melville, *White-Jacket*, 220.

26. Melville, *White-Jacket*, 161.

27. Thomas Seccombe, "Titus Oates (1649–1705), perjurer," *Dictionary of National Biography* (London: Oxford University Press, 1917), 14:741–48; Albert S. Braverman, "Melville's *Billy Budd, Sailor*," *Explicator* 58 (1999): 25–26; Jane Lane [Elaine Dakers], *Titus Oates* (London: Andrew Dakers, 1949), 30 ff. The *DNB* also fails to expand on Oates's chin. According to Oates's modern biographer, "His most striking feature was his chin; it was so long that his mouth, says L'Estrange in one of his *Observators,* was four inches above it. North's description is well-known: 'His Mouth was the Center of his Face; and a Compass there would sweep his Nose, Forehead, and Chin within the Perimeter.' That enormous chin of his was to feature in every broadsheet, wood-cut and lampoon connected with him, from the failure of his Plot to the end of his days" (Lane, *Titus Oates,* 63).

28. Melville, *White-Jacket*, 376.

29. Sedgwick, *Epistemology of the Closet*, 109, 114–27.

30. Anderson, "Genesis of *Billy Budd*," 332–33.

31. Paine, *Collected Writings*, 476.

32. Andrew Marvell, "Upon Appleton House: To My Lord Fairfax," in *Selected Poetry and Prose,* ed. Robert Wilcher (New York: Methuen, 1986), stanza 91.

33. Marvell, "Upon Appleton House," stanzas 18, 21–24, 90.

34. Marvell, "Upon Appleton House," stanza 94.

35. Fliegelman, *Prodigals and Pilgrims,* 161; Merton M. Sealts Jr., *Melville's Reading* (Columbia: University of South Carolina Press, 1988), 178; Salomon Gessner, *The Death of Abel,* trans. Mary Collyer (Baltimore: Warner and Hanna, 1807), 31, 121.

36. Melville, *White-Jacket*, 376.

37. Melville, *White-Jacket,* 174; Melville, *Moby-Dick,* 52; Melville, *White-Jacket,* 169.

38. Woolman, *Journal,* 195; Harrison Hayford, ed., *The Somers Mutiny Affair* (Englewood Cliffs: Prentice-Hall, 1959), 202; Michael Paul Rogin, *Subversive Genealogy: The Politics and Art of Herman Melville* (New York: Knopf, 1983), 81.

39. Melville, *Confidence-Man,* 117, 119.

40. Hayford, *Somers Mutiny Affair,* 30. In their impressive edition of the difficult text of *Billy Budd,* Hayford and Sealts report that Melville described the *Somers* affair in his manuscript as "the execution at sea of a midshipman and two petty officers as mutineers designing the seizure of the brig." On a hint from Newton Arvin, however, Hayford and Sealts suggest that Melville's description was mistaken, since Elisha Small was a plain seaman. They emend their reading text of the novel to "a midshipman and two sailors" (181–82). But it is Arvin, Hayford, and Sealts who are mistaken. Captain Mackenzie explained in his report to the navy that prior to the executions, he mustered at each noose the sailors most likely to have been contaminated by contact with the man to be hanged. Mackenzie stationed the "maintopmen of both watches" at Small's noose, because "for a month or more [Small] had held the situation of captain of the maintop" (Hayford,

*Somers Mutiny Affair,* 43). As Melville himself explains, in chapter 6 of *White-Jacket,* "the Captains of the Tops" are petty officers. (Unlike officers proper, petty officers "mess in common with the crew" and thus are not socially distinct from common sailors [Melville, *White-Jacket,* 27].) Since captain of the maintop was the title of Melville's beloved Jack Chase, it is not surprising that this detail stuck in his mind.

41. Hayford, *Somers Mutiny Affair,* 48, 47.

42. Hayford, *Somers Mutiny Affair,* 149, 42; Melville, *White-Jacket,* 303.

43. Parker, *Herman Melville,* 222–26.

44. Hayford, *Somers Mutiny Affair,* 204–7.

45. Herman Melville, *Collected Poems of Herman Melville,* ed. Howard P. Vincent (Chicago: Packard and Company, 1947), 174.

46. Hayford, *Somers Mutiny Affair,* 149.

47. Hayford, *Somers Mutiny Affair,* 3, 55.

48. Hayford, *Somers Mutiny Affair,* 44–45.

49. Hayford, *Somers Mutiny Affair,* 55.

50. Henry David Thoreau, *Reform Papers,* ed. Wendell Glick (Princeton: Princeton University Press, 1973), 120.

51. Melville, *White-Jacket,* 14, 41.

52. Melville, *White-Jacket,* 271.

53. Melville, *White-Jacket,* 17.

54. Herman Melville, *Billy Budd,* in *Pierre, Israel Potter, The Piazza Tales, The Confidence-Man, Uncollected Prose, and Billy Budd, Sailor,* ed. Harrison Hayford (New York: Library of America, 1984), 1476–77.

55. Paine, *Collected Writings,* 448.

56. Edmund Burke, *Reflections on the Revolution in France and on the Proceedings in Certain Societies in London Relative to That Event in a Letter Intended to Have Been Sent to a Gentleman in Paris, 1790,* ed. J. G. A. Pocock (Indianapolis: Hackett Publishing, 1987), 66.

57. Melville, *White-Jacket,* 95, 276.

58. Melville, *White-Jacket,* 276.

59. Gessner, *Death of Abel,* 121; Hayford, *Somers Mutiny Affair,* 46–47, 71–72.

60. Melville, *Confidence-Man,* 14.

61. Paine, *Collected Writings,* 512. A Jack Chase might also note that Vere here suffers another covert feminization, by the allusion to the myth of Diana (with her changing aspects) and Endymion.

62. Melville, *White-Jacket,* 373–74.

63. Melville, *Confidence-Man,* 175.

64. Melville, *Confidence-Man,* 189.

65. Melville, *Confidence-Man,* 192, 206, 202.

66. Hayford, *Somers Mutiny Affair,* 144; Paine, *Collected Writings,* 448.

67. Melville, *Confidence-Man,* 136.

68. Melville, *Confidence-Man,* 173; A. Smith, *Theory of Moral Sentiments,* 11; Paine, *Collected Writings,* 74.

69. Paine, *Collected Writings,* 657.

70. Stesichorus, Fragment 18, qtd. in Plato, *Complete Works,* 521.

# Index